T0353385

Applied Approach to Privacy and Security for the Internet of Things

Parag Chatterjee
National Technological University, Argentina & University of the Republic, Uruguay

Emmanuel Benoist
Bern University of Applied Sciences, Switzerland

Asoke Nath
St. Xavier's College, Kolkata, India

A volume in the Advances in Information Security, Privacy, and Ethics (AISPE) Book Series

Published in the United States of America by
    IGI Global
    Information Science Reference (an imprint of IGI Global)
    701 E. Chocolate Avenue
    Hershey PA, USA 17033
    Tel: 717-533-8845
    Fax: 717-533-8661
    E-mail: cust@igi-global.com
    Web site: http://www.igi-global.com

Library of Congress Cataloging-in-Publication Data

Names: Chatterjee, Parag, 1992- editor. | Benoist, Emmanuel, 1972- editor.
  | Nath, Asoke, 1953- editor.
Title: Applied approach to privacy and security for the internet of things
  / edited by Parag Chatterjee, Emmanuel Benoist, and Asoke Nath.
Description: Hershey, PA : Information Science Reference, [2020] | Includes
  bibliographical references and index. | Summary: "This book examines the
  conceptual aspects of security and privacy in IoT. It also explores the
  application of IoT systems in smart transports, smart cities, and smart
  healthcare"-- Provided by publisher.
Identifiers: LCCN 2019039273 (print) | LCCN 2019039274 (ebook) | ISBN
  9781799824442 (hardcover) | ISBN 9781799824459 (paperback) | ISBN
  9781799824466 (ebook)
Subjects: LCSH: Internet of things--Security measures. | Embedded Internet
  devices--Security measures. | Computer networks--Security measures.
Classification: LCC TK5105.8857 .A66 2020 (print) | LCC TK5105.8857
  (ebook) | DDC 005.8--dc23
LC record available at https://lccn.loc.gov/2019039273
LC ebook record available at https://lccn.loc.gov/2019039274

This book is published in the IGI Global book series Advances in Information Security, Privacy, and Ethics (AISPE) (ISSN: 1948-9730; eISSN: 1948-9749)

British Cataloguing in Publication Data
A Cataloguing in Publication record for this book is available from the British Library.

All work contributed to this book is new, previously-unpublished material.
The views expressed in this book are those of the authors, but not necessarily of the publisher.

For electronic access to this publication, please contact: eresources@igi-global.com.

Advances in Information Security, Privacy, and Ethics (AISPE) Book Series

ISSN:1948-9730
EISSN:1948-9749

Editor-in-Chief: *Manish Gupta* State University of New York, USA

MISSION

As digital technologies become more pervasive in everyday life and the Internet is utilized in ever increasing ways by both private and public entities, concern over digital threats becomes more prevalent.

The **Advances in Information Security, Privacy, & Ethics (AISPE) Book Series** provides cutting-edge research on the protection and misuse of information and technology across various industries and settings. Comprised of scholarly research on topics such as identity management, cryptography, system security, authentication, and data protection, this book series is ideal for reference by IT professionals, academicians, and upper-level students.

COVERAGE

- Cookies
- Security Classifications
- Privacy-Enhancing Technologies
- Cyberethics
- Technoethics
- CIA Triad of Information Security
- Tracking Cookies
- Information Security Standards
- Access Control
- Privacy Issues of Social Networking

IGI Global is currently accepting manuscripts for publication within this series. To submit a proposal for a volume in this series, please contact our Acquisition Editors at Acquisitions@igi-global.com or visit: http://www.igi-global.com/publish/.

Titles in this Series

For a list of additional titles in this series, please visit:
http://www.igi-global.com/book-series/advances-information-security-privacy-ethics/37157

Large-Scale Data Streaming, Processing, and Blockchain Security
Hemraj Saini (Jaypee University of Information Technology, India) Geetanjali Rathee (Jaypee University of Information Technology, India) and Dinesh Kumar Saini (Sohar University, Oman)
Information Science Reference • © 2020 • 300pp • H/C (ISBN: 9781799834441) • US $225.00

Advanced Security Strategies in Next Generation Computing Models
Shafi'i Muhammad Abdulhamid (Federal University of Technology Minna, Nigeria) and Muhammad Shafie Abd Latiff (Universiti Teknologi, Malaysia)
Information Science Reference • © 2020 • 300pp • H/C (ISBN: 9781799850809) • US $215.00

Advancements in Security and Privacy Initiatives for Multimedia Images
Ashwani Kumar (Vardhaman College of Engineering, India) and Seelam Sai Satyanarayana Reddy (Vardhaman College of Engineering, India)
Information Science Reference • © 2020 • 300pp • H/C (ISBN: 9781799827955) • US $215.00

Cyber Security and Safety of Nuclear Power Plant Instrumentation and Control Systems
Michael A. Yastrebenetsky (State Scientific and Technical Centre for Nuclear and Radiation Safety, Ukraine) and Vyacheslav S. Kharchenko (National Aerospace University KhAI, Ukraine)
Information Science Reference • © 2020 • 345pp • H/C (ISBN: 9781799832775) • US $195.00

Internet Censorship and Regulation Systems in Democracies Emerging Research and Opportunities
Nikolaos Koumartzis (Aristotle University of Thessaloniki, Greece) and Andreas Veglis (Aristotle University of Thessaloniki, Greece)
Information Science Reference • © 2020 • 272pp • H/C (ISBN: 9781522599739) • US $185.00

701 East Chocolate Avenue, Hershey, PA 17033, USA
Tel: 717-533-8845 x100 • Fax: 717-533-8661
E-Mail: cust@igi-global.com • www.igi-global.com

Table of Contents

Section 1

Eoghan Casey, Université de Lausanne, Switzerland
Hannes Spichiger, Université de Lausanne, Switzerland
Elénore Ryser, Université de Lausanne, Switzerland
Francesco Servida, Université de Lausanne, Switzerland
David-Olivier Jaquet-Chiffelle, Université de Lausanne, Switzerland

Kavitha Ammayappan, University of Hyderabad, India
Arun Babu Puthuparambil, Indian Institute of Science, Bengaluru, India
Atul Negi, University of Hyderabad, India

Xinxing Zhao, Singapore Institute of Technology, Singapore
Chandra Sekar Veerappan, Singapore Institute of Technology, Singapore
Peter Loh, Singapore Institute of Technology, Singapore

Detailed Table of Contents

Section 1

Chapter 1

    Eoghan Casey, Université de Lausanne, Switzerland
    Hannes Spichiger, Université de Lausanne, Switzerland
    Elénore Ryser, Université de Lausanne, Switzerland
    Francesco Servida, Université de Lausanne, Switzerland
    David-Olivier Jaquet-Chiffelle, Université de Lausanne, Switzerland

IoT devices produce information that can be used in criminal investigations and cybersecurity incidents to make inferences about identities, locations, chronologies, and relationships between relevant entities. Before this information is relied upon to make critical decisions, its veracity must be assessed critically, and the link between virtual and physical worlds must be evaluated carefully. This chapter presents the forensic science principles needed to exploit the full potential of IoT traces, including uniqueness, exchange, provenance, integrity, reliability, repeatability, evaluating links between virtual and physical entities, and formally assessing alternative hypotheses. This chapter also discusses core forensic processes and activities, demonstrating their application to forensic analysis of IoT devices using practical examples. A typology of IoT traces is proposed and their usefulness during an investigation is discussed. Finally, an investigative scenario is presented to illustrate the opportunities and challenges of exploiting IoT devices and traces for investigative and forensic purposes.

    Kavitha Ammayappan, University of Hyderabad, India
    Arun Babu Puthuparambil, Indian Institute of Science, Bengaluru, India
    Atul Negi, University of Hyderabad, India

Internet of things (IoT) is a buzzword around the globe. Academics and industries are evolving to solve real-world problems with emerging technologies; IoT is one among them. Now, it's very prevalent to see IoT devices in varied application domains like healthcare, hospitality, home, oil and gas, aviation, agriculture and marketing, cold storage chains, food preservation industries, automobile, environmental pollution monitoring sectors, energy industries, marine and fisheries, dairy and poultry, logistics, smart home and smart city, etc. Industries and research institutes are focusing to enrich environment and ecosystem to bring back green world again for the millennials and our future generations to make this globe as a potential place to cherish. In this mission, IoT is playing a major role of protection and preservation. In parallel, hackers are trying to destroy this mission by exploiting varied cyber vulnerabilities. To make IoT systems robust against those vulnerabilities it is necessary to understand the key vulnerabilities in detail.

    Xinxing Zhao, Singapore Institute of Technology, Singapore
    Chandra Sekar Veerappan, Singapore Institute of Technology, Singapore
    Peter Loh, Singapore Institute of Technology, Singapore

Modern processors employ optimization techniques such as out-of-order and speculative execution to maximize the performance. However, they may leave observable side effects that leak the secrets of the system. This phenomenon has led to a proliferation of Spectre and Meltdown attack variants, and this trend will likely continue in the near future. While many makeshift countermeasures have been proposed, they are either not adequately effective or come with inadvertent consequences. New types of processors are designed to deal with these problems; however, those older ones in billions of devices that are currently being used cannot easily or even possibly be replaced. In this chapter, therefore, the authors provide a cross-platform, micro-agent detection system, which can detect four main types of Spectre variants and one variant of Meltdown in real-time in these devices. The empirical performance tests show that the micro-agent system and the in-built detection mechanisms are efficient and effective in detecting such attacks.

Chapter 4

Phidahunlang Chyne, North-Eastern Hill University, India
Parag Chatterjee, National Technological University, Argentina &
University of the Republic, Uruguay
Sugata Sanyal, Tata Institute of Fundamental Research, India
Debdatta Kandar, North-Eastern Hill University, India

Rapid advancements in hardware programming and communication innovations have encouraged the development of internet-associated sensory devices that give perceptions and information measurements from the physical world. According to the internet of things (IoT) analytics, more than 100 IoT devices across the world connect to the internet every second, which in the coming years will sharply increase the number of IoT devices by billions. This number of IoT devices incorporates new dynamic associations and does not totally replace the devices that were purchased before yet are not utilized any longer. As an increasing number of IoT devices advance into the world, conveyed in uncontrolled, complex, and frequently hostile conditions, securing IoT frameworks displays various challenges. As per the Eclipse IoT Working Group's 2017 IoT engineer overview, security is the top worry for IoT designers. To approach the challenges in securing IoT devices, the authors propose using unsupervised machine learning model at the network/transport level for anomaly detection.

Chapter 5

Arundhati Arjaria, Rajiv Gandhi Proudyogiki Vishwavidyalaya, India
Priyanka Dixit, Rajiv Gandhi Proudyogiki Vishwavidyalaya, India

In today's digital era, internet of things and wireless communication needs no introduction as almost everything directly or indirectly is dependent on the same. This scenario also leads to various security issues because devices are connected to internet and this availability makes this exposure vulnerable for various attacks. Recently in internet of things and wireless ad hoc networks, there is an essential issue of how to increase channel utilization without degrading the performance. Some problems are also responsible to increase collision in the network. Here, the authors propose a busy tone-based medium access control scheme to avoid such problems in fully as well as non-fully connected environment. Here in this chapter, they present a brief introduction to internet of things, security challenges regarding IoT, and its association with wireless technology. They also discuss the problems concerning wireless communication, which affects the performance of networks and their solutions.

Chapter 6

How to Authenticate MQTT Sessions Without Channel and Broker

Reto E. Koenig, Department of Computer Science, Bern University of
Applied Sciences, Switzerland
Lukas Laederach, Bern University of Applied Sciences, Switzerland
Cédric von Allmen, Bern University of Applied Sciences, Switzerland

This chapter describes a new but state-of-the-art approach to provide authenticity in MQTT sessions using the means of zero-knowledge proofs. This approach completely voids session hijacking for the MQTT protocol and provides authenticity. The presented approach does not require the broker to keep any secrets for session handling. The presented approach allows completely anonymous but authentic sessions; hence, the broker does not need any priory knowledge of the client party. As it is especially targeted for applications within the world of internet of things (IoT), the presented approach is designed to require only the minimum in extra power in terms of energy and space. The approach does not introduce any new concept, but simply combines a state of the art cryptographic Zero-Knowledge Proof of identity with the existing MQTT 5.0 specification. Thus, no protocol extension is required in order to provide the targeted security properties. The described approach is completely agnostic to the application layer at the client side and is only required during MQTT session establishment.

Section 2

Chapter 7

Emmanuel Benoist, Bern University of Applied Sciences, Switzerland
Serge Bignens, Bern University of Applied Sciences, Switzerland
Alexander Kreutz, Bern University of Applied Sciences, Switzerland

The rise of internet of things (IoT) in medicine has generated tons of new data through connected devices. Medicine and research in medicine are interested in using those data for the personalization of patients' treatment. The authors present the system MIDATA where patients can transfer their medical IoT data and store them. They have also the possibility to share those data with research groups. The solution respects patient privacy. Even an administrator of the site cannot access to the data of the patients. The patient can choose which users can decrypt their data. But users will lose their passwords and keys. So, the authors provide a novel solution for the recovery of the keys. This procedure has different levels: the patient has a new phone but remembers the password; the patient has forgotten the password but can use the phone; and the worst case is when the patient forgot the password and lost the phone, where they developed a novel solution for key recovery.

Chapter 8

Driver assistance systems are advancing at a rapid pace, and almost all major companies have started investing in developing autonomous vehicles. However, the security and reliability in this field is still uncertain and debatable. A vehicle compromised by the attackers remotely can be easily used to create chaos of epic proportions. An attacker can control brake, accelerate, and even steering, which can lead to catastrophic consequences. Therefore, an autonomous vehicle can be weaponized extremely easily if proper security protocols are not implemented. This chapter gives a very short and brief overview of some of the possible attacks on autonomous vehicle software and hardware and their potential implications.

Smart, networked medical devices play a rapidly growing role in healthcare. Those devices and their data have to be integrated into the healthcare system. There are several reasons to reuse those data for well-defined purposes by well-defined partners; this reuse should be controlled by the patient and not depend on the manufacturer infrastructure. Different stakeholders have an understandable reason to access those data under the control of the patient. The authors propose an architecture of a decentralized data broker that receives the data streams from the devices and redistributes them securely to legitimate recipients. This broker is based on the peer-to-peer network Freenet. This network has been defined to be censorship resistant and to protect the privacy of persons sharing data. This covers the needs for protection expected from a secure data broker. The patient can directly define which of the stakeholders will receive which information and the information is encrypted in a way that only that partner can read it.

Security of information is always a challenging domain for any computer network organization. An organization always sets different types of policies with the course of time so that no information can be leaked. Some external or some internal factors of an organization play important roles in revealing the information. An organization mainly depends on its employees. An employee manages the data and information and there exists some chance among employees to reveal the data. There is need to study and set policies for employees so that no full information can be revealed. Information security management system (ISMS) has collection of different types of policies and procedures for systematically managing organizationally sensitive data. ISMSs have to deal with management of employees of an organization to minimize the risk of revealing information. This chapter studies employee management so that an organization can continue its business securely.

The concept of internet of things involves the establishment of ubiquitous computing devices that seamlessly integrate with our living environments, being interconnected via networks to gather information about the surroundings so as to enable the devices to interact with the ambient environment in favorable ways. With the growth of this concept and subsequent development of smart homes, it is to be borne in mind that security is of the utmost importance in such scenarios. In this chapter, the authors highlight the various vulnerabilities prevalent in smart homes, which might be exploited by unscrupulous individuals to launch cyberattacks.

Chapter 12
IoT-Controlled Railway Gate System With ML Object Detection Approach:

Megha Kamble, Lakshmi Narain College of Technology, India
Jaspreet Mehra, Lakshmi Narain College of Technology, India
Monika Jain, Lakshmi Narain College of Technology, India

The growing demand of internet of things (IoT) has rendered advancement in the practical fields towards society. In spite of recent advancements and cost effective IoT solutions for smart railway infrastructure, presently, most of the railway gates in India are opened and closed manually. This is a time-consuming process. It is an error-prone system and raises the accident probability. This chapter evaluates and demonstrates the applicability of IoT to resolve the problem of unmanned automatic railway crossing. The aim is to propose a prototype that will control with the help of microcontroller board, IoT sensor integration, and integrating it to machine learning-based image analysis to detect the intermediate real time obstacle (obstacle on the track). This kind of IoT system will also invite potential attacks, and traditional security countermeasures can be inefficient in dynamic IoT environments. So open challenges related to IoT security threats and emerging security mechanisms for security of the proposed smart railway crossing system are also elaborated.

Foreword

The origin of Internet of Things (IoT) dates back to more than 20 years. Especially in the fast-changing technology space, a common question could be "Does it still make sense nowadays to talk about the fundamentals of Internet of Things?" Even though the answer is affirmative undoubtedly, I would add, "The IoT phenomenon evolves continuously, and we have to continue studying it deeply not for now but especially for the future". The domain of IoT has slowly changed over the years in terms of innovations, solutions, applications, legal issues, ethics and many more aspects. We have witnessed the robust IoT growth with a consequent and relevant impact on several sectors and also on our daily life.

The considerable involvement of different areas like the legal domain, the cybersecurity and data privacy aspects, led me to describe an IoT ecosystem some years ago. We defined it as a complete ecosystem for business and technological innovation, reusability, interoperability, and that includes solving the security, privacy and trust implications. In this context, at least three foundational aspects emerge — privacy, data protection and cybersecurity. Especially in the context of IoT, the interactions between multidisciplinary domains and stakeholders show that data leads the entire ecosystem and all the sectors involved depend significantly on data protection and privacy. Thus, the key lies in designing the IoT systems based on data protection and privacy principles. Then, we identify a 'data protection and privacy ecosystem' that should be the steering force of any IoT ecosystem.

In light of this, I appreciate the work of the authors and editors of this book, not just for presenting a set of interesting contributions in this field, but also for joining the global discussion on data security and privacy in the smart technologies. This book is a comprehensive treatise about the Internet of Things, highlighting methods and applied aspects of security and privacy in IoT-based systems. The effort of the authors is praiseworthy as they paid attention to one of the key issues in IoT — the aspect of cybersecurity and privacy. The deep insights and illustrations on IoT Security and Privacy presented in this book must be considered as one of its strengths.

The data-aspect is highly critical in almost every domain of IoT. For example, In the healthcare sector, doctors, patients, and health-workers use IoT-based medical devices, often exposing themselves to the potential risks of cyber-attacks. Thus, knowing how the security part of the IoT ecosystem works and consequentially the potential risks, helps to avoid serious damages and data breaches. Awareness is one of the key-solutions to acquire opportune knowledge and thus mitigate risks.

I consider this book as a great work by which the authors cover a wide domain of security and privacy aspects in IoT. I hope, the readers will enjoy reading this book, especially for the diverse set of topics addressed in each chapter. This book explains crucial aspects, representing the state-of-the-art issues and innovative pillars in the domain of security and privacy in Internet of Things.

Nicola Fabiano
Data Protection Authority, San Marino

Preface

The Internet of Things (IoT) is not a newbie anymore in today's world. Just even ten years back, people were talking about IoT in the future and the prospects of its widespread development. Nowadays the useful gadgets and tools connected through the IoT have been an integral part of our daily lives. Whether companies or individuals, it is now impossible to live away from the IoT. Security and privacy have been the major concerns for a huge part of the end-users of IoT-based systems. The fear of getting personal data compromised has amplified immensely thanks to the recent incidents of security breaches. As IoT connects several stakeholders and ensures seamless exchange and sharing, a breach of security or unauthorized access to confidential data also makes huge impact in such a scenario due to its extensive span.

Industry 4.0 is transforming product manufacturing by introducing the IoT into all industrial work processes. Purchasing management, stock management, product handling and industrial design, all stages of industrial design have been revolutionized by the arrival of new intelligent and connected machines. The data produced by all these machines and the numerous sensors positioned along the production chain are collected and analyzed. The data and the new processes invented over the last five years have revolutionized the industrial world.

The Internet of Things has also totally changed people's lives. The use of smartphones has increased sharply in the last few years. Homes are increasingly equipped with smart-TVs expanding the domain from TV shows to games and a huge area of multimedia contents online. Streaming companies such as Netflix, Amazon prime or Disney+ have revolutionized the way people consume entertainment. One can also buy connected light bulbs (Philips Hue or IKEA Trädfri for the consumer versions). Baby monitors connect directly to the smartphone. The weighing scale is connected and allows software to directly produce a weight curve for each family member. Voice assistants (Google Home, Alexa and Siri) have totally changed the way we consume music which we can now listen to directly from the Internet (via Spotify, Deezer, Apple music etc.). Little by little, without users even seeing the intrusion coming, our habits have been radically changed. The way we consume music, movies, and also more and more goods and services are now linked to the existence of 24-hour Internet-connected products.

Alongside industry and the home, IoT will revolutionize the way we think about healthcare. Mobile health (mHealth) takes a little longer to take hold than other revolutions but will totally change the relationship between the patients and their health. IoT at home produces very interesting data for patient monitoring and remote patient management. We have for example the weight which is measured by the connected scale, the blood sugar, blood pressure, temperatures which are now measured by sensors directly connected to the Internet or at least to a smartphone. All these data once aggregated will be very useful for long term patient follow-up. Doctors will be able to access the patient's accurate data history. They will also be able to set alarms to warn them when certain values change or exceed a certain threshold. The data will also be used by researchers to analyze the effectiveness of certain therapies and to propose a highly personalized treatment to each patient.

Unfortunately, next to all these opportunities, the IoT that becomes ubiquitous puts us at great risk. The risks are firstly for security and secondly for privacy. For safety, one takes the risk that the product is defective. The more complex a system is, the more difficult it is to test it and therefore the higher the risk. But IoT-devices above all run the new risk of being attacked by a third party from the Internet. Whereas the light bulbs of the 20th century could only switch on and off, the connected light bulbs of the 21st century can connect to the Internet. Like any computer system, they are susceptible to remote control by a malicious person.

Even if it seems harmless for a light bulb to be controlled by an attacker, it can lead to very serious problems. This light bulb can be used in a Botnet to conduct remote attacks (DDoS for example). It can also be used to penetrate the home network to attack other systems. And it can simply be used to know when the house is occupied or when it is empty allowing thieves to enter the house. It is even easier to imagine how a security camera or baby monitor can be diverted from its original purpose. Accessing the accounts (google, amazon, apple) linked to the voice assistants allows you to enter directly into the most private data of the people (list of music listened to, number and name of people at home, list of all movements, agenda, and list of contacts...).

The data produced by IoT systems can be very intrusive. We need to protect user privacy. The risk with privacy is that a minor breach can cause a huge impact. In this case, a loss of user-confidence could lead to the abandonment of all these new technologies. Company and user data must therefore be protected with the best techniques to ensure that it never falls into the wrong hands. It is therefore necessary to ensure that this data cannot be stolen from the IoT device, but also that it is well protected during its transfer over the Internet. The IoT architecture contains many intermediaries (depending on the various architectures). The architecture and security of all intermediaries (smartphone, web server, data server, app viewer, ...) must be optimal.

The revolution of the Internet of Things has already largely started. The benefits have already revolutionized our lives and the life of our companies. New revolutions are in sight such as eHealth. But without security and privacy, users might turn away from these new applications. The risks are multiple and protean, we will have to work on the architectures, on the devices but also on all the systems used to process the data produced by the IoT. A global view is brought in this book and allows to look at the recent advances in the fields related to the security and privacy of IoT systems from several angles.

The security and privacy of the IoT must be present in all phases of the software development life cycle. The first and probably the most important part is during the architecture design. This will define what the device does and how data is exchanged between the different systems. The architecture is based on data exchange protocols. These protocols have to be secure, but you also have to be very careful about how they are implemented. Because even a secure protocol can become insecure if it is incorrectly programmed. The programs (firmware and/or applications) on the device can contain many bugs. IoT devices are essentially small systems with limited power consumption. These restrictions can alter the protection capabilities of such a system. Updating systems is a crucial part of IoT security. If a firmware is never updated, then once a bug is discovered, it is impossible to repair the systems and deploy the necessary patch. If on the other hand one can update the firmware, then this update must be surrounded by a lot of security, because a change in the software could be used by an attacker to take control of the device. In this book, we present aspects of privacy and security protection that affect all stages of the production of IoT systems.

This book is aimed at students, researchers and professionals who want to join the discussion in the field of security and privacy of IoT systems. It covers different aspects of the development life cycle of the equipment, organizations and protocols used in the IoT. This global view is necessary to understand the issues related to the deployment of such infrastructures as a whole. The IoT problem, far from focusing on the device that must be used, covers a whole set of techniques and technologies that must be implemented to safeguard the security and privacy of IoT applications, and this book contributes in this discussion.

Parag Chatterjee
National Technological University, Argentina & University of the Republic,
Uruguay

Emmanuel Benoist
Bern University of Applied Sciences, Switzerland

Asoke Nath
St. Xavier's College, India & University of Calcutta, India

Section 1

Chapter 1
IoT Forensic Science:
Principles, Processes, and Activities

Eoghan Casey
Université de Lausanne, Switzerland

Hannes Spichiger
Université de Lausanne, Switzerland

Elénore Ryser
Université de Lausanne, Switzerland

Francesco Servida
Université de Lausanne, Switzerland

David-Olivier Jaquet-Chiffelle
Université de Lausanne, Switzerland

ABSTRACT

IoT devices produce information that can be used in criminal investigations and cybersecurity incidents to make inferences about identities, locations, chronologies, and relationships between relevant entities. Before this information is relied upon to make critical decisions, its veracity must be assessed critically, and the link between virtual and physical worlds must be evaluated carefully. This chapter presents the forensic science principles needed to exploit the full potential of IoT traces, including uniqueness, exchange, provenance, integrity, reliability, repeatability, evaluating links between virtual and physical entities, and formally assessing alternative hypotheses. This chapter also discusses core forensic processes and activities, demonstrating their application to forensic analysis of IoT devices using practical examples. A typology of IoT traces is proposed and their usefulness during an investigation is discussed. Finally, an investigative scenario is presented to illustrate the opportunities and challenges of exploiting IoT devices and traces for investigative and forensic purposes.

DOI: 10.4018/978-1-7998-2444-2.ch001

INTRODUCTION

Rapid growth in the number, variety and complexity of IoT objects raises major challenges and opportunities for forensic science. These systems are becoming ubiquitous in public spaces, workplaces, schools, homes and other private areas, generating large volumes of data at high velocity in various formats. These digital traces can be analysed to make inferences about identities, locations, chronologies and relationships between relevant entities (Casey, Ribaux, & Roux, 2019). The purpose of forensic science in this context is to study digital traces in a systematic and coherent manner to address the questions of authentication, identification, classification, reconstruction and evaluation for a legal context (Pollitt, Casey, Jaquet-Chiffelle, & Gladyshev, 2018). The legal context can be the typical criminal, civil, and regulatory functions of the legal system, as well as its extensions such as human rights, employment disputes, natural disasters and security matters (e.g., critical infrastructure protection).

IoT devices can be targets, digital witnesses or instrumentalities of crimes and cyberattacks, creating new investigative opportunities, forensic challenges, security risks, legal issues, privacy risks and ethical conundrums. IoT devices can be exploited by a cyberattack, targeting the object itself or connected systems, including critical infrastructure, for various purposes (e.g., cyberstalking, fraud, espionage, botnets, DDOS) (Pour et al., 2019). Traditional criminals can manipulate or disable security systems supported by IoT devices such as door locks, alarms and cameras to facilitate burglary and other non-cyber offenses. Investigators of traditional crimes, including violent crimes, increasingly incorporate information produced by IoT devices to address questions about what happened around the time and place of an offense, and who was involved. However, to mitigate the risk of mistakes, the reliability of information from IoT devices must be assessed critically, and the link between virtual and physical worlds must be evaluated carefully.

The privacy risks associated with capturing information from IoT devices must also be mitigated. Some municipalities have become concerned about the use of technology to investigate crime, strictly controlling use of any *electronic device, system utilizing an electronic device, or similar technological tool used, designed, or primarily intended to collect audio, electronic, visual, location, thermal, olfactory, biometric, or similar information specifically associated with, or capable of being associated with, any individual or group* (Stop Secret Surveillance Ordinance, 2019).

The complexity of issues surrounding IoT devices as sources of evidence and instruments of invasion make it necessary to take a broader forensic science perspective, not just a technical one. Responding to this need, this work applies forensic science principles, processes and activities to IoT devices and traces. This chapter begins with an overview of IoT technology, prior work related to IoT forensics, and types of information produced by IoT devices. The forensic science principles uniqueness, exchange, provenance, integrity, reliability, repeatability, evaluating links between virtual and physical entities, and formally assessing alternative hypotheses are then discussed. This is followed by a synopsis of the core forensic processes – hypothetico-deductive reasoning, authentication, classification, identification, reconstruction and evaluation. Forensic activities that support these core processes include recognition, preservation, examination, documentation, analysis, integration and interpretation. Different potential uses of the information retrieved from IoT traces is discussed, culminating with a suggested forensic approach for IoT based investigation demonstrated using an illustrative case study.

BACKGROUND

In 2015, the IEEE launched an initiative to define IoT, and since then the accepted hardware architecture of an IoT object consists of sensors and actuators, processing units, storage units and communication units. An IoT object becomes a device when the virtual components are added to allow the object to act on both the physical and virtual worlds, which requires middleware, software, digital resources and communication protocols to be added to the hardware architecture (Minerva, Biru, & Rotondi, 2015), as illustrated in Figure 1. In short, an IoT object becomes a device once it connects to a network, cloud or another device such as a smartphone. This work applies forensics principles, processes and activities to such IoT devices and associated traces. IoT traces can be found on the device itself, in the cloud, on connected devices and within network interactions.

Prior work treating IoT devices from a forensic perspective addresses related traces on connected networks and cloud systems (Oriwoh, Jazani, Epiphaniou, & Sant, 2013; Oriwoh & Sant, 2013; Perumal, Norwawi, & Raman, 2015; Zawoad & Hasan, 2015). The approaches proposed in these prior works concentrate on technical issues and neglect forensic science principles and processes. Furthermore, any proposed approach in this area should extend existing forensic methods and published guidelines that are already well established for treating smartphones, networks and cloud environments (Martini & Choo, 2012).

Figure 1. Schematic visualisation of the architecture of IoT

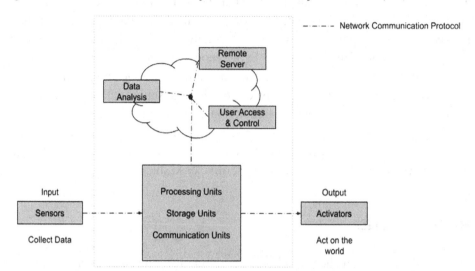

Typology of IoT Traces

The large variety, volume and velocity of IoT traces, as well as their distributed nature, pose practical challenges for forensic personnel both in crime scene management and IoT device analysis (Servida & Casey, 2019). Understanding the typology of IoT traces helps address these challenges in a methodical manner, focusing effort on sources of digital evidence that are most relevant to a given investigation.

Note: This chapter does not specifically address tangible or material characteristics of IoT objects such as identifiers (e.g., serial numbers) or damage (e.g., break points in an alarm system, pinched pin on a connecting outlet). Such details are important to consider in an investigation and can be documented in the same manner as other observable characteristics at a digital crime scene (Casey, 2011).

Fundamentally, because IoT devices can sense activities or take actions (Figure 1), any trace they generate can be categorized as *sensed* or *executed*. IoT traces can be further categorized as *stored* or *transmitted*. Stored IoT traces can generally be forensically preserved in their original state for a certain duration depending on their rate of degradation or external processes (e.g., log rotation, wear leveling). Such traces consist of a byte, a cloud, a web or an app interface, all of which can be found within an IoT environment. It is more difficult to preserve transmitted IoT traces in their original state because they are ephemeral, only existing for a brief moment. Although it is possible to capture a live recording of network communications via cable or radio waves (e.g., ZigBee, Z-Wave), this is often not available after a crime has occurred. Digital traces can be harder to document than material traces and sometimes can only be preserved by copying them in a snapshot that will represent the data in a specific spatiotemporal setting. This representation will also depend on how the data structures are transformed and presented by an interface (e.g., Graphical User Interface, Application Programming Interface).

Types of information that can be obtained from IoT devices and traces are summarized in Table 1. Any type of IoT trace might have an associated time or duration recorded, and this is not explicitly stated in Table 1 examples.

Many of these types of traces can be used to address forensic questions, including the presence or absence of a person or device in a particular place at a specified time, and associated activities.

Table 1. Taxonomy of IoT traces

Class	Event	Trace Example
State	Device was turned on or off, or lost connectivity	System messages describing change of device state
Time	Many activities on IoT devices have associated timestamps	Timestamps on alerts and logs generated by IoT devices
Action	Specific actions occurred near the object	Door opened / closed message
Movement	Motion sensor was activated	Alarm alert, camera recording
Temperature	Change in ambient temperature activated a sensor	Thermostat turns on/off heating/cooling with associated message, Automated assistant initiates a pre-programmed recipe when a certain temperature is detected which generates associated logs.
Location	Person/object was near the object	Person at home or dropped key in garden message
Steps taken	Person walked/ran/climbed	Number of steps taken is recorded
Distance travelled	Person travelled some distance	Distance travelled is recorded
Heart rate	Heart beat active or inactive	Person dies and heart beat stops being registered
Multimedia	Camera or microphone was activated	Photograph / video recorded, sound/voice captured

Case Example

Health application data correlated with murder activities. In March of 2018, Hussein Khavari was found guilty of the rape and murder of 19-year-old medical student Maria Ladenburger in Freiburg, Germany. The health application on his phone revealed "Climbing stairs"-activities at the moment he was suspected to have dragged the body down to the riverside where it was found.

In the context of IoT Forensics, it is necessary to distinguish between *abstract* versus *actual* traces. Although the abstract world can arguably be put aside when analyzing traditional traces such as fingerprints and DNA, IoT traces are inherently abstract because they are translated multiple times before they can be observed (Carrier, 2003).

In order to treat IoT traces effectively, it is necessary to understand how forensic principles apply to these new forms of evidence.

FORENSIC PRINCIPLES APPLIED TO IOT

For over one hundred years, forensic science has been developing principles and practices to exploit traces in order to gain insight into complex crime problems and to shed light on what happened, where, when, how, and sometimes who was involved and why. Applying these principles and practices to IoT traces helps address the aforementioned complex issues.

Uniqueness and Exchange

A fundamental principle that constitutes one of the primary pillars of forensic science is the uniqueness principle, also called the individuality principle (Kirk, 1963), which can be formally stated as follows:

- **Uniqueness Principle:** every object in the universe is unique, including individual traces originating from the same source.

The uniqueness principle implies a vast universe of variations and permutations, creating opportunities and challenges from a forensic perspective. On the one hand, it is theoretically possible to establish the unique source of a given trace, even within a large pool of possible sources. For instance, analysing characteristics of an alert message, it is often possible to establish that it originated from a specific IoT device in a given context, at a certain time. On the other hand, because each object and trace is unique, two cannot be identical. For instance, although two alert messages

6

generated by the same IoT device can contain identical content, they originated at different times and are stored in different locations (e.g., database rows). In reality, challenges arise when certain information is not available or cannot be verified. A video recorded by an IoT device includes a person's face, but the angle and resolution make it impossible to match exactly with a suspect's face. An IoT device log contains activity indicating that a suspect was at work when a murder occurred at his home, but the timestamps cannot be authenticated to confirm his alibi.

Case Example

Amazon Alexa captures user commands, creating a voice recording that could be analysed to classify and/or identify the person speaking. Although everyone's voice is unique, every recorded voice command is also unique, created at a different time from a different location with different tone, background noise, etc. The variations in every recording create challenges for forensic analysis, and it is not always possible to identify who spoke a given voice command.

There is always some uncertainty due to uniqueness, however minute or indiscernible the differences. This is one reason that terminology such as 'match' that suggests certainty is avoid in forensic findings, and that the legal standard of proof in criminal proceedings is 'beyond a reasonable doubt'. This inherent uncertainty drives the requirement in forensic science for a robust evaluative framework discussed in the *Hypothesis Testing and Assessing Alternatives* section below, to reduce the risk of false positives (e.g., misidentifications) and false negatives (e.g., missed identifications). Kwan introduced the Bayesian approach to evaluate the diverse hypothesis on the source of a trace and allow the expert to decide about establishing identity (Kwan, 1977). This subjective decision process applies to establishing identity in a forensic context, as discussed in the *Identification* section below.

Edmond Locard's exchange principle is another pillar of forensic science, which deals with the dynamics of an offense and applies to any activity and associated trace, not only a source and its mark. This principle is based on the observation that nobody can act with the intensity assumed by a criminal action without transferring traces between themselves, the victim(s) and their surroundings (Locard, 1920).

- **Exchange Principle:** the dynamics of an offense cause traces to be exchanged between the offender(s), victim(s) and environments (both physical and virtual).

Often, this principle is paraphrased in English as "every contact leaves a trace" which has the problematic effect of obscuring the importance of activity, whilst also omitting traces being removed or destroyed, and transforming a scientifically valid principle into a statement which cannot satisfy a modern science (Roux, Ribaux, & Crispino, 2012) and as such is difficult to defend in court. The exchange principle is considered as the founding statement of forensic science acting as a fundamental concept to validate the analytic conception of steps: if one attempts to reconstruct what happened, the exchange of traces has to be assumed, otherwise everything that can be done is void.

Case Example

IoT traces do not necessarily result from direct contact between an entity and object. Activities nearby IoT devices cause traces to be generated without making direct contact. For example, an individual walking into a room can activate IoT devices using sounds and movements. In addition, when IoT devices come near each other, they can exchange information automatically, such as hardware identifiers (e.g., MAC address).

So far, no case is known where the exchange principle has not held up for digital traces as well, even though the urban legend of the perfect hacker persists. The complexity of computer systems, especially in the case of logging and file systems, has rendered it effectively impossible to interact with such a system without leaving traces of this interaction. In reality, computer systems have been found to be particularly rich sources of evidence (Pollitt, 2008).

Case Example

The effective impossibility of interacting with a system without leaving a trace is magnified by IoT devices because of their always-on connected nature. Walking into a room that is equipped with IoT objects generates many traces from multiple sources. It is effectively impossible to enter such a room without some traces on IoT devices being generated, and it is equally infeasible to remove all of the traces from the various sources. As a result, forensic challenges created to promote research and development typically contain traces of the creators (Servida & Casey, 2019).

Provenance and Integrity

The trustworthiness of digital evidence is a central requirement in forensic science, reducing the risk that evidence can be altered, replaced with incriminating evidence, or contaminated in some other fashion. Maintaining transparency throughout the lifecycle of evidence enables others to assess the reliability of forensic results. From a legal perspective, this ideally satisfies the fact-finder or decision-maker that the contents of the data have remained unchanged, that the information in the data does in fact originate from its purported source, and that extraneous information such as the apparent date of the data is accurate. The underlying principles can be stated formally as follows:

- **Origination Principle:** Document the original context of evidence to record information about where is was found or obtained, including where and when.
- **Handling Principle:** An audit trail or other record of all processes applied to evidence should be created and preserved throughout its lifecycle. Document what processes, tools, and transformations were applied to evidence throughout its lifecycle in sufficient detail that an independent third party can repeat the same processes and achieve the same result.
- **Integrity Principle:** No action taken by forensic personnel should change data which may subsequently be relied upon to support forensic conclusions.

It is not always possible to establish that digital evidence is the same as the originally seized data, because it is not always possible to compare the acquired data with the original. This is particularly true with an IoT device, which is constantly changing or only partial information can be extracted. Therefore, it is only possible to establish that the data came from a particular device and that the data has remained unchanged since it was acquired. Documentation, particularly chain of custody (a.k.a. continuity of possession), plays an important role in establishing the provenance of traces from IoT objects. Integrity of digital traces is typically established and verified using cryptographic hashes.

When dealing with IoT objects, it may be necessary to dismantle and repair a device. In addition, it is often necessary to use a hardware and/or software tool to copy and transform data into a format that supports forensic processing. The forensic acquisition process should change the original evidence as little as possible and any changes should be documented and assessed in the context of the final analytical results (Casey, 2007).

Case Example

In a home invasion case, the smart hub of the apartment is seized. The investigators document photographically and by taking notes where the hub was found, what cables where branched and what state the device was in. The internal memory of the hub is copied. A hash of the image is created and compared to the original hash. Since the device is not a standard device, all steps and manipulations are documented in detail.

Documenting how evidence was processed does not end at preservation. When analyzing and producing findings from evidence, forensic personnel need to follow a process that is reliable and repeatable; documentation is a critical component, enabling independent evaluation of results.

Reproducibility and Repeatability

Given the grave consequences of mistakes, forensic science is constantly striving to increase the quality and reliability of results by improving forensic processes, technical review, competency testing, and forensic technology. Furthermore, forensic science continually seeks more reliable and refined ways to evaluate and express the value and confidence in results.

It is sometimes necessary for others to repeat a forensic process and reproduce associated results in order to verify their veracity. In some cases, another forensic scientist will repeat a forensic process using different methods or tools. Repeating a forensic process and obtaining different results can reveal mistakes, tool errors, bias, misinterpretation and forensic fraud:

- **Reproducibility Principle:** As with any scientific study, the data, methods, tools, analysis and reasoning of a forensic process are described in sufficient detail that they can be carried out again with the same results.

This principle also emphasizes the importance of documentation; maintaining an account of the specific information, observations and analysis involved in a forensic process provides transparency and helps others assess the work and reliability of results.

An important aspect of the scientific method is that any experiments or observations must be repeatable in order to be independently verifiable. This is particularly important to be able to independently verify findings in a forensic context, when a person's liberty and livelihood may be at stake. Therefore, it may become necessary for one forensic analyst to repeat some or all of the analysis performed by another forensic analyst. To enable such a verification of forensic findings, it is important to document the steps taken to find and analyze digital evidence in sufficient detail to enable others to verify the results independently. This documentation may include the location and other characteristics of the digital evidence, as well as the tools used to analyze the data. (Casey, 2011)

Case Example

During a trial, a second expert is mandated to verify the forensic examination performed by the first expert. By following the documentation of the first expert, the second expert manages to reproduce the same results.

- **Virtual-Physical Principle:** The physical and virtual worlds are linked together, and activities in one influence the other directly or indirectly.

A command sent via a smartphone app in the virtual world can remotely unlock the entrance door to a smarthome in the physical world. A key being used to open the entrance door to a smarthome in the physical world can generate an alert to display on the homeowner's smartphone in the virtual world. The person in possession of the smartphone is indirectly linked to the activities in the physical world via the virtual identity of *the user of the device*. This indirection is not just an academic discussion, it has also been recognised by courts as being an element that requires consideration.

In Commonwealth v. Mangel ("COMMONWEALTH v. MANGEL," 2018), the Pennsylvania Superior Court upheld a decision rejecting the use of a Facebook page supposedly belonging to the defendant due to insufficient authentication. In this case, the Commonwealth claimed that an account with the same name as the defendant, containing other details compatible with the defendant, should be considered as the defendant's account and that messages posted on it should be considered as having been written by the defendant himself. The posts were intended to support the prosecutions claim that the defendant committed an assault at a party in summer 2016.

The opinion of the court differed, observing that essential steps had been omitted, such as asking the defendant whether the account belonged to him, who else might have had access, or obtaining the history of the origin of connections to this account to assess the possibility of someone else accessing the account. In other words, the court considered that the investigators did not sufficiently establish that the virtual identity of the account user was in fact linked to the physical identity of the defendant.

Three approaches exist to bridge the gap between the physical and the digital world:

1. Assessing the possibility of access to the account or the device. Multiple stages of the process to access the resource in question are probed to see whether or not they correspond to the expectations. Whilst this approach has been validated by courts (e.g., Commonwealth v. Mangel), its strength has not yet been evaluated scientifically.
2. Searching for digital recordings of physical properties. People can be identified using biometrics: physical properties such as appearances, characteristics in

voice or movement are given a profile, which is then compared to the properties of the characteristics of the general population. The closer the profile of the contested element is to the profile extracted from known source material, and the better it is distinguishable from the general public, the higher the weight in favour of an identification. (Dessimoz & Champod, 2008)

3. Identifying behavioural characteristics in available data and showing the absence (or presence) of deviations within certain periods. These cues can then be used to infer whether or not the person currently using the phone is the regular user of the device or not (Guido et al., 2016).

IoT traces are of particular interest in this regard, because a large quantity of biometric data is available, relating directly to the physical world. For example, commands spoken to an automated assistant such as Amazon Alexa can be exploited to link the virtual identity of the user with the physical identity of the person by the means of voice recognition.

Testing Hypotheses and Assessing Alternatives

Testing a working hypothesis is integral to scientific practices. This process includes assessing alternative explanations. Attempting to disprove the working hypothesis on the basis of the available evidence is a fundamental aspect of scientific reasoning called falsification:

*   **Evaluation Principle:** When evaluating traces, forensic personnel must consider the likelihood of the traces given one hypothesis, as well as the likelihood of the traces given at least one alternative hypothesis mutually exclusive with the first one.

Case Example: Home Invasion and Burglary

A house was burgled while the owners were on vacation, and their valuable possessions were stolen. When the homeowners reported the theft to police, they did not know the exact date and time of the burglary. Without a specific time range, it would be difficult for police to ask neighbours if they noticed anything unusual, and it would not be feasible to request digital traces from nearby CCTV cameras or cell towers.

Initial examination of logs generated by IoT devices in the home revealed that motion detectors were activated the day before they returned home, starting at 3:36:32 AM on 4 July 2019. An evaluation of the IoT traces in this case could be structured could be structured as follows:

Hypothesis 1: The timestamps of these logs represent correctly the time at which the burglary happened.
Hypothesis 2: The timestamps of these logs do not represent correctly the time at which the burglary happened.
Hypothesis 3: The logs are linked with the burglary activities.
Hypothesis 4: The logs are linked with some other activity.

Further forensic analysis of IoT traces established the accuracy of the timestamps and reconstructed a chronology of events that were compatible with the home intrusion and burglary. The outcome of this evaluation process: it was more probable to observe these logs if a burglary happened than if another activity took place. This well-established timeframe allowed police to conduct a more focused and effective investigation, quickly leading them to two individuals who were seen in the area and were found to be in possession of items stolen from the home.

INVESTIGATIVE USES OF IOT TRACES

When a crime uses IoT devices or occurs in the vicinity of IoT devices, the resulting traces have the potential to answer a broad spectrum of questions essential to an investigation. In general, traces can be used to determine the source of the traces, create a link between a trace and the entity at its source, identify this entity, places of interest, reconstruct the spatio-temporal setting of the events, inform on different aspects of the criminal activity (Ribaux, 2014). IoT traces from sensory devices are of particular value when investigating crimes in the physical world, recording details about activities around the location and time of a crime, including identity-related information and what was said or done by people involved.

For example, home assistant devices have very quickly attracted the interest of investigators (Chung, Park, & Lee, 2017). For their functionality to work, these devices have to be listening to their surroundings constantly. Even though only legitimate commands are supposed to be recorded, it is widely known that such devices tend to record and store other interactions as well. [Source] Recorded sounds can give information about what happened, even if it is just an information about the presence of a person. Identity can be inferred using speaker recognition (Champod & Meuwly, 2000). Considering the difficulty of tampering with cloud data and the possibility to corroborate traces between multiple sources, the connectedness of multiple the IoT devices allows for a higher degree of confidence, in particular in regard to the correctness of timestamps (Casey, 2002).

Connected surveillance cameras have recorded crimes being committed. This gives a visual image of the crime, providing details about what happened and the people involved. If the identity of an individual in the video is contested, biometric approaches such as facial image recognition may be used, following a formal, systematic process (e.g., Analysis, Comparison, Evaluation - Verification [ACE-V]). Although surveillance cameras are not a new phenomenon, the fact that they now are frequently connected to devices that store recordings in the cloud renders the images better protected against intentional destruction. In addition, the connected nature of the devices facilitates independent verification of timestamp accuracy, an aspect that is often a challenge with classical surveillance cameras.

Besides IoT devices fixed to a given location, a series of completely mobile connected objects exists: drones, vehicle and wearable activity trackers. Those devices often store information about the user's location, activity and potentially identity which can be used to link a suspect to the place of a crime or, in other cases, give someone an alibi.

IoT systems may be equipped with detectors of human presence in a room, for example to turn up heating or light based on the measures. Detectors exist as well to see whether or not doors and windows are closed. Even though these kinds of detectors might not provide sufficient information to identify a person, they do foster some degree of conclusion about the activity of people in a space and when those activities took place. Similar information can be gathered based on interaction with devices, such as turning on a connected kitchen or entertainment device.

One other aspect that must be considered, is intentional malicious disruption or misuse of IoT devices. If the perpetrator gains access to the system, he may be able to turn off surveillance cameras as well a sensor for security systems, such as detectors of doors opening or smoke detectors. Resulting IoT traces give information about the temporality of an act, and can be highly indicative of criminal intent. In a fire investigation, if it is unclear whether intentional arson was the cause, the intentional disabling of smoke detectors or sprinkler systems prior to the fire is a highly interesting finding. Additionally, based on the way the access took place, it might also be possible to find traces containing identity-related information related to the perpetrator. For example, when the hardware identifier of the device used to disable the system is captured and can be associated with the perpetrator's mobile phone.

When an IoT device is misused by a perpetrator, it is not just a witnesses to a crime, is becomes the tool used to commit the act. One way this can happen, that has already been observed worldwide, is the use of IoT devices as botnets in Denial of Service attacks (Kolias, Kambourakis, Stavrou, & Voas, 2017). A similar concept was explored by Princeton researchers proposing that a botnet consisting of IoT devices may be used to black out a power grid by simultaneously turning on a large quantity of IoT devices with a high energy demand (Soltan, Mittal, & Poor, 2018). . Whilst in the latter case, IoT devices with a high energy consumption are of particular interest, in both cases, the intended role of the device is of lesser importance. The attacker uses the networking capabilities of IoT devices and does not really care about its other uses. Found traces are therefore susceptible to be similar to the traces found regularly in malware cases.

One could also imagine a case of a connected stove being remotely accessed to set a house on fire, devices being turned randomly on to annoy the inhabitants, or a connected car being used to cause a fatal accident or to abduct someone. In these hypothetical cases, in addition to classical malware traces, one would be interested in IoT traces to reconstruct the events caused by the intruder.

The use of traces can go even beyond constructing a case against a suspect to support operational intelligence (Bitzer, Albertini, Lock, Ribaux, & Delémont, 2015). Operational intelligence is a more specific use of intelligence, where information is exploited to detect repetitions in criminal behavior, follow their evolution and find ways to restrain them (Ribaux, 2014). For instance, the study of burglaries in Switzerland influenced the disposition of police patrols during the day: the studies had shown that burglaries were more likely to happen in winter due to the early sunset. In this case, IoT traces could be helpful in allowing the police to be even more knowledgeable about the timeline of these burglaries or the modus operandi and take measures in preventing them from happening (Birrer, 2010).

The study of criminal situations can be a powerful tool to detect and analyze a set of repetitive activities. As the environment of a criminal act constrains the perpetrator to act in a certain way (Felson, Clarke, & Great Britain Home Office, 1998), the traces that are left will then also present similarities. Those similarities can then be used to discover patterns, as they depend on the activity and its environment. If an author uses a technique or a tool with regularity, traces will then allow us not only to link the cases but also to detect changes in methods of operation and underlying behaviors (Ribaux, 2014).

In summary, IoT traces linked to the identity of the perpetrator and his activities (behavior) in a given context and time period can all be of some importance not only to find and condemn the criminal but also to understand a new criminality and respond strategically (e.g., disrupt or prevent similar crimes in the future).

FORENSIC PROCESSES APPLIED TO IOT

Ongoing efforts to harmonize digital forensics with forensic science principles and, processes define forensic science as "The systematic and coherent study of traces to address questions of authentication, identification, classification, reconstruction, and evaluation for a legal context" (Pollitt et al., 2018). In this context, the study of traces from IoT devices encompasses scientific reasoning, experiments in a controlled laboratory environment, as well as forensic analysis of actual traces encountered in a digital investigation. Examples of how the core forensic processes might be applied to traces from IoT devices include:

- **Authentication:** The recorded event actually occurred. The event occurred at the recorded time.
- **Identification**: The recorded event was performed by a given user account (virtual person). The recorded event was performed by a specific human being (physical person).
- **Classification:** The recorded event was a door unlock. The recorded event was an alarm disable.
- **Reconstruction:** Recorded traces used to create a timeline of events, frequency of activities, interruption of routine activity, link analysis between entities, how a given device functions, mapping events to message ID, functional analysis of possible/impossible scenarios in a given environment.
- **Evaluation:** Producing a value for the level of confidence / strength of evidence, or for the confidence level in the results produced by some other core process. For example, such a value could represent the confidence level in one of the possible scenarios resulting from the reconstruction process.

Hypothetico-Deductive Reasoning

Forensic scientists must employ a formalized logical process that is rigorous and repeatable in order to minimize cognitive bias, and to avoid incorrect assumptions (blind spots) and unfounded conclusions.

Scientific reasoning in the service of a court is somewhat different than in most other sciences where it is attempted to gain general knowledge from the observation of phenomena. In casework, a forensic scientist attempts to learn about the action that caused the observed evidence. This is generally done in a two step process called hypothetico-deductive reasoning. First, potential explanations, so called propositions, of a given situation are explored, ideally covering the most important possible reasons for a situation at hand. Second, for each of those propositions, it is established how likely it would be to observe the evidence found, assuming this particular proposition to be true. This allows for a ranking between the proposition in order of their respective capability to explain the observed evidence. Propositions under which it is impossible to observe the evidence at hand are disproved and can be discarded. Further evidence has then to be gathered until all but one propositions can be discarded or until one proposition is sufficiently high ranked in regards of the others that it can be decided that it is considered as the reason for the traces (Kwan, 1977).

It is important to realize that such scientific reasoning does not lead to certainty in conclusions. Any scientific process is limited by available facts, and must guard against cognitive bias. The focus of an investigation, exposure to case details, which traces are selected for analysis, how a forensic question is phrased, past experience, and other human factors can all contribute to cognitive bias (Sunde & Dror, 2019).

Almost certainly, the [forensic] scientist will be influenced, consciously or sub-consciously, by what she has been told about the case circumstances. There may well also be the influence of her past experience of similar situations and of the explanations that were proven to be true, or otherwise, in those cases. This information and knowledge may provide a valid, robust assessment of the priors but there is a risk of the scientist being swayed [towards one hypothesis] by unreliable or limited prior information, from witnesses for example… (Jackson, Jones, Booth, Champod, & Evett, 2006)

To mitigate these risks, any explanatory hypothesis must be tempered by careful consideration of the facts, or revised as new facts are found. This is the fundamental role of scientific reasoning.

Case Example: Sexual Assault

In an assault case, motion detectors can be seen to activate three times in the period of interest. The investigator states the following hypotheses:

Hypothesis 1: The first activation is the victim arriving at the house, the second the aggressor arriving and the last one is the aggressor leaving.
Hypothesis 2: The first activation is the aggressor arriving at the house, the second the victim arriving and the last one is the aggressor leaving.
Hypothesis 3: At least one of the activations is not in relation to the case.

To discard H3, the investigators check whether or not it is possible to access the house without activating the motion detector. In addition, they test whether or not they can distinguish between a single person arriving and multiple persons arriving.

To differentiate between H1 and H2, the known activities of the victim are put in relation to the timestamps to test whether this rules out one of the possibilities.

Authentication

In general terms, authentication is *the decision process attempting to establish sufficient confidence in the truth of some claim* ((Pollitt et al., 2018)adapted from (Jaquet-Chiffelle, 2009a) adapted from(National Research Council, 2003). In other words, for any authentication process, there is a (sometimes implicit) claim of which truth needs to be established with sufficient confidence. More precisely, an evaluation process is performed and produces a value: the level of confidence in the truth of the claim. The authentication process is successful if and only if this value is above an a priori chosen positive threshold.

Authentication is intertwined with forensic science principles and other forensic processes. For instance, related to the provenance and integrity principles, trace authentication is a common form of authentication in a forensic context, i.e., determining whether a trace is what somebody purports it to be, such as a photograph or message being true and accurate. In this context, authentication considers whether an item has been altered or falsified.

From a forensic perspective, authentication typically deals with the following aspects of evidence, addressing questions of what, when, who, where, and how:

- **Object (what)**: is an item authentic or forged?
- **Time (when):** did an event occur in a specified time period or sequence?
- **Source (where/who/what):** did an item originate from a specific object, person, location, or did two items originate from the same source?
- **Process (how):** did a given cause, or series of causes, result in the observed evidence?

When authentication is not successful, it just means that sufficient confidence in the truth of the claim could not be established; it does not mean that there is enough confidence in the untruth of that claim. The result can be in a grey, inconclusive zone. However, when the negation of the claim can be authenticated, additional forensic questions can arise such as whether digital evidence was altered inadvertently or intentionally, and forensic scientists may be compelled to consider plausible causes, including forgery and fraud.

Identification

Due to its many facets and nuances, identification is one of the most difficult processes in forensic science to define. Identification is *the decision process attempting to establish sufficient confidence that some identity-related information describes a specific entity in a given context, at a certain time* ((Pollitt et al., 2018)adapted from(Casey & Jaquet-Chiffelle, 2017);(Jaquet-Chiffelle, 2009a)). An entity is anything that has a distinct existence; it is the fundamental "thing" that can be identified ((Jaquet-Chiffelle, 2008);(Jaquet-Chiffelle, 2009b)). It refers to any animate or inanimate object (or class of objects), physical or digital. As a special case, identification is called *individualization* when the identity-related information distinguishes a specific entity from all others in a given context and time.

Notably, identity-related information is not limited to what the entity is, but can also what an entity has, knows/chooses or does/prefers (Casey & Jaquet-Chiffelle, 2017). This complexity is perceived in IoT contexts when various traces are combined to reconstruct activities, giving identity-related information in the form of what an individual does. An emerging area of research in digital forensics deals with establishing the link between the virtual and physical worlds to a sufficient level of confidence as discussed in the *Virtual-Physical Link* section above.

Case Example

When a person enters their smart home, they have a code or device that unlocks the door and disable the alarm. Then their presence in the home activates an environmental configuration with personalized music, light color/intensity and temperature. They then have a snack of beer and cheese which is registered by the smart refrigerator. As their activities continue, their identity becomes more evident in the IoT traces.

It can be challenging to link virtual identity to a physical identity, but it is possible in many cases.

Case Example

The question of the identity of the driver of a connected car is raised. Logs of driving habits, seat configuration, the connected smartphone and the radio chain the driver listened to are all elements that favour one driver out of a pool of potential drivers. Each element increases the confidence that this person is the driver of the car at the moment of interest.

There are various ways that identification is applied to IoT traces, including:

- Facial comparison in a photograph or video
- Speaker comparison in a voice recording
- Online account information (virtual identity)
- Use of IoT devices (something you do)

Trace identification is another special case discussed in the *Uniqueness and Exchange* section above, which is the process of recognizing characteristics that distinguish a specific trace from others of the same class, in a given context and time. These distinguishing characteristics can be used to form source conclusions, enabling forensic scientists to determine whether a trace came from a specified source or not. Source conclusions can also address whether multiple traces came from the same source or different sources.

Classification

Classification has two related facets. It is both *the development of taxonomies of traces and the decision process attempting to ascribe a trace with sufficient confidence to its class on the basis of characteristics that are common among traces of the same class, distinguishing them from traces of other classes* (Pollitt et al., 2018). Class characteristics may depend on both the trace and the events (e.g. actual activities) that led to the trace. Forensic classification, like classification in other scientific disciplines, has two facets. One facet is taxonomy, the scientific process that creates and defines classes (as well as rules or conditions to fulfill for an element to belong to a specific class). The other facet is ascription, the process that recognizes an element as belonging to a specific class. An element is ascribed to a class if it is established with sufficient confidence that characteristics of the class describe this element in this classification (context) at a given period of time. This type of information (class characteristics) can help determine which processes can be applied to analyze the trace, and can provide clues about the origin of the trace, potentially leading to source identification.

- Classifying the dialect of a voice recording is useful for narrowing the scope of potential speakers.
- Classifying malware on a computing device can provide useful information, even when the author or attacker cannot be determined.

Reconstruction

Digital and multimedia traces can be useful for establishing action, position, origin, associations, function, and sequence (Chisum & Turvey, 2011). Reconstruction is the process of organizing observed traces to disclose the most likely operational conditions or capabilities (functional analysis), patterns in time (temporal analysis), and linkages between entities – people, places, objects – (relational analysis) (Pollitt et al., 2018). Reconstruction involves combining traces to create an accurate understanding of what occurred related to an offense. With sufficient detail, reconstruction can provide insight into events related to a crime, as well as offense-related behavior (Turvey, 2011).

As noted in the above definition, ultiple subtypes of reconstruction exist: temporal analysis, relational analysis, functional analysis. In addition to determining the sequence and duration of events, temporal analysis can reveal patterns and gaps in the timing of activities. For instance, an alarm being disabled or a fire causing an IoT device failure. Relational analysis looks for associations and interactions between components of the crime. Association is a sub process of relational analysis, establishing links between entities, between traces, or between entities and traces. Functional analysis looks at what was possible or impossible in the given circumstances. For instance, to understand and evaluate digital evidence correctly, it may be necessary to experiment with a specific device or software application to determine how it functions and understand the meaning of data it creates.

Traditionally, reconstructions were formed gradually using traces found and analyzed at different times and places. More recently, visualization tools have been developed that can organize and display digital evidence in a manner that provides an overview of activities from the outset of a forensic analysis. In essence, such approaches enable more advanced analysis, including extracting narratives and theme clustering of text documents (Pollitt, 2013). For example, tools such as IBMs i2 Analyst's Notebook allows for automated importation of data into a relational or temporal graph (Reif, 2019). By importing network logs from a network containing IoT devices using an adapted importation specification allows to quickly gain an oversight into the interactions between those devices during a period of interest. This type of visualization conveys a large amount of information in a condensed form. In this way, digital evidence can be used to perform reconstruction from the beginning of a forensic analysis process, including performing temporal, relational, and functional analysis simultaneously. From this bird's eye view, significant activities or patterns can become apparent, requiring in-depth forensic analysis.

Evaluation

The process of evaluation aims to ensure that the decision maker is well informed about the significance of the sound traces in relation to the questions of interest in the procedure.

Evaluation produces a value that can be fed into a decision process (Pollitt et al., 2018).

It is important to note that forensic scientists are often required to fill different roles: an explanatory one and an evaluative one (Jackson et al., 2006). In both roles, forensic scientists use the scientific process to provide results that have probative value, but in fundamentally different ways. In an explanatory role, forensic scientists apply scientific reasoning to assess the observed traces in order to suggest explanations/ causes, prioritized based on their plausibility, and to highlight missing information. Results of forensic analysis performed in this explanatory role are factual or technical in nature and can be very useful for understanding crime, e.g. technical, investigative or intelligence reports. Articulating such explanatory hypotheses is one of the tasks that forensic scientists perform most frequently, and the results can be very helpful for understanding crime.

Examples of purely technical explanatory results are listed here:

- The IoT device found at the crime scene has the serial number 123456789
- The digital photograph contains embedded data "IoT device model number IOT123"

To avoid misinterpretation by decision makers, it is important to clearly express such results as explanatory hypotheses that have not been evaluated using a formal framework (e.g., Bayesian). The evaluation indeed is not explicit, often not even conscious, with an implicitly accepted level of confidence close to total confidence. While it is accepted practice in the explanatory role to express informally that one possible explanation is more likely than others, it is not appropriate to assert a specific level of confidence or likelihood to the forensic findings in the explanatory role.

Examples of investigative explanatory results are listed here:

- The digital traces produced by IoT devices were more likely caused by an unknown person physically entering the smarthome than some other cause (e.g., remote cyberattack).
- The digital traces produced by IoT devices were more likely caused by an accidental electrical fire than some other cause (e.g., arson).

It is common practice for such statements for investigative purposes to be stated in terms of the explanatory hypothesis to make them more understandable to non-scientists. However, this is not appropriate for the evaluative role - it is crucial to convey formally evaluation in terms of the strength of evidence.

Evaluative reporting differs from the above types of reporting in that it considers the findings given competing accounts of the events. It indicates the relative weight to be given to the findings. (Jackson et al., 2006)

When formalizing their opinions to help judges or other decision makers, forensic scientists shift into an evaluative role and express the uncertainties associated with their findings to help decision makers understand what probative value to attach to the evidence. Evaluation involves weighing of observed traces in relation to a given claim versus alternative, opposing claim(s).

To do so, and to ensure that the forensic expert does not encroach on the domain of the judge or jury, the expert is required to express his or her opinion as an opinion on the strength of the evidence. In a general court setting, multiple, concurring hypotheses are advanced by the parties. The role of the court is it to decide which one they consider to be true. For each of the advanced hypotheses, the expert reasons in an abstract universe, in which the underlying hypothesis is considered to be true. This hypothesis is never questioned and every observation made is reflected as the consequence of this hypothesis. A quantification of the likelihood that the made observations would be made within that particular, hypothetical universe is made. Ideally, this quantification is done on the basis of data resulting from systematic research, but it can also be done based on experience. Systematic research rarely studying the exact situation at hand, often a combination of both is necessary to conduct the quantification process. In comparing this quantification for multiple universes, a value can be obtained informing the court on how much more likely it is to observe the traces under one hypothesis in comparison to the other. (Aitken & Taroni, 2004)

This value can take multiple forms. Especially in regards to material traces, the chosen approach is often to quantify the likelihood as a continuous value between 0 (it is impossible to observe these traces) and 1 (It is certain to observe these traces), a representation that can be understood as conditional probabilities. The resulting value is a likelihood ratio, the ratio between these probabilities, a term that can as such be found in the so called odds form of Bayes Theorem. (Pollitt et al., 2018) Other approaches may consist in the use of discrete values or ordinal scales. An approach combining the latter with the likelihood ratio can be found in verbal scales commonly used to communicate results. (Marquis et al., 2016)

The purpose of evaluation is not to attain certainty, but rather to determine whether the confidence level meets a minimum threshold set by the decision maker (sufficient confidence). For instance, any identification process has some associated uncertainty, including source identification.

FORENSIC ACTIVITIES APPLIED TO IOT

Forensic science applies the following activities to study traces: Survey, Preservation, Examination, Documentation, Analysis, Integration and Interpretation. The following sections explain how these activities apply to IoT.

The Crime Scene

- **Survey:** Finding, detecting, recognizing potential sources of IoT traces.

When searching for pertinent traces, two spaces have to be distinguished: the crime scene and the scene of investigation. The crime scene is defined as every space containing traces in relation to the event, the crime, associated with it. In other words, the crime scene contains all locations where modifications happened as a direct consequence of the crime itself (the event under consideration). For a purely physical crime scene, this encompasses the place where the crime took place, but also the way the author escaped, hiding spots for objects related to the crime and everywhere where eventual victims passed through. (Martin & Delémont, 2002) Expanding the crime scene, it also encompasses cell towers with which mobile devices of the involved communicated, web servers related to the crime as well as the proxies and routers on the way to those web servers. In regards to IoT, the crime scene quickly becomes enormous due to the inherent interconnectedness of devices, especially if the devices are connected to the cloud.

Per definition, the crime scene is not known to the investigator, but remains an abstract construction of all space that contains information about the event. By definition, a crime scene is therefore always virtual.

Much more concrete, the scene of investigation is the collection of all spaces that are observed and treated for investigative purposes. Ideally, the scene of investigation has a high overlap with the scene of the crime, even though it is impossible to know, how much they correspond. The scene of investigation can evolve, taking into consideration the advancement of the investigation, and may contain spaces that turn out to be unrelated to the events.

Case Example

Connected devices at the place where a crime happens record traces linked to this event. They are therefore part of the scene of the crime. This is true as well for cloud servers to which this data is sent to.

In most cases, the investigator will not have access to every server where data from these devices is stored. They therefore will not be part of the scene of investigation. However the scene of investigation may also contain devices that were found on the scene but do not contain relevant traces, since they were not active at the time of the event.

Gathering and Preserving IoT Traces

- **Preservation:** Maximizing the amount of original data acquired while minimizing alterations, including isolating the system on the network, securing relevant log files, and collecting volatile data that would be lost when the system is turned off, and extracting data stored on the system. This step includes subsequent collection or acquisition (Pollitt et al., 2018).

Data pertinent to IoT devices in an investigation can be found in different places, either locally on the devices on-scene, remotely on the cloud servers or on the linked companion devices (e.g., smartphones) which could be both on scene or elsewhere. Handling IoT devices in a forensically sound manner, as discussed above in the Provenance and Integrity section above, is challenging when the device has to be examined live and/or might lose data if it is turned off.

On scene the data can be on the sensors themselves, on base stations for a given product/manufacturer or on products acting as a central aggregator for the data and control of devices of different manufacturers.

Data on sensors is normally very limited in size and time due to the small processing and storage capabilities of IoT devices, these act mostly just as a transit for the data; most of the data on-scene will be found on the base stations and aggregator devices. The data available varies a lot depending on the device but can range from just configuration information to event logs to even full multimedia samples. Traces at this point are in a raw form and it can be difficult to gain access to them. However, the devices most often present debugging interfaces and local network services; depending on how these interfaces are configured an investigator can exploit them to obtain access to the data (Servida & Casey, 2019). These interfaces can also have a misconfiguration, or even nonexistent security, that could also be exploited by malicious actors to access a user's sensitive data. Other techniques include advanced physical access to the device data either via programming interfaces such as JTAG or by desoldering the memory chips and reading them directly (a.k.a. chip-off).

It is important for investigators to have prior knowledge of the most common devices and the possible ways data can be obtained from them; with this knowledge investigators would know the best way to approach a device found on scene. They could then choose to prioritize on-scene analysis or to just collect the device and do advanced analysis in the laboratory.

Case Example

An investigator encounters a known device on scene. He knows on that particular device important activity logs are stored in volatile memory and would be lost on power off. He also knows that a vulnerability exists to extract this data prior to shut down. He therefore prioritizes on-scene analysis: using a tool exploiting the vulnerability he is able to obtain the information directly.

Had he not known the device beforehand this data would have been lost.

The raw form of the data extracted directly from the devices can also be problematic as one has to understand the format before being able to extract traces from it.

At a crime scene, IoT devices can be contaminated by exchange with police devices inadvertent brought into the area. As a precaution, documentation of police devices could be maintained to compare with traces found at the crime scene.

Remote data on the cloud is generally more extensive as there are less constraints about the size of data and the retention period. In this case it is useful to note a distinction between services that store and give access to the data without limit (or at least not apparent) and those that limit access to the data depending on a given subscription plan (access here is paramount, as the data may still be there in another form, eg., backups, just not available to end-users). This data is often accessed through a web interface or web Automated Programming Interface (API). In the opposite way than with data coming from the devices this data has already been transformed by the service and is only a representation of the events that happened on scene. As such it may be incomplete or vary depending on the device/user accessing it. A copy of this data can be obtained manually if the investigator has valid credentials and legal approval to access the account linked to the devices; these credentials could come either from a cooperative suspect or from unprotected configuration files on the IoT devices or the linked smartphones.

Companion devices, such as smartphones, which interact with the IoT devices directly or via the cloud are also an important source of IoT traces. Data on these companion devices is often stored in cache in order to be readily available to the user. Such cached information as well as unprotected configuration files can provide the investigator with information about the event or access to other sources (such as data stored on a cloud). Depending on the way the data is obtained it will be in raw or interpreted form.

When working with raw data obtained from one of these sources an investigator faces the challenge of understanding the content and extracting traces from it (Servida & Casey, 2019). On the other hand, working with data already interpreted by these services means the investigator may be working with incomplete or filtered data. In both cases an uncertainty is introduced in the process, will persist throughout the analysis and will strongly condition the final conclusion. The findings of such an analysis will only be valid, assuming the data obtained is correct and at least reasonably complete (Horsman, 2018).

A nuance of the meaning of preservation in a forensic context is that it is used to refer in an inclusive way to prevention of changes to potential evidence, including collection and acquisition, whereas it is additionally used in some contexts to describe the evidence management activities related to storing and maintaining of digital evidence and provenance information once the potential evidence is in custody (Casey, 2011).

Documenting IoT Traces

- **Documentation:** record traces, along with their associated context, characteristics, forensic activities, and provenance information (Pollitt et al., 2018).

Preventing changes of in situ digital evidence, including isolating the system on the network, securing relevant log files, and collecting volatile data that would be lost when the system is turned off. This step includes subsequent collection or acquisition of traces.

Especially in adversarial legal systems, an intact chain of custody is essential for every piece of forensic evidence. For anyone looking at a piece of evidence at a later stage, it must be possible to understand how and when the evidence was acquired (direct access to original data, or copy of remotely observed data), who could modify subsequently this data (inadvertently or intentionally), where that evidence was stored, who had access to it, and what operations were run on it, with what results, from the moment the evidence was recovered up until it was put into this person's hand. The only way for this to be possible is through a thorough documentation of all interactions and operations, as well as storage on a system with controlled accesses. Additionally, it is considered good practice to document hashes of all disk images and all relevant files as soon as they are obtained. This way, it can be shown later on that the operations that were applied on the data did not modify them. (Casey, 2011)

Utilizing IoT Traces

When IoT traces have been forensically preserved and documented, they are available for examination and analysis to address forensic questions.

- **Examination**: observe traces and their characteristics, recover information or content from data sources, and make the results available for analysis
- **Analysis**: process traces to obtain more information about their characteristics, and make the results available for integration, classification, reconstruction, and evaluation or interpretation. Analysis utilizes the results of the examination forensic activity, and places them into a technical context.

The examination and analysis of an IoT device will be divided between its multiple sources of information such as the object in itself, other connected devices and a cloud service if present. There might also be obstructions to forensic examination and analysis, such as deletion, encryption and encoding. For instance, IoT traces in the cloud might be encoded in an unknown way making their interpretation by a standard tool impossible or incomplete.

Integration is performed to combine results of multiple analysis processes to obtain a more comprehensive understanding of traces, typically to support the forensic reconstruction process, as well as the interpretation and evaluation.

Interpretation involves explaining the meaning of forensic findings to help reach decisions in forensic investigations and to help establish general theories in forensic research. In courtroom contexts, forensic scientists perform evaluations to help decision-makers understand and interpret the implications of the evaluation in the broader context of the case.

Presentation of evidence in a courtroom is a sensitive time during the case lifetime. The exposition should include the context of the case, the relevant uncertainties as well as avoid any kind of miscommunication or bias when explaining the force of the results. Uncertainties are unavoidable as the information carried by traces must be observed or measured: even if the trace is in remarkable condition and the influences around its birth are known, there will still be possible uncertainties coming from the tools used for forensic examination or analysis and from the expert, depending on knowledge and experience. Influences and uncertainties should be taken into account when presenting evidence in court, as well as the way by which this communication is handled.

For instance, a recording coming from a home assistant should be interpreted taking into consideration the state in which the device was found and the tools abilities to examine the traces and to analyze them. This will depend on the structure, format and size of the data and on the quality of the recording - multiple sounds could cause the isolation of one to be challenging or it could be too muffled. During the interpretation, the context of the investigation should be taken into perspective to estimate the value of the information. A weak identification of five gunshots in a recording could have more value in a certain case than the solid identification of the shooter's voice. To convey this value and this reasoning to the courtroom, a language has to be found and be common in the forensic community.

CASE STUDY

Despite the growing prevalence of IoT devices, only a small number of criminal investigations have relied on IoT traces. These devices might be overlooked as sources of evidence or the forensic personnel might not have the necessary knowledge to handle them as sources of evidence. To increase awareness and forensic capabilities, the DFRWS has created IoT forensic challenges with associated datasets that are publicly available. The DFRWS 2017 challenge is perfectly suited to illustrate the use of IoT traces to support an investigative proposition in a murder case. In the simulated case, Betty HALLYM was found dead in the living room of the apartment she lives in with her husband Simon. According to her husband, he found her coming back from the bedroom where he was watching TV and has not heard anything due to his noise cancelling headphones. The HALLYM household is equipped with a series of connected devices which were seized, and their data serves as the foundation for the challenge (James, 2017).

The challenge encompasses both IoT in the proper sense, with an Alexa, a Smart TV, a sensor on the entrance door, Betty's FitBit and Simons headphones, as well as connected devices in the form of the victims and her husband's smartphones. No cloud data was available in this case, but one could imagine demanding the server-side data from the provider and confirming the chronology of the events. Figure 2 shows a relational graph illustrating the core pieces of evidence in the challenge.

The data set can be used to reconstruct the events within the HALLYM apartment in great detail. The Fitbit gives very precise information about the last moment Betty HALLYM moved, giving a very precise time of death. This information could be obtained thanks to the connection of the bracelet with Bettys Phone. This is a typical example of information that would not be available in a classical setting. In this very restrained situation where the external factors (the last time Betty was seen alive and the moment of the discovery of her body) limit the span in which she might have been killed, the connected bracelets measurements further restrict the interval down to almost a moment.

On Betty's phone can also be found a heated discussion that can be interpreted as Betty attempting to break off an affair she was having and leading quite close to the moment of her death. This exchange could be used to infer a motive, either for the husband or for the lover. The use of chats as a trace is not really related to IoT, but has to be mentioned nevertheless because it is a core part in understanding the rest of the traces.

Of primary interest is whether or not the husband Simon was involved. According to him, he was in the bedroom watching two films on YouTube before he found his wife dead on the floor in the living room, after which he attempted to call for an ambulance. This version of the facts consists in a proposition that can undergo an authentication process in accordance with the OSAC core process mentioned earlier. It is attempted to establish sufficient confidence in the veracity of the proposition by following hypothetico-deductive reasoning and evaluations.

Assuming the proposition to be true allows to think about potential traces of interest. If Simon's version were to be true, we would expect to find traces of the SmartTV being turned on and traces of the videos being shown.

Effectively, the Smart TV shows the screening of YouTube videos in the period he claimed having watched them. An Alexa recording can be found where a man can be heard ordering the TV to be turned on. It can also be shown, that his headphones were active and connected to the TV. Also, the last recording made by Alexa is of the same man heard earlier commanding the turning off of the TV and the calling of an ambulance. Whether or not these observations consist "sufficient confidence" is up for discussion, and arguably not for the forensics scientist but for the court to decide, but they do somewhat support his proposition and do not allow his proposition (his version of what happened) to be disproved. Here the influence of the IoT devices on the possibilities of the investigation is enormous. Without IoT devices, it is unlikely that traces in support (or contradiction) can be found, making it impossible for a forensic scientist to formulate a statement on the proposition at hand.

It is not sufficient to say that there is evidence supporting the proposition of Simon's innocence. Supposing accidental and natural death can be ruled out based on the legal examination of the body, Betty has to have been killed by someone else. Based on the found WhatsApp conversation, it is reasonable to propose Betty's lover as a suspect, but also proposing an unknown person is legitimate. If this proposition is assumed to be true, we expect to find traces of the presence of this other person in the data stored by the devices in the apartment.

By carefully observing the data from the hub, traces of the main apartment door opening before and after the events can be found. Also, a third, so far unknown smartphone can be seen connecting to the home network. This is an indicator of another person entering the apartment in the period of interest, likely someone acquainted to the HALLYMs, due to the fact that his phone had been connected on the network before.

The final element that can be used are the rest of the Alexa voice recordings. After the recording of the man presumed to be Simon turning on the TV, a recording of another man and a woman, presumably Betty, having an argument can be found. This is just seconds before the last activity of Betty's fit bit.

Altogether, the traces form a strong support for the proposition of another man, possibly the lover of Betty, being the assailant. In addition, the hypothetico-deductive reasoning process indicates what next investigative to take on. If the person in the recording, supposed to be the assailant, really is Betty's ex-lover, priority should be put into identifying and finding him. Once in police custody, voice recordings of the man can be compared to the Alexa recording and his phone can be seized. Assuming this person to be the lover, it can be expected that the phones id would be the one found on the network.

Figure 2. Temporal visualization of relevant traces in the DFRWS 17/18 challenge.

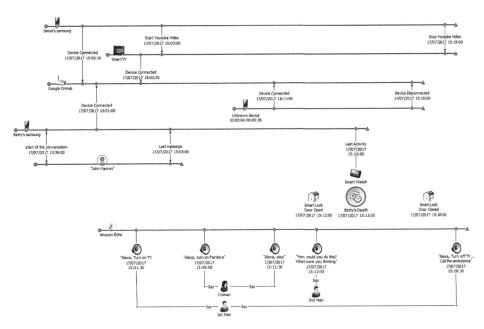

Again, not all traces are exclusive to IoT devices. The traces of the Smartphone connecting to the local network is something that could also be observed in a more traditional home. However, the voice recording and the door sensor strengthen the case, especially since it may be possible to connect to the network from outside the apartment.

In conclusion, discerning between the concurring propositions in this case, whether the husband, the victims lover or an unknown person is the assailant, is incredibly difficult based only on so-called traditional traces. The only elements that indicates the presence of a third person in the apartment would be the connection of a third phone on the home network, trace that may eventually also be explained by someone connecting from the stairwell or a neighboring apartment. Also, no element would be available to test the version given by Simon, putting him in the uncomfortable position of having been in the apartment while his infidel wife was killed. Even physical evidence may not help in such a case as such, since the presence of DNA, finger marks and fiber can be explained either by the fact that Simon and his wife live there together, or by Betty and her lover having an affair

The case at hand having been created for a DFRWS Forensic Challenge, the parallels that can be drawn to real cases are limited. The data is somewhat clinical in the sense that very few general data can be found. In a real case, the relevant data would likely have to be dug up from large quantities of background activity.

Also, the abundance of traces within the data is likely exaggerated. For example, the enactor of Betty uses the word Alexa to trigger the recording of their conversation, something that seems somewhat unlikely to happen in a real case. What remains true, however, are the vast possibilities of information that can be obtained when leading an investigation in a space containing connected devices.

CONCLUSION

Exponential expansion of IoT is driving the rapid evolution of forensic analysis of IoT devices and traces. The increasing volume of data produced by IoT devices can be useful in any type of investigation, including detailed information about events and identities in the physical world, such as who did or said what, when and where. These traces have the potential to invert traditional investigative processes by providing an initial digital reconstruction of events; focused forensic analysis of physical traces can then be performed to confirm key aspects of the case. At the same time, IoT devices can be instruments of surveillance and targets of cyberattack, raising privacy and security concerns.

IoT traces epitomize the decentralization movement in forensic science (Casey, Ribaux & Roux, 2018). IoT devices are distributed by nature, boosting the demand for forensic capabilities at the scene of investigation to fulfil immediate investigative and mission-oriented requirements. As a result, developers of digital forensic tools are competing to supply this in-field demand, thereby commodifying forensic capabilities for treating IoT devices and traces. Without robust knowledge creation and sharing mechanisms, study and understanding of IoT traces is isolated and weak, increasing the risk of mistakes and missed opportunities. The key for a successful future resides in the ability of forensic science institutions to valorize the production and delivery of value-added IoT Forensic knowledge, including forensic expertise, forensic intelligence and big data analysis within a privacy protecting legal framework, to those who need it (Casey, Ribaux & Roux, 2018). uch knowledge management of forensic principles, processes and activities pertaining to IoT devices is valuable for investigating crimes and cyberattacks, and can also be leveraged to improve security of critical infrastructure (Casey & Nikkel, 2020).

The difficulties in forensic analysis of IoT devices and traces are compounded by a lack of standardization in hardware manufacturing and software development, compelling forensic personnel to have a high capacity to adapt to novel devices and traces. This adaptability is possible with strategic research, education, and knowledge sharing across law enforcement, industry, academic and legal communities. The more IoT devices and traces are studied and knowledge is shared, the more experts will understand and how to use the information they carry and the place where to search for it. In addition to technical aspects, it is important to delineate roles, responsibilities, procedures and requisite skills for treating IoT devices and traces in different contexts. Investigators must be able to make sensible decisions when dealing with an IoT device as a potential source of digital evidence, and they require support from forensic specialists to handle more complex situations. Following a defined methodology allows forensic personnel to understand better what it is they are doing, to put more meanings into their actions, and to reduce errors, omissions and duplication of effort.

The results of forensic analysis of IoT traces will only be useful for a legal purpose if they satisfy fundamental forensic science principles and practices outlined in this chapter. Factoring in these principles and practices also facilitates the discussion between forensic expert witnesses and the court, by documenting the work done and the reasoning that was followed, allowing the court to understand the value that might be put into the information carried by traces and their shortcomings. Therefore, these principles and practices must be integrated into IoT Forensic Science research, education, and knowledge sharing in order to answer forensic questions for a legal context. In particular, establishing the link between virtual and physical requires innovative approaches, and more work is needed to evaluate and express the probative value of IoT traces and the links that can be inferred from them.

Ultimately, the forensic considerations and technical aspects must be integrated to make effective use of IoT Forensic Science to protect privacy, strengthen security, and reinforce the criminal justice system.

REFERENCES

Aitken, C., & Taroni, F. (2004). *Statistics and the Evaluation of Evidence for Forensic Scientists*. Wiley. doi:10.1002/0470011238

Birrer, S. (2010). *Analyse systématique et permanente de la délinquance sérielle: place des statistiques criminelles: apport des approches situationnelles pour un système de classification: perspectives en matière de coopération*. Academic Press.

Bitzer, S., Albertini, N., Lock, E., Ribaux, O., & Delémont, O. (2015). *Utility of the clue — From assessing the investigative contribution of forensic science to supporting the decision to use traces* (Vol. 55). Academic Press.

Carrier, B. (2003). Defining digital forensic examination and analysis tools using abstraction layers. *International Journal of Digital Evidence, 1*(4), 1-12.

Casey, E. (2002) "Error, Uncertainty, and Loss in Digital Evidence" International Journal of Digital Evidence, Volume 1, Issue 2

Casey, E. (2007). What does "forensically sound" really mean? *Digital Investigation*, *4*(2), 49–50. doi:10.1016/j.diin.2007.05.001

Casey, E. (2011). *Digital Evidence and Computer Crime - Forensic Science* (3rd ed.). Computers and the Internet.

Casey, E., & Jaquet-Chiffelle, D.-O. (2017). Do Identities Matter? *Policing. Journal of Policy Practice*, *13*(1), 21–34.

Casey, E., Ribaux, O., & Roux, C. (2019). The Kodak syndrome: Risks and opportunities created by decentralization of forensic capabilities. *Journal of Forensic Sciences*, *64*(1), 127–136. doi:10.1111/1556-4029.13849 PMID:29975983

Champod, C., & Meuwly, D. (2000). The inference of identity in forensic speaker recognition. *Speech Communication*, *31*(2), 193–203. doi:10.1016/S0167-6393(99)00078-3

Chisum, W. J., & Turvey, B. E. (2011). *Crime reconstruction*. Academic Press.

Chung, H., Park, J., & Lee, S. (2017). Digital forensic approaches for Amazon Alexa ecosystem. *Digital Investigation*, *22*, S15–S25. doi:10.1016/j.diin.2017.06.010

Commonwealth of Pennsylvania, Appellant v. Tyler Kristian MANGEL, Matthew Robert Craft. Commonwealth of Pennsylvania, Appellant v. Tyler Kristian Mangel, Matthew Robert Craft., No. 181 A.3d 1154 (2018) (Superior Court of Pennsylvania 2018).

Dessimoz, D., & Champod, C. (2008). Linkages between biometrics and forensic science. In *Handbook of biometrics* (pp. 425–459). Springer. doi:10.1007/978-0-387-71041-9_21

Felson, M., Clarke, R. V. G., & Great Britain Home Office, P. a. R. C. U. (1998). *Opportunity makes the thief: practical theory for crime prevention*. London: Home Office, Policing and Reducing Crime Unit, Research, Development and Statistics Directorate.

Guido, M., Brooks, M., Grover, J., Katz, E., Ondricek, J., Rogers, M., & Sharpe, L. (2016). Generating a Corpus of Mobile Forensic Images for Masquerading user Experimentation. *Journal of Forensic Sciences*, *61*(6), 1467–1472. doi:10.1111/1556-4029.13178 PMID:27545967

Horsman, G. (2018). *"I couldn't find it your honour, it mustn't be there!" – Tool errors, tool limitations and user error in digital forensics* (Vol. 58). Academic Press.

Jackson, G., Jones, S., Booth, G., Champod, C., & Evett, I. (2006). *The Nature of Forensic Science Opinion – A Possible Framework to Guide Thinking and Practice in Investigation and in Court Proceedings* (Vol. 46). Academic Press.

James, J. (2017). IoT Forensic Challenge, 2017-2018. Retrieved from https://github.com/jijames/DFRWS2018Challenge

Jaquet-Chiffelle, D.-O. (2008). The Model: A Formal Description, Section 7.2. In D.-O. Jaquet-Chiffelle, B. Anrig, E. Benoist, & R. Haenni (Eds.), *Virtual Persons and Identities, FIDIS deliverable 2.13.* Available at http://www.fidis.net/fileadmin/fidis/deliverables/fidis-wp2-del2.13_Virtual_Persons_v1.0.pdf

Jaquet-Chiffelle, D.-O. (2009a). Identification, Section 4.2. In D.-O. Jaquet-Chiffelle & H. Buitelaar (Eds.), *Trust and Identification in the Light of Virtual Persons, FIDIS deliverable 17.4.* Available at http://www.fidis.net/fileadmin/fidis/deliverables/new_deliverables/fidis-wp17-del17.4_Trust_and_Identification_in_the_Light_of_Virtual_Persons.pdf

Jaquet-Chiffelle, D.-O. (2009b). Identity Core Components, Section 7.2. In D.-O. Jaquet-Chiffelle, H. Zwingelberg, & B. Anrig (Eds.), *Modelling New Forms of Identities: Applicability of the Model Based on Virtual Persons, FIDIS deliverable 17.1.* Available at http://www.fidis.net/fileadmin/fidis/deliverables/fidis-wp17-del17.1.Modelling_New_Forms_of_Identities.pdf

Kirk, P. L. (1963). The ontogeny of criminalistics. *The Journal of Criminal Law, Criminology, and Police Science, 54*(2), 235. doi:10.2307/1141173

Kolias, C., Kambourakis, G., Stavrou, A., & Voas, J. (2017). DDoS in the IoT: Mirai and Other Botnets. *Computer, 50*(7), 80–84. doi:10.1109/MC.2017.201

Kwan, Q. (1977). *Inference of Identity of Source (PhD diss), Sociology.* University of California.

Locard, E. (1920). *L'enquête criminelle et les méthodes scientifiques.* E. Flammarion.

Marquis, R., Biedermann, A., Cadola, L., Champod, C., Gueissaz, L., Massonnet, G., . . . Hicks, T. (2016). *Discussion on how to implement a verbal scale in a forensic laboratory: Benefits, pitfalls and suggestions to avoid misunderstandings* (Vol. 56). Academic Press.

Martin, J.-C., & Delémont, O. (2002). *Investigation de scène de crime: fixation de l'état des lieux et traitement des traces d'objets.* Presses polytechniques et universitaires romandes.

Martini, B., & Choo, K.-K. R. (2012). An integrated conceptual digital forensic framework for cloud computing. *Digital Investigation, 9*(2), 71–80. doi:10.1016/j.diin.2012.07.001

Minerva, R., Biru, A., & Rotondi, D. (2015). Towards a definition of the Internet of Things (IoT). *IEEE Internet Initiative, 1*, 1–86.

National Research Council. (2003). *Who goes there?: Authentication through the lens of privacy*. National Academies Press.

Oriwoh, E., Jazani, D., Epiphaniou, G., & Sant, P. (2013). *Internet of Things Forensics: Challenges and approaches*. Paper presented at the 9th IEEE International Conference on Collaborative Computing: Networking, Applications and Worksharing.

Oriwoh, E., & Sant, P. (2013). *The Forensics Edge Management System: A Concept and Design*. Paper presented at the 2013 IEEE 10th International Conference on Ubiquitous Intelligence and Computing and 2013 IEEE 10th International Conference on Autonomic and Trusted Computing.

Perumal, S., Norwawi, N. M., & Raman, V. (2015). *Internet of Things(IoT) digital forensic investigation model: Top-down forensic approach methodology*. Paper presented at the 2015 Fifth International Conference on Digital Information Processing and Communications (ICDIPC). 10.1109/ICDIPC.2015.7323000

Pollitt, M. (2008). *Applying Traditional Forensic Taxonomy to Digital Forensics*. Paper presented at the Advances in Digital Forensics IV, Boston, MA.

Pollitt, M. (2013). Triage: A practical solution or admission of failure. *Digital Investigation, 10*(2), 87–88. doi:10.1016/j.diin.2013.01.002

Pollitt, M., Casey, E., Jaquet-Chiffelle, D.-O., & Gladyshev, P. (2018). *A Framework for Harmonizing Forensic Science Practices and Digital/Multimedia Evidence*. Retrieved from : doi:10.29325/OSAC.TS.0002

Pour, M., Bou-Harb, E., Varma, K., Neshenko, N., Pados, D., & Raymond Choo, K.-K. (2019). *Comprehending the IoT Cyber Threat Landscape: A Data Dimensionality Reduction Technique to Infer and Characterize Internet-scale IoT Probing Campaigns* (Vol. 28). Academic Press.

Reif, M. (2019). *L'implémentation de CASE aux extractions Cellebrite* (Master Degree Mémoire de Maîtrise). Université de Lausanne.

Ribaux, O. (2014). *Police scientifique: Le renseignement par la trace*. PPUR, Presses polytechniques et universitaires romandes.

Roux, C., Ribaux, O., & Crispino, F. (2012). *From Forensics to Forensic Science* (Vol. 24). Academic Press.

Servida, F., & Casey, E. (2019). IoT forensic challenges and opportunities for digital traces. *Digital Investigation, 28,* S22–S29. doi:10.1016/j.diin.2019.01.012

Soltan, S., Mittal, P., & Poor, H. V. (2018). *BlackIoT: IoT botnet of high wattage devices can disrupt the power grid.* Academic Press.

Stop Secret Surveillance Ordinance. (2019). *File #190110.* C.F.R.

Sunde, N., & Dror, I. E. (2019). Cognitive and human factors in digital forensics: Problems, challenges, and the way forward. *Digital Investigation, 29,* 101–108. doi:10.1016/j.diin.2019.03.011

Turvey, B. E. (2011). *Criminal profiling: An introduction to behavioral evidence analysis.* Academic Press.

Zawoad, S., & Hasan, R. (2015). *FAIoT: Towards Building a Forensics Aware Eco System for the Internet of Things.* Paper presented at the 2015 IEEE International Conference on Services Computing.

Chapter 2
Key Vulnerabilities in Internet of Things:
A Holistic View

Kavitha Ammayappan
University of Hyderabad, India

Arun Babu Puthuparambil
Indian Institute of Science, Bengaluru, India

Atul Negi
University of Hyderabad, India

ABSTRACT

Internet of things (IoT) is a buzzword around the globe. Academics and industries are evolving to solve real-world problems with emerging technologies; IoT is one among them. Now, it's very prevalent to see IoT devices in varied application domains like healthcare, hospitality, home, oil and gas, aviation, agriculture and marketing, cold storage chains, food preservation industries, automobile, environmental pollution monitoring sectors, energy industries, marine and fisheries, dairy and poultry, logistics, smart home and smart city, etc. Industries and research institutes are focusing to enrich environment and ecosystem to bring back green world again for the millennials and our future generations to make this globe as a potential place to cherish. In this mission, IoT is playing a major role of protection and preservation. In parallel, hackers are trying to destroy this mission by exploiting varied cyber vulnerabilities. To make IoT systems robust against those vulnerabilities it is necessary to understand the key vulnerabilities in detail.

DOI: 10.4018/978-1-7998-2444-2.ch002

INTRODUCTION

The term *internet for things* was initially proposed by Kevin Ashton (2009), cofounder of AUTO-ID center at MIT. IoT paradigm has taken real world things getting connected to smarter devices. The industrial internet of is a union of two domains namely manufacturing and software. Manufacturing tends to focus on quality and long product lifespans. The software world tends to focus on speed and agility (Dirk Shama et al., 2020). IoT ecosystem is becoming smarter incrementally by advancing its architecture, end and edge device capabilities, data harvesting mechanism, data processing space, data analytics, security configurations, secure communications, remote debugging, secure storage to provide automated services to achieve minimal delay in setup, quick response time, quick recovery time etc. IoT deployment in healthcare domain mainly focused to have continuous monitoring of patients, in oil and refineries to deal with the challenges on unmanned regions, in smart home and hospitality domains to facility automated safety and security services and to save energy consumption, in automobile sectors to make vehicles more intelligent by having vehicle to vehicle (V2V) communication, to facilitate auto parking, to enable safe and comfortable driving, in manufacturing industry, to view the status of the assets at anytime, anywhere and to get speedy response from dealer and original equipment manufacturer (OEM), in agricultural domain, it is being deployed in precision agricultural and so on. Most of the IoT deployment scenarios have been achieved with the cloud services.

Security is very challenging in IoT since most part of the devices in IoT ecosystem are sensing devices, which usually do not have any processors and secure memory chips to hardcode passwords and calculate secret keys to protect the data that it is generating and transferring to the other component in the eco system. Normally these sensors in IoT eco system will be connected over wired medium and using proprietary protocols. Sensors commonly sense a change in an environment. Sensed data will be transferred mostly to the gateway via serial communication protocol. Physical security of the sensor node is mainly dependent on the stringent access control mechanism and operation of the same at the site.

In simple terms, internet of things can be defined as set of sensors connected with networking and analytics devices for collating critical data aspects of the one or more number of targets to make faster and précised observations and decision-making purposes.

OVERVIEW OF IoT SYSTEMS

IoT Architecture varies with respect to its use cases as it is being used in varied domains such as connected vehicles, smart home, smart cities, agriculture, energy sector, environment pollution protection arena, connected health, automation domains etc. Almost all IoT architecture is backed up by cloud infrastructure which mainly takes care of data analytics. Most of the commercial IoT solutions are based on either open source IoT platforms such as FIWARE, OpenMTC, SiteWhere and Webinos or based on proprietary solutions such as AWS IoT, IBM's Watson IoT Platform, Microsoft's Azure IoT Hub and Samsung's SmartThings. Most of the IoT architecture consists of five layers namely, sensors / actuators, devices, gateway, IoT Integration Middleware and Applications.

The definition on the above components are given below in Table 1 as specified in (J.Guth et al. 2018).

Table 1. Definition of IoT Components

IoT Ecosystem Components	Definition
Sensor	Captures information by responding to a physical stimulus and transfers it to connected device via electrical signals.
Actuator	Receives command from device and translated electrical signal into physical action.
Device	Hardware with a processor and storage; runs software and communicated with IoT integration middleware
Gateway	Has ability to translate different protocols and forwards data over IP and vice versa.
IoT Integration Middleware	Serves as an integration layer. Receives, processes, sends data and thus controls devices. It may have databases, graphical dashboards to manage devices and users. It can be accessed via APIs.
Application	Represents software and connects with Middleware to gain physical environ insight via sensors or manipulate physical world via actuators.

Seven-layer IoT architecture is available and has been proposed by Cisco ("The Internet of Things", 2014). Security is a major concern in these varied IoT architectures. Due to wide presence of different kinds of IoT devices, varied device hardware, softwares, operating system and protocols, IoT environment looks more of a heterogenous environment which presents lot of increasing challenges to protect IoT Devices. Most of the IoT devices', life span in the field is more without the option to upgrade and patch, which offers unlimited period to attackers to identify and execute exploits against those field IoT devices. Depending on the architecture, viable end-to-end security need to be defined and implemented to have secure communication in the IoT ecosystem.

Layer one devices can be either hub, cables or repeaters. Layer two devices are bridges, modem, network interface card. Layer 3 devices are routers, brouters. Layer four devices are gateways and firewalls. Figure 1 presents the general outline on IoT architecture.

Figure 1. General IoT Architecture

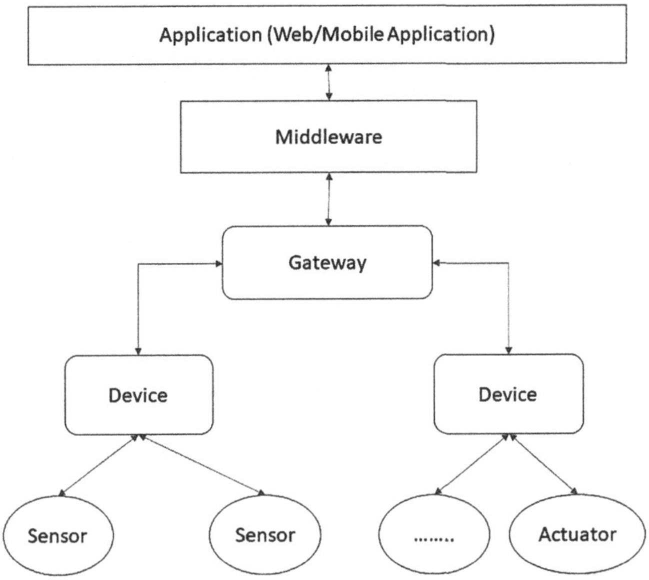

KEY VULNERABILTIES, EXPLOITS AND SECURITY RISKS IN IOT ECOSYSTEM

Vulnerabilities Exploitable in IoT via Communication Protocols

MQTT

Message Queuing Telemetry Transport (MQTT) Communication protocol being used in IoT devices widely, do provide authentication but not encryption. The reasons for preferring MQTT protocol is due to it's lightweight small code footprint and small bandwidth requirement. It is an ISO standard publish-subscribe based messaging protocol. Using MQTT, sensors deployed in IoT ecosystem periodically publish results of their measurements to a message broker. Each device needs to subscribe for a specific topic to receive a message from message broker when the topic gets updated. Hackers use black box penetration testing approach to explore the target using techniques such as shodan, Masscan, Nmap etc. In MQTT, message brokers which had connection code '0' are more vulnerable to exploit, since due to the lack of client authentication procedure. Also, MQTT broker did not block repeated authentication attempts which could led to DoS attack (Giuseppe and Maria, 2020). Message broker allowed anonymous publisher and subscriber to connect with it. Using this insecure handshake bot master could have controlled bot nets (Giuseppe and Maria, 2020).

Mutual authentication could be the one of recommended solution to overcome the above-mentioned attack scenario.

MQTT broker did not deal with proper authorization control, which could enable attackers to launch privilege escalation attacks and tried to get unauthorized resources. Proper authorization check should be in broker to prevent possible attacks.

Crafted MQTT messages from clients could make brokers unresponsive. Stack overflow at MQTT broker could be achieved from MQTT client by sending a SUBSCRIBE packet with atleast 65,400 "/" characters ("CVE 2019-11779", 2019).

DoS on MQTT broker might have achieved via a CONNECT packet with malformed UNSUBSCRIBE request packet ("CVE 2019-11779", 2019) from clients.

To achieve authenticated and encrypted communication between MQTT broker and MQTT client, it is advisable to use MQTTS protocol which makes use of TLS handshake to authenticate and establish an encryption key between broker and client (Openest, 2020).

HTTP Traversal Attack

It had been discovered as part of the research on IoT devices in the most recent firmware for Blipcare device. The device might allow to connect to web management interface on a non-SSL connection using plain text hypertext transport protocol (HTTP). When the user uses the web management interface of the device to provide user's Wi-Fi credentials so that the device could connect to it and had Internet access. This device acts as a Wireless Blood pressure monitor and is used to measure blood pressure levels of a person. This might had allowed an attacker who was connected to the Blipcare's device wireless network to easily sniff these values using a man in the middle (MITM) attacker ("CVE-2017-11578", 2017). Vulnerabilities to HTTP traversal attack ("CVE-2019-11603", 2019; Bosch, 2019) allowed remote attackers to read files outside the http root. TLS 1.2 and higher versions need to be used while establishing a handshake between the communicating nodes to avoid sniffing of secret credentials which are used to authenticate and establish the communication.

CoAP

In IoTivity through 1.3.1, certain constrained application protocol (CoAP) server interfaces might had been used for launching Distributed Denial of Service (DDoS) attacks using source IP address spoofing and user datagram protocol (UDP)-based traffic amplification ("CVE-2019-9750", 2019). This has been exploited due to specific response message mishandling (Giuseppe and Carla, 2020). To avoid message mishandling, strong input validation might be a potential recommended approach.

CoAP based systems also have been impacted by memory leak and remote code execution vulnerabilities due to overflow vulnerabilities exist in CoAP libraries and mishandling invalid options (Giuseppe and Carla, 2020).

XMPP

Extensible messaging and presence protocol (XMPP) is an application layer protocol meant for instant messaging services like google hangouts, whatsapp messenger and later used in voice over internet protocol. Slowly IoT applications used XMPP -IoT lightweight version and authors of (Malik et al., 2018) claim that XMPP is vulnerable to crafted messages during a session which could lead to shotgun parsers exploits. Denial of service (DoS) attack might had been achieved by sending a malformed XMPP authentication request to systems such as Cisco Unified Communications Manager Instant Messaging and Presence Service, Cisco TelePresence Video Communication Server (VCS), and Cisco Expressway Series which could allow an unauthenticated, remote attacker to cause a service outage for users attempting to authenticate, resulting in a DoS condition. Successful exploit might had allowed the attacker to cause an unexpected restart of the authentication service, thus might had prevented users from successful authentication ("CVE-2019-1845", 2019).

To overcome exploits using crafted messages, strong input validation need to be present at the target device.

AMQP

Spoofing vulnerability had been discovered when Azure IoT device provisioning Advanced Message Queuing Protocol (AMQP) Transport library improperly validates certificates over the AMQP protocol ("CVE-2018-8119", 2018). Certificate pinning need to be done to avoid impersonation of the legitimate devices. Cryptographic credentials used for authentication need to be secured inside the device to avoid extraction and tampering.

UDP

A vulnerability has been discovered in IoT Field Network director which uses UDP protocol. This vulnerability causes unauthenticated remote attackers to exhaust system resources which could lead to DoS attack("CVE-2019-1644", 2019). This is possible because of improper management of UDP ingress packets. Packets need to be validated for source authenticity and request from a specific source need to be limited and other denial of service prevention mechanisms need to be analyzed and implemented for an effective prevention against DoS attack.

Vulnerability Exploitable Due to Hard Coded Credentials

Attacker gets super user control of an IoT device via telnet session due to default and unremovable support credentials ("CVE-2018-11629", 2018) as cited below as an example ("CWE-798", 2018).

```
DriverManager.getConnection(url, "scott", "tiger");
```

Hardcoding passwords need to be strictly prohibited and if there is no other alternative for identifying the target without hardcoding, it should be changed once device communicates for the first time. Device should be provided with least privilege to avoid unnecessary exploits scenarios.

Vulnerability Exploitable via Web Based Management Interface

A web based management interface for an IoT device, could allow a cross site request forgery attack (CSRF) via an unauthenticated remote attacker. This usually happens due to insufficient CSRF protections in the web based management interface which is used to control the affected device. Basically, CSRF attack can make the intended victim to follow a malicious link which might perform an attack with the privilege level of the affected user while the user has an active session with the device. As per ("CVE-2019-1957", 2019) a vulnerability in the web interface of IoT field network director could allow an unauthenticated remote attacker to trigger high CPU usage, which results in a denial of service attack on the affected device. The vulnerability is due to improper handling of Transport Layer Security (TLS) renegotiation requests. An attacker could exploit this vulnerability by sending renegotiation requests at a high rate. A successful exploit could increase the resource usage on the system, eventually leading to a DoS condition. Again, web based user interface of IoT field network director software could allow a remote attacker to gain read access to information stored in the affected system. This is due to improper handling of XML external entity entries while parsing certain XML files.

To achieve cross site request forgery (CSRF) protection, try to use language-based prevention mechanism for example in Java you can use spring security for having authentication and authorization. CSRF tokens should be mandated for all state changing requests (OWASP Foundation, 2001). Customized logic to prevent CSRF need to be designed when there are no alternatives found.

Vulnerability Exploitable via Remote Code Execution

As described in ("CVE-2018-8531",2018), remote code execution vulnerability exists in Azure IoT Hub Device Client SDK which uses MQTT protocol allows to access objects from the memory. This bug could corrupt memory so that attacker could execute arbitrary code in the context of current user and thus the attacker gains the level of rights that the current user has in the system. Based on the level of privilege attacker could take control on the system. This also affects Azure IoT Edge.

Elevation of Privileges

Azure IoT Java SDK generates symmetric keys for encryption, allowing an attacker to predict the randomness of the key. As an impact, attacker could derive the keys from the way, they are generated and use them to access a user's IoT hub ("CVE-2019-0729", 2019). This seems to be a design flaw in the random number generation algorithm which need to be strengthened via foolproof implementation designs.

Vulnerabilities Exploitable in P2P IoT Technology

ILinkP2P is a P2P software and is a common feature in IoT devices. It facilitates access without user intervention for device configurations. It is found in security cameras, smart doorbells, video recorders, baby monitors etc. Exploitable vulnerabilities have been discovered in iLnkP2P. Enumeration vulnerability in iLnkP2P enables attackers to discover exploitable devices that are in online ("CVE-2019-11219",2019). Another exploit in iLnkP2P is a bug in authentication ("CVE-2019-11220",2019). An authentication flaw of iLnkP2P allows remote attackers to actively intercept device traffic in cleartext, including video streams and device credentials. Algorithm to generate device IDs (UIDs) for devices in iLnkP2P leaves attackers to predict the internal logic which allows remote attackers to establish direct connections to arbitrary devices ("CVE-2019-11219",2019). If attacker can able to guess UID which is a combination of alphabetic prefix with six-digit number, it can use that to establish a direct connection to the device and can own the device for any number of malicious purposes.

Mostly users of the IoT devices can't able to change security settings. Default security settings and security credentials are to be used. To have better security of IoT deployment, customers of such IoT devices need to demand better security from vendors (J. Curtis, 2019). Due to effective utilities of IoT, off late it has become our day today companion, in that case, expecting customers to secure their IoT devices do not make much sense as we have different segments of people.

Exploitable Vulnerability via Buffer Overflow

Lack of input validation for data received from user space could lead to an out of bound array issue in snapdragon consumer IoT platform ("CVE-2018-13914",2018). Improper validation of array index could lead to unauthorized access while processing debugFS in Snapdragon Consumer IoT ("CVE-2018-13913",2018). Truncated access authentication token leads to weakened access control for stored secure application data in snapdragon industrial IoT ("CVE-2018-13908", 2018). Signature verification of the 'skel' library could potentially be disabled as the memory region on the remote subsystem in which the library is loaded is allocated from user space in Snapdragon Consumer IoT and Snapdragon Industrial IoT ("CVE-2018-11967",2018). Data length received from firmware is not validated against the maximum allowed size which results in buffer overflow in Snapdragon Consumer IoT and Snapdragon Industrial IoT ("CVE-2018-11925",2018).

Exploitable Vulnerabilities in Secure Boot

As specified in ("CVE-2019-2278",2019) user key-store signature could be ignored in boot and which could lead to bypass boot image signature verification in snapdragon consumer IoT. Also Bootloader could be interrupted via uboot shell command and thus secure boot can be bypassed.

Remote Code Execution

("CVE-2019-2255",2019) presents a vulnerability which is exploitable in Snapdragon Consumer IoT, Snapdragon Industrial IoT etc. Using this vulnerability an unprivileged user could craft a bitstream such that the payload encoded in the bitstream gains code execution.

Vulnerability Exploitable Via Stack

("CVE-2019-11603", 2019; Bosch, 2019) among other things described a vulnerability via stack trace leakage in remote access to backup and restore. Using this, remote attackers gather information about file system structure.

Vulnerability Exploitable via Server

("CVE-2019-11603", 2019; Bosch, 2019) also described about a server-side vulnerability which affects the components of the IoT ecosystem like Gateway during backup and restore functionality. Here due to server-side request forgery, remote attacker could forge GET requests to arbitrary URLs and attacker can able to read sensitive zip files from the local server.

Directory Traversal Vulnerability

("CVE-2019-11603", 2019; Bosch, 2019) also talks about directory traversal vulnerability during remote access and backup process which could affect IoT Gateway component through which remote attackers can able to write or delete files at any location. It is a http attack, through which attacker can access restricted directories and run commands from outside the web server's root directory. This can be mitigated by making use of latest versions of Web server software with full patches. Additionally, input validation is very critical to prevent this type of attack by not executing the input request if it is suspicious.

Device Based Vulnerabilities

Lack of hardware based security features like secure data memory (Flash Memory, EPROM, SRAM), hardware security modules (HSM) makes IoT devices more vulnerable for exploits. Storing crypto credentials like secret keys, private keys, symmetric keys in a flash memory allows the possibility for data leakage via reverse engineering and accessing the memory location contents via any open interface in the device. But due to small factor of IoT devices, all the above-mentioned features are difficult to have as part of IoT devices. At least, to achieve minimum security like authentication and confidentiality, IoT devices should have relevant hardware capabilities. Most of the IoT system can be hacked with the default login and password credentials via user interface.

OS Based Vulnerabilities

Layer 3 and 4 devices are part of the IoT ecosystem which could be vulnerable due to exposed interfaces like ssh, telnet, ftp, bootloader command shell. Likewise, open debug interfaces like JTAG and serial wire debug used to access the memory space on the chip and their contents. Open interfaces and unused services, logins via ssh should be disabled in IoT devices, and other IoT ecosystem components to overcome exploits via these vulnerabilities.

KEY CHALLENGES IN SECURE IoT DEPLOYMENT

1. IoT devices don't have virus protection and malware protection software in them and therefore they can serve as bots.
2. Static key usage in IoT devices is generally considered as insecure, why because, static keys need to be hardcoded in every device of its kind and if it is compromised once, the same key usage leaves the communication open to exploitation.
3. Deploying/hardcoding security parameters in IoT devices is a real challenge when product manufacturers are not owning the hardware platform. Since they can't hardcode the seed value in One Time Programmable memory/secure element/secure memory of the hardware. To provide those security credentials, product manufacturers should be dependent on the hardware vendor which would leave opportunity for data leakage.
4. If manufacturing of the devices is getting outsourced, hardcoding secret parameters at the factory will be problematic due to third party involvement and again ends up in data leakage. In such scenarios, the approach is to use asymmetric key usage using certificates and verifying certificate with certifying authority. This may not be achievable in IoT due to low device processing capabilities, less memory space and low battery power availability in IoT devices.
5. Generation of dynamic key in an IoT mesh environment is again cumbersome due to lack of secure element to store and have seed values / private keys.
6. If firmware encryption is desired to protect intellectual property rights, but the hardware belongs to other stake holder of the product, the stake holder who provides the software solution shall not have any robust mechanism to hardcode decryption key without revealing it to the other stake holder who has more control on the device since it owns the hardware.
7. Possibility of reverse engineering the binary, if one gets the unencrypted binary.

8. Most of the conventional IoT devices, encryption at rest is not possible due to lack of cryptographic chip support at the hardware level.

Attacks Surface in IoT and Their Coverage

All the above discussed exploits are falling under the specified categories of exploits mentioned in (Lindsey, 2020; "Threat post" n.d.) and the same is taken for reference. The percentage of occurrence of specific exploits are also mentioned in Table 2.

Table 2. Coverage of IoT Attack Surface

Attack Surface			Coverage of Attack Surface
1. User Practice			26%
Phishing (8%)	Password (13%)	Cryptojacking (5%)	
2. Exploits			41%
SQL Injection (4%)	Buffer overflow (5%)	Zero Day (3%)	
Network Scan (14%)	Remote Code Execution (5%)	Command Injection (5%)	
Others (5%)			
3. Malware			33%
Botnet (6%)	Backdoor Trojan (7%)	Ransomware (8%)	

ANALYTICS OF CVE DATA RELATED TO IoT DEVICES AND TECHNOLOGIES

To perform analytics on IoT related vulnerabilities, a set of regular expressions (table - 3) were used on lower-case description of all CVEs. The regular expressions are used to match commonly used IoT devices and related technologies.

The below regular expressions were run on all the CVEs until 2nd Oct 2019; and matched 414 CVEs. The statistics of attributes are given in table - 4. The data was further analyzed using Simple K-Means and with two clusters; and the results are given in table - 5. The results of basic analytics indicate that the *Access Complexity* of attacks on IoT devices is Low in general, and are possible to be carried out on Network without authentication. In terms of impact, most of the attacks allow an attacker to get an unauthorized information, and likely to cause disruption of service, and allows an attacker to perform modification.

Table 3. List of regex ("Common Vulnerabilities and Enumerations", n.d.) used to match IoT related CVEs

'[, .]iot[^a-z0-9]',
'[, .]iiot[^a-z0-9]',
'[, .]freertos[^a-z]',
'[, .]contiki-ng[^a-z]',
'[, .]contiki-os[^a-z]',
'[, .]openwrt[^a-z]',
'[, .]raspberry[-]pi[^a-z]',
'[, .]arduino[^a-z]',
'[, .]beaglebone[^a-z]',
'[, .]smart[-]?watch[^a-z]',
'[, .]wifi[-]?bulb[^a-z]',
'[, .]ip[-]?camera[^a-z]',
'[, .]internet[-]?camera[^a-z]',
'[, .]smart[-]?home[^a-z]',
'[, .]smart[-]?lock[^a-z]',
'[, .]smart[-]?plug[^a-z]',
'[, .]smart[-]?tv[^a-z]',
'[, .]smart[-]?viewer[^a-z]',
'[, .]smart[-]?cloud[-]?tv[^a-z]',
'[, .]set[-]?top[-]?box[^a-z]',
'[, .]baby .+ monitor[^a-z]',
'[, .]radio[-]?thermostat[^a-z]',
'[, .]security[-]?cam[^a-z]',
'[, .]security[-]?camera[^a-z]',
'[, .]smart[-]?lighting[^a-z]',
'[, .]google glass',
'[, .]fitbit[^a-z0-9]',
'[, .]home router[^a-z]',
'[, .]robot vacuum cleaner[^a-z]',
'[, .]defibrillator[^a-z]',
'[, .]pacemaker[^a-z]',
'[, .]infusion[-]pumps?[^a-z]',
'[, .]insulin[-]?pumps?[^a-z]',
'[, .]quadcopter[^a-z]',

Table 4. Statistics of IoT related CVEs

Attribute	Values		
Access Complexity	Low (78%)	Medium (21%)	High (1%)
Access Vector	Network (64%)	Local (29%)	Adjacent Network (7%)
Allows unauthorized disclosure of information	True (85%)	False (15%)	
Authentication	None (91%)	Single (9%)	
Confidentiality Impact	Partial (51%)	Complete (34%)	None (15%)
Provides Administrator Access	False (99.8%)	True (.2%)	
Victim must voluntarily interact with attack mechanism	False (90%)	True (10%)	
Availability Impact	Partial (37%)	Complete (36%)	Neutral (27%)
Allows disruption of service	True (72%)	False (28%)	
Allows unauthorized modiðcation	True (72%)	False (28%)	
Integrity Impact	Partial (41%)	Complete (31%)	None (28%)

Table 5. Simple K-Means analysis of IoT related CVEs

Attribute	Full-Data 414	Cluster-0 310 (75%)	Cluster -1 104 (25%)
Access Complexity	Low	Low	Low
Access Vector	Network	Network	Network
Allows unauthorized disclosure of information	True	True	True
Authentication	None	None	None
Confidentiality Impact	Partial	Partial	Partial
Provides Administrator Access	False	False	False
Victim must voluntarily interact with attack mechanism	False (90%)	True (10%)	
Availability Impact	Partial	Partial	None
Allows disruption of service	True	True	False
Allows unauthorized modiðcation	True	True	False
Integrity Impact	Partial	Partial	None

CONCLUDING REMARKS

Vulnerabilities in IoT ecosystem are not different from vulnerabilities of any networked device. This chapter provides an overview of published vulnerabilities recorded against IoT ecosystem from MITRE. The enumerated list of vulnerabilities with respect IoT ecosystem provides a glimpse of the nature of the vulnerabilities and associated exploits. This chapter also presents some of the key challenges in IoT secure deployment.

REFERENCES

Andy, S., Rahardjo, B., & Hanindhito, B. (2017). Attack scenarios and security analysis of MQTT communication protocol in IoT system. In *4th International Conference on Electrical Engineering, Computer Science and Informatics (EECSI)*, (pp. 1–6). IEEE. 10.1109/EECSI.2017.8239179

Ashton, K. (2009). That 'internet of things' thing. *RFID Journal*, 22(7), 97–114.

Bosch. (2019). *Multiple Vulnerabilities in ProSyst mBS SDK and Bosch IoT Gateway Software.* https://psirt.bosch.com/Advisory/BOSCHSA-562575.html

Cisco. (2014). *The Internet of Things Reference Model.* Retrieved from http://cdn.iotwf.com/resources/71/IoT_Reference_Model_White_Paper_June_4_2014.pdf,2014

Common Vulnerabilities and Exposures. (n.d.). https://cve.mitre.org

CVE-2017-11578. (2017). https://nvd.nist.gov/vuln/detail/CVE-2017-11578

CVE-2018-11629. (2018).Retrieved from https://nvd.nist.gov/vuln/detail/CVE-2018-11629

CVE-2018-11925. (2018). Retrieved from https://nvd.nist.gov/vuln/detail/CVE-2018-11925

CVE-2018-11967. (2018). Retrieved from https://nvd.nist.gov/vuln/detail/CVE-2018-11967

CVE-2018-13908 .(2018).Retrieved from https://nvd.nist.gov/vuln/detail/CVE-2018-13908

CVE-2018-13913. (2018). Retrieved from https://nvd.nist.gov/vuln/detail/CVE-2018-13913

CVE-2018-13914. (2018). Retrieved from https://nvd.nist.gov/vuln/detail/CVE-2018-13914

CVE-2018-8119. (2018). Retrieved from https://nvd.nist.gov/vuln/detail/CVE-2018-8119

CVE-2018-8531. (2018). Retrieved from https://nvd.nist.gov/vuln/detail/CVE-2018-8531

CVE-2019-0729. (2019) Retrieved from https://nvd.nist.gov/vuln/detail/CVE-2019-0729

CVE-2019-11219. (2019). Retrieved from https://nvd.nist.gov/vuln/detail/CVE-2019-11219

CVE-2019-11220. (2019). Retrieved from https://nvd.nist.gov/vuln/detail/CVE-2019-11220

CVE-2019-11603. (2019). https://nvd.nist.gov/vuln/detail/CVE-2019-11603

CVE-2019-1644. (2019). Retrieved from https://nvd.nist.gov/vuln/detail/CVE-2019-1644

CVE-2019-1845. (2019). Retrieved from https://nvd.nist.gov/vuln/detail/CVE-2019-1845

CVE-2019-1957. (2019). Retrieved from https://nvd.nist.gov/vuln/detail/CVE-2019-1957

CVE-2019-2255. (2019). Retrieved from https://nvd.nist.gov/vuln/detail/CVE-2019-2255

CVE-2019-2278. (2019). Retrieved from https://nvd.nist.gov/vuln/detail/CVE-2019-2278

CVE-2019-9750. (2019). https://nvd.nist.gov/vuln/detail/CVE-2019-9750,2019

CWE-798: Use of Hard-coded Credentials. (2018). Retrieved from http://cwe.mitre.org/data/definitions/798.html

Franklin. (2019). *Peer-to-Peer Vulnerability Exposes Millions of IoT Devices.* Retrieved from https://www.darkreading.com/vulnerabilities—threats/peerto-peer-vulnerability-exposes-millions-of-iot-devices/d/d-id/1334564

Giuseppe Nebbione and Maria Carla Calzarossa. (2020). *Security of IoT Application Layer Protocols: Challenges and Findings.* MDPI, Future Internet.

Guth, J., Breitenbucher, U., Falkenthal, M., Fremantle, P., Kopp, O., Leymann, F., & Reinfurt, L. (2018). *A Detailed Analysis of IoT Platform Architectures: Concepts, Similarities, and Differences. In Internet of Everything.* Springer.

Malik, M. I., McAteer, I. N., Hannay, P., Firdous, S. N., & Baig, Z. (2018). XMPP architecture and security challenges in an IoT ecosystem. *Proceedings of the 16th Australian Information Security Management Conference*, 62.

O'Donnell. (2020). *Threat post*. https://threatpost.com/half-iot-devices-vulnerable-severe-attacks/153609/

OPenest. (n.d.). https://openest.io/en/2020/01/03/mqtts-how-to-use-mqtt-with-tls/

OWASP Foundation. (n.d.). https://owasp.org/

Shama, D., Puhlmann, F., Morrish, J., & Bhatnagar, R. M. (2019). *Enterprise IoT, Strategies and Best Practices for Connected Products and Services*. O'Reilly Media Inc.

Threat Post. (n.d.). https://media.threatpost.com/wp-content/uploads/sites/103/2020/03/11092116/word-image-24.png

Chapter 3
Real–Time, Cross–Platform Detection of Spectre and Meltdown Attack Variants

Xinxing Zhao
Singapore Institute of Technology, Singapore

Chandra Sekar Veerappan
Singapore Institute of Technology, Singapore

Peter Loh
Singapore Institute of Technology, Singapore

ABSTRACT

Modern processors employ optimization techniques such as out-of-order and speculative execution to maximize the performance. However, they may leave observable side effects that leak the secrets of the system. This phenomenon has led to a proliferation of Spectre and Meltdown attack variants, and this trend will likely continue in the near future. While many makeshift countermeasures have been proposed, they are either not adequately effective or come with inadvertent consequences. New types of processors are designed to deal with these problems; however, those older ones in billions of devices that are currently being used cannot easily or even possibly be replaced. In this chapter, therefore, the authors provide a cross-platform, micro-agent detection system, which can detect four main types of Spectre variants and one variant of Meltdown in real-time in these devices. The empirical performance tests show that the micro-agent system and the in-built detection mechanisms are efficient and effective in detecting such attacks.

DOI: 10.4018/978-1-7998-2444-2.ch003

INTRODUCTION

With the advancement of IoT technology, we have already seen some of the changes in how we interact with everyday digital objects (e.g., smart wearable devices, smart home appliances, etc.). The visions for IoT are that millions and billions of electronic devices will be connected to each other and the network allowing individuals to communicate with various machines, and machines to interact with other machines. To increase the processing power to accommodate the needs of the newly IoT devices as well as the traditional devices (e.g., laptops, desktops), more and more vendors have been shifting focus from the processing technology (because of the physical limitations, e.g. it is becoming very hard to keep shrinking transistor size,) and increasing clock frequency to increasing the number of cores and optimizing of the instruction pipeline. By parallelizing the pipelines that allow the instructions in the instruction stream to be executed ahead of time or even out-of-order, massive performance gains can be achieved. In order to keep the pipelines always full and hence keep the performance gain, modern processors use optimizations techniques such as branch prediction and out-of-order execution to predict the control flow, data dependencies and possibly even the actual data. As it is always possible that a prediction is wrong, the pipeline may be partially flushed and any results ensuing from that prediction to ensure the correctness of any function, discarded. From here, the name of transient execution is derived (Kocher et al. 2019; Lipp et al. 2018). As instructions are executed transiently (e.g., after the prediction), and their results removed if the predictions are indeed wrong, it is comparable to the processors idling at the architectural level during the transient execution process.

Although the effects of transient execution at the architectural level will be discarded in the end, the side effects from microarchitecture level and the implications might remain. As some of these side effects can be leveraged to leak secrets of the system to third-parties, attacks such as Spectre (Kocher et al. 2019), Meltdown (Lipp et al. 2018), and Foreshadow (Van Bulck et al. 2018) are derived from these phenomenons. The CPUs that are susceptible to these attacks are from all the major vendors, Intel, ARM, AMD. In other words, all the IoT devices (including the traditional desktops and laptops) with processing powers inside are susceptible to one type or another these transient attacks.

New types of the aforementioned attacks may continue to emerge in the near future, and the patches or makeshifts are not effective enough (Sebastian 2018) or incur inadvertent consequences (Steven 2018). Although new processors can be designed to root out the problem, however, there are billions of devices currently being used that are susceptible to these attacks. Therefore, in this chapter, we present the design of a cross-platform, light weight, micro-agent system that can detect the Spectre and Meltdown attack variants in real-time, and therefore provide adequate protection on platforms with heterogeneous operating platforms, including networked computational IoT networks.

The contributions of this work include the following:

1. A previous research work has been updated and revamped (Loh et al. 2016), and the current version of the CELLS (a micro-agent system, more detail in the later part) is written with QT (QT Creator 2019). As QT supports not only the mainstream operating systems, but also mobile and embedded platforms, it offers a practical basis to develop the secure agent framework which aims to protect the IoT devices and more traditional endpoint devices, such as laptops, desktops and gateways. The extended CELLES now works on Windows, Linux and MacOS, android phone and raspberry Pi systems. In other words, a device-independent cross-platform framework with the aim to provide security protection capacities for a big range of IoT devices (the framework design is modular and scalable to extend endpoint protection to more IoT devices) has been developed.

2. The micro-agent system and its current detector can work on all the mainstream operating systems, i.e., Windows, Linux and MacOS as well as Android-based mobile platforms.

3. The detector can detect the 4 main variants of Spectre attacks and 1 variant of Meltdown attack and once the anomaly happens, the detector can inform the administrator in real-time, thereby protecting the systems from attacks in real-time.

4. The system can be used to protect the older legacy systems such as Windows 8, 7 and even Windows XP from these types of attacks.

5. The system can be easily deployed onto a big distributed system e.g. a network of heterogeneous IoT devices or a cloud platform, which will help improve the detection and protection scope.

6. The detection capabilities in the micro-agent system can be developed and scaled via a system of plug-and-play detection libraries to detect more types of IoT endpoint attacks.

7. IoT endpoint or edge computing devices that may be supported by our security framework include smart meters, smart wearables and appliances, unmanned autonomous vehicles, SCADA controllers etc.

BACKGROUND

In this part more details will be given about some of the important microarchitecture components of modern CPUs, which can improve the performance, and why and how can they leak the information from the running programs to the attackers.

The Out-of-Order Execution of Modern Processors

In computer engineering, out-of-order execution is one of the optimization techniques that the execution units of CPU exploit to maximize usage of instruction cycles that would otherwise be wasted. In this paradigm, the instructions are not necessarily executed in a sequential program order (the original order). Instead, they are executed as soon as they can be executed with the available data input and the execution units, therefore the instructions can be executed in parallel. In doing so, the processor can avoid being idle while waiting for the preceding instruction to complete and can, in the meantime, process the next instructions that are able to run immediately and independently. In the end, these completed instructions will be queued in the reorder buffer of the processor, and they are retired according to their original sequential program order. Only at this point the retired instructions are committed and made visible externally.

The Speculative Execution of Modern Processors

Speculative execution is another optimization technique that is used in modern processors to boost the performance. As programs and their corresponding instructions usually are not executed linearly, and they have branches (e.g., conditional branches) or data dependencies between the instructions. Had it not been for the various mechanisms that predicted the outcome of a branch or a data dependency of the program, the CPU would have stalled to deal with these branches and the data dependencies, and the performance would have decreased significantly as a result. Instead, the CPU continues executing the instructions along the predicted path (these transient results will be stored into the reorder buffer). Therefore, it would boost the performance if the predictions were correct. However, if it did predict incorrectly, the CPU needs to revert back to the last correct state by squashing the transient results stored in the recorder buffer, and the end result equals to that as if the CPU had stalled in resolving the path.

Micro-Architectural Side-Channel Attacks

Modern CPUs use successively smaller but faster caches (e.g., L3, L2 and L1 level of caches), and the frequently used data are buffered into these hierarchical caches to hide the memory latency between the faster processor and the slow memory. Some of the caches in the hierarchy are private to their cores while others are shared among all the cores. When different programs run on the same hardware, changes in the micro-architectural level by one program might affect other programs. This means that unintended information may be leaked from one program to another program (Ge et al. 2018). The early stage of micro-architectural side channel attacks makes use of timing variability (Kocher 1996) and steals keys from cryptographic primitives through L1 cache (Osvik et al. 2006). Over the years, more and more micro-architectural components are found out to be exploitable to leak information, such as instruction cache in Acıiçmez 2007, other levels of caches (L2 and L3) (Irazoqui et al. 2015; Liu et al. 2015; Yarom et al. 2014), the branch history (Acıiçmez et al. 2007) and the *Branch Target Buffer* (BTB) (Evtyushkin et al. 2016; Lee et al. 2017). The attack interests have expanded from key stealing to co-location detection (Ristenpart et al. 2009), breaking ALSR (Evtyushkin et al. 2016; Gruss et al. 2016), keystroke monitoring (Gruss et al. 2015). And the recent attacks have been extended to cross-core and cross-CPU attacks (Irazoqui 2016; Zhang 2012), cloud-based attacks (Inci 2016; Zhang 2014). There are quite a number of attack techniques that can leak the secret information, such as Evict + Reload (Gruss et al. 2015), Flush + Reload (Gullasch et al. 2011; Yarom et al. 2014), Flush + Flush (Gruss 2016) and Prime+ Abort (Disselkoen et al. 2017), etc. Take the Flush + Reload as an example on how these techniques might leak the information to the attackers. It exploits the shared, inclusive last-level cache (e.g., L3 level or L2 for some cases, shared by different cores). As it can identify accesses to specific memory lines (lines are fixed size chunks divided from the cache memory) in the cache, it has a high fidelity and hence more dangerous. An attacker starts with choosing some cache line that is shared with the victim, then flushes the targeted memory location using the x86's *clflush* instruction and waits there for the victim to access the cache line. After the victim executes for some time, the attacker reloads the memory line, measures the time it took for the reloading. If during the waiting period, a victim accessed the monitored cache line, then the reloading and reading operation will be fast, because the data will be readily there in the cache. On the other hand, the reloading operation will be significantly slower, if the victim has not accessed the line during the waiting, as the data will need to be brought from memory. Therefore, an attacker can know which data is used during the waiting time, just by measuring the timing difference it takes to reload the data from the cache line.

SPECTRE AND MELTDOWN AT HIGH-LEVEL

Before giving more details about the Spectre and Meldown and their variants, these attacks will be described from a high level perspective, and these two types of attacks and their variants share some similar patterns.

First, the attacker sets the micro-architecture into a desired state, e.g., by flushing internal predictors or data caches. Then he triggers the execution of some transient instructions, and these instructions access some unauthorized data through a microarchitectural covert channel. After that, the CPU flushes and squash the results of these transient instructions due to an exception or a mis-predicted branch or data dependency. The attackers abuse the transient instructions to use it as the sending end of a microarchitectural covert channel, e.g., by loading a secret-dependent memory location into the CPU cache. And finally, he reconstructs the secret from microarchitectural state. The unauthorized data that the transient instructions brought to the cache (though squashed in the architectural level) will be recovered at the receiving end of the covert channel, e.g., by Flush + Reload, mentioned above and deduce the secret data.

Spectre vs Meltdown

As mentioned, Spectre and Meltdown and their variants share some common patterns in that they abuse the transient instructions. With different instantiations of the process described in the previous paragraph, a wide spectrum of different attack variants can be derived. However, there are fundamental differences as to which type of CPU properties are exploited between these two main categories of attacks. Spectre and its variants are based on dedicated control or data flow prediction mechanism, while Meltdown and its variants make use of a faulting instruction that is forwarded to instructions ahead in the pipeline to get unauthorized data. These fundamental differences determine the nature and the scope of the attacks of the Spectre-type and Meltdown-type. To be more specific, for Spectre-type, they manipulate these transient instructions and can compute based on these data that the application is able to access architecturally. It bypasses software defined security boundaries and tricks a program into accessing arbitrary locations in the program's memory space. An attacker steers a victim into computing based on the memory locations that the victim can access but attacker cannot, and therefore read the content of accessed memory and obtain sensitive data. Whereas for the Meltdown-type, the execution of transient instructions can completely "melt down" architectural isolations and breaks the most fundamental isolation between user applications and the Operating System. This type of attack allows a program to access the memory, and thus also the secrets of other programs and the Operating System by computing on unauthorized results of faulting instructions. Therefore, Meltdown attacks bypass hardware-level security boundaries, leak these data that are supposed always to remain architecturally inaccessible for the application.

Figure 1. Spectre-type attacks and Meltdown-type attacks
(Canella et al. 2018)

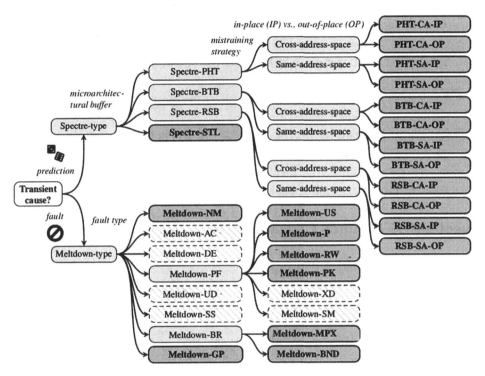

Some of the attacks in Figure 1 are only theoretically possible (the ones encircled with dashed lines). As we know, Meltdown attacks usually exploit these transient executions after a faulting instruction (e.g., an exception), but some of the operations, e.g., divide-by-zero error, will not cause an exception (on ARMs) or do have an exception and have transient executions but the register will be set to '0'(on AMD and Intel). And some of the operations, although raise exceptions, but there are no transient executions after them, e.g., out-of-limit segmentation faults.

SPECTRE-TYPE ATTACKS

As mentioned, Spectre attacks make use of prediction mechanisms for the various of branches and data dependencies. One of obvious ways to categorize them is according to which corresponding microarchitectural internal buffer or component they exploit.

There are currently four main types of Spectre attacks based on the different root cause that triggers the misprediction leading to transient execution.

1. Spectre-PHT (Kocher et al. 2019) exploits the *Pattern History Table* (PHT) to predict the outcome of conditional branches.
2. Spectre-BTB (Kocher et al. 2019) exploits the *Branch Target Buffer* (BTB) for predicting branch destination addresses.
3. Spectre-RSB (Maisuradze et al. 2018; Koruyeh et al. 2018) primarily exploits the *Return Stack Buffer* (RSB) for predicting return addresses.
4. Spectre-STL (Horn 2018) exploits memory disambiguation for predicting *Store To Load* (STL) data dependencies.

Spectre-PHT (Bounds Check Bypass)

Korcher et al. first introduced the Spectre variant 1(CVE-2017-5753), an attacker can poison the Pattern History Table to exploit conditional branch mis-prediction. In a computer program, conditional branch refers to the act of switching execution to a different instruction sequence as a result of executing a particular sequence of instructions only if certain conditions are satisfied, and it is commonly used to maintain the memory safety invariants. Take the following code snippet for example (Kocher et al. 2019).

```
if (x< array1_size)
    y= array2[array1[x]* 4096]
```

Assume this code is part of a function, x is an unsigned integer from an untrusted source. The array of unsigned bytes array1 and its size array1_size and another byte array array2 of size 1MB are accessible by the running process. At the architectural level, the snippet begins bound check on x, and it is essential for security, as it prevents the processor to read out-of-bounds of the fixed length buffer array1. However, before the result of the bound check is known, CPU will speculatively execute the code following the if condition, because the resources in the system are not available (e.g., existence of congestions, complex dependencies, other cache misses related to this bound check) to give an immediate bound checking result. So by providing valid values of x to the process (a training that could be provided by an attacker), the Pattern History Table will be poisoned, and it predicts that the next x value (which is out-of-bounds and provided by the attacker) will also be within the bounds, and the if will likely be true. Suppose the attacker can cause some of the following conditions that:

- The next x value provided by the attacker is out-of-bounds, such that the resolving of array1[x] will get a secret byte k in the victim's memory space;
- That array1_size is not cached, and the array2 is also not cached, however the k is cached;
- The series of values of x provided to the process previously are valid, leading to the prediction that the if will likely be true.

Assume the above compiled code runs on a system, x value will be used to compare with the array1_size, and as array1_size is not cached, this reading will be a cache miss. The process will face a significant slowdown until the value (of array1_size) will be brought from the memory. It could have taken some time before the result is determined, however, the speculative execution kicks in, it assumes that the if condition will be true, and continues to work. It adds the x value to the base address of the array array1, and array1[x]=k is resolved quickly, as this secret k is cached. The program continues to use this k and resolves array2[array1[x]* 4096], and as the array2 is also not cached, the address needs to be brought from the memory. At this point of the time, the bound check results might have just determined, and the processor realizes that the speculative executions in this case were wrong and goes back to the last correct state in the architectural level (squashing the transient results, rolling back to the original state). However, the reading of array2[k* 4096] will affect the cache state, and the address of which depends on the k. The final step of this whole process is that attacker can use the Flush + Reload to measure which location in the array2 was brought to the cache. It keeps trying to read different values in the array2, until array2[k* 4096] is hit, and the reading process of which is significantly faster than others, thus the secret k is leaked.

There is a proof-of-concept (PoC) code in C that in the appendix of (Kocher et al. 2019) which works for x86 processors. According to them the unoptimized code can read roughly 10KB/s on an i7-4650U with a low error rate. Processors from Intel, ARM and AMD are all susceptible to Spectre-PHT style attacks.

Spectre-BTB (Branch Target Injection)

In the same paper (Kocher et al. 2019), the authors also introduced another Spectre type, the variant 2 (CVE-2017-5715). An attacker poisons the Branch Target Buffer

(BTB), and it can manipulate the transient execution to a mis-predicted branch target to read arbitrary memory from another process. During the speculative execution, modern processors predict the result of branch instructions. There are various prediction mechanisms for the direct and indirect branches. For direct branches, a subset of virtual address bits of the branch instruction is used by the processor to index the BTB and to predict the target, while for the indirect branches, the global accumulative branching history that is stored will be used for the indexing of the BTB. And the indirect branch instructions can jump to more than two arbitrary target addresses that are computed at runtime. If there is no immediate results as to the destination of the target address due to a cache miss and the mis-trained branch predicator, the speculative may continue with the location chosen by an attacker, and the execution of that misdirected location might leave measurable side effects for the attacker and this will in turn lead to the leakage of secrets. The poisoning of the indirect branch is very similar to the techniques used by return-oriented programming (ROP) attacks (Shacham et al. 2007). The difference is that, the attack abuses and poisons the BTB. Instead of finding application level vulnerabilities, it finds "gadgets" in the victim's address space, and chains them together to form arbitrary instruction sequences, and to leak the secrets from the transient domain. An example PoC code of this variant can be found from (Msmania 2018) It uses call[rax] to demonstrate the indirect jump. One can observe the processor speculatively runs the code at the previous jump destination while fetching a real destination from the address stored in the register rax. In the variant, an attacker can train the branch predictor to cause the processor to mis-predict a branch to the address which the attacker wants to run from. Processors from Intel, ARM and AMD are all susceptible to Spectre-PHT style attacks.

```
indirect_call:
  mov rax, rcx
  mov rcx, rdx
  mov rdx, r8
  clflush [rax]
  call [rax]
  ret
```

Spectre-RSB (Return Address Injection)

The authors in (Maisuradze & Rossow 2018; Koruyeh et al. 2018) introduced another type of Spectre variant which manipulates the Return Stack Buffer (RSB). The RSB is a common per-core component in modern CPUs used to predict return address. It stores the return address following the N (typically of size 16 entries) most recent call instructions. When the return (ret) is encountered, the CPU uses the top address stored in the RSB to predict the return address to facilitate the speculative execution. Mis-prediction happens when the address that it holds in RSB differs from the return address it is supposed to be. Such can happen naturally, for example, when restoring kernel/enclave/user stack pointers upon protection domain switches. It can, however, also happen by the manipulation of an adversary code. The attacker might explicitly overwrite return addresses on the software stack or transiently execute the call instruction, causing a value to be pushed to the RSB and updates it, but the effects of it will not be committed at the architectural level. This allows the attacker to push an address in the stack that is outside the legal program that can access and diverts the control flow to some "code gadget" and therefore leaks the secrets. There is a basic attack example from (Koruyeh et al. 2018) in the following.

```
1.  Function gadget()
2.  {
3.  push %rbp
4.  mov %rsp,%rbp
5.  pop %rdi // remove frame/return address
6.  pop %rdi // from stack stopping at
7.  pop %rdi//next return address
8.  nop
9.  pop %rbp
10. clflush(%rsp)//flush the return address
11. cpuid
12. retp//triggers speculation return to 17
13. }//committed return goes to 23
14. Function speculative(char *secret_ptr)
15. {
16. gadget(); //modify the Software stack
17. secret = *secret_ptr; //Speculative return here
18. temp &= Array[secret * 256]; //Access Array
19. }
20. Function main()
21. {
22. Speculative(secret_address);
23. for(i=1 to 256)//actual return to here
24. {
25. t1=rdtscp();
26. junk=Array[i*256];//check cache hit
27. t2=rdtscp();
```

```
28.}
29.}
```

The attacker code starts at line 22, it provides an argument which is not legal (the address of a secret). And the speculative function calls the gadget()at line 16, it serves two purposes: First, the return address will be pushed into the RSB. Second, jump to the function at line 1 which will manipulate the software stack to create a mismatch between the stack and the RSB. When the return retp at line 12 executes, the speculative execution continues from line 17 which gets the secret (this secret can be retrieved using flush +reload tecnique), as the clflush(%rsp)(flush the return address from the cache) in line 10 flushes the address in the cache, and gives a speculative window. Processors from Intel, ARM and AMD are all susceptible to Spectre-PHT style attacks.

Spectre-STL (Speculative Store Bypass)

Speculative execution in the modern CPUs not only works in the control flow, it also works in the prediction of dependencies of data flow. For example, one common type of the Store To Load (STL) dependencies requires all the preceding stores that write to the same location be executed first (many microarchitectures block loads until all preceding store address are known) before a memory load can be executed. However, when the disambiguator predicts that a load does not have such a dependency, the load takes its data from the L1 data cache. Eventually, the prediction is verified. If an actual conflict is detected, the load and all succeeding instructions are re-executed (INTEL 2017). Horn (Horn 2018) has shown that the memory disambiguator can be exploited to bypass the store instructions. The Spectre-STL type can use transient instructions to leak unsanitized stale values through a microarchitectural covert channel, and also the use of stale pointer might break the type and memory safety guarantees in the transient domain (INTEL 2017).

There is a PoC code (Horn 2018), and the authors have tested it on two intel processors (Skylake i7-6600U @ 2.60GHz, Haswell E5-1650 v3 @ 3.50GHz) and one AMD (PRO A8-9600 R7).

MELTDOWN-TYPE ATTACKS

As previously mentioned, Spectre-type attacks exploit prediction mechanisms to predict branches and data dependencies to trigger the transient execution, whereas Meltdown-types take advantage of these transient instructions following a CPU exception. As in modern CPUs, out-of-order execution is a common optimization technique that improves the performance, and in microarchitectural level, the transient instructions following the exception might be used to compute the unauthorized data and results (that will be squashed in the architectural level). The side effects of these executions and the unauthorized data and results can be deduced by covert channels attacks using such as Flush + Reload. We will give more details of different known variants of Meltdown-types in the following.

Meltdown-US (Supervisory-Only Bypass)

Memory isolation is a fundamental feature for security in modern Operating Systems. An Operating System (OS) ensures that a user program cannot read another program's memory or the kernel memory. That is why multiple programs can run concurrently on the same OS or multiple users can run concurrently on a single machine in the cloud. Modern OSs typically use a supervisor bit to achieve the isolation of a user program memory and the kernel: basically, a supervisor bit of the processor is set when entering the kernel mode, whereas upon switching to user processes, the bit is cleared. This hardware isolation feature allows the OSs to map the kernel into the address space of every processes, therefore the transition from user to kernel mode will be very efficient, for example, when handling the interrupts. Because of this efficiency, there is practically no memory mapping change upon switching from the user mode to the kernel mode.

This type of attack allows an adversary to break the isolation completely – it uses a simple way for any user to read the entire kernel memory and the physical memory that is mapped in the kernel. We now provide more details about how this can happen.

Out-of-order execution is the feature of modern CPUs that improve the performance. The processor units can avoid execution stall (e.g., memory fetch unit stops and waits until the arrival of data from memory) by running the operations out-of-order, i.e., they execute ahead and schedule the later part of the operations to the idle units of the core. From security perspective, that feature allows a user process (an unprivileged one) to load data from privileged address space of kernel and physical memory into a temporary CPU register, and even perform some computations based on that resister value, e.g., access an array based on the register value. This will cause serious problems that the research community has not previously noticed of.

```
1. raise_exception();
2. // the next line should never be executed
3. access probe_array[data*4096])
```

From the architectural level, after the exception (the code above), the access of array should not have happened, however, due to the out-of-order execution, the code in the line 3 might have already executed. If it turns out these out-of-order operations indeed should not have been executed, the register state will be reversed back and any related results will be squashed. The outcome is comparable to that of the execution units idling the whole time. In this sense it is considered safe and without any security implications.

However, these operations (memory lookups of the out-of-order executions) have side-effects on the microarchitectural level and change cache state, which in turn can be used to leak out the secret (the register value that was not supposed to be read) by side-channel attacks, e.g. Flush+ Reload.

Figure 2. The Meltdown attack with Exception Handling/Suppression (Lipp et al. 2018)

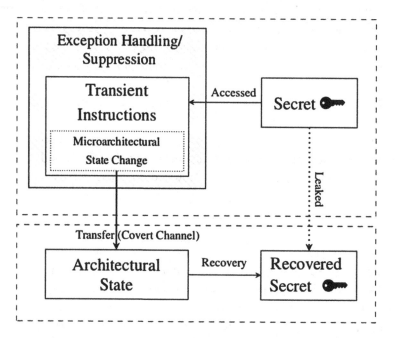

Trying to access pages that normal users are not supposed to read, e.g., these kernel pages will cause an exception and which in turn generally leads to the termination of an application. A user code which targets a secret at a user inaccessible address space will also cause an exception. Therefore, the adversary needs to deal with the exceptions, if he wants to continuously get the values in the privileged address space. The authors in (Lipp et al. 2018) provide two possible ways that dealing with the exceptions: 1. exception handling, e.g., it is possible to install a handler to deal with certain types of exception, such as a segmentation fault. This allows room for manipulating and preventing the application from crashing. 2. exception suppression. This way it can prevent an exception from ever happening. For example, transactional memory (Jiang et al. 2016) can group memory into one atomic operation and can reverse back to its previous state should an error occur. An execution raised within a transaction will cause a reset in the architectural state, but the execution will continue without disruption. In summary, it takes the following 3 steps for an adversary to get a secret from the system.

Step 1: The adversary chooses a memory location which has the secret and he does not have the privilege to access, and has it loaded to a register.
Step 2: Transient instructions access a cache line, and compute based on the secret content in the register.
Step 3: Use side-channel attack techniques, such as Flush + Reload, to determine which cache line it accessed and deduce the secret stored at the chosen memory location.

By repeating the above steps at different memory location, the adversary can read all the kernel memory, including the physical memory (for Linux and Mac OS, the entire physical memory is directly mapped into the kernel; also, large part of Windows system memory) that is mapped into the kernel. According to authors in (Lipp et al. 2018), their work can dump kernel and physical memory with 3.2KB/s to 503KB/s on different machines with different specifics. The tests setups are mainly on Intel processors (in cloud and lab PCs), and one Samsung Exynos 8890 on an Android phone. An attack PoC code example can be found here (IAIK 2018).

Meltdown-P (Virtual Translation Bypass, AKA Foreshadow)

Van Bulck et al. 2018 first introduce the Foreshadow attack, which is a type of Meltdown attack (because it exploits the out-of-order execution feature, and previously it was categorized as one of the Spectre attacks) that specifically targets Intel SGX technology. Intel Software Guard eXtensions (SGX) (Intel 2016) is a Trusted Execution Environment (TEE) that enables secure program execution in untrusted environments. The program and the data it operates on, are placed inside a secure enclave. There they are protected from modification or inspection, even in the presence of a highly-privileged adversary corrupting the Operating System, hypervisor, or firmware (BIOS). SGX also provides a remote attestation protocol that allows software to prove to a remote party that it is running on a genuine SGX-enabled Intel processor, as opposed to a (potentially malicious) simulator.

The previous known attacks that target Intel SGX rely on application-specific information leakage from either side-channels (Lee et al. 2017; Van Bulck et al. 2017) or software vulnerabilities (Lee et al. 2017; Weichbrodt et al. 2016]. It is generally believed that well design of the enclaves and good code practice (e.g., no branching on secrets, so as to avoid side channel attacks) can eliminate the possibility of leakage of information. However, Van Bulck et al. presented the Foreshadow attack, and it defeats this belief that it relies solely on elementary Intel x86 CPU behavior and does not exploit any software vulnerability, or even require knowledge of the victim enclave's source code. As mentioned above, that meltdown type attacks depend on the out-of-order execution of transient instructions after an exception that is raised, and the meltdown-us type can read the kernel memory from user-space. However, if there were an unauthorized access to the enclave memory, a page fault exception will usually not be raised. Instead, dummy values of the aborted page will be provided silently. As a result, the above meltdown-us type cannot mount an attack on SGX. To deal with the limitation, the authors (Van Bulck et al. 2017) provided a way that clears the "present" bit in the page-table entry that maps the secret in enclave. Therefore, next time when accessing the enclave memory illegally, there will be an exception raised, and this time the adversary can use similar attack (as meltdown-us) methods. There is a PoC provided by the authors (Jovanbulck 2019), interested reader might have a try.

There are two new related variants (Weisse et al. 2018) to this Foreshadow attack identified by Intel, and they are named Foreshadow-NG (Next Generation). The attacks can read any and all information that is in the L1 cache e.g. kernel memory belonging to the OS, memory protected by the SMM. Even worse, A malicious guest VM (running on the cloud) can potentially read memory belonging to the VM's hypervisor or memory belonging to another guest VM running on the cloud, causing a huge potential risk to the cloud infrastructure. In some cases, according to the authors (Weisse et al. 2018), the Foreshadow-NG attacks effectively render the previously released mitigations against transient execution attacks ineffective.

Meltdown-GP (System Register Bypass)

This type of attacks allow an adversary to read privileged system registers, first discovered by ARM (ARM 2018) and later, Intel (INTEL 2018) announced that their CPUs are also susceptible. As mentioned, one of the key components for a Meltdown attack is an exception that need to be raised. Here, for the Meltdown-GP, the exception is a general protection fault (#GP), which is caused by an unauthorized access to privileged system registers (e.g., via rdmsr). The attack then follows almost the same pattern as Meltdown-Us (the transient executions compute on the unauthorized data after the exception) attack and leaks the unauthorized data through a side channel attack.

Meltdown-NM (FPU Register Bypass)

This type of attacks allows an adversary to read floating-point unit (FPU), SIMD registers and virtual machines of other processes (Stecklina & Prescher 2018). Modern processors use continuingly large set of registers in supporting efficient floating point and SIMD computation. Upon a context switch, the OS needs to save all the registers values in order to restore them when the context is switched back. This is a burden for the OS, and it decreases the efficiency of the context switch. Therefore, there is an optimization technique - the OS puts off the context switch of FPU and SIMD register set until the first instruction is executed that needs to access to these registers. In the meanwhile, the old values in the registers are left there hoping that the current task will not use them at all. This technique is called lazy FPU context switching, and a processor allows for turning off the FPU and marked it as "not available". Once it is marked as not available, the first instruction which accesses the FPU will cause a device-not-available (#NM) exception, permitting the OS to save the FPU state of previous execution context, then marking the FPU as available again. To exploit this optimization technique in modern CPUs, the authors provides a three-step attack technique to leak the register values.

Step 1: The victim performs operations and loads the data into FPU registers.

Step 2: The CPU switches to the adversary, turning off the FPU and marks it as "not available".

Step 3: The adversary now utilizes an instruction that uses the FPU to switch to the adversary, which in turn causes a device-not-available (#NM) exception.

Now the whole process behaves once again similar to the Meltdown-US attack. Before the faulting instruction is retired, the CPU has already executing the transient instructions that use the data in the FPU from the previous context. With a microarchitectural covert channel attack (e.g., again the Flush + Reload), the data can be retrieved.

Meltdown-RW (Read-Only Bypass)

Different from the Meltdown-US attack, that the adversary can steal the kernel secrets from the user space, this (Meltdown-RW) type of attacks allows an adversary to get the secrets in the same privilege level by bypassing the page-table access rights (bypass the Read/Write page-table entries). This renders the software-based sandboxes ineffective, as the sandboxing depends on the hardware-based read-only memory (and the attack type bypasses it). According to the authors in (Kiriansky & Waldspurger 2018), this attack works on both ARM and x86 processors.

Meltdown-PK (Protection Key Bypass)

Memory protection keys for user space (PKU) feature (INTEL 2017) means that from the user space, the processes can directly change the access permissions, without the need of a syscall/hypercall. And this feature is supported by Intel Skylake-SP server CPUs, therefore, user-spaces applications on these servers can easily implement hardware-enforced isolation of trusted parts. The authors in(Canella et al. 2018) provided an attack, that by creating a memory mapping and using PKU to remove both write and read access, as a result the accessing of that memory will cause a page fault (#PF) exception, and now we can mount the same process again as the Meltdown-US attack. According to them this type of attack is especially problematic, as for now there is no software workaround, and the solution lies in a new hardware design in future CPUs and possibly also in redesign of microcode.

Meltdown-BR (Bounds Check Bypass)

When a program tries to index an offset in an array that is out-of-bound, a dedicated x86 CPUs instruction (bound instruction) will raise a bound range exceeded exception (#BR). The IA-32 ISA defines a bound opcode for this purpose, and modern Intel CPUs are equipped with Memory Protection eXtensions (MPX) for array bounds checking efficiency. The authors in (Canella et al. 2018) exploits the transient executions following a #BR exception, encodes the secrets that are not architectural level visible. The authors use their proofs-of-concept exploitations to leak the secrets by either ISA 32 bound (Intel, AMD) or the more advanced MPX protection (Intel only).

THE DEFENSES AND THE SOLUTIONS

For the defense, some big companies such as Microsoft, Apple, Google have already released patch-ups for different products to work around these problems. To a certain extent, they mitigate the problems. However, still some problems are caused inadvertently, such as downgrade of system performance (Stephen 2018), or even cause boot-up problems (Sebastian 2018). There are some types of attacks, such as the above-mentioned meltdown PKU, for which there might be no work around solution yet. Of course, to root out the problems, new generations of CPUs can be designed, but the problem is that, currently there are billions of devices susceptible to these transient execution attacks, and a more effective way must be provided to protect them.

The Proposed Solution: Agent-based Protection System

The agent system that has been developed, called CELLS (Loh et al. 2016), has the ability to work across the different platforms. The current version of CELLS can work on Windows, MacOS, Linux (including the Raspberry Pi devices) systems, and Android Phones (Qualcomm Quad-Core Processor Snapdragon 425). In the long run it will be extended to more mobile and embedded platforms, as the framework is written with the QT creator (suitable for multi-platforms), therefore can cover more systems that the IoT devices depend on. The vision of the agent system is to provide a universal way to protect all sort of IoT devices (traditional endpoint devices included). The system has a one-to-many control mechanism, the CELLS Leader talks to the many followers that are working on different IoT devices, end-devices included (As shown in Figure 3, Figure 4 and Figure 5). At the moment, communication between Leader / Followers including commands and message are not encrypted. The installation of Followers CELLS and their related Qt libraries takes around 50MB disk space at an endpoint device. This size can be reduced with various optimization techniques, as small size is a critical requirement for covering more resource constrained IoT devices.

The newly extended CELLS system has many desirable functions that support it to work in a possibly highly hostile environment. Some of the main functions are presented in the following.

- **Clone:** The agents can be cloned and be configured individually and sent to the different end-devices, e.g., five agents are cloned on a laptop (the server of the CELLS system), configured and sent to the five endpoint devices, with possibly different operating systems, to be secured. The clone function also serves another important role, that the agent might be deleted by certain malware (Veerappan et al. 2018), which has advanced proactive detecting abilities, or accidently by a user. After receiving a message that the agent got deleted, the control mechanism of the agent system can send another agent to the same location to continue the protection of the endpoint device.

Figure 3. The Leader (Control Panel)

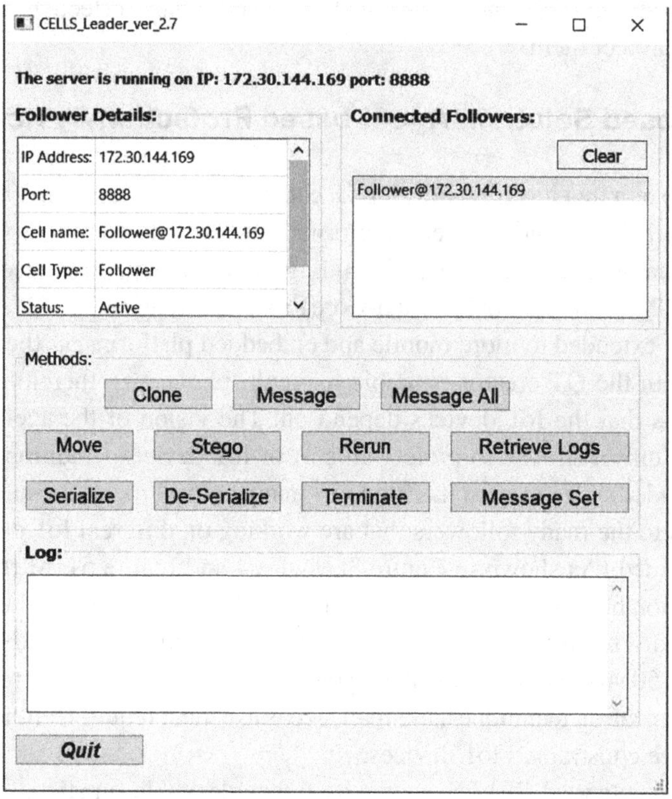

Figure 4. The Follower Agent

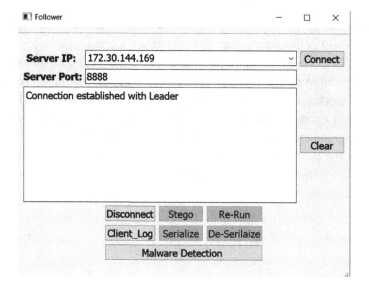

Figure 5. The follower on a phone

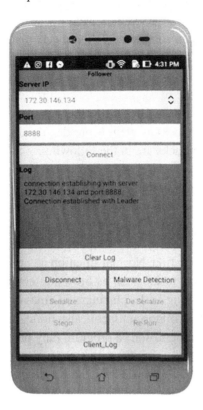

- **Move:** The agents can be moved from one device to another device, for example, the place that an agent was cloned might different from the location where it actually is working. The system needs some information such as IP address and the port number to send the agent over to the desired location. This function is supported by a server extension installed on endpoint machines to receive the agents.
- **Message** and **Message All:** The system can send a message to one of the agents or to all the agents that are in the same network.
- **Terminate:** The system can terminate an agent that is working in an endpoint device from a control device.
- **RetriveLogs:** the system will record any events in log files and can retrieve them for analysis if it is needed.
- **Steganography** and **Rerun:** The follower agent even can hide itself in a picture in order to avoid the scanning process of certain malwares (Veerappan 2018). The system can reactivate this hidden agent (suspended) into by executing the Rerun function.

- **Detection:** The current detection mechanisms are particularly designed for transient execution attacks (aka. Meltdown, Spectre and their variants). The follower agent can run the detection mechanisms to detect the transient execution attacks (Zhao et al. 2018). This ability can be evolved over time (to detect more variants of transient executions attacks if not all of them mentioned in the above part), and can be customized, e.g., not only can detect transient execution attacks, but also other attacks types (especially for the protection of IoT devices) as well. More details about the detector to detect transient execution attacks are in the following.

When running the samples of the transient execution attacks (four Spectre variants and one Meltdown that the authors are currently working on), one important fact that is universal can be observed - some CPU parameters (these specific parameters are the same for all Intel CPUs) will jump significantly to a very high level as compared to the normal situation. Normal situation means that, the system operates on the common day-to-day tasks, such as browsing certain websites, watching a video from YouTube, copying a file, playing a HD movie from the local hard disk, or even idling, etc. Another important fact is also noticed, that mouse movements, keyboard entries and clicking to start a program (any program), etc., the values of these parameters also jump to a significantly high level, sometimes even higher than the values that introduced by a transient execution attack.

Figure 6. The Principle of the Detection Mechanism

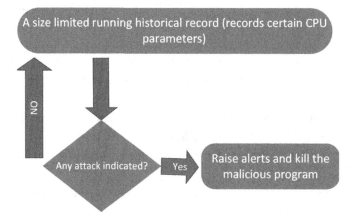

However, the duration of that jump into higher level will usually be very short, a few seconds only. With these two important observations, the detection mechanism is formed. As sketched in the Figure 6, that the program has a running historical record (with a limited size and adjustable) to note down the values of certain CPU parameters, when a transient execution attack happens, these values will jump to a significant higher level, and constantly stay there for the whole attacking process, by observation, a semi-optimized threshold can be chosen. If the average of the current running record is constantly higher than this semi-optimized threshold, the program will raise the alerts; Where as if there is no such attack, the running record will update the new values that it collects from the CPU parameters and delete the older ones.

There is one important fact that the authors want to emphasize here, that the detection mechanism is cross-platform and applied to all the major operating systems on the Intel processors.

The Performance of the Protection System

In this part, the performance of the proposed detection program will be presented, and as the detection mechanism only needs a few seconds to detect the different attacks, therefore it provided a much-needed real-time capability.

Figure 7. The Detection of Spectre-PHT on Windows

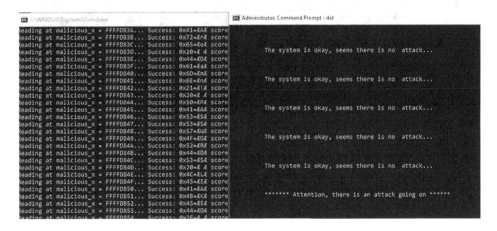

According to the paper (Kocher et al. 2019), their non-optimized Spectre attack code can read approximately 10KB/s on an i7 Surface Pro 3 and the Meltdown [the meltdown] test dumps the kernel memory at up to 503 KB/s. Therefore, in order to get any meaningful information and leak it to the attackers from the system, the attack process might take minutes, if not hours. To emulate this continuously attacking process, the authors execute and loop an attack executable file (PoC) in the background and test the effectiveness of the detector. Our prototype developed detector can detect the Spectre main variants on Windows 10, Linux and MacOS systems, also can detect the Meltdown-US on Windows 10 and Linux systems.

As can be seen from Figure 7, the developed detector can detect one variant of Spectre attacks which poisons the Pattern History Table (PHT), and it can detect this attack within 4 seconds.

In Figure 8, it shows that the detector can detect another Spectre type that poisons the Branch Target Buffer (BTB) to steer the transient execution to a mis-predicted branch target on a Windows System, and it can detect the attack in 5 seconds.

Figure 8. The Detection of Spectre-BTB on Windows

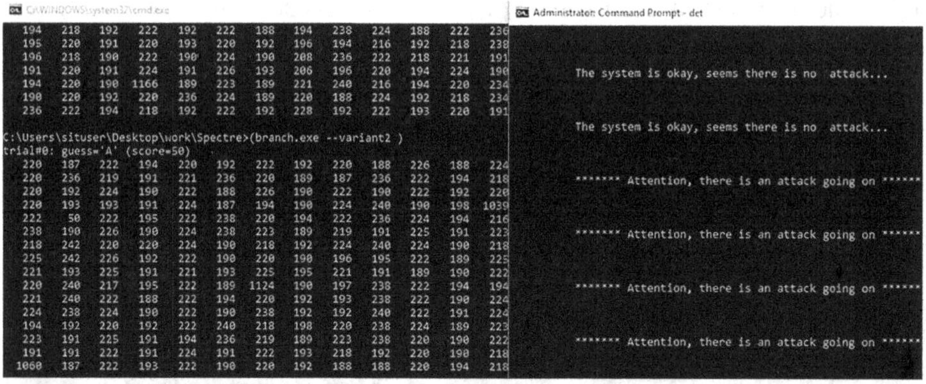

In Figure 9, that the detector can detect yet another Spectre type (Spectre-RSB) that hijacks return flow to the interesting code gadgets on a Windows System, and it can detect the attack in 8 seconds, this attack PoC is from Koruyeh et al. 2018. There are many attack types in this paper and this is the basic type attack similar to Spectre-PHT.

In Figure 10, it shows that the detector can detect the fourth main Spectre type, which is the Spectre-STL that abuses the memory disambiguator to bypass store instructions to leak unsanitized stale information on the Linux System. And it can detect the attack within 7 seconds.

Figure 9. The Detection of Spectre-RSB on Windows 10

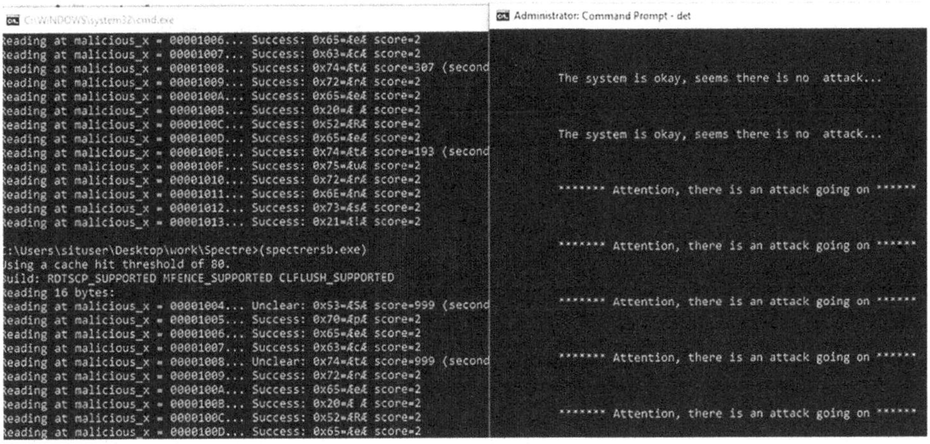

Figure 10. The Detection of Spectre-STL on Linux system

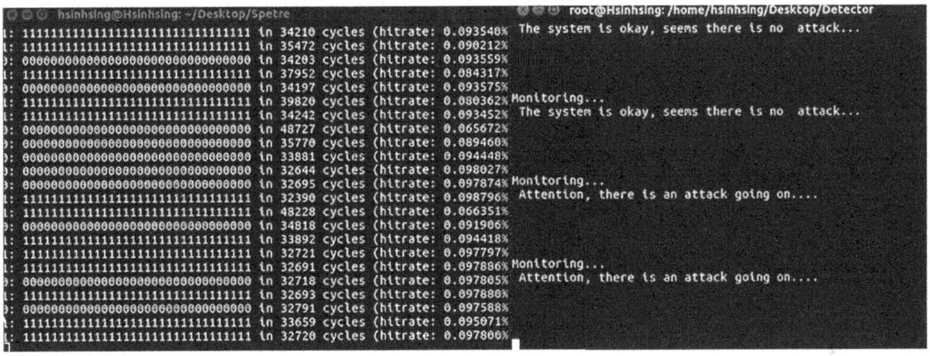

As can be seen from Figure 11, the detector can detect the Spectre-PHT attacks on MacOS, and it can detect this attack within 8 seconds. In Figure 12, it can detect the Spectre-PHT attacks on Linux system with 5 seconds.

In Figure 13, it shows that the detector can detect Meltdown-US on a Windows 10, and it detects the attack in 9 seconds. And in Figure 14, the detector can detect Meltdown-US on a Linux System, and it detects the attack in 8 seconds.

Table 1 summarizes the types of attacks that the authors are currently working on, and timing latencies of the detector incurred in detecting the attacks (in terms of seconds).

Figure 11. The Attack and Detection of Spectre-PHT on Mac system

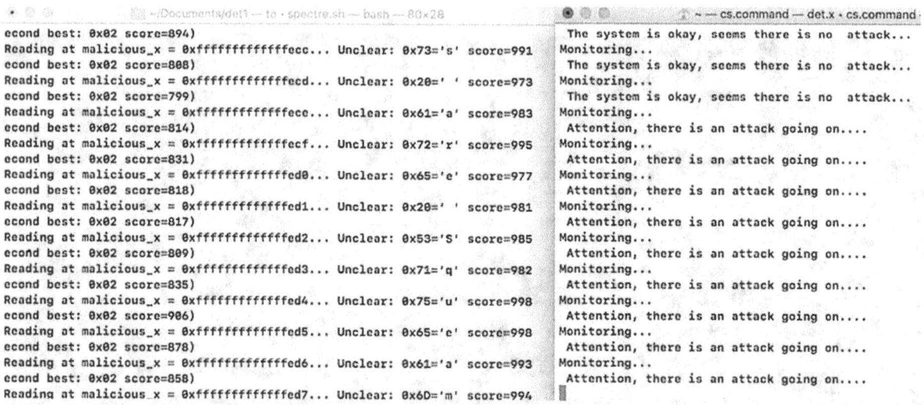

```
econd best: 0x02 score=894)                                          The system is okay, seems there is no  attack...
Reading at malicious_x = 0xffffffffffffffecc... Unclear: 0x73='s' score=991   Monitoring...
econd best: 0x02 score=808)                                          The system is okay, seems there is no  attack...
Reading at malicious_x = 0xffffffffffffffecd... Unclear: 0x20=' ' score=973   Monitoring...
econd best: 0x02 score=799)                                          The system is okay, seems there is no  attack...
Reading at malicious_x = 0xffffffffffffffece... Unclear: 0x61='a' score=983   Monitoring...
econd best: 0x02 score=814)                                          Attention, there is an attack going on....
Reading at malicious_x = 0xffffffffffffffecf... Unclear: 0x72='r' score=995   Monitoring...
econd best: 0x02 score=831)                                          Attention, there is an attack going on....
Reading at malicious_x = 0xffffffffffffffed0... Unclear: 0x65='e' score=977   Monitoring...
econd best: 0x02 score=818)                                          Attention, there is an attack going on....
Reading at malicious_x = 0xffffffffffffffed1... Unclear: 0x20=' ' score=981   Monitoring...
econd best: 0x02 score=817)                                          Attention, there is an attack going on....
Reading at malicious_x = 0xffffffffffffffed2... Unclear: 0x53='S' score=985   Monitoring...
econd best: 0x02 score=809)                                          Attention, there is an attack going on....
Reading at malicious_x = 0xffffffffffffffed3... Unclear: 0x71='q' score=982   Monitoring...
econd best: 0x02 score=835)                                          Attention, there is an attack going on....
Reading at malicious_x = 0xffffffffffffffed4... Unclear: 0x75='u' score=998   Monitoring...
econd best: 0x02 score=906)                                          Attention, there is an attack going on....
Reading at malicious_x = 0xffffffffffffffed5... Unclear: 0x65='e' score=998   Monitoring...
econd best: 0x02 score=878)                                          Attention, there is an attack going on....
Reading at malicious_x = 0xffffffffffffffed6... Unclear: 0x61='a' score=993   Monitoring...
econd best: 0x02 score=858)                                          Attention, there is an attack going on....
Reading at malicious_x = 0xffffffffffffffed7... Unclear: 0x6D='m' score=994
```

FUTURE RESEARCH DIRECTIONS

As mentioned above, currently there are five types of transient execution attacks that can be detected by the extended micro-agent system (the CELLES) on the mainstream operating systems such as Windows, Linux and MacOS, although the CELLES system itself can work on more systems (not only on mainstream systems but also) on Android phones and Raspberry Pi devices. In near future, the authors would like to extend the detector to detect more types of transient execution attacks, and work on more types of microprocessors (currently the detector can work on Intel processors, but not on AMD and ARM). Another research direction is that the authors want to extend the current detection mechanisms to accommodate (not just for the transient attacks, but also for the arising types and possibly existing types of attacks, the point being that the detection abilities can be evolved with time and can be customized as needed) more IoT devices, such as smart meters, wearable devices, etc. As can be seen from the Figure 5, that is the current version of CELLS on the Android system. It is not yet equipped with the malware detection abilities, but soon it will be extended to have them. Customers can click the 'Malware Detection' button and it will link to the Google Play Store and a bunch of detection programs (developed by the authors and other researchers or the companies that use this product) can be downloaded and customized by the users. Another example is for the Raspberry Pi devices, as they are getting more and more popular, therefore they also attract the attacker's attention, the authors will also dedicate themselves to the malware analysis and the malware detection in the area.

Figure 12. The Attack and Detection of Spectre-PHT on Linux system

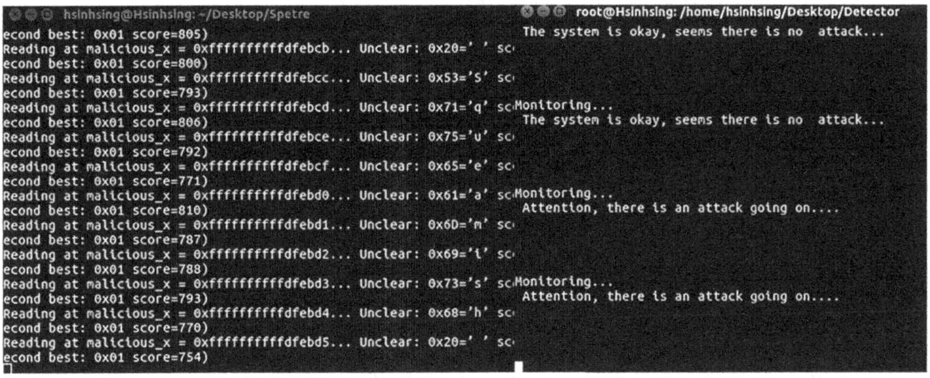

Figure 13. The Attack and Detection of Meltdown-US on Windows 10

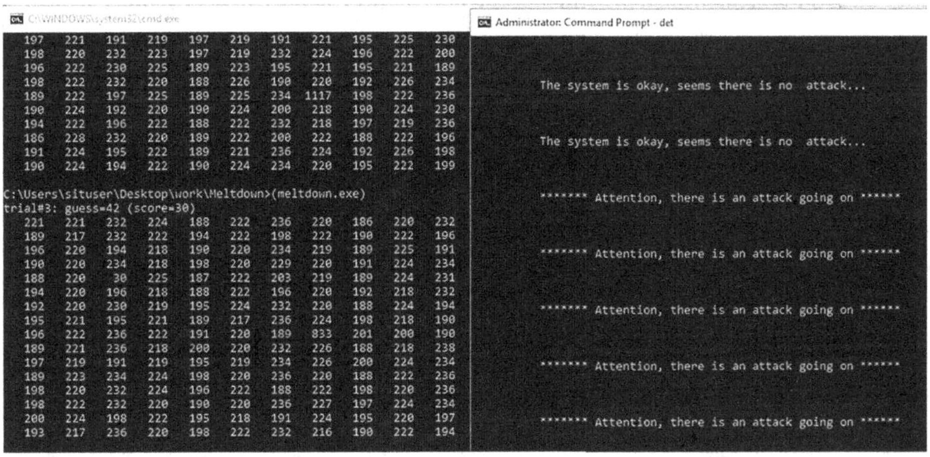

CONCLUSION

The vision with IoT technology has mainly two perspectives: Firstly, it is with the "Internet-centric" architecture. It mainly involves Internet services that can provide the huge amount of processing capabilities to process the data generated by the "Things". The second perspective being the "Things-centric" architecture. The main focus will be the smart devices. From the security point of view, there are a few trends for the technology of IoT that particularly relates to the area that the authors want to research on. First of all, these devices are getting more and more powerful (e.g., new mobile, wearable or connected devices), therefore if they are compromised by attackers, they can cause potentially catastrophic damages. Second, the smart devices will be everywhere and in every sector of life, billions of them, this also means there is a big chance that these devices can be compromised. In view of these trends, there is an urgent need to respond to these critical IoT-enabled infrastructures. The authors deem therefore developing a system which can provide a platform-neutral way to protect the IoT devices (traditional endpoint devices included) in general is of crucial importance. And this research project took its first step towards this goal. It aims to provide a micro-agent system which can work cross platform and, to protect endpoint devices (IoT devices included) efficiently in real time from certain types of Internet attacks (for the time being, more attention has been paid to the transient execution attacks on modern CPUs, more detection capabilities for more range of IoT devices will be provided soon). The developed micro-agent system (CELLS), can run not only on the mainstream operating systems (Linux, Windows, Mac Os), but also on systems such as Android and Raspberry Pi systems, and in future it will be running on more embedded devices. The detection capabilities for the transient attacks are currently only on Intel processors, and they will be extended to other type microprocessors (AMD and ARM) in future, therefore can protect more types of IoT devices, and that is the ultimate goal for this research. One of the highlights of CELLS's subsystem system is Malware detection / Ransomware activity detector. This feature enables end users/customers to use their own proprietary anti-malware software on top of the CELLS framework and deploy across their endpoints. This helps enhance the CELLS capabilities as an endpoint protection solution including newer threats and enhance collaboration with potential commercial anti-malware solutions providers.

Figure 14. The Attack and Detection of Meltdown-US on Linux

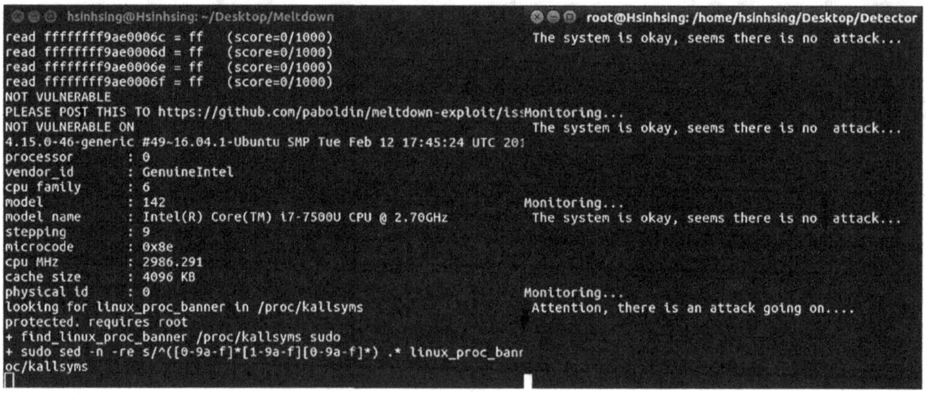

The authors report their research methodology and the initial results to the research community and encourage more researchers to continue this work and to equip the micro-agent system with more detection capabilities to protect IoT-enabled commercial and industry-space devices, as the future is already here.

Table 1. The performance of the detector

Type	S-PHT W	S-BTB W	S-RSB W	S-STL L	S-PHT M	M-US W	M-US L	S-PHT L
Time	4s	5s	8s	7s	8s	9s	8s	5s

S-PHT W = Spectre PHT on Windows
M-US L = Meltdown-US on Linux
S-PHT L = Spectre-PHT on Linux
S-PHT M = Spectre PHT on MacOs.
S-STL L= Spectre STL on Linux

ACKNOWLEDGMENT

This research project was supported by the Singapore Ministry of Education Translation and Innovation Fund [MOE2016-TIF-1-G-022].

REFERENCES

Acıiçmez, O. (2007). Yet another microarchitectural attack: exploiting I-Cache. In *Comp* (pp. 11–18). Security Arch. WS.

Acıiçmez, O., Gueron, S., & Seifert, J. P. (2007). New Branch Prediction Vulnerabilities in OpenSSL and Necessary Software Countermeasures. *International Conference on Cryptography and Coding (IMA)*. 10.1007/978-3-540-77272-9_12

ARM. (2018). *Vulnerability of speculative processors to cache timing side-channel mechanism*. Developer support of security update.

Canella, C., Van Bulck, J., Schwarz, M., Lipp, M., Von Berg, B., Ortner, P., Piessens, F., Evtyushkin, D., & Gruss, D. (2018). *A Systematic Evaluation of Transient Execution Attacks and Defenses*. arXiv:1811.05441

Creator, Q. T. (2019). *Software development made smarter*. Retrieved from https://www.qt.io

Disselkoen, C., Kohlbrenner, D., Porter, L., & Tullsen, D. (2017). Prime+Abort: A Timer-Free High-Precision L3 Cache Attack using Intel TSX. Usenix Security.

Evtyushkin, D., Ponomarev, D. V., & Abu-Ghazaleh, N. B. (2016). Jump over ASLR: Attacking branch predictors to bypass ASLR. MICRO.

Ge, Q., Yarom, Y., Cock, D., & Heiser, G. (2018). A survey of microarchitectural timing attacks and countermeasures on contemporary hardware. *J. Cryptographic Engineering*, 8(1), 1–27. doi:10.100713389-016-0141-6

Gruss, D., Maurice, C., Fogh, A., Lipp, M., & Mangard, S. (2016) Prefetch Side-Channel Attacks: Bypassing SMAP and Kernel ASLR. CCS.

Gruss, D., Maurice, C., Wagner, K., & Mangard, S. (2016). Flush+Flush: A Fast and Stealthy Cache Attack. DIMVA'16.

Gruss, D., Spreitzer, R., & Mangard, S. (2015). Cache Template Attacks: Automating Attacks on Inclusive Last-Level Caches. *USENIX Security Symposium*.

Gullasch, D., Bangerter, E., & Krenn, S. (2011). Cache Games - Bringing Access-Based Cache Attacks on AES to Practice. IEEE: Security & Privacy.

Horn, J. (2018). *Speculative execution, variant 4: speculative store bypass*. Retrieved from https://bugs.chromium.org/p/project-zero/issues/detail?id=1528

IAIK. (2018). *Meltdown Proof-of-Concept*. Retrieved from https://github.com/IAIK/meltdown

Inci, M. S., Gulmezoglu, B., Irazoqui, G., Eisenbarth, T., & Sunar, B. (2016). Cache Attacks Enable Bulk Key Recovery on the Cloud. CHES'16. doi:10.1007/978-3-662-53140-2_18

INTEL. (2016). *Intel Software Guard Extensions (Intel SGX)*. Retrieved from https://software.intel.com/en-us/sgx

INTEL. (2017b). *Intel 64 and IA-32 Architectures Optimization Reference Manual*. INTEL.

INTEL. (2018). *Intel Analysis of Speculative Execution Side Channels*. Retrieved from https://software.intel.com/security-software-guidance/api-app/sites/default/files/336983-Intel-Analysis-of-Speculative-Execution-Side-Channels-White-Paper.pdf

INTEL. (2017a). *Intel Xeon Processor Scalable Family Technical Overview*. Retrieved from https://software.intel.com/en-us/articles/intel-xeon-processor-scalable-family-technical-overview

Irazoqui, G., Eisenbarth, T., & Sunar, B. (2015). S$A: A shared cache attack that works across cores and defies VM sandboxing—and its application to AES. *IEEE Security & Privacy*. doi:10.1109/SP.2015.42

Irazoqui, G., Eisenbarth, T., & Sunar, B. (2016). Cross processor cache attacks. AsiaCCS. doi:10.1145/2897845.2897867

Jovanbulck. (2019). *Foreshadow*. Retrieved from https://github.com/jovanbulck/ sgx-step/tree/master/app/foreshadow

Kiriansky, V., & Waldspurger, C. (2018). *Speculative Buffer Overflows: Attacks and Defenses*. arXiv:1807.03757

Kocher, P. (1996). Timing Attacks on Implementations of Diffie-Hellman, RSA, DSS, and Other Systems. Proc. Advances in Cryptology (CRYPTO '96), 104-113.

Kocher, P., Horn, J., Fogh, A., Genkin, D., Gruss, D., Haas, W., Hamburg, M., Lipp, M., Mangard, S., Prescher, T., Schwarz, M., & Yarom, Y. (2019). Spectre attacks: Exploiting speculative execution. *IEEE Security & Privacy*. doi:10.1109/ SP.2019.00002

Koruyeh, E. M., Khasawneh, K., Song, C., & Abu-Ghazaleh, N. (2018). Spectre returns! speculation attacks using the return stack buffer. WOOT.

Lee, J., Jang, J., Jang, Y., Kwak, N., Choi, Y., Choi, C., Kim, T., Peinado, M., & Kang, B. B. (2017). Hacking in darkness: Return-oriented programming against secure enclaves. In USENIX Security (pp. 523–539). Academic Press.

Lee, S., Shih, M., Gera, P., Kim, T., Kim, H., & Peinado, M. (2017). Inferring Fine-grained Control Flow Inside SGX Enclaves with Branch Shadowing. *USENIX Security Symposium*.

Lipp, M., Schwarz, M., Gruss, D., Prescher, T., Haas, W., Fogh, A., Horn, J., Mangard, S., Kocher, P., Genkin, D., Yarom, Y., & Hamburg, M. (2018). Meltdown: Reading Kernel Memory from User Space. *USENIX Security Symposium*.

Liu, F., Yarom, Y., Ge, Q., Heiser, G., & Lee, R. (2015). Last level cache side channel attacks are practical. *36th IEEE Symposium on Security and Privacy (S&P 2015)*. 10.1109/SP.2015.43

Loh, P. K. K., & Loh, B. W. Y. (2016). Celles — A novel IOT security approach. In *Conf. Rec. 2016 IEEE Int. Conf. TENCON* (pp. 3716– 3719). IEEE.

Maisuradze, G., & Rossow, C. (2018). Ret2spec: Speculative execution using return stack buffers. CCS.

Msmania. (2018). *Meltdown/Spectre Proof-of-Concept for Windows*. Retrieved from https://github.com/msmania/microarchitectural-attack

Osvik, D. A., Shamir, A., & Tromer, E. (2006). Cache Attacks and Countermeasures: The Case of AES. CT-RSA.

Ristenpart, T., Tromer, E., Shacham, H., & Savage, S. (2009.) Hey, you, get off of my cloud: exploring information leakage in third-party compute clouds. CCS. doi:10.1145/1653662.1653687

Sebastian, M. (2018). *Intel admits Meltdown/Spectre patches cause severe reboots.* Retrieved from https://www.datacenterdynamics.com/news/intel-admits-meltdownspectre-patches-cause-server-reboots/

Shacham, H. (2007). The geometry of innocent flesh on the bone: Return- into-libc without function calls (on the x86). CCS.

Stecklina, J., & Prescher, T. (2018). *LazyFP: Leaking FPU Register State using Microarchitectural Side-Channels.* arXiv:1806.07480

Stephen, N. (2018). *Intel: Problem in patches for Spectre, Meltdown extends to newer chips.* Retrieved from https://www.reuters.com/article/us-cyber-intel/intel-problem-in-patches-for-spectre-meltdown-extends-to-newer-chips-idUSKBN1F7087

Van Bulck, J., Minkin, M., Weisse, O., Genkin, D., Kasikci, B., Piessens, F., Silberstein, M., Wenisch, T. F., Yarom, Y., & Strackx, R. (2018). Foreshadow: Extracting the Keys to the Intel SGX Kingdom with Transient Out-of-Order Execution. *Proceedings of the 27th USENIX Security Symposium.*

Van Bulck, J., Piessens, F., & Strackx, R. (2017). SGX-Step: A practical attack framework for precise enclave execution control. In *Proceedings of the 2nd Workshop on System Software for Trusted Execution.* ACM. 10.1145/3152701.3152706

Veerappan, C. S., Loh, P. K. K., Tang, Z. H., & Tan, F. (2018). Taxonomy on Malware Evasion Countermeasures. In *Conf. Rec. 2018 IEEE Int. Conf. WF-IoT* (pp. 558-563). IEEE.

Weichbrodt, N., Kurmus, A., Pietzuch, P., & Kapitza, R. (2016). Asyncshock: exploiting synchronization bugs in Intel SGX enclaves. In *European Symposium on Research in Computer Security.* Springer. 10.1007/978-3-319-45744-4_22

Weisse, O., Vanbulck, J., Minkin, M., Genkin, D., Kasikci, B., Piessens, F., Silberstein, M., Strackx, R., Wenisch, T. F., & Yarom, Y. (2018). *Foreshadow-NG: Breaking the Virtual Memory Abstraction with Transient Out-of-Order Execution.* Technical report.

Yarom, Y., & Falkner, K. (2014). FLUSH+RELOAD: A High Resolution, Low Noise, L3 Cache Side-Channel Attack. In *23rd USENIX Security Symposium* (pp. 719–732). San Diego, CA: USENIX Association.

Zhang, Y., Juels, A., Reiter, M. K., & Ristenpart, T. (2012). Cross-VM side channels and their use to extract private keys. In CCS (pp. 305–316). doi:10.1145/2382196.2382230

Zhang, Y., Juels, A., Reiter, M. K., & Ristenpart, T. (2014). Cross-tenant side-channel attacks in PaaS clouds. In CCS (pp. 990– 1003). doi:10.1145/2660267.2660356

Zhao, X., Veerappan, C. S., Loh, P. K. K., Tang. Z. H., & Forest, T. F. (2018) Multi-Agent Cross-Platform Detection of Meltdown and Spectre. In *Proc. 2018 IEEE Conference on Control, Automation, Robotics and Vision* (pp. 1834—1838). 10.1109/ICARCV.2018.8581146

Chapter 4
Anomaly Detection in IoT Frameworks Using Machine Learning

Phidahunlang Chyne
North-Eastern Hill University, India

Parag Chatterjee
National Technological University, Argentina & University of the Republic, Uruguay

Sugata Sanyal
Tata Institute of Fundamental Research, India

Debdatta Kandar
North-Eastern Hill University, India

ABSTRACT

Rapid advancements in hardware programming and communication innovations have encouraged the development of internet-associated sensory devices that give perceptions and information measurements from the physical world. According to the internet of things (IoT) analytics, more than 100 IoT devices across the world connect to the internet every second, which in the coming years will sharply increase the number of IoT devices by billions. This number of IoT devices incorporates new dynamic associations and does not totally replace the devices that were purchased before yet are not utilized any longer. As an increasing number of IoT devices advance into the world, conveyed in uncontrolled, complex, and frequently hostile conditions, securing IoT frameworks displays various challenges. As per the Eclipse IoT Working Group's 2017 IoT engineer overview, security is the top worry for IoT designers. To approach the challenges in securing IoT devices, the authors propose using unsupervised machine learning model at the network/transport level for anomaly detection.

DOI: 10.4018/978-1-7998-2444-2.ch004

INTRODUCTION

The escalated advancement of system innovations and the quick development of the number of heterogeneous networks that are interconnected and which consistently trade vast information volumes have made a prolific ground for the advancement of adaptable cyber-attack classification and in the event of different types of network anomalies. It is estimated that by 2020, the complete number of Internet-associated gadgets being utilized will be 25 to 50 billion. As the numbers develop and advances become more developed, the volume of information distributed will increment. Internet associated gadgets innovation alluded to as the Internet of Things (IoT), keeps on expanding the current Internet by giving network and connection between the physical and digital universes. Notwithstanding expanded volume, the IoT creates Big Data portrayed by speed in terms of location dependency and time, with an assortment of various modalities and fluctuating information quality. Intelligent analysis and processing of this Big Data is the way to creating brilliant IoT applications. IoT and comparative conditions are at a very fascinating momentum of both the network of inventions and their developments. Tan and Wang(2010), and Wu et al. (2010) discussed in their papers that IoT alludes to an ongoing worldview that has quickly made progress in the present day wireless communications. IoT is then another innovative trend joining new computing and communication standards. Within this new trend, there are smart gadgets that have an advanced substance and are universally interconnected on a system and to the worldwide Internet (Armentano et. al., 2018). Regular items may incorporate knowledge and the capacity to sense, translate and respond to their condition, joining the Internet with rising innovations, for example, the used of Radio Frequency Identification (RFID) as mentioned by Sharma and Siddiqui(2010) as well as Ziegler and Urbas (2011), real-time locations and installed sensors. The IoT idea depends on the thought of a widespread nearness of 'things' or 'articles, for example, RFID labels, sensors, actuators, cell phones, and so on, with computerized recognizable proof and tending to plans that empower them to coordinate with neighbours so as to accomplish a few shared objectives. In the business area, the most evident results of IoT may emerge in modern computerization and manufacturing, in coordination, in business or procedure management and in astute plans for intelligent transportation. Let us explore IoT in the next subsections.

IoT Architecture

IoT is a blend of embedded technologies including wired and wireless communications, sensor and actuator gadgets, and the physical articles associated with the Internet as mentioned by Atzori et al.(2010) and Cecchinel et al. (2014). One of the long-standing targets of computing is to streamline and enhance human activities and experiences. IoT requires data to either represent better services to users or improve the IoT system execution to achieve this intelligently. Thusly, frameworks ought to have the capacity to access raw information from various assets over the system and investigate this data in request to extricate learning.

IoT requires intelligent processing and reliability inside the system. To give this, system engineering contains three layers: the sensing layer, the transport layer, and the application layer. The detecting/sensing layer contains edge devices that are made out of an assortment of sensors and actuators that gather information and send it through the transportation layer to the application layer for analysis. The transport layer comprises of system communications including Wi-Fi, Bluetooth, ZigBee, and 802.15.4. The transport layer contains the gateways/passages that process the data also, hand-off the data over the system. The application layer contains the logical connection between the user and the Internet through smart applications. Figure 1 is a pictorial representation of the IoT Architecture.

Figure 1. IoT Architecture[1]

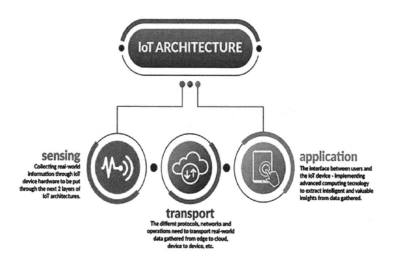

Security Concerns

According to the 2018 report, India ranked third in cyber attacks after Mexico and France according to the Business Today survey updated on March 13, 2019. According to the UK-based endpoint security provider recent survey Sophos has found 76% businesses were hit by cyber attacks in 2018, meanwhile around 68% cyber attacks in organizations were globally recorded in 2018. In India, most of the attacks are on financial services, oil and gas and energy sectors. Ransomwares, Viruses, Phishing are an ever increasing threat. Some of the major cyber security incidents that have cropped so far are the "Agent Smith virus" which has infected 25 million Android devices around the world, out of which 15 million are in India. "LockerGoga Ransomware" is another cyber attack which has struck the systems of Norwegian aluminium manufacturer Company Norsk Hydro which modified the user account in the infected system by changing their passwords. Analysis initially shown that LockerGoga, doesn't appear to have the capability to propagate like "WannaCry" which hit worldwide on May, 2017 or Petya/NotPetya which belong to a family of encrypting ransomware that was initially discovered in 2016. Computer makers such as Asus disclosed a supply chain attack in the second half in 2018 that had compromised the Company's Live Updates Tool to push Malware to almost 1 million customers. Then there was Barium supply chain hack in 2017 of the popular computer Cleanup Tool CCleaner.

Criminal groups are likely to continue attacking businesses, health care providers, educational institutions, financial organizations as well as local governments. Coming back into IoT there are a few difficulties with actualizing security inside an IoT network as discussed by Mahmoud et al. (2015). Few of them include authorization and authentication of devices, ensuring data privacy and integrity, ensuring high availability, detecting vulnerabilities and secure computing. To start with, IoT frameworks are heterogeneous and the line between normal and abnormal is usually blurred. There are distinctive kinds of devices, techniques for communication, kinds of information being exchanged and shared, different asset dimensions of devices, and framework setups. Each unique component adds to the challenge of successfully secure IoT. A second challenge inheres in the number of devices that are associated together. Numerous IoT devices have constrained measures of capacity, memory, and processing ability and they regularly should almost certainly work on lower power, for instance, when running on batteries. Security approaches that depend vigorously on encryption are not a solid match for these compelled devices since they are not equipped for performing complex encryption and decoding rapidly enough to have the capacity to transmit information safely in real time.

Most IoT arrangements comprise of three fundamental levels. IoT arrangement segments that keep running in every level need to fuse explicit security measures to ensure against different vulnerabilities.

1. Devices/Gateways level: Protect against a "fake" server that sends malicious commands, or ensures against a hacker that attempts to tune in to private sensor information being sent from the devices.

2. Network/Transport level: Protect against a "fake" device that sends false measurements that may degenerate the information that is being persevered in the application.
3. Applications level: Protect against the invalid utilization of information, or ensure against the manipulation of expository procedures that are running in the application level.

Objective of the Chapter

To address the challenges in securing IoT devices, the authors propose using unsupervised machine learning techniques for anomaly detection only in the domain of the Network/Transport level. Unsupervised AI indicates to reveal beforehand obscure examples in information, however more often these patterns are poor approximations of what supervised AI can accomplish. Anomaly detection can naturally find irregular information focuses on the dataset. This is helpful in pinpointing deceitful transactions, discovering faulty pieces of hardware, or recognizing an anomaly brought about by a human mistake amid data entry

BACKGROUND STUDY

In the course of the most recent decade, AI has gained phenomenal ground in regions as diverse as image recognition, self-driving vehicles and making complex games on the go. These victories have been to a great extent acknowledged via preparing profound neural systems with one of two learning supervised learning and reinforcement learning. The two ideal models require training sets/signals to be structured by a human passed on to the computer. On account of supervised learning, these are the "objectives, (for example, the correct caption of an image); on account of reinforcement learning, they are the "rewards" for effective conduct, (for example, getting applause after a performance). The breaking points of learning are along these lines characterized by the human mentors. Unaided learning is also known as Unsupervised learning is a worldview intended to make self-ruling knowledge by rewarding/compensating agents (that is, computer programs) for finding out about the information they see without a specific undertaking at the top of the priority list.

A key inspiration for unaided/unsupervised learning is that, while the information passed to learning algorithms is amazingly wealthy in interior structure (e.g., pictures, recordings, and content), the objectives and compensations utilized for training are normally meagre (e.g., a solitary one or zero to mean achievement or disappointment in a game). This proposes the heft of what is found out by an algorithm must comprise of understanding the information itself, instead of applying that understanding to specific assignments.

Xiao et al. (2018) focus on the machine learning based IoT authentication, access control, secure offloading and malware detection schemes to protect data privacy. They also investigated the attack model for IoT systems, and reviewed the IoT security solutions based on machine learning techniques including supervised learning, unsupervised learning and reinforcement learning. The authors in Canedo et al.(2016) approach the challenges in securing IoT devices; using machine learning within an IoT gateway to help secure the system. They investigated using Artificial Neural Networks in a gateway to detect anomalies in the data sent from the edge devices. Mouaatamid et al. (2016) mentioned three categories of security requirements in WSN and RFID i.e, Denial of Service, Privacy and Impersonation. Based on these different attacks were classified. Unsupervised learning depends on two essential suspicions. To begin with, they assume that the vast majority of the system associations are ordinary traffic and just a little measure of rate is abnormal. Second, they envision that pernicious traffic is measurably unique in relation to typical traffic. In view of these two suspicions, data gatherings of comparative examples that show up every now and again are thought to be typical traffic and those information clusters that are rare are viewed as malignant. The most widely recognized unsupervised calculations are self-organizing maps (SOM), K-means, C-means, expectation-maximization meta-algorithm (EM), adaptive resonance theory (ART), and one-class support vector machine. One mainstream procedure is self-organizing maps (SOM). The primary target of the SOM is to diminish the component of information perception.

AI methods are presently getting significant consideration among the anomaly identification to address the shortcomings of information base location procedures. Peculiarity discovery can successfully aid in finding fraudulent attacks, finding strange activities in enormous and complex Big Data sets. This can demonstrate to be helpful in zones, for example, banking security, common sciences, medication, and marketing, which are inclined to noxious exercises. With the machine, a learning association can strengthen the pursuit and increment adequacy of their advanced business activities as envisioned by Perera (2015).

Unsupervised Learning Algorithms

1. *Clustering:* Clustering is the effort of gathering a group of objects so that objects in a similar group/cluster are increasingly comparative to one another than to those in different clusters. It is a primary job of exploratory data mining, and a typical strategy for measurable information or data analysis, utilized in numerous fields, including AI, image analysis, data recovery, pattern

recognition, data compression, and bioinformatics. A few different types of commonly used clustering are:

a. K-Means Clustering – grouping the data/information points into a number (K) of mutually exclusive clusters. A great deal of the multifaceted nature encompasses how to pick the correct number for K.

b. Hierarchical Clustering – clustering the data/information points into parent and child groups. You may part your clients among younger and more established ages, and afterward part every one of those clusters into their own individual groups too.

c. Probabilistic Clustering – clustering the data/information points into groups on a probabilistic scale.

2. *Unsupervised Deep Learning:* Obviously, unsupervised learning has likewise been stretched out to deep learning and neural nets. This section is as yet beginning, yet one well-known use of the neural net in an unsupervised manner is called an Autoencoder. Like a Neural Net, an Autoencoder uses weights to attempt to form the input data values into the ideal output; however, the astute bend here is that the output is a similar thing as the input. At the end of the day, the Autoencoder attempts to make sense of how to represent the input data as itself, utilizing a little measure of information than the first. Autoencoders have demonstrated valuable in PC vision applications like object recognition, and are being investigated and stretched out to scopes like speech and audio. This is also stretched out to Self-Organizing maps which will be adapted in our proposal, there is also the Hebbian Learning and Deep belief Nets which we will not discussed in this chapter.

3. *Anomaly Detection:* Anomaly detection is a case of an unsupervised AI approach. Unsupervised algorithms do not have a label or target result ahead of time. These algorithms discover similarities or regularities in the information data– for instance gathering comparable clients, in light of procurement information. Anomaly detection initially builds up what normal behaviour is, then compares it to the observed behaviour and generates an alert if significant deviations from normal were identified. For this situation, the authors don't begin with a known set of conditions that the authors will attempt to group. Rather, we search for deviations from typical reading, and we apply that assessment in real time.

Classification of Anomalies

Machine Learning has four common classes of applications: classification, predicting next value, anomaly detection, and finding structure. Among them, Anomaly detection detects data points in data that does not fit well with the remainder of the information. It has a wide scope of uses, for example, fraud detection, surveillance, diagnosis, data cleanup, and predictive maintenance. With the advent of IoT, anomaly detection would likely to play a key role in IoT use cases such as monitoring and predictive maintenance.

Static rule based systems are brittle and complex for identifying rules. Therefore, statistical or machine learning based approach, which automatically learns the general rules, are preferred to static rules as mentioned in [4].

Raza et al. (2013) presented a hybrid approach to deal with intrusion detection inside IoT frameworks. Their work endeavours balance a signature approach with an anomaly approach. Zhang et al. (2005) presented a unified anomaly system for network anomography. They propose to isolate anomaly detection into two classifications; frameworks using temporal correlation methods, and systems using spatial correlation methods to recognize typical traffic.

Types of Network Abuse

The types of network abuse that ranges in IoT frameworks are listed below.

1. Denial of Service (DoS) attacks: The attackers flood the target server with superfluous requests to prevent IoT devices from obtaining services. A standout amongst the most hazardous kinds of a DoS attack is when DDoS attackers utilize a large number of Internet convention to delivers IoT administrations, making it troublesome for the server to recognize the authentic IoT devices from attackers as mentioned by Andrea et al. (2015).

2. Man-in-the-middle attacks: A man-in-the-middle attacker sends send counterfeit signals to interfere with the on-going radio transmissions of IoT gadgets and further drain the bandwidth, vitality, central processing units(CPUs), and memory assets of IoT sensors amid their failed communication attempts as discussed by Han et al. (2017). It additionally sends spoofing signals which mimic a legal IoT gadget with its personality as discussed by Xiao et al. (2016). For example, the medium access control (MAC) address and RFID tag to gain unlawful access to the IoT framework and can additionally launch attacks with the objective of secretly monitoring, eavesdropping, and modifying the private communication between IoT devices was mentioned by Andrea et al. (2015).

3. Brute force attack: As manufacturers keep on contending on who might get the most recent gadget in the hands of purchasers first? Not many of them are thinking about the security issues related to information access with IoT devices. The Mirai botnet, utilized in the absolute biggest and most problematic DDoS assaults mentioned by Antonakakis et al. (2017) is maybe a standout amongst the best instances of the issues that accompany shipping devices with

default passwords and not advising customers to change them when they get them. The main motivation behind why Mirai malware was so successful is that it distinguished vulnerable IoT devices and utilized default usernames and passwords to sign in. In this manner, an organization that utilized manufacturers default accreditations on their devices is setting the users and their valuable data in danger of being vulnerable to a brute-force attack.

Numerous researchers such as Ahmad et al. (2017), Yang (2017), Yasumoto et al. (2016) and Ding and Fei (2013) concentrated on the anomaly identification of streaming data. Initially, in IoT based devices, streaming data are typically created very rapidly and in huge volumes, so any conventional off-line anomaly detection algorithm that endeavours to store or filter the entire dataset multiple times for anomaly identification will eventually come up short on memory space, which would be impractical and unfeasible to carry out effectively.

Furthermore, in light of the fact that the anomaly behaviour rarely happened, the streaming data more often contains very typical data and uncommon anomalous focuses, which made the anomaly detector training troublesome and difficult to become familiar with the given precise model for the significant unbalanced dataset. Concept drift is another significant thought while managing anomalous behaviour in streaming data as mentioned in Wang et al. (2003), Ditzler and Polikar (2012) and Zhou et al. (2009).

Types of Anomalies

The types of anomalies that ranges in IoT frameworks are listed below.

1. Point Anomalies: An observation that deviates from the trend in which a solitary case of data is anomalous if it is excessively distant from the rest.
2. Contextual Anomalies: The variation from the normal is context specific. This sort of anomaly is common in time series data.
3. Collective Anomalies: A huge set of data instances collectively aids in identifying oddities or an anomaly is detected with reference to the entire dataset.

In Zarpelao et al. (2017), authors analyze, evaluate and classify anomaly detection systems and system specifics in IoT. In the network level analyzes, wireless communications is one of the security concerns as it encourages malicious operations of the adversary. Even though it is ensured with cryptographic and verification systems, things are exposed to wireless attacks from either inside the network or from the internet. Another test is dynamic topology, which provides the grounds for the adoption of intruder nodes, Moreover, routing conventions, flow control and access control attempts to work with less computational expense and overhead, which consequently leads to security challenges.

The issue of characterizing and investigating anomalies absolutely with information perceptions (unsupervised learning) and the absence of already described information is the focal point of much consideration inside the research network. Unsupervised learning works on the assumptions that unusual traffic is on a very basic level distinctive to the typical traffic structures. It is expected that by considering these distinctions, variations from normal and abnormal information can be found.

Unsupervised Anomaly Detection is the most adaptable setup, which does not require any labels. Besides, there is likewise no distinction between training and a test dataset. The thought is that an unsupervised anomaly detection algorithm scores the information exclusively dependent on characteristic properties of the dataset. Regularly, distances or densities are utilized to give estimation what is typical and what is an outlier. This article just spotlights on this unsupervised abnormality identification setup. Unsupervised learning does not require labelled data as in the supervised learning but instead researches the comparability between the unlabeled information to cluster them into various clusters. For instance, IoT devices can utilize the multivariate relationship analysis to identify DoS assaults as discussed by Tan et al. (2013) and apply the infinite Gaussian mixture model (IGMM) in the physical (PHY)- layer authentication with security insurance as mentioned in Xiao et al. (2013)

Unsupervised Learning Model Illustration of Anomaly Detection

In IoT devices, attacks were mainly physical cyber attacks, which results from breaches in the IoT devices sensors. As the authors mainly focus on network attacks, it includes monitoring and eavesdropping, network traffic analysis, camouflage, denial of service attacks, node subversion, node malfunction, node capture, node outage, message corruption, false node, replication attacks and routing attacks.

IoT devices can apply unsupervised learning techniques to evaluate the runtime behaviours of the apps in anomaly detection. Our approach to anomaly detection includes utilizing a Markov chain model, a strategy from AI, to learn examples of typical system conduct. When the authors have a learned probabilistic model of typical conduct, which would then be able to look at it against observed network messages to detect anomalous behaviour. A learned model of ordinary conduct enables us to evaluate the likelihood of each observed network messages, given the previously observed sequence of messages. At that point, messages were called with the minimal assessed probabilities anomalous and alarm a framework administrator to investigate.

As illustrated in Figure 2, attackers can attack directly from IoT devices or within the network, attackers here doesn't only mean a hacker but it may be a malware or botnets. The IoT device filters the TCP packets and selects the features among various network features including the frame number and length, labels them, and stores these features in the database. The input raw data are then segregated into clusters where interpretation is done and as it is unsupervised the data are untrained and then fed into the Markov model which will assembles a Markov chain in the network traffic to detect a sequence of occasions and to recognize the uncommon sequences.

The nearest neighbour technique can detect anomalies by computing the distance of a data instance to its kth nearest neighbour or by calculating the relative distance of each data instance.

Figure 2. Illustration of Unsupervised Anomaly Detection

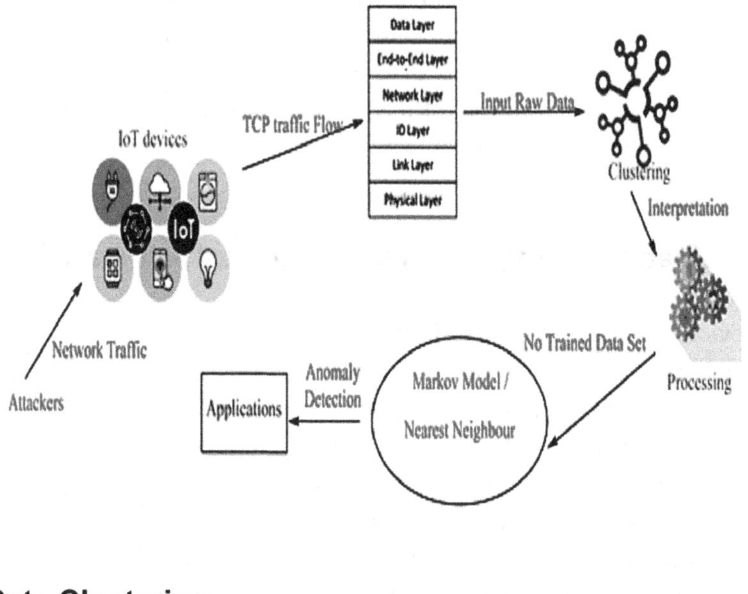

Raw Data Clustering

Clustering is the most well-known type of programmed unsupervised data analysis. It tends to be seen as a sort of vector quantization process in which the point by point information inside an informational collection are abstracted and, compacted to a little arrangement of class portrayals, one for each class, that outline the attributes of the information in every data subset characterized as groups or clusters. So clustering is an expressive information investigation task, that goes for finding the natural structure in accumulation of objects by gathering them into a cluster, in view of the values of their features, to such an extent that those inside each cluster are more firmly identified with each other than objects allocated to various groups.

Clustering is an unsupervised learning task. In this manner, given a set of unlabelled information a clustering calculation endeavours to amass them to increasingly significant groups. As a second step, a label will be allocated to each cluster, giving a means to summing up over the information objects and their highlights, as opposed to supervised learning, where for the informational index label or target is as of now given to the preparing or training set. Clustering is valuable particularly for enormous and high dimensional datasets as it gives a disentanglement of the basic information dispersion, and it additionally reveals shrouded structure and learning. In cluster analysis, a significant parameter to be characterized is a proportion of likeness (or difference) between the individual objects being clustered. A standout amongst the most prevalent strategy to quantify the similitude between two vectors, assume d-dimensional space, is the Euclidean distance:

$$d\left(a,b\right) = \sqrt{\sum_{i=1}^{n}\left(a_i - b_i\right)^2} \tag{1}$$

It is proposed to adapt Self Organizing Maps (SOM) neural network to cluster the IoT network attacks. Self-organizing maps (SOM) were presented by Kohonen (1982 and 1990), and have turned into an exceptionally prominent apparatus utilized for the representation of high dimensional information spaces, grouping/ vector quantization (VQ) and in the meantime spatial ordering preserving of the information space reflected by the requesting of the codebook vectors or cluster centroids. The fundamental thought of SOM is to delineate information designs onto an n-dimensional framework of neurons or units. That network shapes what is known as the output space, rather than the input space that is the first space where the information designs are, as delineated in Figure 3.

The development of the SOM pursues a particular strategy beginning with the initialization of the synaptic weights in the system, standardized somewhere in the range of 0 and 1, to defeat the way that specific factors may overpower others in the learning procedure. Weights are picked by haphazardly picking smaller number from a number generator. Likewise, the element map isn't sorted out from the earlier. When the initialization is done, the meaning of the SOM pursues three significant procedures; competition, collaboration and synaptic adjustment as proposed by Haykin (2009).

Figure 3. Self Organizng Maps (Kohenen Model)[5]

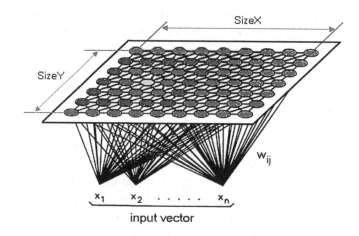

input vector

SOM Algorithm

Three fundamental advances are associated with the use of the SOM algortihm after the initialization stage: sampling, similarity matching, and synaptic loads update.

Algorithm SOM

Parameter Requirements: X: the informational/data collection;
c_d: the component of the information design;
M: the SOM grid measurement;
the quantity of cycles;
$\eta_0, \sigma_0, \tau_1, \tau_2$: parameters;

1. Initialization. For every neuron n in the cross section introduce the synaptic weight vectors $w_n(0)$ with little irregular values.
2. repeat
3. Sampling. Draw a pattern x from X at arbitrary;
4. Similarity Matching. Locate the best-coordinating (winning) neuron i(x) at time-step k by utilizing the base separation model or Euclidean distance:

$$i(x) = \arg\min \left\| x(k) - w_n(k) \right\|, 1 \le n \le M \tag{2}$$

5. Updating. Alter the synaptic-weight vectors of all energized neurons by utilizing the update equation

$$w_n\left(k+1\right) = w_n\left(k\right) + \eta\left(k\right)h_{n,i(x)}\left(k\right)\left(x\left(k\right) - w_n\left(k\right)\right) \tag{3}$$

where $\eta(k)$ is the learning-rate parameter and $h_{n,i}(k)$ is the neighbourhood function revolved around the triumphant neuron $w(x)$; both $\eta(k)$ and $h_{n,i}(k)$ are fluctuated progressively amid learning for best results.

When the SOM calculation has merged, the outcome is a topological portrayal of the information space, as in contiguous neurons in the cross section will in general have comparative synaptic-weight vectors and will relate to a specific class or highlight that shows the significant measurable attributes of the input information.

Data Processing

Today, devices create more data than interpersonal organizations. Every device can send information a few times each second, and with a large number of associated devices, a common data processing platform may be required to manage billions of such approaching events each day. Despite the fact that handling this measure of information is clearly a significant technological test, obviously, the device information itself – even when stored in a pre-processed structure – is not noteworthy. To get noteworthy bits of knowledge, the gathered information must be investigated.

The authors portray our methodology, feature a few perceptions made amid different ventures, and view the segments that a framework for data analysis normally incorporates:

- Data preprocessing: This part module is intended to take care of numerous issues, for example, information purifying and the generation of domain-specific highlights.
- Data investigation: The fundamental job of this part is to discover inconsistencies in the information. The test is to pick a suitable data mining algorithm and to calibrate its parameters
- Data representation: Here the principle task is to envision the outcome for the end client just as to give methods for visual examination. The test is to pick visual methods that are suitable for the assignment being tackled and the specified issues in area of interest.

Processing and preparing data for IoT based communication is a basic test. To react to this test, various types of data processing, for example, edge analytics, stream investigation, and IoT analysis at the database must be employed. The choice to apply any of the referenced procedures relies upon the specific application and its needs as discussed by Bonomi et al. (2012). Fog and cloud processing are two expository strategies adopted in handling and preparing data before exchanging to different things. The entire assignment of IoT is condensed as pursues: first, sensors and IoT gadgets gather the data from nature. Next, learning ought to be extricated from the crude information. At that point, the information will be prepared for transfer to different items, gadgets, or servers through the Internet.

Unsupervised Anomaly Detection Techniques

- *Markov Chain model based*

Markov chains and Hidden Markov chains can measure the likelihood of an arrangement of events occurring. This methodology assembles a Markov chain for the underline procedure, and when a sequence of occasions has occurred, the authors can utilize the Markov Chain to quantify the likelihood of that succession happening and utilize that to recognize any uncommon sequences.

Markov chain models are based on learning a transition matrix from training data proposed by Murphy (2012). For this situation, our training data is a huge arrangement of network data which the authors believe to contain as a rule ordinary conduct as discussed by Haque et al. (2017). Changes allude to a succession of just two messages. The whole training data indexes can be spoken to as a succession of messages, $M = \{M_1, ..., M_n\}$. At that point, the related progress lattice contains components $T_{ij} = T(M_{k+1} = j|T_k = i)$. These probabilities can be evaluated by computing them dependent on our training data set, which gives us the greatest probability measure of the actual transition grid. Note that it is difficult to measure the actual change framework since a complete learning of all conceivable system message groupings as well as their relative frequencies must be known.

1. Let n_i be the number of times message i is seen in the succession $\{M1, ..., Mn-1\}$.
2. Let n_{ij} be the number of times seen as message i go to message j. For the last message in the list, it might be the case that it only appears that one time. In that case, set $\hat{T}_{ii} = 1$
3. Then $\hat{T}_{ij} = \dfrac{n_{ij}}{n_i}$

Note that since the authors can just quantify messages they observed, there is no way of n_i being 0, aside from potentially being the last message in the list.

Therefore, the authors arrive at a transition matrix where every component $T_{i,j}$ is the maximum probability measure for the likelihood that arrange message j legitimately pursues message i.

Subsequent to taking in the transition grid from a training set of messages falling in normal behaviour, the authors might want to check that the learned model indeed picked up the patterns of normal behaviour. To do this, the learned transition matrix can be utilized to produce a synthetic message sequence and analyze it to the sequence observed in the training set. In the event that the synthetic and authentic message sequences are comparable, the authors can conclude that they have taken in a model of ordinary conduct, and they will move on to assessing its value for abnormality identification.

- *One Class Support Vector Machine (SVM)*

In unsupervised case, potentially only one class of normality is present and the data points are between the normality case and the origin of the kernel feature space. This algorithm can handle non-linear cases but can also struggle when hyper parameters has to be defined which are far from being trivial to define and can struggle if there are high dimensional datasets. Several researchers such as Mulay et al. (2010), Perdisci et al. (2006), Erfani et al. (2016), Wang et al. (2004) and Heller et al. (2003) adapted Support Vector Machines for anomaly detection. Improvised versions of SVMs were discussed by Amer et al. (2013) and Li et al. (2003) for enhanced anomaly detection.

- *Tree Based Methods*

Another class of algorithms is Tree Based Method. The authors have here particularly the Isolation Forest which is basically a set of randomized decision trees that are in a way more intuitive than the one class SVM because it can easily distinguish inliers and outliers. The main advantage of their algorithm is that it can be parallelized. Various authors proposed the used of decision trees for anomaly detection and intrusion detection system as discussed by authors in Liu et al. (2012), Sindhuet al. (2012), Muniyandi et al. (2012) and Mulay et al. (2010).

- *Distance and Density Based Methods*

Derived from the k nearest neighbours that basically has feature space where distances are computed and the thumb rule is that if one data point is lonely and the neighbours too are segregated then it is an inliers else it is an outlier. This provides an advantage to identify local outliers but not predominantly as other points. This method is complicated for computing distances especially in dimensionality because the more data we have in our datasets the more costly it is to compute distances. Density-based anomaly detection put together inconsistency identification with respect to the k-closest neighbour's calculation as discussed by Amer and Goldstein (2012).

Consider two clusters representing normality and a few points that were sampled at random over the space that represents the outliers. The idea is to fit the algorithms on those data points and then apply decisions function over a pre-defined grid of the given domain to be able to plot decisions maps to identify the regions that contains inliers and outliers. But practically, in IoT the authors have to deal with multidimensional datasets therefore, numerical binary features has to be considered with more data points and more dimensions. The labels at benchmark times were actually needed, to train the proposed model and hide those labels. The classic Receiver Operating Characteristic (ROC) curves has to be plotted with false positive ratios in the Y- axis and true positive ratios in the X-axis, and interpretation of these results similarly to a classification problem has to be done.

It is presumed that normal data points happen around a thick dense neighbourhood and anomalies are far away. The closest arrangement of data points is assessed utilizing a score, which could be Euclidean separate or a comparable measure subject to the kind of information (absolute or numerical). Nearest neighbour based anomaly detection techniques can comprehensively arranged into two categories:

1. *K-nearest neighbor:* Techniques that use the distance of a data instance to its kth nearest neighbour as discussed by Amer and Goldstein (2012) and Kriegel et al. (2011) as the anomaly score. k-NN is a basic, non-parametric lethargic learning system used to order information dependent on likenesses in separation measurements, for example, Euclidean, Manhattan, Minkowski, or Hamming separation. A reverse k-nn anomaly detection was introduced by Radovanović et al. (2014).

2. *Relative density of information:* This is also called the local outlier factor (LOF). This idea depends on a separation metric called reachability distance. Techniques that compute the relative density of each data instance to compute its anomaly score as mentioned by Sugiyama, and Borgwardt (2013) and Angiull and Fassetti (2007).

The simplest way to deal with recognizing abnormalities is by visualizing the data in a plot. As k-NN utilizes basic examples in the data for predictions, any errors in these expectations are consequently indications of information signs, which do not acclimate toward overall trends. However, by this methodology, any calculation that creates a prescient model can be utilized to identify peculiarities. For example, in regression analysis, an anomaly would stray altogether from the best-fit line. When peculiarities have been recognized, they can be expelled from the datasets used to prepare prescient models. This will diminish noise in the information, along these lines fortifying the precision of prescient models.

System Model Flowchart

A stream of raw input data from various IoT devices are initially fed into the network. Typical breaches and network attacks were discussed in Subsection 3.1. The raw input data will be further analyzed for a learned probabilistic model to be able to be evaluate the likelihood of the observed messages or incoming streams of data. The observed input data are segregated into clusters in a clustering based unsupervised data analysis by utilizing SOM as mentioned in Subsection 3.2. Then the data is interpret and fed into the Markov Model which will assembles a Markov chain in the network traffic to detect a sequence of occasions and to recognize the uncommon sequences by checking the query fed into the database for pre-defined knowledge for detecting malicious behaviour. This model acts as a defence layer for providing network security in which framework collaborations are monitored and important cautions are issued after distinguishing anomalous conduct in the system as well as to identify malevolent practices of obscure outer system assailants. This model framework can breakdown and distinguishes typical conduct of the IoT system to recognize assaults and threats, and the system is warned with the goal that more harm is anticipated. The authors follow similarity based models, where each data is compared with other data of the network and collective data and non-similarity with other data of the network is identified as an anomaly. If the data delineates from the normal data it is detected as an anomaly otherwise it will pass on to the next layers.

CONCLUSION AND FUTURE PERSPECTIVES

One of the preeminent approaches to identify anomaly patterns is to extract every unusual pattern happening in the framework, develop new algorithms and store it in the cloud. Algorithms should be intended to track the characteristics and structure of minority class, adopt new approaching patterns dynamically by contrasting it and previous historical information. Develop new algorithms to find multi-class imbalanced figuring out how to comprehend connections between various classes. IoT frameworks should utilize numerous layers of defences, for instance, isolating devices onto separate systems and utilizing firewalls, to compensate for device restrictions. The intrusion detection schemes based on unsupervised learning techniques sometimes have miss detection rates that are not negligible for IoT systems. If there are no training data, still it is possible to do anomaly detection using unsupervised learning and semi-supervised learning. However, after building the model, analyzing it's performance is complex as nothing is available to test it against. Hence, the results obtained need to be tested in the field before placing them in the critical path.

Figure 4. Flowchart of the Proposed Anomaly Detection Model

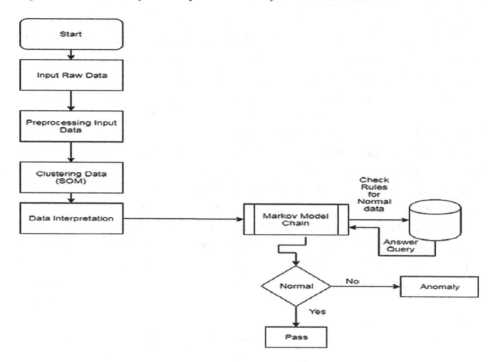

Since there are no labels in unsupervised learning, it's close to difficult to get a sensibly target proportion of how exact your calculation is. In grouping for instance, how we might know that whether K-Means found the correct group? The number of clusters is commonly not known from earlier, yet there are a couple of "execution" or "assessment measurements one can use to derive an ideal group against the estimation of K. The greatest "drawback" in k-means is that we expect that our clusters come in circular or globular shapes; that is infrequently the situation with "genuine world" information. Interestingly, choosing the "ideal" k is simply one more hyper parameter advancement methodology. One of the most momentous properties of IoT information/data, however, lives in its roughness: on the grounds that IoT gadgets are gathering information through different complex sensors, the information they create is normally crude. This implies real information handling is fundamental before business worth can be extricated and incredible AI applications can be manufactured. Truth be told, isolating the important or meaningful signal from the clamor and changing these unstructured information streams into organized information is the most vital, yet unsafe, advance when building a brilliant IoT application. Another test originates from the way that IoT gadgets may not constantly be associated with the cloud and hence may require some neighborhood reference

106

information for disconnected preparing, just as the ability to work in independent. This is the place an edge-computing design winds up intriguing, as it empowers information to be at first handled at the degree of the edge gadgets. This methodology is especially alluring when upgraded security is wanted; it is likewise invaluable on the grounds that such edge gadgets are fit for separating information, lessening clamor and improving information quality on the spot. Researchers have also been working on algorithms that might give a more objective measure of performance in unsupervised learning.

FUNDING AGENCY

This research received no specific grant from any funding agency in the public, commercial, or not-for-profit sectors.

REFERENCES

Ahmad, S., Lavin, A., Purdy, S., & Agha, Z. (2017). Unsupervised real-time anomaly detection for streaming data. *Neurocomputing, 262,* 134–147. doi:10.1016/j. neucom.2017.04.070

Amer, M., & Goldstein, M. (2012, August). Nearest-neighbor and clustering based anomaly detection algorithms for rapidminer. In *Proc. of the 3rd RapidMiner Community Meeting and Conference (RCOMM 2012)* (pp. 1-12). Academic Press.

Amer, M., Goldstein, M., & Abdennadher, S. (2013, August). Enhancing one-class support vector machines for unsupervised anomaly detection. In *Proceedings of the ACM SIGKDD Workshop on Outlier Detection and Description* (pp. 8-15). ACM.

Andrea, I., Chrysostomou, C., & Hadjichristofi, G. (2015, July). Internet of Things: Security vulnerabilities and challenges. In *2015 IEEE Symposium on Computers and Communication (ISCC)* (pp. 180-187). IEEE.

Angiulli, F., & Fassetti, F. (2007, November). Detecting distance-based outliers in streams of data. In *Proceedings of the sixteenth ACM conference on Conference on information and knowledge management* (pp. 811-820). ACM. 10.1145/1321440.1321552

Antonakakis, M., April, T., Bailey, M., & Bernhard, M. ElieBursztein, Jaime Cochran, ZakirDurumeric (2017). Understanding the mirai botnet. *26th USENIX Security Symposium (USENIX Security 17),* 1093-1110.

Armentano, R., Bhadoria, R. S., Chatterjee, P., & Deka, G. C. (2018, October). The Internet of things: foundation for smart cities, eHealth and ubiquitous computing. Boca Raton, FL: CRC Press. ISBN 9781498789028

Atzori, L., Iera, A., & Morabito, G. (2010). The internet of things: A survey. *Computer Networks*, *54*(15), 2787–2805. doi:10.1016/j.comnet.2010.05.010

Bonomi, F., Milito, R., Zhu, J., & Addepalli, S. (2012, August). Fog computing and its role in the internet of things. In *Proceedings of the first edition of the MCC workshop on Mobile cloud computing* (pp. 13-16). ACM.

Canedo, J., & Skjellum, A. (2016, December). Using machine learning to secure IoT systems. In *2016 14th Annual Conference on Privacy, Security and Trust (PST)* (pp. 219-222). IEEE.

Cecchinel, C., Jimenez, M., Mosser, S., & Riveill, M. (2014, June). An architecture to support the collection of big data in the internet of things. In *2014 IEEE World Congress on Services* (pp. 442-449). IEEE. 10.1109/SERVICES.2014.83

Ding, Z., & Fei, M. (2013). An anomaly detection approach based on isolation forest algorithm for streaming data using sliding window. *IFAC Proceedings Volumes*, *46*(20), 12-17.

Ditzler, G., & Polikar, R. (2012). Incremental learning of concept drift from streaming imbalanced data. *IEEE Transactions on Knowledge and Data Engineering*, *25*(10), 2283–2301. doi:10.1109/TKDE.2012.136

El Mouaatamid, O., Lahmer, M., & Belkasmi, M. (2016). Internet of Things Security: Layered classification of attacks and possible Countermeasures. *Electronic Journal of Information Technology*, (9).

Erfani, S. M., Rajasegarar, S., Karunasekera, S., & Leckie, C. (2016). High-dimensional and large-scale anomaly detection using a linear one-class SVM with deep learning. *Pattern Recognition*, *58*, 121–134. doi:10.1016/j.patcog.2016.03.028

Han, G., Xiao, L., & Poor, H. V. (2017, March). Two-dimensional anti-jamming communication based on deep reinforcement learning. In *2017 IEEE International Conference on Acoustics, Speech and Signal Processing (ICASSP)* (pp. 2087-2091). IEEE.

Haque, A., DeLucia, A., & Baseman, E. (2017, November). Markov chain modeling for anomaly detection in high performance computing system logs. In *Proceedings of the Fourth International Workshop on HPC User Support Tools* (p. 3). ACM.

Heller, K., Svore, K., Keromytis, A. D., & Stolfo, S. (2003). *One class support vector machines for detecting anomalous windows registry accesses*. Academic Press.

Joglekar, S. (2015). *Self-Organizing Maps with Google's Tensor Flow*. Retrieved from https://codesachin.wordpress.com/2015/11/28/self-organizing-maps-with-googles-tensorflow/

Kohonen, T. (1982). Self-organized formation of topologically correct feature maps. *Biological Cybernetics*, *43*(1), 59–69. doi:10.1007/BF00337288

Kohonen, T. (1990). The self-organizing map. *Proceedings of the IEEE*, *78*(9), 1464–1480. doi:10.1109/5.58325

Kriegel, H. P., Kröger, P., Sander, J., & Zimek, A. (2011). Density-based clustering. *Wiley Interdisciplinary Reviews. Data Mining and Knowledge Discovery*, *1*(3), 231–240. doi:10.1002/widm.30

Li, K. L., Huang, H. K., Tian, S. F., & Xu, W. (2003, November). Improving one-class SVM for anomaly detection. In Proceedings of the 2003 International Conference on Machine Learning and Cybernetics (IEEE Cat. No. 03EX693) (Vol. 5, pp. 3077-3081). IEEE.

Liu, F. T., Ting, K. M., & Zhou, Z. H. (2012). Isolation-based anomaly detection. *ACM Transactions on Knowledge Discovery from Data*, *6*(1), 3. doi:10.1145/2133360.2133363

Mahmoud, R., Yousuf, T., Aloul, F., & Zualkernan, I. (2015, December). Internet of things (IoT) security: Current status, challenges and prospective measures. In *2015 10th International Conference for Internet Technology and Secured Transactions (ICITST)* (pp. 336-341). IEEE.

Mulay, S. A., Devale, P. R., & Garje, G. V. (2010). Intrusion detection system using support vector machine and decision tree. *International Journal of Computers and Applications*, *3*(3), 40–43. doi:10.5120/758-993

Muniyandi, A. P., Rajeswari, R., & Rajaram, R. (2012). Network anomaly detection by cascading k-Means clustering and C4. 5 decision tree algorithm. *Procedia Engineering*, *30*, 174–182. doi:10.1016/j.proeng.2012.01.849

Murphy, K. P. (2012). *Machine learning: a probabilistic perspective*. MIT Press.

Perdisci, R., Gu, G., & Lee, W. (2006, December). Using an Ensemble of One-Class SVM Classifiers to Harden Payload-based Anomaly Detection Systems. In ICDM (Vol. 6, pp. 488-498). doi:10.1109/ICDM.2006.165

Perera, S. (2015). *Introduction to Anomaly Detection: Concepts and Techniques.* Retrieved from https://iwringer.wordpress.com/2015/11/17/anomaly-detection-concepts-and-techniques/

Radovanović, M., Nanopoulos, A., & Ivanović, M. (2014). Reverse nearest neighbors in unsupervised distance-based outlier detection. *IEEE Transactions on Knowledge and Data Engineering, 27*(5), 1369–1382. doi:10.1109/TKDE.2014.2365790

Raza, S., Wallgren, L., & Voigt, T. (2013). SVELTE: Real-time intrusion detection in the Internet of Things. *Ad Hoc Networks, 11*(8), 2661–2674. doi:10.1016/j.adhoc.2013.04.014

Sharma, M., & Siddiqui, A. (2010, April). RFID based mobiles: Next generation applications. In *2010 2nd IEEE International Conference on Information Management and Engineering* (pp. 523-526). IEEE.

Simon, S. O. (2009). *Haykin Neural Networks and Learning Machines.* Academic Press.

Sindhu, S. S. S., Geetha, S., & Kannan, A. (2012). Decision tree based light weight intrusion detection using a wrapper approach. *Expert Systems with Applications, 39*(1), 129–141. doi:10.1016/j.eswa.2011.06.013

Sugiyama, M., & Borgwardt, K. (2013). Rapid distance-based outlier detection via sampling. In Advances in Neural Information Processing Systems (pp. 467-475). Academic Press.

Tan, L., & Wang, N. (2010, August). Future internet: The internet of things. In *2010 3rd international conference on advanced computer theory and engineering (ICACTE)* (Vol. 5, pp. V5-376). IEEE.

Tan, Z., Jamdagni, A., He, X., Nanda, P., & Liu, R. P. (2013). A system for denial-of-service attack detection based on multivariate correlation analysis. *IEEE Transactions on Parallel and Distributed Systems, 25*(2), 447–456.

Wang, H., Fan, W., Yu, P. S., & Han, J. (2003, August). Mining concept-drifting data streams using ensemble classifiers. In *Proceedings of the ninth ACM SIGKDD international conference on Knowledge discovery and data mining* (pp. 226-235). ACM. 10.1145/956750.956778

Wang, Y., Wong, J., & Miner, A. (2004, June). Anomaly intrusion detection using one class SVM. In *Proceedings from the Fifth Annual IEEE SMC Information Assurance Workshop*, 2004. (pp. 358-364). IEEE. 10.1109/IAW.2004.1437839

Wu, M., Lu, T. J., Ling, F. Y., Sun, J., & Du, H. Y. (2010, August). Research on the architecture of Internet of Things. In *2010 3rd International Conference on Advanced Computer Theory and Engineering (ICACTE)* (Vol. 5, pp. V5-484). IEEE.

Xiao, L., Li, Y., Han, G., Liu, G., & Zhuang, W. (2016). PHY-layer spoofing detection with reinforcement learning in wireless networks. *IEEE Transactions on Vehicular Technology, 65*(12), 10037–10047. doi:10.1109/TVT.2016.2524258

Xiao, L., Wan, X., Lu, X., Zhang, Y., & Wu, D. (2018). *IoT security techniques based on machine learning.* arXiv preprint arXiv:1801.06275

Xiao, L., Yan, Q., Lou, W., Chen, G., & Hou, Y. T. (2013). Proximity-based security techniques for mobile users in wireless networks. *IEEE Transactions on Information Forensics and Security, 8*(12), 2089–2100. doi:10.1109/TIFS.2013.2286269

Yang, S. (2017). IoT stream processing and analytics in the fog. *IEEE Communications Magazine, 55*(8), 21–27. doi:10.1109/MCOM.2017.1600840

Yasumoto, K., Yamaguchi, H., & Shigeno, H. (2016). Survey of real-time processing technologies of iot data streams. *Journal of Information Processing, 24*(2), 195–202. doi:10.2197/ipsjjip.24.195

Zarpelao, B. B., Miani, R. S., Kawakani, C. T., & de Alvarenga, S. C. (2017). A survey of intrusion detection in Internet of Things. *Journal of Network and Computer Applications, 84*, 25–37. doi:10.1016/j.jnca.2017.02.009

Zhang, Y., Ge, Z., Greenberg, A., & Roughan, M. (2005, October). Network anomography. In *Proceedings of the 5th ACM SIGCOMM conference on Internet Measurement* (pp. 30-30). USENIX Association.

Zhou, J., Fu, Y., Wu, Y., Xia, H., Fang, Y., & Lu, H. (2009). Anomaly detection over concept drifting data streams. *Journal of Computer Information Systems, 5*(6).

Ziegler, J., & Urbas, L. (2011, September). Advanced interaction metaphors for RFID-tagged physical artefacts. In *2011 IEEE International Conference on RFID-Technologies and Applications* (pp. 73-80). IEEE. 10.1109/RFID-TA.2011.6068619

KEY TERMS AND DEFINITIONS

AI/Machine Learning: AI is the logical investigation of algorithms and factual models that computer frameworks use to play out a particular role successfully without utilizing explicit instructions, depending on examples and inference rules. It is viewed as a subset of fabricated brainpower.

Anomaly Detection: Anomaly detection (additionally known as outlier discovery) is the identification of uncommon things, occasions, or perceptions, which raise doubts by varying fundamentally from most of the data.

Botnet: A botnet is a group of nodes associated in a planned manner for vindictive purposes. Every node in a botnet is known as a bot. These bots structure a system of trading off nodes, which is constrained by an outsider and used to transmit malware or spam or to dispatch attacks.

Data Pre-Processing: Data Pre-processing is a strategy that is utilized to change over the raw information into a clean data collection. At whatever point the information is assembled from various sources it is gathered in a crude configuration which feasible for the analysis. Hence, data pre-processing is necessary.

Denial of Service Attacks: A denial-of-service (DoS) attack is an attack intended to close down a machine or system, making it out of reach to its destination. DoS assaults achieve this by flooding the target with traffic or sending it data that prompts an accident.

Inliers: Inliers are characterized as a perception that is clarified by fundamental probability density function.

Markov Chain Model: A Markov chain is a numerical framework that encounters advances starting with one state then onto the next as indicated by certain probabilistic principles.

ENDNOTE

[1]   Future IoT Architectures: A Cypress-Based Hands-On Graduate Class, Matthew Salmanpour.

Chapter 5
Collision Avoidance Methodology in Internet of Things and Wireless Ad hoc Network

Arundhati Arjaria

ⓘD https://orcid.org/0000-0001-5107-1544
Rajiv Gandhi Proudyogiki Vishwavidyalaya, India

Priyanka Dixit
Rajiv Gandhi Proudyogiki Vishwavidyalaya, India

ABSTRACT

In today's digital era, internet of things and wireless communication needs no introduction as almost everything directly or indirectly is dependent on the same. This scenario also leads to various security issues because devices are connected to internet and this availability makes this exposure vulnerable for various attacks. Recently in internet of things and wireless ad hoc networks, there is an essential issue of how to increase channel utilization without degrading the performance. Some problems are also responsible to increase collision in the network. Here, the authors propose a busy tone-based medium access control scheme to avoid such problems in fully as well as non-fully connected environment. Here in this chapter, they present a brief introduction to internet of things, security challenges regarding IoT, and its association with wireless technology. They also discuss the problems concerning wireless communication, which affects the performance of networks and their solutions.

DOI: 10.4018/978-1-7998-2444-2.ch005

I. INTRODUCTION

In today's scenario, Internet of Things can be seen as a global infrastructure for the information society, which is capacitating enhanced applicability by interconnecting (real and virtual) things depends on pre deployed and advanced interoperable information and communication technologies (ICT).

Here, things are objects of the physical/real sphere or of the information sphere (virtual world) which have the capability of being identified and incorporate into intercommunication systems. Things have affiliated information or data, which can be static and dynamic.

Physical things present in the real world and are capable of being sensed, instigated and associated. For example surrounding environment, industrial robots, goods and electrical equipment. Virtual things present in the information world and are capable of being stored, processed and accessed. Examples of virtual things are multimedia content and application software.

Figure 1.
Source: Recommendation

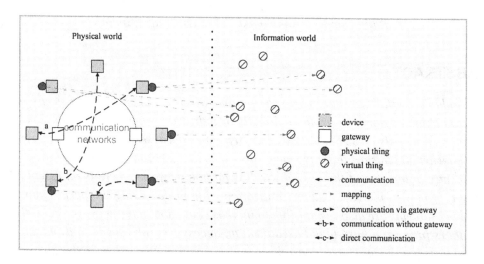

ITU-T Y.2060

Internet of Thing is a new era development. In order to accomplish the goal of pervasive computing system, various technical methodologies work effectively in Internet of Things. Some of them are Wireless communication, wireless sensor networks etc. Among other technologies, these are playing an important part in completing the Internet of Things topic.

With the rapid development in IoT applications, several security issues have raised drastically. As devices and things are becoming integral part of Internet infrastructure, therefore these issues need to be deal with. When most of the things will be associated with Internet, these issues will become more obtrusive; with extended Internet global disclosure will literally disclose more security breaches. Such security flaws will be subsequently exploited by hackers, and later can be misused in uncontrolled environments with billions of IoT devices [Vaidya 2002]. In addition, the IoT will also increase the potential attack surfaces for hackers and other cyber criminals. A study conducted by Hewlett Packard [Weniger 2003] revealed that 70% of the most commonly used IoT devices contain serious vulnerabilities. IoT devices are vulnerable to security threats due to their design by lacking certain security features such as insecure communication medium, insufficient authentication and authorization configurations. As a matter of fact, when IoT become everywhere, everyone whether individuals or companies will be concerned. Additionally, cross linking of objects presents new potentials to influence and to exchange. This leads to a variety of new potential risks concerning information security and data protection, which should be considered. Further, lack of security will create resistance to adoption of the IoT by companies and individuals. Security issues and challenges can be addressed by providing proper training to the designers and developers to integrate security solutions into IoT products and thus, encouraging the users to utilize IoT security features that are built into the devices [Weniger 2003]. Our motivation to conduct this study is that most of the previous studies had focused on academic solutions only and had ignored other type of solutions from technical and industrial sides. However, these three sectors should work cooperatively and synchronously in order to reach integrated solutions as well as all the considerations from the three aspects should be taken into an account. Therefore, this paper provides a review on the main issues of IoT in terms of security as well as addresses some considerations that must be taken into account before and during the design stages to fill the gap of the literature regarding this issue by providing some solutions from three aspects including technical, academic, and industrial solutions. The main contribution of this paper is to provide the necessary insights on how certain utilization of such technologies can be facilitated by certain mechanisms and algorithms. This is believed to guide future studies to the use of certain solutions for certain problem based on the suggested algorithms and mechanisms by academic researchers with attention to technical and industrial solutions too.

Here is the introduction of wireless communication.

Wireless communications have become more and more common place over the past decade, working their way not only into business, military and disaster applications, but also everyday life. With this wide acceptance comes the desire to push this technology to perform new applications, one of these being a mobile ad-hoc network.

Collision avoidance in contention-based medium access control (MAC) protocols for wireless ad hoc networks is very important, as simple MAC protocols such as carrier sense multiple access (CSMA) cannot avoid the "hidden terminal and exposed terminal" problem completely and performance can degrade to that of the ALOHA protocol in ad hoc networks [Kumar 2006].

Many collision-avoidance protocols [Bharghavan 1994, Mirhahhak 2011] have been proposed and the most popular collision avoidance scheme today consists of a sender-initiated four-way handshake in which the transmission of a data packet and its acknowledgment is preceded by request-to-send (RTS) and clear-to-send (CTS) packets between a pair of sending and receiving stations.1 Other stations that overhear RTS or CTS packets will defer their access to the channel to avoid collisions. For the sake of simplicity, it can be also called RTS/CTS-based scheme. Among all these proposed collision-avoidance protocols, the IEEE 802.11 distributed foundation wireless medium access control (DFWMAC) protocol [Mirhahhak 2011] is very popular in the performance studies of routing protocols for ad hoc networks, even though it was originally intended for wireless LANs with no or very few hidden terminals. Though there has been considerable work on the performance evaluation of IEEE 802.11 and similar protocols [Bianchi 2000, Luo 2004, Abusalah 2008, Shushan 2011], most of the analytical models are largely confined to single- hop networks [Bianchi 2000, Cali, Xiao 2000] or cases when the number of hidden terminals is very small [Murthy 2004, Luo 2004]. We deem it very important to investigate the performance of the four way sender-initiated collision avoidance scheme with a truly multi-hop network model as potential interference from hidden stations always exists, which is a salient characteristic of multi-hop ad hoc networks.

Among the existing MAC protocols [Bianchi 2000], only the Dual Busy Tone Multiple Access (DBTMA) protocol [Bianchi 1996] is able to solve the problems for both hidden terminals and the exposed terminals using two out-of-band busy tones to indicate the on-going transmissions, in which one busy tone indicates the transmitting busy and the other indicates the receiving busy. However, the analytical and simulation results shown in [Bianchi 1996] are evaluated under that condition that the interference range of each mobile host is assumed to be the same as the transmission range. It should be noticed that the promising performances obtained under such ideal situation may not match the ad hoc network environment. In fact, more and more researchers have realized the problem of large interference range in the ad hoc networking environment [Bharghavan 1994][Cali][Xiao 2000]. The large interference is defined as that the range of interfering is larger than the transmission range, which is caused by large transmitter-receiver distance in an ad hoc network.

In this case, none of these proposed MAC protocols [Bianchi 2000] works as well as what is expected in theory.

II. RELATED STUDY

Many schemes have been proposed in the current literature to reduce severe collisions of DATA packets at the MAC layer. MACA [1] in which Request-To-Send (RTS) and Clear-To-Send (CTS) packets mechanism for the collision avoidance is used. A ready station or sender transmits an RTS packet to request the channel to the receiver. The Receiver replies to the sender by sending a CTS packet. MACA reduces the data packet collision which causes by hidden terminals by using RTS/CTS packets and MACAW [Bharghavan 1994] proposes the use of RTS and CTS packets for the collision avoidance on the shared channel. MACAW also uses DS packet to advertise the use of the shared channel in which RTS-CTS-DS-DATA-ACK message exchange for a data packet transmission is used. The Data sending (DS) packet was used in this protocol to notify all stations in the transmitter range that it is using the channel. The ACK packet was used for the acknowledgment.

However, both of them solve neither the hidden nor the exposed-terminal problems. The FAMANCS scheme [Bianchi 2000] uses long dominating CTS packets which act as a receive busy tone to prevent any competing transmitters in the receiver's range from transmitting. This requires each station hearing the interference to keep quiet for a period of one maximum data packet to guarantee no collision with the ongoing data transmission, which is not efficient especially when the RTS/CTS negotiation process fails or the DATA packet is very short.

Multi-channel random MAC schemes have also been investigated in the past few years [Bianchi 1996]–[Govindaswamy 2011]. One common approach to avoid collisions between control packets and data packets is to use separate channels for different kinds of packets. The DCA scheme [Angin 2008] uses two channels; one control channel for RTS/CTS and one or more data channels for DATA/ACK; however, it does not mitigate the hidden terminal problem.

Some busy tone based approaches are also used to resolve the hidden and exposed terminal problems. Busy Tone multiple access (BTMA) scheme is used where there is a base station which broadcast a busy tone signal to let the potential hidden terminals that channel is busy by sensing the channel.

Dual busy Tone Multiple Access (DBTMA) is an extension of BTMA in which a distributed approach is used of sending the busy tones. In this method two out-of-band busy tones are used, transmit busy tone (BTt) and receive busy tone (BTr), to protect the RTS packets and data packets respectively. This scheme can solve the hidden terminal problem but can not receive the exposed terminal problem. The dual busy tone multiple access (DBTMA) schemes ([Kumar 2008], [Masoumeh 2009]) use a transmit busy tone to prevent the exposed terminals from becoming new receiver, a receive busy tone to prevent the hidden terminals from becoming new transmitter, and a separate data channel to avoid collisions between control packets and data packets. However, the DBTMA schemes have no acknowledgements for DATA packets which is needed for unreliable wireless links, and the potential collisions between the acknowledgements and other packets can greatly degrade the performance. PAMAS [Weniger 2004] uses a separate control channel to transmit both RTS/CTS packets and busy tone signals. It gives a solution to the hidden terminal problem and mainly focuses on power savings.

III. SYSTEM MODEL

Consider a scenario of ad hoc wireless network where data and voice traffic are transmitted. A communication channel is by which all the stations send there frames in the network. Any overlap of transmissions at a receiver can cause a collision, and due to this none of the overlapped frames can be correctly received. The successful simultaneous transmissions are possible due to spatial reuse. In this paper, one hop transmissions are taken into consideration.

Here, we had taken the IEEE 802.11 MAC protocol to describe the problems in this research. These problems not only associated with the IEEE 802,11 MAC but many MAC schemes which uses backoff mechanism also suffers from these same problems. Along with all this we had also taken multiple data rate support of the wireless ad hoc network into consideration. Multiple Data Rates depend upon the bit error ratio of the communication channel.

A. Problem Statement

This section, describes the problems in multi-hop ad-hoc networks when the IEEE 802.11 MAC protocol is deployed. The hidden and exposed station problems are two well known problems. Here, in this section the hidden and exposed Station problems are defined appropriately

1) Hidden Station Problem

The hidden and exposed Station problems are two well known problems. For example, in Fig. 1, it indicates that the station A is in the transmission range on station B and station C in also in the station B's transmission range. A hidden station problem occurs in this case so it must be important that the transmission range and sensing range should be different.

2) Exposed Station Problem

The exposed station problem occurs when a transmitter is in the transmission range of an ongoing transmission and wants to sends data packer to the intended receiver which is not in the transmission range on that ongoing transmission, so the intended transmitter has to wait unnecessarily for that ongoing transmission to be completed, as shown in Fig. 2,where station C is in the transmission range of station B which is the transmitter and station D is in the transmission range of station C, so in this case, station C has to wait until station B completes its transmission, in this station B and station C are exposed to each other.

B. RTS/CTS Mechanism

The basic RTS/CTS scheme operates as follows. When a sender A has data to send, it first sends RTS frame to the intended receiver station B. Upon receiving the RTS frame, station B replies a CTS frame back to station A. If station A successfully receives the CTS frame, it starts sending data frame; or it backs off for an increasing period of time and tries again.

C. Problem With the RTS/CTS Scheme

MACA/PR [*Gunes* 2002] presented a scenario in which the RTS/CTS scheme fails to solve the hidden terminal problem. The fundamental reason for the failure is that the RTS/CTS scheme relies on the successful and timely delivery of the RTS/CTS frames. With the significant dynamicity in network topology and traffic condition in ad hoc networks, collisions involving the RTS/CTS frames are frequent, which increase the chance of the hidden terminal problem.

In summary, all MAC protocols mentioned above, except DBTMA, depend directly on the RTS/CTS frames to relieve the hidden terminal problem and may fail in case of the collision of the CTS frames. DBTMA, however, effectively prevents such problem by utilizing busy tones, which are long-lasting and collision-free signal for reserving channel capacity, as compared to the short and collision-prone RTS/CTS frames.

D. The Desired Protocol Behavior

The desired MAC protocol for wireless ad hoc networks should at least resolve the hidden terminal problem, the exposed terminal problem. Therefore, in the ideal protocol it should be guaranteed that there is only one receiver in the interference range of the transmitter and there is also only one transmitter in the interference range of the receiver. The exposed stations may start to transmit in spite of the ongoing transmission. The hidden stations cannot initiate any transmission but may receive packets. Thus, to maximize the spatial reuse or network capacity, it should allow multiple transmitters to transmit in the sensing range of any transmitter and multiple receivers in the sensing range of any receiver to receive. In addition, the transmitter should know whether its intended receiver is blocked or is just outside of its transmission range in case that it does not receive the returned CTS to avoid packet discarding and the wrong protocol behavior at the higher layer, such as unnecessary rerouting requests.

IV. PROPOSED PROTOCOL

In our scheme, a single channel is split into two sub-channels: a data channel for data frames and a control channel for control frames. Two busy tones transmit busy tone (BTt) and receive busy tone (BTr), are assigned two separate single frequencies in the control channel. Here Busy Tone Receiver (BTr) associated with the transmitter and Busy Tone Transmitter (BTt) associated with the receiver. A station that is transmitting/receiving data turns on BTt/BTr, which can be heard by all stations within its transmission range. The difference of our scheme from DBTMA is that, by adjusting the receiver's sensitivity, we set the channels' carrier sense ranges such that the BTt channel's carrier sense range covers the two-hop neighborhood of the sensing station, while the BTr channel's carrier sense range covers the one-hop neighborhood of the sensing station. In this protocol we have considered multiple data rate environment to solve all these problems. Basically IEEE 802.11 standard supports four kinds of data rates that are 1, 2, 5.5 and 11 Mbps. It depends on the Bit Error Rate of the communication channel that which data rate is supported by the network. If the Bit error rate is higher than lower data rate is supported (1 Mbps and 2 Mbps) and if the bit error rate is lower than higher data rate is supported (5.5 Mbps and 11 Mbps). We calculated the Bit Error Rate of the channels and addressed these entire problems on the various data rates.

V. OPERATION PROCEDURE

The protocol operates as follows:

When a sender has to transmit data, it first senses the channel for BTr to make sure that the intended receiver is not currently receiving data from another "hidden" station. If intending receiver is not receiving from another source, the sender transmits a RTS frame to the intended receiver. Upon receiving this RTS frame, the receiver senses for BTt to make sure that the data it is expected to receive will not collide with another ongoing data transmission nearby. If BTt is not present, it replies with a CTS frame and turns on BTr until data is completely received. Upon receiving the CTS frame from the intended receiver, the sender begins data transmission and turns on BTt until data transmission is completed. We have used four kinds of data rates to resolve the hidden and exposed terminal problem that is 1 Mbps, 2 Mbps, 5.5 Mbps and 11 Mbps. and after simulating the network in various data rate environment it has shown that our scheme is working in all kinds of data rate environment.

VI. PERFORMANCE EVALUATION

A. Simulation Environment

The simulations are done in NCTUns 5.0 simulator. The NCTUns network simulator and emulator (NCTUns) is a high-fidelity and extensible network simulator capable of simulating various devices and protocols used in both wired and wireless networks. It uses a distributed architecture to support remote simulations and concurrent simulations.

Table 1. Simulation Parameters

Parameters	Value
Data Transmission Range	200 m
RTS Threshold Value	250 Bytes
Data Packet Size	1200 Bytes
Data Interference Range	200 m
Channel Rate	2Mbps
Duration	100 ms
Basic Rate (RTS/CTS) Transmission	2 Mbps

B. Results and Discussion

We evaluated the performance of the network on various topologies. We evaluate the performance of the network under various topologies. The system performance is evaluated under some specific topologies firstly as shown in Figure 2. Figure 2 shows the network topology in which here are total 5 stations, here station 2 is the receiver station and rest of the stations are transmitter stations.

Figure 2. Network Topology with 5 mobile stations

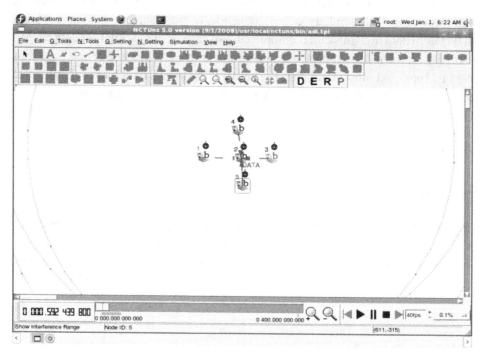

Figure 3 describes the hidden terminal problem, in which there are total 6 stations, station 1 and station 3 are the transmitter stations and station 2 is the receiver station. According to hidden station problem, station 1 and station 3 both are the transmitter stations and try to send data frame to station 2 at the same time simultaneously because both are hidden to each other and this causes collision to station 2.

In our proposed scheme, when station 1 tries to send data frame to station to, for that period of time station 3 postpones its transmission until node 1 finishes its transmission as shown in Figure 4.

Figure 3. Network Topology with 6 mobile stations

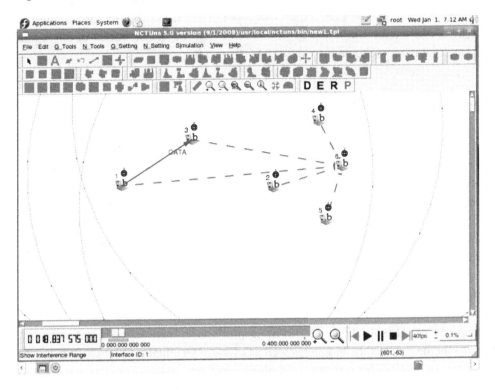

Figure 4. Aggregate throughput of the network

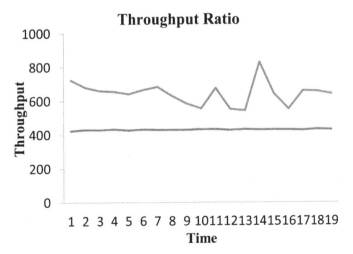

Figure 4 shows the aggregate throughput ratio of our proposed scheme for hidden terminals. We have calculated the throughput of the network after simulating the network and we fond in our proposed scheme that the measurement of aggregate throughput in our scheme provides the better results.

VII. CONCLUSION

In this chapter, we have briefly described the introduction to wireless networks and internet of Things and also identified the problems that are the main cause of performance degradation of the wireless networks, and Internet of Things namely, different cyber attacks that are the main reasons behind various security breaches, the hidden terminal problem, the exposed terminal problem and also discussed the solutions for same. The mechanism increases the probability of successful data transmission and consequently improves the network throughput. These problems are the main cause of collision occurrence in wireless ad hoc networks with Internet of Things. To alleviate these problems, we proposed a new protocol which uses two channels: one for control packets and the other for DATA packets; a busy tone channel is used to solve the hidden terminal problem and exposed terminal problems. Our scheme reduces the hidden as well as exposed terminal problem and increases the throughput of the network in multiple data rate environment as compare to IEEE 802.11e MAC scheme. This results to avoid the collision of the network and improves the performance of the network. Simulation results prove that our protocol increases spatial reuse and decreases collision probability.

REFERENCES

Abomhara, M., & Køien, G. M. (2014). Security and privacy in the Internet of Things: current status and open issues. In *International Conference on Privacy and Security in Mobile Systems (PRISMS)*. IEEE. 10.1109/PRISMS.2014.6970594

Abusalah, L., Khokhar, A., & Guizani, M. (2008). "A survey of secure mobile ad hoc routing protocols," IEEE Commun. *Surveys & Tutorials, IEEE, 10*(4), 78–93. doi:10.1109/SURV.2008.080407

Angin, O., Campbell, A., Kounavis, M., & Liao, R. (1998, August). The Mobiware Tollkit: Programmable Support for Adaptive Mobile Computing. *IEEE Personal Communications Magazine, Special Issue on Adapting to Network and Client Variability, 5*(4), 32–44. doi:10.1109/98.709367

Arjaria. (2013). A Scalable MAC Scheme Supporting Multimedia Applications in Wireless Ad-hoc Networks. *International Journal of Modern Engineering Management Research.*

Arjaria & Khan. (2011). Busy Tone Based IG-MAC Protocol Using Multiple Data Rates In Ad-Hoc Networks. *Proceedings of International Journal of Advance in Communication Engineering, 3.*

Bensaou, B., Wang, Y., & Ko, C. C. Fair Medium Access in 802.11 Based Wireless Ad-Hoc Networks. *First Annual IEEE & ACM International Workshop on Mobile Ad Hoc Networking and Computing.*

Bharghavan, V., Demers, A., Shenker, S., & Zhang, L. (1994). MACAW: A Media Access Protocol for Wireless LANs. *Proc. of ACM SIGCOMM '94.* 10.1145/190314.190334

Bharghavan, V., Demers, A., Shenker, S., & Zhang, L. (1994). MACAW: A media access protocol for wireless LAN's. *Proc. ACM SIGCOMM.* 10.1145/190314.190334

Bharghavan, V., Lee, K., Lu, S., Ha, S., Li, J. R., & Dwyer, D. (1998). Timely Adaptive Resource Management Architecture. *IEEE Personal Communication Magazine, 5*(8), 20-31.

Bianchi, G. (2000, March). Performance Analysis of the IEEE 802.11 Distributed Coordination Function. *IEEE Journal on Selected Areas in Communications, 18*(3), 535–547. doi:10.1109/49.840210

Bianchi, G., Fratta, L., & Oliveri, M. (1996). Performance Evaluation and Enhancement of the CSMA/CA MAC Protocol for 802.11 Wireless LANs. *Proc. of PIMRC '96,* 392–396. 10.1109/PIMRC.1996.567423

Cali, Conti, & Gregori. (n.d.). *Dynamic Tuning of the IEEE 802.11 Protocol to Achieve a Theoretical Throughput Limit.* Academic Press.

Cali, F., Conti, M., & Gregori, E. (2000, December). Dynamic tuning of the IEEE 802.11 protocol to achieve a theoretical throughput limit. *IEEE/ACM Transactions on Networking, 8*(6), 785–799. doi:10.1109/90.893874

Cali, F., Conti, M., & Gregori, E. (2000, September). IEEE 802.11 Protocol: Design and Performance Evaluation of an Adaptive Backoff Mechanism. *IEEE Journal on Selected Areas in Communications, 18*(9), 1774–1786. doi:10.1109/49.872963

Choi, N., Seok, Y., & Choi, Y. (2003). Multi-channel MAC Protocol for Mobile Ad Hoc Networks. *Proc. IEEE VTC 2003.*

Fullmer, C. L., & Garcia-Luna-Aceves, J. J. (1997). Solutions to Hidden Terminal Problems in Wireless Networks. *Proc. ACM SIGCOMM '97*. 10.1145/263105.263137

Gen, H. P.-C. S. A. (2015). *Controllers, R. Hewlett-Packard Enterprise Development LP.*

Govindaswamy, V., Blackstone, W. L., & Balasekaran, G. (2011). Survey of Recent Position Based Routing Mobile Ad-hoc Network Protocols. Proceedings of *2011 UKSim 13th International Conference on Modelling and Simulation*, 467-471. 10.1109/UKSIM.2011.95

Guimar, R., Morillo, J., Cerd, L., & Barcel, J. (2004). *Quality of service for mobile Ad-hoc Networks: An Overview*. Technical Report UPC-DAC-2004-24, Polytechnic University of Catalonia.

Gunes, M., & Reibel, R. (2002). An IP address configuration algorithm for Zeroconf mobile multihop ad hoc networks. *Proceedings of International Workshop on broadband wireless ad hoc networks and services.*

Karimi, M., & Pan, D. (2009). Challenges for Quality of Service (QoS) in Mobile Ad-Hoc Networks (MANETs). *Proceedings of IEEE 10th Annual Wireless and Microwave Technology Conference, WAMICON '09*, 1-5. 10.1109/WAMICON.2009.5207262

Kumar Sarkar, S., Basavaraju, T. G., & Puttamadappa, C. (2008). *Ad-hoc Mobile Wireless Networks Principles, Protocols, and Applications*. Auerbach Publications.

Lee, S. B., Gahng-Seop, A., Zhang, X., & Campbell, A. T. (2000, April). INSIGNIA: An IP-based Quality of Service Framework for Mobile Ad-hoc Networks. *Journal of Parallel and Distributed Computing, 60*(4), 374–406. doi:10.1006/jpdc.1999.1613

Li, Cai, & Xu. (2007). Spanning-tree based autoconfiguration for mobile ad hoc networks", Wireless Personal Communications. *Springer Science, 43*(4).

Li, L., Cai, Y., & Xu, X. (2009). *Cluster based autoconfiguration for mobile ad hoc networks. Wireless Personal Communications* , 49.

Luo, H., Lu, S., Bharghavan, V., Cheng, J., & Luo, H. (2004). A Packet Scheduling Approach to QoS Support in Multi-hop Wireless Networks. *Mobile Networks and Applications, 9*(3), 193–206. doi:10.1023/B:MONE.0000020643.70011.c7

Mirhahhak, M., Schult, N., & Thomson, D. (2000). Dynamic Quality-of-Service for Mobile Ad-hoc Networks. *Proceedings of the 1st ACM International Symposium on Mobile Ad-hoc Networking & Computing*, 137 - 138.

Mohsin, M., & Prakash, R. (2002). IP address assignment in a mobile ad hoc network. *Proceedings of the IEEE MILCOM 2002.* 10.1109/MILCOM.2002.1179586

Murthy, C. S. R., & Manoj, B. S. (2004). *Ad-hoc Wireless Networks Architectures and Protocols.* Prentice Hall.

Perkins, Malinen, Wakikawa, Belding-Royer, & Sun. (2001). *IP address autoconfiguration for ad hoc networks.* IETF draft.

Sun, Y., & Belding-Royer, E. M. (2003). *Dynamic address configuration in mobile ad hoc networks.* UCSB Technical Report 2003-11.

Swarnapriyaa, U. G., & Vinodhini, S. Anthoniraj, R., & Anand. (2011). Auto Configuration in Mobile Ad Hoc Networks. *Proceedings of the National Conference on Innovations in Emerging Technology,* 61-66.

Tayal, A. P., & Patnaik, L. M. (2004). An address assignment for the automatic configuration of mobile ad hoc networks. *Personal and Ubiquitous Computing, 8*(1), 47–54. doi:10.100700779-003-0256-5

Tobagi, F. A., & Kleinrock, L. (1978). The Effect of Acknowledgment Traffic on the Capacity of Packet-Switched Radio Channels. *IEEE Transactions on Communications, 26*(6), 815–826. doi:10.1109/TCOM.1978.1094159

Vaidya, N. H. (2002). Weak duplicate address detection in mobile ad hoc networks. *Proceedings of the ACM mobi-Hoc 2002,* 206–216. 10.1145/513800.513826

Vidhyasanker, Manoj, & Siva Ram Murthy. (2006). Slot Allocation Schemes for Delay Sensitive Traffic Support in Asynchronous Wireless Mesh Networks. *International Journal of Computer and Telecommunications Networking, 50*(15), 2595-2613.

Wang, Y., & Garcia-Luna-Aceves, J. J. (2002). Performance of Collision Avoidance Protocols in Single-Channel Ad Hoc Networks. *Proc. of IEEE ICNP 2002.* 10.1109/ICNP.2002.1181387

Weniger, K. (2005, March). PACMAN: Passive autoconfiguration for mobile ad hoc networks. *IEEE JSAC, Special Issue on Wireless Ad Hoc Networks, 23*(3), 507–509. doi:10.1109/JSAC.2004.842539

Weniger, K. (2003). Passive duplicate address detection in mobile ad hoc networks. *Proceedings of the IEEE WCNC 2003.* 10.1109/WCNC.2003.1200609

Weniger & Zitterbart. (2004). Address Autoconfiguration in Mobile Ad Hoc Networks: Current approaches and Future Directions. *IEEE Network,* 6-11.

Weniger & Zitterbart. (2004). *Address Autoconfiguration in Mobile Ad Hoc Networks: Current approaches and Future Directions*. IEEE Network.

Wu, L., & Varshney, P. (1999). Performance Analysis of CSMA and BTMA Protocols in Multihop Networks (I). Single Channel Case. Information Sciences. *Elsevier Sciences Inc.*, *120*, 159–177. doi:10.1016/S0020-0255(99)00047-X

Wu, S.-L., Lin, C.-Y., Tseng, Y.-C., & Sheu, J.-P. (2000). A New Multi-Channel MAC Protocol with On-Demand Channel Assignment for Mobile Ad Hoc Networks. *Int'l Symp. on Parallel Architectures, Algorithms and Networks (I-SPAN)*, 232-237.

Xiao, H., Seah, W. G., Lo, A., & Chua, K. C. (2000). A Flexible Quality of Service Model for Mobile Ad-hoc Networks (FQMM). *Proceedings of IEEE Vehicular Technology Conference (VTC 2000- Fall)*, 397-413.

Zhao, S., Aggarwal, A., Frost, R., & Bai, X. (2011). A Survey of Applications of Identity-Based Cryptography in Mobile Ad- Hoc Network. *IEEE Communications Surveys and Tutorials*.

Chapter 6

How to Authenticate MQTT Sessions Without Channel and Broker Security

Reto E. Koenig
*Department of Computer Science, Bern University of Applied Sciences,
Switzerland*

Lukas Laederach
Bern University of Applied Sciences, Switzerland

Cédric von Allmen
Bern University of Applied Sciences, Switzerland

ABSTRACT

This chapter describes a new but state-of-the-art approach to provide authenticity in MQTT sessions using the means of zero-knowledge proofs. This approach completely voids session hijacking for the MQTT protocol and provides authenticity. The presented approach does not require the broker to keep any secrets for session handling. The presented approach allows completely anonymous but authentic sessions; hence, the broker does not need any priory knowledge of the client party. As it is especially targeted for applications within the world of internet of things (IoT), the presented approach is designed to require only the minimum in extra power in terms of energy and space. The approach does not introduce any new concept, but simply combines a state of the art cryptographic Zero-Knowledge Proof of identity with the existing MQTT 5.0 specification. Thus, no protocol extension is required in order to provide the targeted security properties. The described approach is completely agnostic to the application layer at the client side and is only required during MQTT session establishment.

DOI: 10.4018/978-1-7998-2444-2.ch006

INTRODUCTION

MQTT is designed as a robust, session-oriented protocol especially suitable for the world of IoT, where the clientID plays the central role for session management. The MQTT specification requires the clientID to be provided within the first data frame of the protocol during session establishment. The semantics of the clientID is to provide the unique way a session can be (re)established between a client and the broker, without any further information. So the clientID is required to be unique per broker over time, hence, no collision of clientIDs should ever happen. As the clients are not aware of each other, but usually provide their own clientID, it must be drawn from large set of possible clientIDs so the probability of a collision of clientIDs is negligible. The protocol specification defines a minimum clientID space of order 63^{23}. Hence, allows the theoretical security parameter of 2^{λ} with an approximate $\lambda = 137$.

The specification of MQTT does not directly address the immanent possibility of active session hijacking. This attack vector allows an adversary to take over the session by simply (re-)establishing a connection using the clientID of the victim. Only indirectly, the MQTT specification tries to weaken that immanent attack vector by providing the possibility for channel security via Transport Layer Securit (TLS) or even worse, by securing a whole network via Virtual Private Network (VPN), and of course the heavy security requirement of the broker to be fully trusted in terms of secrecy of the clientID. However, the MQTT protocol specification gives room for customized authentication and even provides protocol intrinsic authentication solution via simple username password or via ACLs for ID-based session handling. These ID-based approaches, however, pose several disadvantages in the context of client management and security, as they require a separate and out-of-band on-staging-phase comprising the broker in order to manage clients by the identification scheme. Moreover, all these methods require the broker to keep secrets shared amongst different clients and the broker.

The presented approach provides a fully anonymous identification scheme based on the Schnorr Non-Interactive Zero-Knowledge Proof (Schnorr NIZKP) identification scheme (Hao 2017) without any of the drawbacks mentioned above. It makes use of well-known cryptographic properties and allows the security model of the broker to be lowered from "fully trusted" to "honest but curious... without any privacy constraints". Again, there is no new concept introduced, but well-known concepts are simply combined in order to provide the desired property.

The following sections will introduce the security and adversary model this approach is operating in. This way, a discussion about the targeted adversary and the trust and security assumptions is possible. Then the cryptographic and protocol prerequisites are provided in order to understand the implementation that follows.

The paper concludes by providing some quantitative and qualitative analysis of the approach.

SECURITY MODEL

The main security parameter is denoted by $\lambda \in N$. We write $a \leftarrow A(x)$ if a is assigned to the output of algorithm A with input x. An algorithm is efficient if it runs in probabilistic polynomial time (*ppt*) in the length of its input. For the remainder of this paper, all algorithms are ppt if not explicitly mentioned otherwise. If $\emph{S}$ is a set, we write $a \leftarrow_R \emph{S}$ to denote that a is chosen uniformly at random from $\emph{S}$. For a message $m = \left(m[1], m[2], \dots, m[l] \right)$, we call $m[i]$ a block, while $l \in N$ denotes the number of blocks in a message m. For a list we require that we have unique, injective, and efficiently reversible encoding, which maps the list to $0, 1$.

The security model that covers the approach consists of three actors, namely the channel, the broker and the client. There are no security assumptions required for the channel except of eventual availability. The channel is allowed to be modelled as an unreliable broadcast channel. The memory of the broker can be modelled as public readable memory, thus no secrecy is required on the broker side concerning the management of the clientIDs. The client is required to be able to keep a secret which might be either completely intrinsic to the client e.g. provided by a Physical Unclonable Function (PUF), or injected via application level.

The security properties of the actors define the adversary model. The adversary which is assumed to be restricted to be in ppt only is allowed to have full knowledge about the channel and the memory of the broker at any time (*full-take*). The adversary, however, is not able to extract the secret from the client.

PREREQUISITES

In the following section the prerequisites are described in order to understand the solution. As this solution proposes a cryptographic approach within the given protocol specification, both aspects are described here.

Cryptographic Prerequisites

The cryptographic protocol used for this solution is the Schnorr identification scheme as described in the RFC-8235. In order to render this paper self-contained, a brief summary of the RFC-8235 is given here. Please refer to the full RFC document for further details (Hao 2017).

The Schnorr NIZKP can be implemented over a finite field or an elliptic curve. The technical specification is basically the same, except that the underlying cyclic group is different. For simplicity, this document describes the approach within the finite field, whereas in the RFC-document, both versions are described.

Let p and q be two large primes with $q \vee p - 1$. Let G_q denote the subgroup of Z_p of prime order q, and g be a generator for the subgroup.

Statement

$NIZKP\left[(x): y = g^x\right]$ Alice knows the discrete logarithm x of the value y to the base g (within Z_p).

Public input

p, q, g, Z_p, G_q, and the cryptographic hash function $H(x)$.

Prover's (Alice) private input.

$x \in Z_q$ such that $y = g^x \bmod p$.

P $\xrightarrow{(t,s)}$ V

Alice chooses random, calculates, calculates, calculates
Verification.
Bob *accepts* the proof only if $y \in Z_p$ and $g^s = t \cdot y^c \bmod p$.

Protocol Prerequisites

The MQTT protocol (Banks et al. 2019) describes the possibility for authentication exchange in section 3.15 and section 4.12. The authors of the MQTT protocol were aware of the problem of session hijacking and replay attacks. Especially in section 5.4.5 of the protocol specification, they give hints on how to mitigate the attack attempts. But all these mitigation approaches are not focusing on the problem at hand but augment the security assumptions of the channel or even of the network, by requiring the channel to be secured (*TLS*) or even by asking for a secure network environment (*VPN*).

As already advertised in the security model, the approach does not require such heavy security assumptions. It is based on a challenge response mechanism already foreseen by the specification, very much like the described Salted Challenge Response Authentication Mechanism (*SCRAM*) in the non-normative part of the protocol description. Thus the approach perfectly fits within the given protocol boundaries.

PROTOCOL DESCRIPTION

The main idea of this protocol is to choose the *clientID* as a group element $y \in G_q$. In the notation for the multiplicative group, the client chooses $y = g^x$ with $x \leftarrow_R Z_q$. In order to void replay attacks, the broker provides the client with a nonce n to be used as *public data* for the Non-interactive Zero-Knowledge Proof. Only if the client is able to provide the proof (t, s) within the same network connection as the provided challenge, the broker proceeds with a CONNACK containing the reason code *0x00 (Success)*, in all other cases it disconnects with $DISCONNECT$ and some reason code e.g. *0x83 (Implementation specific error)*. This way, the client provides an anonymous identification each time it establishes a fresh connection.

Implementation

A first approach would be a general purpose Schnorr NIZKP system, but the generality comes with a price, in the form of substantial processing time and large public parameters required to construct a proof.

The approach proposed in this paper consists in choosing a key pair (sk, pk) which verifies whether sk is the private key corresponding to the public key pk in a digital signature scheme. This choice allows us to reduce our proof of knowledge problem to that of digitally signing messages, whose implementation is simpler and more efficient than any known general purpose Schnorr NIZKP system (Aranha 2017).

Let the following be the primitives of a secure digital signature scheme:

$$Sign(sk, m) = s \vee m \tag{1}$$

$$Verify(pk, s \vee m) = \begin{cases} m, & \text{if } s \text{ is valid} \\ \perp, & \text{otherwise} \end{cases} \tag{2}$$

Equation 1 signs the message m using the private key sk, and prepends the signature s to the message m. Equation 2 verifies whether s is a valid signature for m produced by the private key sk corresponding to the public key pk then outputs the original message m if the signature is valid, or $\perp$ if it is invalid.

It is assumed that the given digital signature scheme satisfies completeness, validity and zero-knowledge to be useful in this context.

The implementation requires some addition to the client and broker software, that provide the MQTT ability.

The following Figure 1 visualizes a the enhanced authentication process. For further examples within this paper the authentication method, which is needed to trigger enhanced authentication on the broker, is named *SMOKER*. The process uses the signature primitives mentioned in Equation 1 and 2 and the key pair $\left(sk, clientID \leftarrow_{mqtt} pk\right)$. As pk must serve as clientID, it must get mapped into the set of MQTT-$clientID$s.

Client

Prior to the connection the client calculates its $clientID$ by deriving a value pk from its secret key sk (can be the result of a puf or an out-of-band injected value). This is then mapped into the to the allowed set of MQTT-$clientID$s $clientID \leftarrow_{mqtt} pk$. After the client established a connection to the broker, the client starts a MQTT session by sending the connect frame containing the authentication flag in expectancy of a broker authentication response, where a nonce $m \leftarrow_R \{0,1\}^{256}$ has to be provided. The client signs the received nonce using the secure signature scheme.

The client then sends the signed nonce $s \vee m$ as an authentication response within the same connection to the broker. If the client needs to re-establish the session, the very same procedure is executed as if the client would establish the session for the very first time.

Broker

If a client is connecting to the broker, the provided $clientID$ is only accepted, once the authentication succeeds within the same connection. The broker generates a random nonce $m \leftarrow_R \{0,1\}^{256}$ as a response to the first authentication frame within a new connection. The response delivered from the client consists of the signed nonce. The broker verifies the signature and thus extracts m' from $s \vee m$ which must be equal to the originally transmitted m. Only if this verification is successful, the $clientID$ is accepted and the broker behaves in its usual way.

Figure 1. Successful MQTT session establishment using the SMOKER authentication method.

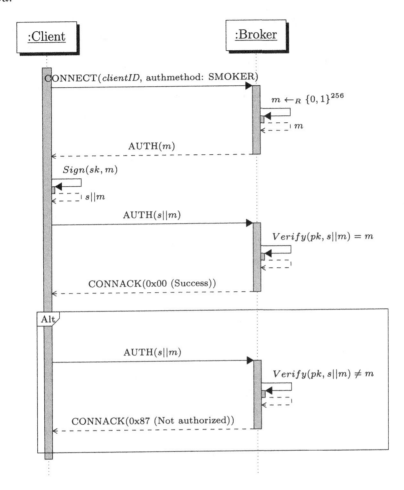

Connecting With an Unknown Authentication Method

As shown in, the given authentication method, requested by the client, must be supported by the broker – otherwise a CONNACK with the reason code 0x8C (Bad authentication method) (Banks et al. 2019 Table 3-1) must be returned and the connection is closed by the broker. An empty authentication method is not further handled by the extended authentication mechanism and is delegated to the brokers default implementation.

Figure 2. MQTT connect with an unknown authentication method.

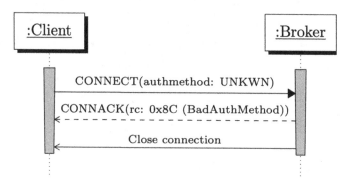

ClientID Stealing

Common broker implementations are disconnecting an active client session if another client is connecting with the same clientID. The specification is very clear (Banks et al. 2019, sec. 3.1.3.1):

"The broker must not accept connections with the same clientID"

As the clientID does not need to be treated as a secret anymore, the broker must ensure that an unauthenticated client is not able to steal a clientID of a proper authenticated client. In this case the broker must reject the connection by sending a CONNACK packet with a *0x85 (Client Identifier not valid)* reason code. Conversely, a connecting client that successfully authenticates, must be preferred over any other unauthenticated client with the same clientID – the unauthenticated client must get disconnected immediately.

ANALYSES

First a fair warning: Due to the 'short' maximum length of the *clientID* covered by the MQTT specification in relation to cryptographic constraints, it is important to implement the proof or signature using the mathematics of elliptic curves. This way, the security parameter λ provided by the MQTT specification provides a maximum $\lambda = 70$. According to cryptographic sources (Giry 2008), this is already a very low security. But using finite fields would lower λ by at least another factor of 20 and would not sustain an attack of any computational moderate potent adversary. Therefore, as an advice, the client and the broker must be enabled to accept a clientID set of order $\geq 2^{256}$. Using the alphabet supported by the MQTT specification this results in a minimum of 43 characters for the clientID in order to get a minimum $\lambda = 128$.

Energy and Space Requirements

In terms of computing power, the client must be able to execute two operations on an elliptic curve and one cryptographic hash per connection. The expensive calculations on the elliptic curve can even be lowered down to a single operation if the *clientID* derived from the according secret can be stored in the system. The computing power on the broker side must allow to calculate a minimum of two operations on the elliptic curve and one cryptographic hash per connection. Furthermore, the broker is required to provide a high entropy challenge nonce m per connection. Either, the broker gets true randomization, which is a very difficult task, or the broker uses an initialization vector (secret iv) seed to initialize a pseudo random generator function. It can keep seeding the pseudo random generation function by the answers it receives from the client connections. This way, the entropy of the client secret can be used to influence the available entropy on the broker, where natural sources of entropy are sparse by nature.

Passive Adversary

The provided implementation allows the broker to reside in a very relaxed security model. No secret is required anymore concerning the *clientID*. The provided implementation further does not require any special treatment of the channel used for communication, as no secret is sent over the channel at all. As long as the underlying network protocol provides authenticity in terms of source and destination during connection, the MQTT session cannot be hijacked at all. The only remaining party within a strict security model is the client. It must be able to keep the secret safe from being extracted.

Active Adversary

As long as the adversary is not in possession of the secret x kept by the client, it cannot provide a valid proof of knowledge to the broker. However, if the adversary model is relaxed, it can start a Man In The Middle (MITM) attack. This allows the adversary to impersonate the client without the client nor the broker to gain any knowledge of that. Thus, the client is required to be sure about the public identity of the desired broker. This brings us back to TLS (and all its pros and cons) with server certificate, in order to provide server-identity 'only' in order to prevent the man-in-the-middle attack. So, one might argue, that the title of this paper might be miss leading, but it must be stressed out, that TLS is not required to prevent clientID stealing, but for broker identity in order to prevent the active adversaries MITM attack.

REFERENCES

Aranha, Barbosa, Cardoso, Mariano, & Diego. (2017). *Nizkctf: A Non-Interactive Zero-Knowledge Capture the Flag Platform.* https://arxiv.org/abs/1708.05844.X

Banks, A., Briggs, E., Borgendale, K., & Gupta, R. (2019). *MQTT Version 5.0.* https://docs.oasis-open.org/mqtt/mqtt/v5.0/mqtt-v5.0.html.X

Giry, D. (2008). *Keylength – Cryptographic Key Length Recommendation.* http://www.keylength.com

Hao, F. (2017). *Schnorr Non-Interactive Zero-Knowledge Proof.* RFC 8235. https://tools.ietf.org/rfc/rfc8235.txt.X

Section 2

Chapter 7
Patient Empowerment in IoT for eHealth:
How to Deal With Lost Keys

Emmanuel Benoist
Bern University of Applied Sciences, Switzerland

Serge Bignens
Bern University of Applied Sciences, Switzerland

Alexander Kreutz
Bern University of Applied Sciences, Switzerland

ABSTRACT

The rise of internet of things (IoT) in medicine has generated tons of new data through connected devices. Medicine and research in medicine are interested in using those data for the personalization of patients' treatment. The authors present the system MIDATA where patients can transfer their medical IoT data and store them. They have also the possibility to share those data with research groups. The solution respects patient privacy. Even an administrator of the site cannot access to the data of the patients. The patient can choose which users can decrypt their data. But users will lose their passwords and keys. So, the authors provide a novel solution for the recovery of the keys. This procedure has different levels: the patient has a new phone but remembers the password; the patient has forgotten the password but can use the phone; and the worst case is when the patient forgot the password and lost the phone, where they developed a novel solution for key recovery.

DOI: 10.4018/978-1-7998-2444-2.ch007

INTRODUCTION

The rise of Internet of Things (IoT) in medicine has generated tons of new data through connected devices such as blood pressure, glucose monitoring or activity sensors. Medicine and research in medicine are interested in using those data for the personalization of patients' treatment. Physicians might monitor the evolution of chronic diseases over a long period of time. These data can also be used to generate alarms if vital constants exceed certain limits. Hospitals and doctors are therefore very interested in the IoT data produced by their patients. Teams of medical researchers want to have the data sets as complete as possible in order to be able to do the best work and discover the most effective treatment or evaluate current treatments.

Hafen and Bignens in (Shabo et al. 2016) described the MIDATA system that allows patients to store the data produced by all connected objects in their IoT, their smartphone and other health related personal data on one platform. Patients can decide with which other users, health professionals or research projects they want to share their data, but they remain owner of their data. The data on the MIDATA system are all encrypted. The patient provides a decryption key to recipient corresponding to the data he or she agrees to share. Each set of data on MIDATA is encrypted and the keys are only accessible to the users that the patient has authorized.

The big problem with encrypted data is that they cannot be read without a decryption key. It's the basic principle of the system, but it's also a very serious problem. Unfortunately, users regularly lose their passwords. If a password is lost in a conventional system, a process exists for resetting the password. If this process ends positively, then the password is changed and the users can access their data again. If the data are encrypted and the users lose their encryption key, so it is impossible to access the data. For vital data such as IoT data for medicine, loss of data can have a negative impact on the quality of care and it may have dramatic consequences.

In this chapter, we present a system to protect the user keys. This system must operate with the minimum of human interaction to limit costs.

STAKEHOLDERS

In this chapter, we will call *patients* all the users placing data in the MIDATA system regardless of their medical status. They can be healthy or ill. Patients and other stakeholders (physicians, nurses, researchers, …) having an account in the system will be referred to as *users*.

Internet of Things in eHealth generates a lot of data that are of interest for the treatment of patients. The first users interested with the data are the physicians treating the patients. They need to access all the data with as less filters in between as possible. The data they want need to be delivered as soon as possible and to be as accurate as possible.

In most of the systems, the physicians access the data through the proprietary interface of the IoT device maker. They need to log on a server that is owned by the device maker and access data that are centralized on it. Hence the physicians have only access to a limited number of devices, since the hospitals will not provide interfaces to a large number of device manufacturers.

The second set of recipients of the data are the researchers. They need to access as much data as possible to have large figures of the disease they study. Normally, researchers do not need to know to which person the data belong to. They should work only with anonymous data.

In a centralized architecture, the makers of the IoT devices play a central role, because all the data transfer goes through their servers. They have the control on all the data and the persons that can read them.

IOT IN EHEALTH

Farahni et al (2018) presented the main challenges of IoT for medicine. For them, IoT will revolutionize the treatment of patients. We will move from hospital-centered treatment to Patient-Centered Care (PCC). This will enable us to respond to the various challenges of the current healthcare system: the population is ageing, urbanization is growing and we will face a shortage of healthcare workforce. All this will force us to find innovative solutions. They show how the IoT can participate in finding solutions to these problems.

Yang et al. (2018) present a system where the IoT and big-data merge. Within this framework, the protection of privacy is an absolute imperative. They present a solution based on group keys that are shared by patients and medical staff. To achieve both security and privacy, they use two algorithmic tools, the Decisional Bilinear Diffie-Hellman (DBDH) Assumption and the Linear Secret Sharing Scheme (LSSS).

IoT systems for eHealth almost all require a gateway (mostly a smartphone). Pereira et al. (2018) showed that one can build a system without such a gateway. This system is based on low power consumption ESP8266 modules. They do not provide a cryptographic solution for the privacy of the patients.

Literature shows that IoT solutions for eHealth will help to solve some of the major issues medicine is facing. But this has to be done with respect to the patient and to patient's privacy.

ARCHITECTURE

The MIDATA system is composed of three main components: the server and its portal, mobile applications and data importers. External services might be connected, for instance to make data analysis.

The server is hosting the medical data of the different patients belonging to one cooperative. The server is secured in a way, that all data are encrypted and a two-factor authentication is needed for the login. We don't go here in more details about server hardening. The description of the encryption features is presented in the next sections. Only the patient has the key to decrypt data. The patient can give access to some chosen partners for some defined data sets by opening for them the cryptographic keys of the safe containing the data. Physicians and researchers connect to the server to access the data. They cannot read data for which the patient has not given the key.

The patients mostly use mobile applications dedicated to a research project to enter data into the system. For instance, the patients may enter their temperature, blood pressure, stress level or the severity of their allergy symptoms or answer to questionnaires. The patients might also connect IoT devices that allow a direct connection to the app. Local data stored on the smartphone (number of footsteps, km of bike, temperature in the house, localization of the patient, etc.) can also be accessed.

Data collected by IoT devices need to be stored on the MIDATA server. Most IoT devices in the health industry send their data directly to the device maker's server. Thus, MIDATA has to get a copy of these data and stored them in the patient's account. To be able to access the data on the manufacturer's server, patients have to authorize MIDATA to access their account on the remote server, usually using OAuth. This gives the patients the opportunity to group data from different sources into their account. Datasets are downloaded from the different servers into one single database that is controlled by the patients.

The patients have a central place where all their data can be securely stored. The data will be available on the MIDATA server even if they are no longer available on the IoT provider server.

SECURITY ISSUES

Since all the data belonging to one person are stored together on the MIDATA server, this makes a good target for a cyber-attack. Some attackers could be interested in bribing the administrators of the site. They could also try to attack (using SQL-Injections or any security flow) the server to acquire patients' data. Since 100%

security is very difficult to obtain, this could happen. The data stored in MIDATA's database are very sensitive. No-one should have the opportunity to access to them without having been authorized.

The data contained in MIDATA belong to the patients. They should have the control on who can access to them. In most of the web sites hosting data, the control is delegated to the administrators of the web site. The patients must believe the administrators will properly handle data. They must believe that the data are not resent to anybody. In our system, an administrator alone cannot access data and cannot give access to data. The data stored inside the MIDATA database are encrypted with a patient specific key. Patients control the use of the key and data cannot be seen by anybody they did not authorize to see it, even an administrator of the site cannot do it.

The security is mainly based on a password that is used to crypt the patients key. With this key, the patients can choose who will have access to which part of their data. They have the possibility to open the access to a dataset (or to all the data if they want) to a physician or to a group of researchers. They can also choose not to do so and to restrict the view of their data to only themselves.

Unfortunately, in the real-world, people lose their passwords. This is not a real problem for most of the applications. In a normal application, the password is stored inside a database. The password is stored hashed. When the user wants to log, the password received from the user is hashed and compared with the stored data. Then the password is not used anymore until the next time the user wants to log in. If the password is lost, a recovery procedure allows the user to enter a new password that is hashed and stored inside the database. The user can simply use this new password for login.

In our case this is not so easy. The password is used to encrypt data (or precisely, to encrypt a key). If we change the password, there is no way to access the key and hence the data anymore. We need a password restore procedure that allows users to recover their key. This function must be efficient in order to save costs but must also be secure in order to prevent an administrator to access the data without the consent of a patient.

ENCRYPTION OF DATA

Patient data is stored on the server. In order for the patients to retain control of their data, they must be the only one able to read them. If and only if they choose to do so, they can share the data with a healthcare professional or researcher. MIDATA's goal is to put the patient back at the center of the data flow and to give back the power over the data to the patient.

MIDATA receives data via several paths:

- First, an IoT device produces data and sends it to its manufacturer's server. In this case, the user must allow (via OAuth) the MIDATA server to download the data from the manufacturer's server. Data are then transformed into FHIR data (HL7 medical data format defined in FHIR Work Group (2011)). The data is then stored on the MIDATA server.
- Secondly, IoT data or data entered manually by the patient are collected by various apps (smartphone applications) developed by MIDATA or by third parties. These apps send the data to the MIDATA server, which then stores the data. Each app sends the data to the MIDATA server using the standard FHIR API.

The data cannot be stored in clear text on the server. Otherwise any person with administrator rights could have access to it. In the same way, an attacker managing to take control of the server could read and exploit the data. We must therefore protect these data by encrypting them.

We have set up an architecture allowing each user to have a pair: private key, public key. The details of the management of these keys are given in the next section. Anyone can access everyone's public keys. All the public keys are stored in clear text on the server. Private keys are protected and are only accessible by the owner himself or herself.

The server encrypts the data as soon as it receives them using the patient's public. This way, only the user with the corresponding private key will be able to read and share the data. In reality, encrypting large amounts of data using public key cryptography is very expensive. That is the reason why we encrypt data using a symmetric algorithm (AES) and it is this symmetric key that we encrypt using the patient's public key.

Figure 1. Data are aggregated inside the app

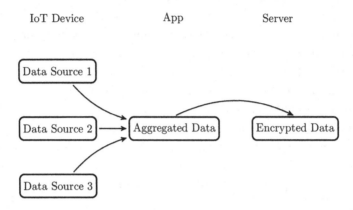

Figure 2. Data are encrypted with a symmetric session key that is encrypted with the patient's public key

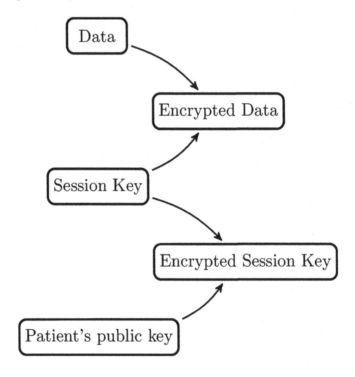

Figure 1 shows the data flow between the applications and the MIDATA database. The data flow from the IoT devices and are collected within the app. The app aggregates the data and puts them into FHIR format. The data is then transferred to the MIDATA server. A symmetric session key is generated (Figure 2). This key is used to encrypt the received data. The key is immediately encrypted using the patient's public key. The key is never stored in clear text on the server disk. It is erased from memory as soon as possible. The only way to decrypt this key is to know the patient's private key (which is not stored on the server).

Figure 3. To share data, the session key is encrypted with physician's private key

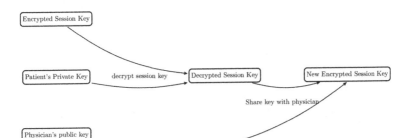

Figure 3 shows the data sharing process. The patient decides to share their data with a third party. This can be a physician, a health professional or a researcher. The patients must use their private key to decrypt the session keys corresponding to the data they want to share. Then they encrypt these keys using the public key of the data recipient (the physician's public key for example). The particularity of asymmetric cryptography is that it can encrypt the data with a key while it will not be able to decrypt these data since it does not have access to the corresponding private key. The recipient of the data will then be able to decrypt the session key using his or her own private key and then decrypt the data using the session key.

For the encryption of data, we use both symmetric and asymmetric cryptography. For symmetric cryptography, we use the algorithm Advanced Encryption Standard (AES). For asymmetric cryptography, we use Rivest Shamir and Adelman (RSA).

PASSWORD AND KEY MANAGEMENT

A user can access the MIDATA system from one or more smartphone applications. The security of data is based on their encryption. Each user will generate different private keys and the corresponding public keys will be used to encrypt the data. The user must have access to all his or her private keys on each of these applications.

Figure 4. Backup of the keys generated in the App

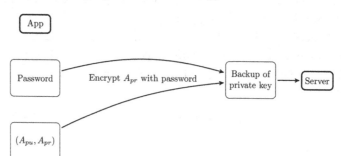

In order to limit the view of the data only to what is necessary, we added a restriction: apps access data through a dedicated channel. A Data Access Filter defines which type of data might be retrieved through the app channel.

The users cannot be asked to take care of the backup of their keys. The users are asked to remember a password. This password is used to decrypt each user's main key. In this way, with the same password, a user can access the stored data from different smartphones and different apps.

We have developed a system that relies only on the user remembering a password. We have also developed a password recovery system in case the users lose their password. In this case, there are two procedures. If the users still have their smartphone, they will be able to use the phone to access the keys. If they do not have their smartphone anymore, a more cumbersome procedure involving at least two of the administrators will be used.

KEYS SHARED BETWEEN THE APP AND THE SERVER

Each user receives two pairs of public and private keys. One to be used inside the apps, the other to be used server side.

The first pair of keys is used inside the app. The app generates one Public key A_{pu} and one private key A_{pr}. A_{pu} is the *App public key*, and A_{pr} is the *App private key*. The App private key A_{pr} is encrypted using the user's password and stored on the server.

The password is never transferred to the server and remains inside the app. For the login, the hash of the hash of the password (i.e. password is hashed 2 times) is stored on the server. The password is given to the app. The app does not send the password to the server but hashes it before. Then the hashed password is sent to the server, that hashes it a second time to compare with the value stored in the database. For security reasons a salt is added for both hash functions. The server never accesses the password. So even an attacker having the control of the server cannot read the passwords and decrypt the private key A_{pr}.

Figure 5. Transfer of the keys generated in the Server

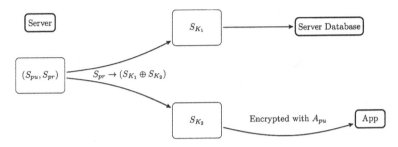

The server generates for every user a pair of asymmetric keys *Server public key* S_{pu} and *Server private key* S_{pr}. The private key S_{pr} is never stored on the hard disk (or in any database) of the server. One generates a one time padding S_{k1} (this is a random number having the same length as the key S_{pr}) and the key is encrypted into S_{k2} using the following formula: $S_{k2} = S_{k1}$ XOR S_{pr}. S_{k1} is stored inside the server. S_{k2} ist encrypted using A_{pu} (public key of the key inside the app).

Figure 6. Data encryption

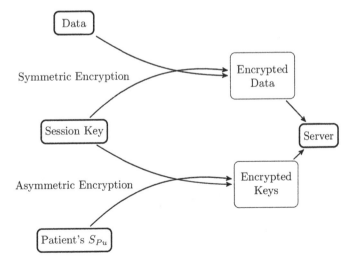

S_{pr} is reconstructed by each login, S_{k2} encrypted is sent to the app, where the private key A_{pv} is used to decrypt it. S_{k2} is sent back to the server, where it is used to reconstruct S_{pv} (Server private key). Another one-time pad is generated, a new S_{k1} and S_{k2} pair is generated, new S_{k2} is encrypted using A_{pu} (the app public key). The encrypted key it stored inside the database.

Data Encryption

Server private and public keys are used to encrypt data. Encryption is not done using asymmetric crypto (since it is to slow) but using symmetric keys. Those symmetric keys are stored in an Access Permission Set together with the ID of the record they are used to encrypt. Those Access Permission Sets are encrypted using the public key of the users that are allowed to see the content. So, one can easily delegate and transfer the rights to read a content provided one has this right.

The application is moreover responsible to check for the credentials, to see if the person reading an access permission set record has the right to forward the key. This part is not done cryptographically.

Figure 7. Key sharing

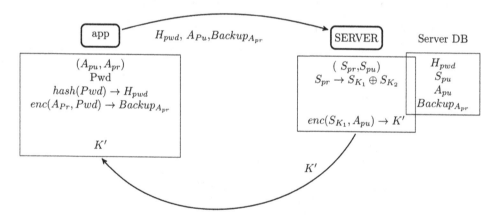

PASSWORD RECOVERY

Patients will lose their password (and maybe very often). If a key is lost, all data are lost and cannot be recovered. Hence a password recovery procedure must be put in place.

The key A_{pr} (private key of the application) is stored encrypted inside the app. It is encrypted using a symetric key composed of two parts (also combined using a XOR). *Secret* and *Secret2*. *Secret* is stored inside the phone, *secret2* is stored inside the server.

If the password is lost, the server asks the client to enter a one time password (OPT) (sent by email). Once the OTP is given the app sends it to the server; *secret2* is then sent to the app. It is combined (XOR) with *Secret* and allows the decryption of the private key A_{pr}. The key is then encrypted using the new password and the hash of the password is sent to the server.

If the patient lost the phone. The private key can be reinitialized using the password since an encrypted version of A_{pr} encrypted using the password is stored on the server.

If the patient lost the phone AND the password, this is more complex, but it does not happen very often.

Five (or it could be 7) persons working at MIDATA have generated a public-private key pair (Recovery key) on their own computer. They keep the private recovery key for themselves and never share it. The public keys are made public so that the apps can also access them.

The user's app private key A_{pr} is split into 5 parts using Shamir Secret Sharing Scheme (SSSS). At least 2 (or it could be 3) of these parts are required to reconstruct the original key. Each of the parts is encrypted with one of the public recovery keys. The encrypted parts are sent to the server and stored there. As the server does not have any of the private recovery keys it cannot decrypt the app private key.

In order to recover the user's app private key each of the persons doing recovery receives one of the encrypted parts. At least 2 (or 3) of the persons decrypt the part using their private recovery key on their own computer.

The decrypted parts are sent to the server and the server may now reconstruct the app private key if enough parts of the key have been decrypted. At no point in time there is enough information at one place to decrypt all of the user keys.

The idea is that no-one can access alone to the keys. The procedure is strict and complex, and therefore costs money.

CONCLUSION AND FURTHER WORK

The data stored in MIDATA is shared by the patient with the chosen stakeholders. The patients regained the power over their data. In IoT, very often the data are stored by companies and users (here our patients) have no power over their sharing. The MIDATA project allows patients to regain control of their most private and important data. First, it allows to keep these data for a long enough period of time, whereas manufacturer support for an IoT system is by definition limited. It then allows the patient to choose with which professionals, doctors, hospitals or researchers these data are shared and under what conditions.

The data centralized in MIDATA are very sensitive. It is therefore natural that they're encrypted. Unfortunately, the cost of this encryption could be the irretrievable loss of these data in case of loss of the password or smartphone. So, we have put in procedures to reset a password automatically or even manually in extreme cases. This system is designed in such a way that nobody, not even the system administrator can have sole access to the keys. The centralized data are therefore such that only patients and those who have been given their consent may access it.

The system currently works with data collected by the apps developed by MIDATA's team or by other partner companies. The system is already importing data from different IoT makers (currently Fibit and Nokia, Strava and LibreView are being implemented by third party) . The interfaces still need to be opened to other manufacturers of IoT products. As soon as a manufacturer offers a FHIR interface to data and uses OAuth for authorization, it can easily be integrated inside the MIDATA ecosystem.

REFERENCES

Badr, S., Gomaa, I., & Abd-Elrahman, E. (2018). Multi-tier blockchain framework for IoT-EHRs systems. *Procedia Computer Science*, *141*, 159–166. doi:10.1016/j.procs.2018.10.162

Farahani, B., Firouzi, F., Chang, V., Badaroglu, M., Constant, N., & Mankodiya, K. (2018). Towards fog-driven IoT eHealth: Promises and challenges of IoT in medicine and healthcare. *Future Generation Computer Systems*, *78*, 659–676. doi:10.1016/j.future.2017.04.036

FHIR Work Group. (2011). *HL7 FHIR Release 4*. Retrieved from https://hl7.org/fhir/

Pereira, C., Guimarães, D., Mesquita, J., Santos, F., Almeida, L., & Aguiar, A. (2018). Feasibility of Gateway-less IoT E-health Applications. In *2018 European Conference on Networks and Communications (EuCNC)*, (pp. 324-328). IEEE. 10.1109/EuCNC.2018.8442531

Shabo, A., Sahama, T. R., Hofdijk, J., Hafen, E., Bignens, S., Goossen, W., Yasnoff, W., & Ball, M. (2016). *IMIA Working Group on Health Record Banking-How Complex Systems Can Cooperate Towards Having Individual's Consolidated Data*. Academic Press.

Yang, Y., Zheng, X., Guo, W., Liu, X., & Chang, V. (2018). Privacy-preserving fusion of IoT and big data for e-health. *Future Generation Computer Systems*, *86*, 1437–1455. doi:10.1016/j.future.2018.01.003

Chapter 8
Security and Privacy Vulnerabilities in Automated Driving

Suchandra Datta
St. Xavier's College, Kolkata, India

ABSTRACT

Driver assistance systems are advancing at a rapid pace, and almost all major companies have started investing in developing autonomous vehicles. However, the security and reliability in this field is still uncertain and debatable. A vehicle compromised by the attackers remotely can be easily used to create chaos of epic proportions. An attacker can control brake, accelerate, and even steering, which can lead to catastrophic consequences. Therefore, an autonomous vehicle can be weaponized extremely easily if proper security protocols are not implemented. This chapter gives a very short and brief overview of some of the possible attacks on autonomous vehicle software and hardware and their potential implications.

I. INTRODUCTION TO AUTOMATED DRIVING

An automated driving system is a complex combination of various components that can be defined as systems where perception, decision making, and operation of the automobile are performed by electronics and machinery instead of a human driver, and as introduction of automation into road traffic. This includes handling of the vehicle, destination, as well as awareness of surroundings. While the automated system has control over the vehicle, it allows the human operator to leave all responsibilities to the system.

DOI: 10.4018/978-1-7998-2444-2.ch008

In SAE's automation level definitions, "driving mode" means "a type of driving scenario with characteristic dynamic driving task requirements (e.g., expressway merging, high speed cruising, low speed traffic jam, closed-campus operations, etc.)"

- Level 0: Automated system issues warnings and may momentarily intervene but has no sustained vehicle control.
- Level 1 ("hands on"): The driver and the automated system share control of the vehicle. Examples are systems where the driver controls steering and the automated system controls engine power to maintain a set speed (Cruise Control) or engine and brake power to maintain and vary speed (Adaptive Cruise Control or ACC); and Parking Assistance, where steering is automated while speed is under manual control. The driver must be ready to retake full control at any time. Lane Keeping Assistance (LKA) Type II is a further example of level 1 self-driving.
- Level 2 ("hands off"): The automated system takes full control of the vehicle (accelerating, braking, and steering). The driver must monitor the driving and be prepared to intervene immediately at any time if the automated system fails to respond properly. The shorthand "hands off" is not meant to be taken literally. In fact, contact between hand and wheel is often mandatory during SAE 2 driving, to confirm that the driver is ready to intervene.
- Level 3 ("eyes off"): The driver can safely turn their attention away from the driving tasks, e.g. the driver can text or watch a movie. The vehicle will handle situations that call for an immediate response, like emergency braking. The driver must still be prepared to intervene within some limited time, specified by the manufacturer, when called upon by the vehicle to do so.
- Level 4 ("mind off"): As level 3, but no driver attention is ever required for safety, e.g. the driver may safely go to sleep or leave the driver's seat. Self-driving is supported only in limited spatial areas (geofenced) or under special circumstances, like traffic jams. Outside of these areas or circumstances, the vehicle must be able to safely abort the trip, e.g. park the car, if the driver does not retake control.
- Level 5 ("steering wheel optional"): No human intervention is required at all. An example would be a robotic taxi.

In the formal SAE definition below, note in particular what happens in the shift from SAE 2 to SAE 3: the human driver no longer has to monitor the environment. This is the final aspect of the "dynamic driving task" that is now passed over from the human to the automated system. At SAE 3, the human driver still has the responsibility to intervene when asked to do so by the automated system. At SAE 4 the human driver is relieved of that responsibility and at SAE 5 the automated system will never need to ask for an intervention (Self-driving car retrieved from https://en.wikipedia.org/wiki/Self-driving_car Access Time:10:37 HRS 20th May,2019)

The challenge for driverless car designers is to produce control systems capable of analyzing sensory data in order to provide accurate detection of other vehicles and the road ahead. Modern self-driving cars generally use Bayesian simultaneous localization and mapping (SLAM) algorithms, which fuse data from multiple sensors and an off-line map into current location estimates and map updates. Waymo has developed a variant of SLAM with detection and tracking of other moving objects (DATMO), which also handles obstacles such as cars and pedestrians. Simpler systems may use roadside real-time locating system (RTLS) technologies to aid localization. Typical sensors include Lidar, stereo vision, GPS and IMU. Control systems on automated cars may use Sensor Fusion, which is an approach that integrates information from a variety of sensors on the car to produce a more consistent, accurate, and useful view of the environment.

Driverless vehicles require some form of machine vision for the purpose of visual object recognition. Automated cars are being developed with deep neural networks, a type of deep learning architecture with many computational stages, or levels, in which neurons are simulated from the environment that activate the network. The neural network depends on an extensive amount of data extracted from real-life driving scenarios, enabling the neural network to "learn" how to execute the best course of action.

Presently autonomous cars combine a multitude of sensors including radars, cameras, LIDAR, GPS to perceive their surrounding driving environment. The multiplicity of enabling technologies embedded within connected and autonomous vehicles (CAVs) promises prevention and mitigation of accidents, reduction in greenhouse gas emissions and more efficient utility of energy and infrastructure. With this, the in-vehicle communication network supports an increasing wealth of electronic control units (ECUs), sensors, actuators and interfaces. A primary goal of driver-less vehicles is the reduction of road fatalities predominately caused by human error. Numerically it has been found that human error is responsible for 57% of all road accidents whilst being a contributing factor in over 90% of the cases(Treat, J. R., Tumbas, N. S., McDonald, S. T., Shinar, D., Hume, R. D., Mayer, R. E., Stanisfer, R. L. and Castellan, N. J. (1977)). Mechanical faults and environmental factors caused accidents in only 5.4% and 4.7% of the cases respectively. However, it is again humans who pose the greatest threat to CAVs. The creators of the enabling technologies may unwittingly create systems with defects or vulnerabilities that allow malicious hackers the opportunity to exploit these vulnerabilities. CAV cyber-risk is of particular concern to insurers, regulators and policing authorities and an appropriate method to risk assessment is required.

The problem with autonomous cars is not the manufacturing process itself but the volume of probable outcomes that could arise from even the tiniest of miscalculations. However, there is more to worry about than just manufacturing defects. What really is significant – when it comes to traveling in self-driving vehicles is their security, that is, the ability to ward off cybercriminals. As the Internet of Things (IoT) is an embedded feature that can help cars of the future navigate through busy roads, making split-second decisions, the risks of falling prey to a malicious hacker is likely the most significant concern manufacturers face going forward. It is to be borne in mind that any device connected to a network attracts hackers who would be interested in gaining control of the device, steal data as well as gain an advantage over other devices through the compromised device. One of the drawbacks of IoT is the inherent interconnectedness of devices, once a device is under the control of a criminal, he can send potentially misleading information to all other devices in communication with the hacked machine without suspecting anything to be amiss. Hacked cars would be an undeniable security threat to the inmates of the vehicle, neighboring vehicles, pedestrians. Hence it is of interest to be aware of the various security vulnerabilities prevalent in autonomous cars. This chapter outlines the latter with focus on how algorithms work and where the loophole exists for such attacks to be carried out.

II. SECURITY VULNERABILITIES IN SELF DRIVING CARS

As new discoveries in fields of machine learning, deep learning, and computer vision continue to surface, new technology is developed to make our lives easier. However parallel to making our lives easier, it is also imperative to develop systems which make our lives safer, for creating systems with numerous loopholes which unscrupulous individuals can utilize is detrimental to the interests of the general masses. Any device connected to networks may be hacked, controlled, destroyed; numerous devices might be controlled to launch the devious distributed denial of service attacks. With respect to self-driving cars, it is imperative to develop fail safe measures to keep attackers at bay for any security compromise would result in widespread destruction. Hacked cars are a scary proposition for the passengers, a threat to the other neighboring cars and a menace in general. The sophisticated technology used to create these systems offer numerous pathways for breaking into it.

The existing literature documents several successful cyber-attacks on autonomous vehicles. These include attack on security keys used by the ECUs, tyre pressure monitoring systems (TPMSs), wireless key fobs and more. The most dangerous attacks are where hackers assume physical control of the vehicle such as braking systems, auto-steering, or cruise controls. Attacks can also be classified as: standalone and connected attacks. In case of absence of connectivity, hackers/attackers require physical access to the vehicles and attacks are confined to a single vehicle only. However, if the autonomous vehicles are connected to a common network for communication, hackers can utilize it to carry out cyber attacks wirelessly on multiple vehicles, thereby creating chaos. Hence, CAVs can be more easily compromised and weaponized to infect other vehicles. These connection mechanisms include vehicle-to-vehicle (V2V), vehicle-to-infrastructure (V2I) and vehicle-to-x (V2X), where x denotes any internet-enabled device.

Types of Attacks include:

1. Global Positioning System (GPS)

To locate and navigate the vehicle, one uses GPS data with great accuracy. To overcome the difficulties in getting GPS data, the count of satellites increased in the public domain where one can easily access the data. Provision of free access to the data with transparent architecture helps the hackers to mislead or manipulate the data to provide the wrong directions or to control the routing of the vehicle. This leads to the security and safety issues of the passengers (Amara, Dinesh & Chebrolu, Naga & R, Vinayakumar & Kp, Soman., 2018))

Qihoo 360 is a Chinese Internet security firm whose researchers claim to have hacked into a Tesla Model S with complete control over the car's lock, lights and horn. They employed a method to create a GPS emulator that can falsify the GPS location of in-car navigation systems and smartphones with minimum cost. SDR or software defined radio tools is used for this purpose(Retrieved from https://www.forbes.com/sites/parmyolson/2015/08/07/gps-spoofing-hackers-defcon/#6f46c8d14efb Access Time:09:00 HRS 21th May,2019) . SDR is system where components like filters, modulators, demodulators, amplifiers and the like are implemented in software not in hardware as it is done traditionally. Signal processing is carried out by a general purpose processor rather than special purpose electronic circuits. The SDR tools includes HackRF which is described by Forbes as the Swiss army knife for the hacking community just as Python is considered to be the army knife for the machine learning community. The board has the capacity to transmit a range of radio frequencies from low(used by FM) to high(Used in WiFi), shifting between them the way computers switch between applications. The developers of the board outline that it is capable of observing signals in transit, intercepting and reverse-engineering it to find out the information being sent and maybe used to inject new information laden signals into the network with only a laptop needed. Wireless signals will no longer be safe by virtue of belonging to a unique frequency since such a vast range is covered by the device. GPS spoofing is hence made easy where the hacker simply spoofs GPS signals for fake maps which appear to be the real depiction of the location but are in fact only a fabrication to confuse automated cars. Instead of connecting to legitimate satellite systems the software is forced to connect to the hackers software system instead. The virtual route selected is often one that would be feasible for the car to take under the current circumstances so it suppresses a recalculation warning.

Currently, however, only examples of "proof-of-concept style attacks can be found in literature(Simon Parkinson*, Paul Ward†, Kyle Wilson†, Jonathan Miller, 2017). For example, in 2013 students from the University of Texas demonstrated how they could generate counterfeit GPS signals which would gradually overpower authentic GPS signals, resulting in the deviation of a superyacht's course. The superyacht's control then reacted to the changing GPS signals by reporting location discrepancies to the crew who then initiated correction by setting a new course (Retrieved from https://news.utexas.edu/2013/07/29/ut-austin-researchers-successfullyspoof-an-80-million-yacht-at-sea, accessed: 2019-05-20 time: 20:00hrs). The hardware involved in the above attack was developed by Humphreys et al., and by their own admission, is the only GPS spoof reported in open literature which is capable of precisely generating counterfeit GPS signals(D. P. Shepard, T. E. Humphreys, and A. A. Fansler, 2012). Using GPS for criminal activity such as being able to redirect vehicles of high-value or those transporting goods for theft or widescale disruption will be desirable. Research efforts to develop GPS spoofing countermeasures have been taking place since GPS was developed as open-standard technology. There are many simple validation mechanisms that can be put in place to prevent spoofing. For example monitoring identification codes, satellite signals, and the use of time intervals can help detect spoofing attempts. Warner et al(I. Abdic, L. Fridman, D. McDuff, E. Marchi, B. Reimer, and B. Schuller, 2016) detail how the observed signal strength would be expected to be around − 163 decibel watts. A GPS simulator, such as that developed by Humphreys et al. would provide a signal strength many orders of magnitude larger than any possible satellite at the Earth's surface. In addition, GPS signals can be monitored to ensure that their relative change is within a threshold. Warner et al. also discuss the potential of monitoring the GPS signal to check that its strength does vary as expected and is not too perfect. However, if the sophistication of the attack is sufficient to appear genuine, these validation checks will fail and the GPS device will be spoofed.

A counterpart of GPS spoofing is GPS jamming in which a device called a GPS jammer is used to send radio frequency signals in the same frequency range as the GPS satellite signal. This results in interference and it becomes difficult to identify the car's current location. It randomly generates signal in that specific range which amounts to a lot of white noise. In comparison with spoofing, jamming only requires that enough radio noise on the GPS frequency (1575.42 MHz) is transmitted to prevent authentic signals from being distinguishable by the GPS receiver. Although illegal to use, GPS jamming devices are readily available. Such devices can be used to ensure that a vehicle's tracking device cannot determine its location through GPS. Executing this attack on CAVs has the potential to disable a vehicle's navigation mechanism, which would be a large inconvenience for the driver and would disable any autonomous navigation capabilities utilising GPS. There is also the possibility of using secondary measurement systems to aid in preventing both spoofing and jamming attacks. However, this does rely on the different positioning system using a different frequency which is not also been attacked. Other measurements are in existence which could be used as a secondary source. For example Russian Federation's GLONASS, China's BeiDou, the European Union's Galileo, and India's NAVIC(S.-S. Jan and A.-L. Tao, 2016). However, as their transmission mechanisms are fundamentally the same and just use different frequencies, the use of a secondary satellite navigation system would only prevent against jamming attacks if the attacker did not transmit on the different frequencies. The use of multiple measurement systems for spoofing attacks is much more significant as the attacker would be required to spoof multiple systems which inevitably increases the complexity of the attack.

2. Inertial Measurement Units (IMU)

IMU is the combination of the Gyroscope and Accelerometers which provides the data of velocity, acceleration and orientation of the vehicle (Amara, Dinesh & Chebrolu, Naga & R, Vinayakumar & Kp, Soman, 2018). IMU also check the change in the environmental dynamics like the gradient. The data provided by the sensors can be modified not to recognize the curvature or gradient of the road. It causes the vehicle to modify its speed incorrectly on the gradient roads which in turn slow down the following vehicles.

IMU is a device which is involved in measuring the three rotational and three linear acceleration components or the six degrees of freedom of a vehicle. It might also include a 3-axis magnetometer. These units are typically used with other sensor fusion software which combines and processes data from multiple sensors to provide measurements of heading and orientation. The raw data picked up by the sensors in an IMU is subjected to mathematical operations to get a clearer idea of the ambient surroundings, a process known as sensory fusion. A reference maybe created by combining the accelerometers sense of gravity with the data from the gyroscope. IMU plays a major role in the correct maneuvering of automated cars, which in turn makes them devices which would be a hacker's favorite pick. For instance, IMU's are responsible for the general safety of the vehicle and the occupants. It may happen that multiple sensors fail simultaneously. In this situation, IMU's are capable of calculating position and acceleration independently. It can slow down a vehicle and bring it to a stop on its own under stressful situations. Attitude control for vehicles involves controlling the orientation of the latter with respect to an entity like an inertial frame of reference. Attitude can be tracked accurately with IMU's of good calibration. They can dynamically control and position changes, detect skidding when tires lose traction and the data they generate is often input to other algorithms. IMU's are involved in accurate lane keeping especially important at turns. To steer the car dynamically, maintain a lane accuracy of 30cm(compared to only 10cm of human drivers). In addition to being indispensable with respect to safety, IMU could be used to stop algorithms from being stuck in local minima. For example, LIDAR and HD maps are being tested by Cruise and Waymo in their increasingly advanced level 4 self-driving cars. Convolutional signal processing is used to match LIDAR scans with HD maps but that is computationally very expensive. The more accurately the initial position of the object can be determined, the less computation needed to find the best match. It is important to note that often the GPS location detected may not be accurate for several reasons, most common being interference with the radio waves in presence of other radio sources, inside tunnels or even by buildings and trees, atmospheric conditions where troposphere and ionosphere may have impact on radio signals, multipath effects where it bounces off buildings, receiver clock errors, error in satellite orbital's location, poor satellite geometry where satellites are clustered together or in a single line. To make sure the vehicle does not veer off course even if the GPS is not working properly, IMU's are necessary. GPS and IMU are complementary to each other, working in unison.

The sensory data maybe compromised to be false but realistic enough to manipulate the control systems in a way which would be beneficial to unscrupulous individuals (Parkinson∗, Paul Ward†, Kyle Wilson†, Jonathan Miller, 2017). Compromising a primitive sensor would impair a vehicle's functionality. The vehicle would be fed fabricated data to trick it into believing it was on a steep gradient and would slow down. This can be considered as a form of DOS attack or Denial of service attack. The only way to perpetrate such attacks would be by means of physical access to the device, failing which one must intercept the signals between the sensor and a corresponding control unit. Such communication could be transferred via cables or close proximity wireless connection method. Sensor readings are to be validated by a control unit to ensure that it is within tolerance as expected. If the attacker knows of the tolerance value, he can modify the behavior of the vehicle without alarming the ECU(Engine Control Unit) to enter into safe mode. This impact may have deeper impacts, even beyond the compromised vehicle. If one vehicle is slowed down on a busy highway, all other vehicles using that same network would also necessarily slow down. Tools like CarShark is used to observe traffic on existing networks like Controller Area Network(CAN) bus system. Research performed by Karl Koscher et al. demonstrated this utility on a CAN bus network using CarShark. Their work involved performing a detailed packet analysis and modification of the captured packets to simulate a MITM or man in the middle attack on the CAN network, whilst observing vehicle behavior. It demonstrated changing packet data to falsify the speedometer readings while traelling(K. Koscher, A. Czeskis, F. Roesner, S. Patel, T. Kohno, S. Checkoway, D. McCoy, B. Kantor, D. Anderson, H. Shacham et al, 2016). Prevention of low-level attacks maybe mitigated by using encrypted communication on the vehicle's communication network. This makes sure that counterfeit signals cannot be arbitrarily injected into the network. Rigorous monitoring of the signals behavior to make sure it is within range and not exhibiting abnormal behavior is another safety measure which can be taken. Another measure is to include an additional source of measurement like combining GPS data with IMU data to calculate whether or not the car is actually on a steep slope or being a victim to malicious signals from hackers.

3. Light Detection and Ranging (LIDAR)

Light Detection and Ranging (LiDAR) is used to localize the environment, obstacle detection, and avoidance. It based on the technology, time taken by the light to travel to and fro to the vehicle determines the distance at which the object is located(Amara, Dinesh & Chebrolu, Naga & R, Vinayakumar & Kp, Soman., 2018) If the hacker sends a signal of the same frequency to the vehicle scanner device and to assume the object is detected. It makes the Autonomous vehicle to move slowly or stop which can cause unforeseen incidents.

Light detection and Ranging (LiDAR) sensors are used to generate a map of the vehicles environment for localisation, obstacle avoidance, and navigation. LiDAR is a surveying technology that measures distance through measuring the time of flight of a pulse of light to determine the distance between the sensor and an object. This technology is capable of quickly producing 3D maps of the environment, making it possible to develop a computational model of the 3D environment. It shoots beams of laser light which gets reflected off nearby objects and the time it took for the light to return to the sensor is calculated. Since millions of light beams are transmitted per second, it is possible to get a 3D visualization of the surroundings with exact measurements of objects upto around 60cm subject to the sensitivity and accuracy of the sensor. LiDAR was conceived in the 1960's after the birth of laser. Stanley, the winner of the 2005 Grand DARPA Challenge employed 5 SICK LIDAR sensors, GPS, gyroscopes, accelerometers, forward facing camera, 1.6GHz Pentium Linux PC's. LIDAR can also track objects and differentiate between a person walking and one on a bike, estimating their speed and even which direction they are going towards. It can also be used for object recognition, trajectory planning etc. This technology has been shown to be a viable aid in autonomous vehicles; however, as there is no guarantee over the validity of the constructed 3D model, it opens the potential for spoofing, deceiving and jamming with low cost hardware.

Work conducted by Stottelaart et al. demonstrates the potential for jamming LiDAR by directly emitting light back at the scanner unit which is of the same frequency as the laser reflecting on the target(B. G. Stottelaar, 2015). A similar attack has recently been performed by researchers from the University of Cork(Retrieved from https://spectrum.ieee.org/cars-that-think/transportation/self-driving/researcher-hacks-selfdriving-car-sensors Access Time:10:21 PM 17.06.2019.). However, what is interesting is that in their research, not only do they manage to compromise a LiDAR laser using low-cost hardware (raspberry Pi and a low-power laser), but they also manage to make the vehicle's control unit assume that there is a large object in front of the vehicle and force it to stop. Furthermore, they also demonstrate the potential to overwhelm the LiDAR sensor preventing the vehicle from moving. Mitigation techniques exist which involve utilising different wave lengths to try and reduce the potential for jamming and spoofing attacks involving off-the-shelf laser devices and increase the required hardware to perform the attack(B. G. Stottelaar, 2015). Other mechanisms discussed by Stottelaart et al. include the use of vehicle-to-vehicle communication to collaboratively share measurements. However, this has the potential for a compromised measurement to be used beyond the compromised vehicle. Another, and arguably more feasible solution, is to implement random probing. This involves the device frequently changing the interval between scanning speeds to make it difficult for the attacker to synchronise their laser to the correct frequency.

4. Monoscopic and Stereoscopic Cameras

Cameras are used to detect lane detection, traffic sign/signal recognition, headlight detection, obstacle detection, etc. Functioning of cameras can be partially disabled by using high beam torches or headlights of the opposite vehicles. It may introduce the safety concerns like false detection or not detection of the objects. Complementary metal oxide (CMOS) sensors used in the camera can be blinded by high power lights. Cameras (stereo- or mono-vision) and infrared systems are used in CAVs to provide static and dynamic obstacle detection, object recognition, and 360 degree information when fused with other sensors. The difference between mono and stereo-vision systems is the number of cameras which are used. Mono-vision systems need additional support from other sensors to improve accuracy in determining aspects such as depth(Simon Parkinson*, Paul Ward†, Kyle Wilson†, Jonathan Miller, 2017). Stereo systems use an overlapping region of two cameras to help determine depth. Cameras are often fused with other sensors on CAVs. For example, the Google Driverless Car fuses LiDAR with stereo-vision and Enhanced Maps (Emaps) for road scenery understanding (J. Du, J. Masters, and M. Barth, 2004). There are many other applications of cameras in CAVs such as lane detection, traffic sign recognition, headlight detection etc. Cameras typically contain a Charge-Coupled Device (CCD) or Complementary Metal Oxide Semiconductor (CMOS) sensor which can be partially disabled from a 3- metre distance through using a low-powered laser, such as a Class 2 laser found in a CD player. A potential attack demonstrated by Stottelaart et al. can be taken against auto exposure (B. G. Stottelaar, 2015) where sensitivity and exposure is reduced when extra light is introduced. The extra light could be from a high powered torch or a vehicle's headlights. This has the potential to hide information such as traffic signs, road edges and pedestrians. According to an MIT Technology Review, the Google Driverless Car is susceptible to this problem where low sunlight is able to blind the vehicle's cameras (L. Gomes, 2014)

The recent tragic events of Tesla clearly illustrates the significance of this problem where neither the car nor the driver identified a white commercial trailer against the brightly lit sky. American crash investigators have thrown open their files on a fatal motorway collision between a Tesla Model S and a truck, confirming Tesla's earlier statement that its autopilot failed to notice the truck blocking the car's path. The accident, which happened in May last year on US Highway 27A in Florida's Levy County, left the 40-year-old driver, Joshua Brown, a US Navy Seal turned networking hardware company owner, dead after the collision. Freshly unsealed US National Transportation Safety Board investigation documents reveal that Brown's last action was to set the cruise control to 74mph. That's enough above the 65mph speed limit but no so far that the cops would bust you unless ticket quotas were tight. According to data recovered from the car, Brown's final trip lasted 37 minutes, from buckling in until the crash. During that time he had his hands on the wheel for 25 seconds and relied on the car's software the rest of the trip. The car issued six audible warning alerts that he'd spent too long with his hands off the wheel. But then a truck slowly pulled out of a side road onto the highway, and the Tesla smashed into its trailer and passed underneath "in a cloud" of debris, according to the report. The trailer lacked side guards that would have stopped the car from going under and Brown suffered fatal head injuries(N. Deepika, V. V. S. Variyar, 2017). This raises the concern of whether shining high-powered lights at a CAV may introduce safety concerns. Furthermore, given the uncertainty of the environment, perhaps it is possible for a natural event to occur which creates light conditions suitable to disrupt camera systems. An adversary could easily perform an attack of this nature by directing a bright light at a vehicle. Compact, high-powered 6 lights are readily available which have potential to blind a vehicle's cameras. It is also worth noting that an intense light source might be accidentally reflected towards a vehicle. For example, a vehicle or building with a particularly reflective and concave surface might provide sufficient focusing of the sun to disable a vehicle's cameras. An example of this can be found with at 20 Fenchurch St. London which was nicknamed "walkie scorchie" and had been known to melt car paint and parts(Retrieved from ., " http://www.bbc.co. uk/

news/uk-england-london-23930675, Access Time: 08:52PM 18.06.2019). The potential implications of an attack of this nature are large. Disabling a vehicle's vision system could result in the vehicle not detecting a physical obstruction. This would be a localized incident; however, natural conditions may cause a wide-spread problem resulting in many localized incidents.

5. Vehicular Adhoc Network (VANET) Attacks (More Explanation Needed)

In order for vehicles to communicate with the driver, other cars, and the road, they need to employ many different communication technologies. Three broad classifications of communication mechanisms exist in the literature. These are vehicle-to-vehicle (V2V), vehicle-to-infrastructure (V2I), and the "Cloud". V2V communication provides the mechanism for vehicles to communicate with each other in a peer-to-peer mechanism, that is, no client/server architecture is required. The system uses the unlicensed 5.9GHz band range, known as the IEEE 802.11. This wireless range frequency spectrum has been allocated a harmonised basis in Europe and the United States, although the systems are not yet compatible. The principle is that when two vehicles or ITS stations are in radio communication range, they can connect automatically and establish an ad hoc network where all connected stations can share information such as position, speed, direction, etc. V2I communication mechanisms provide a means for vehicles to connect to the electronic devices controlling and monitoring the physical environment within which the vehicles are travelling. The infrastructure can then use this information to optimise the traffic control infrastructure to maximise traffic flow, minimizing fuel usage and pollution. A V2I is often described as a centralised control infrastructure, whereas a V2V is decentralised. Example uses of V2I include the control of vehicle acceleration and velocity to optimise travel times, fuel consumption, and congestion levels. 1) Attack Types: Coupling CAVs with an array of different communication mechanisms will inevitably result in them being accessible through a publicly accessible infrastructure (i.e. the internet), or broadcast into public space. This opens the potential for CAVs to experience large-scale, automated and highly damaging attacks. There is great potential for attacks that are damaging to the current information technology to be carried over to CAVs. The list below looks at some of the prominent categories of attack types(Simon Parkinson*, Paul Ward†, Kyle Wilson†, Jonathan Miller, 2017)

Attacks on Internal Networks

These attacks mainly target to extract personal and private data of the passengers. Passcode and key attacks are the most common type of attacks in this category.

Passcode and Key attackspasscode and keys are one of the safety features of the connected cars. Multiple attempts may crack the pass-word or keys which work on the IR based technologies can be easily hacked. Brute force attack on the passcode can crack the passcodes of the connected cars. Blue-tooth connectivity can be affected and leaks the private data of the passenger (Amara, Dinesh & Chebrolu, Naga & R, Vinayakumar & Kp, Soman, 2018) Password and key attacks are where security restriction mechanisms are continuously tested using different values to see if they can be compromised. Attacks of this nature can generally be classified into the three different categories of a 1) dictionary attack, 2) rainbow table attack, and 3) brute force attack. A dictionary-based attack will use a list of words, which are used individually and in combination, to repeatedly attempt to crack the password. A rainbow table attack is similar in nature; however, it uses a list of pre-computed hashes, constructed from all the possible passwords and a given algorithm. This reduces the time required to crack a password to the time taken to identify the correct hash in the table. A brute force attack is similar to that of a dictionary attack; however, it is also able to identify non-dictionary words by working through all alpha-numeric combinations. This can be a slow process due to the large potential combinations, but it is a complete process meaning that the correct password will eventually be identified. Brute force attacks have been used for compromising VANETs(Simon Parkinson∗, Paul Ward†, Kyle Wilson†, Jonathan Miller, 2017). An example of a Rainbow table attack is that performed by Flavio Garcia from the University of Birmingham to crack the 96-bit Megamos Crypto algorithm used by many vehicle manufacturers. Building the 1.5 Terabyte rainbow table took less than one week, but exhaustive search only takes seconds(Simon Parkinson∗, Paul Ward†, Kyle Wilson†, Jonathan Miller, 2017)(R. Verdult, F. D. Garcia, and B. Ege, 2015). This has potential implications for vehicle owners as it demonstrates that security mechanisms can easily be compromised and the vehicle can easily be stolen. Although this attack is quite complex to perform in that specialist hardware and software is required, there is significant potential for off-the-shelf solutions to become available as attacks of this type will become financially motivated. Attacks of this type can be prevented by implementing stronger mechanisms (i.e. larger keys, more secure algorithms); however there will always be an underlying risk that cannot be eliminated. It is also possible that as technology progresses, and computational power increases, current encryption mechanisms that are deemed secure may become easy to crack

Attacks on External Networks

These attacks include V2X attacks (Vehicle to X where X is any connected internet device), V2V attacks (Vehicle to Vehicle attacks) and V2I (Vehicle to Infrastructure) Network attacks.

Connecting car concept and emerging technologies in vehicular networks and which can communicate with other cars and infrastructure giving many advantages along with opening up the network and providing the network access point for the attackers to exploit. It can connect to a smartphone, cloud and other devices and communicate which is described as the V2X communication .Generally communicating channel between the car and smartphone is established through Wið, Bluetooth and GSM protocols which are inherently vulnerable and contain known bugs and vulnerabilities which can be exploited by the attackers. Connecting to a smartphone is always a risk for a vehicle as it is interacting with an external unfamiliar device. Sending and receiving data from the cloud is a threat as the data centre may get compromised and then vehicle starts communicating with the miscellaneous server. Dedicated Short Range Communication (DSRC) protocol in V2V networks is a duplex communication protocol channel used particularly for automotive use operating at 5.9 GHz with a bandwidth of 75 Mhz, WAVE(Wireless Access in vehicular environments) and IEEE802.11 p are the protocols that are generally used in theV2X communication. All of them have known vulnerabilities which can be exploited by an attacker. Vehicle to Vehicle (V2V) Network Attacks: The communication between the host vehicle and adjacent vehicles for overtaking, lane changing, at intersection cars, exchange data through V2V networks. Impersonation attack consists of a malicious car which connects with the host vehicle with a false identiðcation by spoofing then it establishes communication sending the malicious and receiving the sensitive data capturing it than logging and storing it[2]. The major drawback of V2V communication is the use of insecure and unencrypted protocols which makes attackers to eavesdropping the traffic and data between the host vehicle and other vehicle communication and then get the sensitive information like authentication keys leading to authentication attacks Vehicle to Infrastructure (V2I) Network Attacks: The vehicle connects with the infrastructure establishing a communication channel for receiving and transmitting information. The vehicle connects with intelligent trafðc signs and cellular network nodes which can be compromised, infected and impersonated by an attacker thus gaining a access through a backdoor intruding into the vehicle network and ECU's

Denial of Service (DoS)/Distributed Denial of service (DDoS) attacks are where the normal service of a system is disrupted either by a single or multiple attacking machines. Researchers have demonstrated how DDoS attacks can be performed against VANETs and that it is possible to identify malicious connections for prevention. Different types of DoS attacks can be performed by overwhelming 1) a single network node, 2) vehicle to vehicle (V2V), or 3) vehicle to infrastructure (V2I). All these attacks are damaging and aim to disrupt the infrastructure. However, V2I DoS attacks are likely to cause widespread disruption to communication mechanisms. Attacks of this 11 type prevent important communication between vehicles and will ultimately disrupt traffic flow. More significantly, attacks of this type may cause vehicle collisions as potential warning mechanisms may never reach the intended recipient. Furthermore, as with most countermeasures, they can inevitably be broken given enough time and persistence. The implications of compromising VANETs are significant as they are used for functionality such as communicated braking, platooning, traffic information systems, as well as the local infrastructure. Denial of service is one of the most vulnerable threats that connected cars may experience. Service of the sys-tem denied by the several attacking mechanisms which results in disruption of the traffic ñow and damages to the infrastructure. It may cause the collision of the vehicles, a life threat for the passenger.

6. Hardware Attacks

These are mainly OBD port-based attacks. OBD stands for onboard diagnostics and OBD port is present in almost all the vehicles manufactured from2008. OBD port is used for collecting the diagnostics data of the vehicle. It gives the data about the vehicle faults and performance. It interacts with the ECU's communicating through CAN bus. It is a hand held device like USB which has to be connected to the vehicle through the port generally present below the dashboard opposite to adjacent driver seat which then connects to the computer through a wired connection using USB port or through a wireless connection using Bluetooth. Once connected PC can send and receive the data to and from the vehicle ECU's and with a possible exploitation can also manipulate the data packets and inject malicious packets into the vehicle network (Amara, Dinesh & Chebrolu, Naga & R, Vinayakumar & Kp, Soman, 2018). The OBD can access the network infrastructure within the vehicle (to be precise all CAN busses). This is an intended level of access as the OBD port is a means of maintenance and upgrading ECU firmware. The OBD port does have a reduced threat level when compared to wireless connection mechanisms as it is located physically within the car; however, once access has been acquired, it is possible to perform significant modification to the ECU's functionality. Examples could include modifying the codebases responsible for engine, lighting, and braking functionality. In addition, it has also been identified that criminal organisations may aim to extract the intellectual property of OEMs, as well as stealing driver sensitive data (Simon Parkinson∗, Paul Ward†, Kyle Wilson†, Jonathan Miller, 2017). The mechanisms of access control within the OBD protocol are relatively weak but allow the attacker to easily extract and modify firmware and parameters, for example, by reducing the mileage count to increase a vehicle's value. This has implications for a potential buyer as they may be sold something which is not genuine. It is also possible that individuals may want to falsify log information on the ECU to hide their involvement in a vehicle accident, or even to commit insurance fraud(Simon Parkinson∗, Paul Ward†, Kyle Wilson†, Jonathan Miller, 2017).

ECU Firmware Tampering Attack

An **Electronic Control Unit (ECU)** is any embedded system in automotive electronics that controls one or more of the electrical systems or subsystems in a vehicle. Types of ECU include Engine Control Module (ECM), Powertrain Control Module (PCM), Transmission Control Module (TCM), Brake Control Module (BCM or EBCM), Central Control Module (CCM), Central Timing Module (CTM), General Electronic Module (GEM), Body Control Module (BCM), Suspension Control Module (SCM), control unit, or control module. Taken together, these systems are sometimes referred to as the car's computer (Technically there is no single computer but multiple ones.) Sometimes one assembly incorporates several of the individual control modules (PCM is often both engine and transmission). Some modern motor vehicles have up to 80 ECUs. Embedded software in ECUs continues to increase in line count, complexity, and sophistication. Managing the increasing complexity and number of ECUs in a vehicle has become a key challenge for original equipment manufacturers (OEMs) (Retrieved from https://en.wikipedia.org/wiki/Electronic_control_unit Access Time: 02:56PM 22.06.2019). ECU (Engine control unit) is hence an electronic control module for the sensors and actuators of any subsystem in a vehicle and a typical vehicle consists of more than100 ECU's. ECU code is propitiatory making it safe and secure but attackers started targeting recent attacks by reñashing the ECU with custom ðrmware altering its state and inducing malicious and unintended actions. It is called a direct access attack as we assume that attacker has physical access to the ECU. Attacker updates the ðrmware of ECU using the external interface thus altering the functionality of ECU. By altering the ECU memory and tampering with the security keys whilst parallel maintaining the integrity of the ECU ðrmware code and its updates using the hashing techniques and authentication for software updating the attackers are able to accomplish their motives without alerting the system or the humans using the system. Engine control sensors are used to acquire data to regulate engine activity. This includes sensors such as; temperature, air flow, exhaust gas, and engine knock and are all used to acquire performance data which is used to adjust engine conditions. For example, air-flow is used to adjust the amount of fuel required by the engine to achieve the desired output. These sensors have been used on vehicles long before the introduction of levels of automation and connectivity between vehicles. However, as vehicles become connected to a wider networked infrastructure, the sensors become susceptible to outside attacks. Furthermore, data generated by such sensors now have influence beyond the generating vehicle. These sensors are connected to an internal network, such as the CAN. Fortunately, such sensors often require physical access to the vehicle to attack. However, as connectivity increases, care needs to be taken to ensure that these primitive sensors are not vulnerable.

Rogue Updates

Rogue updates are where software running on a vehicle's ECUs is updated with software which was not produced by the manufacturer and has hidden vulnerabilities. Many researchers have discussed the requirements for a distribution model where manufacturers can update the firmware on large numbers of vehicles without a large financial overhead. The research community are in agreement that Firmware updates Over The Air (FOTA) is a credible solution. However, they are also in agreement that there are large potential security implications. Furthermore, secure protocols need to be developed that use cryptographic techniques to guarantee with a certain level of confidence that the update is legitimate. These solutions can provide convincing architectures; however, without wide-scale testing there will always be uncertainty over their security.

Firmware updates in the connected cars are one of the sources for the Rogue updates. These updates are not from the manufacturer and lack of proper updates with safety and security. They are prone to the severe cyber attacks which leak private data of the vehicle. It allows hackers to provide enough security weakness to introduce malware and control the õrmware of the connected cars. The exploitation can be through 1) Physical Access 2) Remote Access

1. Physical Access: Nowadays physical layer is integrated with the ECU's directly which increases the potential for cyber attacks. Hackers can directly exploit the sensor data, control and communication modules. The attacks can be direct or indirect attacks targeting vehicular electronic modules or overloading effect on the physical layer.

2. Remote Access: Remote Access can be done through different connections like WiFi, Bluetooth, 4G, etc. ECU's are directly connected to the CAN bus which is not intended.3 Connectivity to internet leads to the potential threat of injecting malware or virus õles into the õrmware. Automakers are not sure about the threats or actions to be taken to eradicate them. Even Automakers are not sure of the recovery actions to be performed.

Network Protocol Attacks

Network protocol attacks are where communication protocols are analysed to identify potential exploitation mechanisms. Once identified, an attack can then be mounted against the acquired knowledge. Researchers have demonstrated that attacks can be mounted and detected against the FlexRay, and CAN protocols. Due to a lack of confidentiality protection, an attacker can read all data sent on the FlexRay bus, as well as send spoofed packets, which can modify vehicular behaviour . It is clear that protocols are carefully analysed by the scientific community to identify exploits, and once identified, suitable mitigation action will be taken. However, such a reactive approach is not feasible as the number of CAVs on the road increases. Phishing is a form of social engineering where a user masquerades as a trusted entity to gain sensitive information or compromise the system. Phishing attacks are currently the most common form of attacks on PC-based architectures and are often performed through unsolicited email. There is currently an absence of literature detailing significant phishing attacks in CAVs; however, should a user's device that is connected to a CAV be compromised through phishing, the adversary will be able to mount attacks on the vehicle through the connected network via the device. Attacks of this nature are likely to become more wide-spread as the integration between the vehicle and user applications is tightened, for instance, as in the recent integration of email systems and the vehicle's entertainment and information system. There are many damaging potential impacts that could happen as a result of a phishing attack, but as detailed in marketing material from FireEye, it is anticipated that ransomware attacks would soon be developed to seize control of the vehicle and render it unusable until the user pays a premium for it to be unlocked. Phishing and ransomware attacks have the potential to be very damaging for the user as the system may become unusable, which can have considerable financial consequences. The cellular (synonymous with mobile) network architecture is used by vehicles as a mechanism for long-range communication. There are many different technologies that use a cellular network infrastructure. In CAVs, connection mechanisms which have a high bitrate are most desirable for performing tasks such as continuous streaming of data. For example, a survey publication discusses the use of 3G as mechanism in inter-vehicle communication. However, in principle, a CAV can be developed to utilise any cellular-based architecture. Addressable cellular data networks are used in CAVs to distribute data such as crash reporting, diagnostics, anti-theft, and convenience (e.g., weather and traffic updates). Cellular enables attackers to conduct remote attacks on a vehicle as it can be performed over a long distance in a largely anonymous fashion(Treat, J. R., Tumbas, N. S., McDonald, S. T., Shinar, D., Hume, R. D., Mayer, R. E., Stanisfer, R. L. and Castellan, N. J., 1977). There is an absence of literature detailing attacks that specifically target cellular infrastructure with most of the literature focussing on those targeting to exploit internet-enabled technology regardless of whether it is connected using a cellular network or connected through a WiFi hotspot.

Keyless Entry and Ignition Systems

It is widely accepted that in primitive systems, remote central locking signals can be captured and replicated to gain access to a vehicle, and more importantly, disable the alarm and immobiliser allowing thieves sufficient time to start and steal the vehicle. Manufacturers have invested heavily in implementing systems that are much harder to circumvent. These often involve using some kind of cryptographic key change protocol. However, vulnerabilities are still being identified allowing adversaries to gain access to luxury vehicles. A news article by The Guardian details that luxury Range Rovers with keyless locking systems are being targeted by thieves. Furthermore, the requirement for new keys to be programmed to a vehicle presents the opportunity to programme a new key and drive the vehicle away. This is something that is being exploited in premium Audi RS4 vehicles where thieves are able to add a new key into the system once they gain physical access to the vehicle. Although this is a premeditated sophisticated attack to exploit a known vulnerability, Audi have dismissed any liability. Researchers from the University of Birmingham developed techniques of cracking encryption mechanisms used for keyless entry; however were initially prevented from publishing their research by UK government over fears of enabling criminals with knowledge to easily steal luxury vehicles.

7. Adversarial Attacks on Autonomous Vehicles

Deep Learning is based on the probabilistic estimation for the classiõcation tasks predicting the data belonging to a particular class with a certain level of probability and when the probability is higher then in that case we say that class has higher conõdence (Amara, Dinesh & Chebrolu, Naga & R, Vinayakumar & Kp, Soman., 2018).Deep learning algorithms like Deep Neural Net-works (DNN's) are start of the art techniques that are used in the autonomous vehicles for perception and sensing(N. Deepika, V. V. S. Variyar, 2017). But DNN's are prone to certain adversarial attacks making the autonomous vehicles vulnerable to such attacks. Adversarial attack is a form of attack in which the small noise or perturbations are added to the original data misleading and deceiving the DNN's decision making which may create dangerous consequences[17](Retrieved from URL https://arxiv.org/abs/1801.00553 Access Time: 20-05-2019 19:00hrs).In (I. Evtimov, K. Eykholt, E. Fernandes, T. Kohno, B. Li,A. Prakash, A. Rahmati, 2017) physical perturbations are created by adding stickers to a stop traffic sign at certain positions and the traffic sign detection algorithm failed to classify it correctly.

Deep Learning in Self-Driving Cars

Localization, perception, prediction, planning and control are the major activities carried out by self-driving vehicles. For localization data from sensors is utilized by means of sensor fusion. To get the maximum possible accuracy Kalman filters or particle filters are applied. In statistics and control theory, Kalman filtering, also known as linear quadratic estimation(LQE), is an algorithm that uses a series of measurements observed over time, containing statistical noise and other inaccuracies, and produces estimates of unknown variables that tend to be more accurate than those based on a single measurement alone, by estimating a joint probability distribution over the variables for each timeframe. The filter is named after Rudolf E. Kálmán, one of the primary developers of its theory. The Kalman filter has numerous applications in technology. A common application is for guidance, navigation, and control of vehicles, particularly aircraft and spacecraft(Retrieved from https://en.wikipedia. org/wiki/Kalman_filter Access Time: 11:37AM 18.06.2019). Perception makes use of computer vision in order to perceive the surroundings. In prediction, the car attempts to predict the behavior of ambient cars, including the direction they might take, at what speed and the like. Deep learning models are used in areas like prediction where RNN(Recurrent Neural Networks) maybe used, reinforcement learning and A* search algorithms are used in path planning.

Design of perception and control systems in the driving domain have benefited significantly from learning-based approaches that leverage large-scale data collection and annotation in order to construct models that generalize over the edge cases of real-world operation. Leveraging the release large-scale annotated driving datasets, automotive deep learning research aims to address detection, estimation, prediction, labeling, generation, control, and planning tasks. Current efforts are briefly summarized as follows(Lex Fridman∗, Daniel E. Brown, Michael Glazer, William Angell, Spencer Dodd, Benedikt Jenik, Jack Terwilliger, Aleksandr Patsekin, Julia Kindelsberger, Li Ding, Sean Seaman, Alea Mehler, Andrew Sipperley, Anthony Pettinato, Bobbie Seppelt, Linda Angell, Bruce Mehler, Bryan Reimer, 2017):

- Fine-grained Face Recognition: Beyond classic face recognition studies, fine-grained face recognition focuses on understanding human behavior toward face perception, such as facial expression recognition eye gaze detection. In the driving context, explore the predictive power of driver glances or use facial expression to detect emotional stress for driving safety and the driving experience(I. Abdic, L. Fridman, D. McDuff, E. Marchi, B. Reimer, and B. Schuller, 2016).
- Body Pose Estimation: Work on human body pose expands the performance, capabilities, and experience of many real-world applications in robotics and

action recognition. Successful approaches vary from using depth images, via deep neural networks, or with both convolutional networks and graphical models(]J. J. Tompson, A. Jain, Y. LeCun, and C. Bregler, 2014). Specifically for driving, (D. Sadigh, K. Driggs-Campbell, A. Puggelli, W. Li, V. Shia, R. Bajcsy, A. L. Sangiovanni-Vincentelli, S. S. Sastry, and S. A. Seshia, 2014) use driver pose, which is represented by skeleton data including positions of wrist, elbow, and shoulder joints, to model human driving behavior.

- Semantic Scene Perception: Understanding the scene from 2D images has long been a challenging task in computer vision, which often refers to semantic image segmentation. By taking advantage of large scale datasets like Places, Cityscapes, many approaches (] H. Zhao, J. Shi, X. Qi, X. Wang, and J. Jia, 2017), (P. Wang, P. Chen, Y. Yuan, D. Liu, Z. Huang, X. Hou, and G. Cottrell, 2017) manage to get state-of-the-art results with powerful deep learning techniques. As a result, precise driving scene perception for self-driving cars is now actively studied in both academia and industry(] M. Bojarski, D. Del Testa, D. Dworakowski, B. Firner, B. Flepp, P. Goyal, L. D. Jackel, M. Monfort, U. Muller, J. Zhang et al, 2016).

- Driving State Prediction: Vehicle state is usually considered as a direct illustration of human decision in driving, which is also the goal for autonomous driving. In terms of machine learning, it serves as the ground truth for various tasks from different perspectives such as driving behavior (D. Sadigh, K. Driggs-Campbell, A. Puggelli, W. Li, V. Shia, R. Bajcsy, A. L. Sangiovanni-Vincentelli, S. S. Sastry, and S. A. Seshia,, 2014) and steering commands. Many aspects of driver assistance, driver experience, and vehicle performance are increasingly being automated with learning-based approaches as representative datasets for these tasks are released to the broad research community. The MITAVT study aims to be the source of many such datasets that help train neural network architectures that provide current and future robust solutions for many modular and integrated subtasks of semi-autonomous and fully-autonomous driving.

Adversarial Attacks on Deep Learning Models

If the attacker has control over one or more ECU's then he might be able to spoof messages from the camera owing to lack of authentication on the CAN bus. The hacker will modify the image captured from the camera, creating an adversarial example which would be misclassified by a steering angle controller for the vehicle(Alesia Chernikova∗, Alina Oprea∗, Cristina Nita-Rotaru∗ and BaekGyu Kim, 2019). The attack must be stealthy so as to avoid suspicion by humans looking at the camera, avoid detection by the anomaly detection software for threat detection.

Carlini and Wagner(N. Carlini and D. Wagner, 2017) proposed the L2 attack for image classification where the adversarial examples are generated by solving an optimization problem for an image x with original class I to find the perturbation that transforms x into a targeted class t where t is not equal to i. This attack is to be used for direct classification. For regression the classification attack maybe adapted in the sense that objective function will be changed to maximize the MSE or mean square error metric difference between the predicted response on the adversarial image and the true response. This way the attacker tries to change the prediction value further away from the true value. Adversarial images can be used to trick multiple different types of models without being specifically trained for that architecture, making it highly transferable, finding application in black box attacks where the attacker knows nothing about the model parameters, type of model or the dataset on which it has been trained. To achieve these types of attacks, an algorithm called Fast Gradient Step Method can be used where subtle noise is introduced at every stage of optimization to shift the output value either towards or away from a desired target class. The amplitude of noise is to be shifted slightly so that images tampered with and original ones do not look any different to the naked eye. The amplitude here means change in the intensity of a pixel value.

Aspects of Adversarial Attacks

- Adversarial Falsification – False positive attacks generate a negative sample which is misclassified as a positive one (Type I Error). In a malware detection task, a benign software being classified as malware is a false positive. In an image classification task, a false positive can be an adversarial image unrecognizable to human, while deep neural networks predict it to a class with a high confidence score. False negative attacks generate a positive sample which is misclassified as a negative one (Type II Error). In a malware detection task, a false negative can be the condition that a malware (usually considered as positive) cannot be identified by the trained model. False negative attack is also called machine learning evasion. This error is shown in most adversarial images, where human can recognize the image, but the neural networks cannot identify it(Xiaoyong Yuan, Pan He, Qile Zhu, Xiaolin Li, 2018).
- Adversary's Knowledge – White-box attacks assume the adversary knows everything related to trained neural network models, including training data, model architectures, hyper-parameters, numbers of layers, activation functions, model weights. Many adversarial examples are generated by calculating model gradients. Since deep neural networks tend to require only raw input data without handcrafted features and to deploy end-to-end

structure, feature selection is not necessary compared to adversarial examples in machine learning. – Black-box attacks assume the adversary has no access to the trained neural network model. The adversary, acting as a standard user, only knows the output of the model (label or confidence score). This assumption is common for attacking online Machine Learning services (e.g., Machine Learning on AWS1, Google Cloud AI2, BigML3, Clarifai4, Microsoft Azure5, IBM Bluemix6, Face++7). Most adversarial example attacks are white-box attacks.

- Adversarial Specificity – Targeted attacks misguide deep neural networks to a specific class. Targeted attacks usually occur in the multiclass classification problem. For example, an adversary fools an image classifier to predict all adversarial examples as one class. In a face recognition/biometric system, an adversary tries to disguise a face as an authorized user (Impersonation) . Targeted attacks usually maximize the probability of targeted adversarial class. – Non-targeted attacks do not assign a specific class to the neural network output. The adversarial class of output can be arbitrary except the original one. For example, an adversary makes his/her face misidentified as an arbitrary face in face recognition system to evade detection (dodging). Non-targeted attacks are easier to implement compared to targeted attacks since it has more options and space to redirect the output. Non-targeted adversarial examples are usually generated in two ways: 1) running several targeted attacks and taking the one with the smallest perturbation from the results; 2) minimizing the probability of the correct class. Some generation approaches (e.g., extended BIM, ZOO) can be applied to both targeted and non-targeted attacks. For binary classification, targeted attacks are equivalent to non-targeted attacks.

- Attack Frequency – One-time attacks take only one time to optimize the adversarial examples. – Iterative attacks take multiple times to update the adversarial examples. Compared with one-time attacks, iterative attacks usually perform better adversarial examples, but require more interactions with victim classifier (more queries) and cost more computational time to generate them. For some computational-intensive tasks (e.g., reinforcement learning), one-time attacking may be the only feasible choice.

- Perturbation- Small perturbation is a fundamental premise for adversarial examples. Adversarial examples are designed to be close to the original samples and imperceptible to a human, which causes the performance degradation of deep learning models compared to that of a human. There exists three aspects of perturbation: perturbation scope, perturbation limitation, and perturbation measurement. (1) Perturbation Scope – Individual attacks generate different perturbations for each clean input. – Universal attacks only create a universal perturbation for the whole dataset. This perturbation can be applied to all clean input data. Most of the current attacks generate adversarial examples individually. However, universal perturbations make it easier to deploy adversary examples in the real world. Adversaries do not require to change the perturbation when the input sample changes. (2) Perturbation Limitation – Optimized Perturbation sets perturbation as the goal of the optimization problem. These methods aim to minimize the perturbation so that humans cannot recognize the perturbation. – Constraint Perturbation sets perturbation as the constraint of the optimization problem. These methods only require the perturbation to be small enough.

III. CONCLUSION

Self driving cars will eventually become a commonality in the future which further increases the importance of proper strong security enforcement in such vehicles. These vehicles would turn out to be an integral part of the IoT framework. Depending on time and location, they would turn the heater on inside the car and drive the owner to destinations with minimum human intervention. However the decrease in human intervention must be compensated with increase in impenetrability of the cars otherwise self driving cars would turn out to be a societal nightmare. Autonomous vehicles are a collection of sophisticated technology components plugged together, each with its own particular vulnerability. The GPS might be spoofed, the hacker could interfere with the IMU, the cameras, the LIDAR, networks can be jammed and deep learning models tricked into producing a wrong output. Such areas must be shielded from outside forces in order for self driving cars to be utilized without mishap.

REFERENCES

Abdic, I., Fridman, L., McDuff, D., Marchi, E., Reimer, B., & Schuller, B. (2016). Driver frustration detection from audio and video in the wild. In *KI 2016: Advances in Artificial Intelligence: 39th Annual German Conference on AI*. Springer.

Akhtar, N., & Mian, A. (n.d.). *Threat of adversarial attacks on deeplearning in computer vision: A survey*. https://arxiv.org/abs/1801.00553

Amara, Chebrolu, Vinayakumar, & Soman. (2018). *A Brief Survey on Autonomous Vehicle Possible Attacks, Exploits and Vulnerabilities*. Academic Press.

Bojarski, M., Del Testa, D., Dworakowski, D., Firner, B., Flepp, B., Goyal, P., Jackel, L. D., Monfort, M., Muller, U., & Zhang, J. (2016). *End to end learning for self-driving cars*. arXiv preprint arXiv:1604.07316

Carlini, N., & Wagner, D. (2017). Towards evaluating the robustness of neural networks. *Proc. IEEE Security and Privacy Symposium*. 10.1109/SP.2017.49

Chernikova, Oprea, Nita-Rotaru, & Kim. (2019). *Are Self-Driving Cars Secure? Evasion Attacks against Deep Neural Networks for Steering Angle Prediction*. arXiv:1904.07370v1

Deepika, N., & Variyar, V. V. S. (2017). Obstacle classiðcation and detection for vision based navigation for autonomous driving. *2017 International Conference on Advances in Computing,Communications and Informatics (ICACCI)*, 2092–2097. 10.1109/ICACCI.2017.8126154

Du, J., Masters, J., & Barth, M. (2004). Lane-level positioning for in-vehicle navigation and automated vehicle location (avl) systems. In *Intelligent Transportation Systems, 2004. Proceedings. The 7th International IEEE Conference on*. IEEE. 10.1109/ITSC.2004.1398868

Evtimov, I., Eykholt, K., Fernandes, E., Kohno, T., Li, B., Prakash, A., Rahmati, A., & Song, D. (n.d.). *Robust physical-world attackson machine learning models*. https://arxiv.org/abs/1707.089455

Fridman, Brown, Glazer, Angell, Dodd, Jenik, Terwilliger, Patsekin, Kindelsberger, Ding, Seaman, Mehler, Sipperley, Pettinato, Seppelt, Angell, Mehler, & Reimer. (n.d.). *MIT Autonomous Vehicle Technology Study: Large-Scale Deep Learning Based Analysis of Driver Behavior and Interaction with Automation*. arXiv:1711.06976v3

Gomes. (2014). *Hidden obstacles for googles self-driving cars: Impressive progress hides major limitations of googles quest for automated driving*. Academic Press.

Jan, S.-S., & Tao, A.-L. (2016). Comprehensive comparisons of satellite data, signals, and measurements between the beidou navigation satellite system and the global positioning system. *Sensors*, *16*(5), 689. doi:10.339016050689 PMID:27187403

Koscher, K., Czeskis, A., Roesner, F., Patel, S., Kohno, T., Checkoway, S., McCoy, D., Kantor, B., Anderson, D., & Shacham, H. (2010). Experimental security analysis of a modern automobile. *2010 IEEE Symposium on Security and Privacy*, 447–462. 10.1109/SP.2010.34

O'Hanlon, B. W., Psiaki, M. L., Bhatti, J. A., Shepard, D. P., & Humphreys, T. E. (2013). Real-time gps spoofing detection via correlation of encrypted signals. *Navigation*, *60*(4), 267–278. doi:10.1002/navi.44

Parkinson, Ward, Wilson, & Miller. (2017). Cyber Threats Facing Autonomous and Connected Vehicles: Future Challenges. *IEEE Transactions on Intelligent Transportation Systems, 18*(11).

Sadigh, D., Driggs-Campbell, K., Puggelli, A., Li, W., Shia, V., Bajcsy, R., Sangiovanni-Vincentelli, A. L., Sastry, S. S., & Seshia, S. A. (2014). *Datadriven probabilistic modeling and verification of human driver behavior*. Formal Verification and Modeling in Human-Machine Systems.

Sadigh, D., Driggs-Campbell, K., Puggelli, A., Li, W., Shia, V., Bajcsy, R., Sangiovanni-Vincentelli, A. L., Sastry, S. S., & Seshia, S. A. (2014). *Datadriven probabilistic modeling and verification of human driver behavior*. Formal Verification and Modeling in Human-Machine Systems.

Shepard, D. P., Humphreys, T. E., & Fansler, A. A. (2012). Evaluation of the vulnerability of phasor measurement units to gps spoofing attacks. *International Journal of Critical Infrastructure Protection*, *5*(3), 146–153. doi:10.1016/j.ijcip.2012.09.003

Stottelaar, B. G. (2015). *Practical cyber-attacks on autonomous vehicles*. Available: http://essay.utwente.nl/66766/

Tompson, J. J., Jain, A., LeCun, Y., & Bregler, C. (2014). Joint training of a convolutional network and a graphical model for human pose estimation. *Advances in Neural Information Processing Systems*, 1799–1807.

Treat, J. R., Tumbas, N. S., McDonald, S. T., Shinar, D., Hume, R. D., Mayer, R. E., Stanisfer, R. L., & Castellan, N. J. (1977). *Tri-level study of the causes of traffic accidents*. Report No. DOT-HS-034-3-535-77 (TAC).

Ut austin researchers successfully spoof an $80 million yacht at sea. (n.d.). https://news.utexas.edu/2013/07/29/ut-austin-researchers-successfullyspoof-an-80-million-yacht-at-sea

Verdult, R., Garcia, F. D., & Ege, B. (2015). Dismantling megamos crypto: Wirelessly lockpicking a vehicle immobilizer. *Supplement to the 22nd USENIX Security Symposium (USENIX Security 13)*, 703–718.

'walkie-talkie' skyscraper melts jaguar car parts. (n.d.). http://www.bbc.co.uk/news/uk-england-london-23930675

Wang, P., Chen, P., Yuan, Y., Liu, D., Huang, Z., Hou, X., & Cottrell, G. (2017). *Understanding convolution for semantic segmentation.* arXiv preprint arXiv:1702.08502

Yuan, X., He, P., & Zhu, Q. (2018). *Adversarial Examples: Attacks and Defenses for Deep Learning.* arXiv:1712.07107v3

Zhao, H., Shi, J., Qi, X., Wang, X., & Jia, J. (2017). Pyramid scene parsing network. *The IEEE Conference on Computer Vision and Pattern Recognition (CVPR).*

Chapter 9
Using Freenet as a Broker for Multi-Party Data Exchange in IoT for Health

Emmanuel Benoist
Bern University of Applied Sciences, Switzerland

Jan Sliwa
Bern University of Applied Sciences, Switzerland

ABSTRACT

Smart, networked medical devices play a rapidly growing role in healthcare. Those devices and their data have to be integrated into the healthcare system. There are several reasons to reuse those data for well-defined purposes by well-defined partners; this reuse should be controlled by the patient and not depend on the manufacturer infrastructure. Different stakeholders have an understandable reason to access those data under the control of the patient. The authors propose an architecture of a decentralized data broker that receives the data streams from the devices and redistributes them securely to legitimate recipients. This broker is based on the peer-to-peer network Freenet. This network has been defined to be censorship resistant and to protect the privacy of persons sharing data. This covers the needs for protection expected from a secure data broker. The patient can directly define which of the stakeholders will receive which information and the information is encrypted in a way that only that partner can read it.

DOI: 10.4018/978-1-7998-2444-2.ch009

INTRODUCTION

We face an immense technological development in the area of the smart medical devices. The market of the devices that treat serious medical conditions is dominated by the established big players. They deliver complete support systems and take responsibility for their function. They provide an integrated information system for treating data from the device to the different stakeholders through their own infrastructure. They control from their servers which information is sent to which partner and for what purpose.

That this leaves little room for smaller, independent companies, especially for startups with little commercial experience. At the universities there are numerous projects in which the students develop e.g. novel sensors and after obtaining their PhD make no effort to translate it into a product. If they try and build a startup company, having good experience but only in one area, they rarely succeed. The challenge for them is to provide an integrated end to end system starting with an Internet of Things (IoT) device to the dispatching of data to the various stakeholders. There are here various skills and one should help them concentrate on their main goal: providing the best possible IoT devices for medicine.

In traditional architectures all data produced by an Internet of Things (IoT) device for medicine pass through a central infrastructure managed by the device manufacturer. In case of startups entering the market, this single point of failure is a big issue for the acceptance of their product. The market does not foresee the future of those firms. If the manufacturer of an IoT device for medicine goes bankrupt or decides to stop the maintenance of one device, then the servers are not available anymore. Since data can not be sent, the system is not usable anymore. This is particularly problematic for implantable devices or life saving devices. We propose the use of a decentralized data broker based on the Freenet peer to peer network for storing and sharing the data produced by the IoT devices for medicine.

Those devices produce a stream of data that is principally destined for the hospital and physicians to support the treatment, but can be also used for quality assurance and the verification in the sense of the Evidence Based Medicine. In order to provide a level field for all players, independent of their size, we need a neutral broker for multi-party data exchange. This broker must be vendor independent and should not be able to read or even see which data are transfered to whom.

We propose the use of Freenet, a censorship resistant peer to peer network for playing the role of the data broker. This is a peer to peer network designed to be privacy preserving that meets very high security requirements.

In Section 2 we present the different existing architectures for Internet of Things for health. In Section 3 we present the different stakeholders and their needs for data. In Section 4 we show the different architectures that are used in the mobile health industry. In Section 5 we see the risks the architecture is facing, from eavesdropping to complete destruction of the device. In Section 6 we present the Freenet peer to peer network. In Section 7 we present how we use Freenet as a data broker. In Section 8 we show how our architecture solves security problems. The last section, Section 9 presents our conclusion and the future work.

RELATED WORK

An overview of the Internet of Things can be found in (Al-Fuqaha et al. 2015), with the focus on the middleware (Razzaque et al. 2015). An overview of IoT systems for healthcare is given in (Islam et al. 2015), (Yuehong et al. 2016) and (N. Zhu et al. 2015). The privacy and security issues are discussed in (Arias et al. 2015), (Moosavi et al. 2016), (Roman, Zhou, and Lopez 2013), (Singh et al. 2015) and (Weber 2010). An ethical view on the fair sharing of information is given in (Shilton et al. 2009). Possible architecture solutions are discussed in (Catarinucci et al. 2015), (M. S. Hossain and Muhammad 2016), (Paschou et al. 2013) and (T. Zhu et al. 2017). Stream processing and event detection is presented in (Ma et al. 2014).

As we see from the literature, there are many existing and proposed approaches to the subject, but the size of the chapter does not permit a profound discussion or comparison. As this field is in full development, we recommend to follow current presentations of ideas and products. Technology is only one side of the problem, balancing the need for privacy and the public good is a challenging, nontrivial ethical issue. This has been discussed at the Computers, Privacy & Data Protection (CPDP2017) Conference[1] in Brussels. The complete videos are available, e.g. the panel "Data protection and data-driven innovation for health care and biomedical research"[2].

STAKEHOLDERS AND THEIR DATA NEEDS

In the mobile health ecosystem we can name several legitimate stakeholders. This configuration is based on the general presentation of multi-party IoT systems in (Sliwa 2016). Medical devices produce data streams that could be used by those stakeholders.

The principal method to reduce the risk of data misuse is to distribute only the necessary data extracts, encrypt them between the endpoints and to control well the subsequent access to them. For example, data transferred to a research institute, being basically medical without personal information, could be re-assigned to the known patients using additional knowledge. Therefore only a limited number of registered, competent people should have access to those data. Additional privacy policy compatible with the local legislation on privacy protection must be enforced in the different partners receiving data.

The data extract will depend on the type of the recipient and should be sufficient to perform the required action but as limited as possible. Let us consider those issues on an example. Our data exchange system is used by patients with various cardiac problems. The severity of the cases, safety requirements and costs justify establishing a dedicated support system. The patients use one or more medical devices - wearable, implantable or portable. These devices transmit data to a local concentrator (typically a smartphone), that has enough computing power to preprocess the data, e.g. extract significant events from an electrocardiogram, to encrypt them with the public keys of the different stakeholders and to send them to the broker. Stronger, portable (tabletop) devices can transmit data on their own. The condition of a typical patient allows him to live normally, there is however a risk of a rapid aggravation and of an emergency. Therefore he has an implanted ECG (electrocardiogram) sensor that permits continuous monitoring. It is supplemented by several other sensors that together permit a sharper detection of an event.

We will now identify the stakeholders, present their general data needs and discuss reasonable data extracts for them in more detail.

The hospitals and doctors need timely and precise information about the health condition of the patients they handle. They also want to know which methods and devices are optimal in which case, what will be the result of of the scientific analysis.

The devices provide synchronous measurement values of various vital parameters. If those measurements are required by the therapy, missing value will be treated as an event that calls for an action. In case of medical emergency (e.g. a heart attack), asynchronous message will be transmitted and will trigger a rapid intervention, like sending an ambulance. Patients' data are stored in their personally identifiable Electronic Medical Records.

The recommendations regarding the methods and devices will be provided by the researchers. They do not need to identify individual patients but have to analyze the anonymous, individual connected histories. They need good information about the diagnosis, applied therapy and the result. The result may also depend on gender, age, or other demographic factors. Therefore a stratification of the population into groups based on such factors may be necessary. It should be possible to assign a patient to a group without revealing his/her identity. This means that the information packet (e.g. a measurement) has to be stripped of personal data. The researcher may also evaluate the devices. The device model and its settings are an important part of the therapy specification, as a correct device may be used in a wrong operation mode. Similarly, externally observable device failures will be registered.

The producers need detailed technical information regarding the performance of their devices. In the case of the malfunction, aside from actual events (red alarm) they should detect possible events (yellow alarms) what will permit them to fix the problem and to upgrade the device before a serious event happens. This detailed information is considered a trade secret, not to be shared with other stakeholders and especially with other, competing producers. For a device that operates in a wireless Body Area Network the signal quality can be reported as well as the percentage of transmission errors and packet repetitions. For the software, memory usage will be useful, with the check for memory leaks. Unusual states (no connection, subsystem missing, storage error, inconsistent local database) should be reported. In every software some unpredicted states may be not properly handled and cause a crash. An exceptional software restart should be detected and reported with enough supplementary (debugging) information to allow to analyze precisely the incident. The physical part of the device should be also monitored. Some intelligent prostheses measure the intensity of use and detect the mechanical stress that can lead to a mechanical damage[3].

The identities of the patients are irrelevant, although the lifecycles of individual devices may have to be observed. This means including information about exact model, software release and possibly the production lot. The connection between the patients and the devices should not be known by the producer. If however a possible malfunction of an individual device is detected, this information should be transferred to the hospital, in order to repair or replace it. Medical approval authorities, like FDA in the USA, perform the postmarket surveillance (vigilance) of the devices and require to be notified about safety related incidents. Based on this information, they may recall malfunctioning devices. They also oversee the efficacy of the devices and therapy methods. This information helps to decide which of them are to be reimbursed. The authorities need the quality information in a very condensed form: reports about actual safety related events and the statistics regarding medical efficacy of therapy methods. As a government institution, they define the content and the form of the required information.

These recommendation should be presented in an understandable form to the general public.

The patients benefit from this entire system. They are treated by optimally chosen therapy methods and devices. Their data are partly used for the direct support of the therapy. They can also be reused for the verification and optimization of these therapies. Typically, secondary reuse is allowed only if the patient gives his/her consent to do so. The patient will be empowered and will receive the control directly inside the device or the aggregator to whom which data will be sent.

EXISTING ARCHITECTURES

The following IoT applications rely on various architectures. We present what is similar to all of them and what is different. We then try to determine how the information flow can be missused and by whom.

Here are some existing IoT systems for eHealth: scale, blood pressur meter, glucometer, implantable insuline pump, implantable heart defibrilator.

We can compare those systems on different dimensions. On one side, some of the systems are sensors (scale, blood pressur meter, glucometer), and some of them are a combination of sensors and actuators (implantable insuline pump and implantable heart defibrilator). Some of them are implanted (implantable heart defibrilator) some have implanted components (implantable insuline pump), some can be implanted or not (glucometer, blood pressur meter) and some must remain external (scale).

As far as IT infrastructure, systems involved in IoT for eHealth are also very different.

- Some systems are closed and contain only the possibility to be accessed locally. Some implantable heart defibrilator can not communicate with the external world and must be managed locally.
- Some systems use a local aggregator (can be a smartphone or a table top system) to connect to a server.
- Some systems connect directly to the server.

Users can access data directly from the system using a local interface (for instance a small screen) or more often need an application

The systems can be totally independant, and only have an interface to deliver information. They can also have an interface to receive orders, to be configured or to be updated. The firmware update is a way to change the system of an IoT device. This may be possible even if the system can not use Internet directly.

In all the cases, we have a system that is designed by the manufacturer and data are sent to its infrastructure (its server or a chosen MQTT broker). The infrastructure is then responsible for the transporting and the sharing of the right information with the right partner.

RISK ANALYSIS

Main risks in the Medical IoT are first on the security for the integrity of the devices, and then on the security privacy of data.

The devices can be attacked by malicious actors. They will try to insert malwares inside the devices, this can be done exploiting the system or forging a fake firmware update. On the one side, if the system suffers a vulnerability, attackers can build an exploit and take the control of it. Typically, this occurs when the device has a flow and the attacker can take the control of it using a rogue input. This can be for instance buffer overflow (Cowan et al. 1998), SQL-Injection(Clarke-Salt 2009) or a misconfiguration (Hwang 2015). On the other side, the attack will target the update of the software run in the device (the firmware). Attacker will replace legitimate software with a new one containing a malware.

Another risk is for data being lost or stollen. Data can be lost if there is no server or if the device or the aggregator of data (smartphone) can not find the server any more. This will occur if the server is target of a DDoS attack (Nazario 2008). This will also arrive if the server is turned off because the firm does not exist anymore or decides not to support the device any more. In any case, the data are sent by the device and can not be treated by anybody. The firm can not receive information, neither will the hospital, physicians or any other stakeholder.

The risks if a firm disappears, is that data can not reach any of the targets. This risk can not be taken by hospitals, physicians, and patients. Hence, this is a major hurdle for Small and Medium Enterprises (SME) to enter the very competitive market of medical IoT devices. We present a solution based on a established peer to peer network to play the role of the data broker.

FREENET AS A DATA BROKER

The role of the data broker is to transfer securely data from the IoT device (or the corresponding aggregator) and the different partners (firm(s), hospital, physicians, patients). The solution must be vendor independant and reliable, even if the firm must stop the support of the device, even if the firm does not exist anymore, the devices will have the possibility to send data to the different partners.

Freenet (I. Clarke et al. 2001; I. Clarke et al. 2002) is a peer to peer network designed for storing and sharing of data. The goal of Freenet is to offer a way to exchange data in a way protecting both the anonymity of the authors and the readers. This network has been designed to give a solution to fight against censorship and allow the sharing of information in a secure way. This system can be used to share information, without risk to be spied on. The system has been conceived to resist a state sponsored attack. For instance, the data are decentralized, to prevent any central point of failure (I. Clarke et al. 2002).

In (project 2019) the developpers of Freenet describe the project as a large storage device. *"When you store a file in it, you receive a key which can be used to retrieve the file. When you supply Freenet with a key, it returns the appropriate file (if it is located).".* You can access to a file if you know the key. So only people knowing the key can access to information. Freenet offers the possibility to use a *Keyword signed key* that the partners can chose for a file transmitted to the network. Then people will have the possibility to access the file using that key.

In (I. Clarke et al. 2001) the designers of the system present the *five main design goals*

- *Anonymity for both producers and consumers of information*
- *Deniability for storers of information*
- *Resistance to attempts by third parties to deny access to information*
- *Efficient dynamic storage and routing of information*
- *Decentralization of all network functions*

In our case, some features are not interesting per se, but cover exactly what we expect from our data broker.

- *Anonymity for both producers and consumers of information*: Nobody should be able to know which patient generated which data and also whom it was targeted to.
- *Deniability for storers of information*: In order to be deniable, information must be encrypted in a way that the servers storing them do not have the possibility to read them. This is what we expect from the different members of the network. They should not be able to read the information.
- *Resistance to attempts by third parties to deny access to information*: This resistance is already interesting for fighting against denial of service attacks. It is even more important if the firm producing the device does not exist anymore or decides not to support the device any more.
- *Efficient dynamic storage and routing of information*: The system must be efficient and robust, since life saving data will be transmitted, any loss of information can lead to the death of a patient.
- *Decentralization of all network functions*: There is no single point of failure and SME can trust a system that is not owned and can not be controlled by any bigger competitor.

ARCHITECTURE OF THE DATA BROKER

IoT medical devices can communicate directly to the broker or be connected to an aggregator (for instance a smartphone) that is responsible to send information to the broker.

Information sent to the data broker must be packaged in a way, that only the legitimate reader(s) will be able to access them. Devices must be configured by the hospital where they are deployed or later reconfigured by patients if they have the ability to do so. The system (device or aggregator) receives the public key of the hospital, together with the public keys of the different stakeholders that should receive data. The patient is then responsible for validating the different partners that will receive the data.

Information is encrypted inside the device or its aggregator, under the control of the patient data is encrypted with the public keys of the different recipients. Encrypted data is transfered to the Freenet to addresses that were beforehand decided for each of the partners. Each partner knows only one single address and can neither access nor guess any of the other addresses.

Data is sent to one address per partner. Each partner (hospital, researchers, manufacturer, or authorities) can read only the data that are present at the address they know. They do not have the possibility to access data at another address. Even if it were possible, data are encrypted using the public key of the recipients, hence prohibiting any access to third parties.

SECURITY

The system has to ensure a secure transmission of the selected data towards the predefined recipients. The system is based on the Public Key Infrastructure (PKI) in which each partner (patient or a data recipient) owns a pair of keys (private and public) and a certificate signed by one or more Certificate Authorities (CA). Each data item made available by the patient on this platform has a list of recipients to be validated by him/her (Benoist and Sliwa 2014). The generated data are then encrypted by a one-time symmetric key and sent to the server. The symmetric key is then encrypted with each public key of all recipients. The different versions of the encrypted key are then stored on the server at the predefined address. In this way each recipient can read the data prepared for him, because he can download the encrypted data as well as the key for reading them. This key will be decrypted with his private key. . The data to be aggregated do not need to be later connected to a patient. At the source, he/she encrypts them with a one-time symmetric key that is itself encrypted with with the public key of the recipient. The informations necessary for the stratified aggregation (region, age range and whatever else necessary) and sends them to the server where they are not anymore connected to the patient. The recipient receives the anonymous data and can perform statistics without knowing the origin of the data. The patient can control the degree of aggregation and the demographic factors used for the stratification. If he/she does not accept the proposed parameters, he/she can refuse to share the data. As mentioned above, some recipients - like government agencies - can overrule this decision.

The details of the management of the PKI keys exceed the scope of this paper.

This architecture provides answers to the main security issues that we depicted. It is not possible to a third party to read any data. Data are encrypted and only the owner of the corresponding private key can understand the meaning of data. One can not see that a person is communicating with one server or another one, so privacy of the patients is protected. For instance it is not possible to see that one patient is sending information to the register for breast cancer, or to the manufacturer of a heart defibrilator. Hence it is not possible to guess that one person has one specific disease based on those information. The device (or aggregator) is only communicating with the Freenet network and nobody knows what it is about.

There is no single point of failure anymore. Since the system does not rely on one single server (or a set of servers), there is no way to stop it. Freenet is a system that has been conceived to be resistent to attacks and can not be shut down (I. Clarke et al. 2001). Even if the manufacturer of the device does not exist anymore or does not provide any support anymore, data will still be transmitted from the device to the other stakeholders.

CONCLUSION AND FUTURE WORK

Smart medical devices that aim for the high-level segment of the market - severe medical conditions, application in actual therapy, higher price / reimbursement - need a system to objectively and continuously monitor their function and safety. We propose a decentral data broker that ensures a secure and privacy preserving data distribution to the legitimate partners.

An important step towards the implementation is the analysis of the possible mapping of the presented design on existing protocols (MQTT, FHIR, HL7, ...) and platforms. The system handles data of critical importance, and especially the communication with the hospitals, i.e. direct health support, needs an efficient and reliable platform. The aspect of the delay between the sending of the data and its reception is a big issue that need to be monitored. Freenet is nowadays fast and reliable, we need to measure if it will resist under stress conditions and how reliable it would be if used by hundreds of thousands of patients.

In order to make such data exchange system work in real conditions, its technical implementation is crucial, but other ethical, organizational and legal problems must also be solved. It is a challenging but rewarding task.

REFERENCES

Al-Fuqaha, Guizani, Mohammadi, Aledhari, & Ayyash. (2015). Internet of Things: A Survey on Enabling Technologies, Protocols, and Applications. *IEEE Communications Surveys & Tutorials, 17*(4), 2347–76.

Arias, O., Wurm, J., Hoang, K., & Jin, Y. (2015). Privacy and Security in Internet of Things and Wearable Devices. IEEE Transactions on Multi-Scale Computing Systems, 1(2), 99–109. doi:10.1109/TMSCS.2015.2498605

Benoist, E., & Sliwa, J. (2014). How to Collect Consent for an Anonymous Medical Database. HEALTHINF, 405–12.

Catarinucci, L., De Donno, D., Mainetti, L., Palano, L., Patrono, L., Stefanizzi, M. L., & Tarricone, L. (2015). An Iot-Aware Architecture for Smart Healthcare Systems. IEEE Internet of Things Journal, 2(6), 515–26. doi:10.1109/JIOT.2015.2417684

Clarke, Miller, Hong, Sandberg, & Wiley. (2002). Protecting Free Expression Online with Freenet. *IEEE Internet Computing, 6*(1), 40–49.

Clarke, Sandberg, Wiley, & Hong. (2001). Freenet: A Distributed Anonymous Information Storage and Retrieval System. In *Designing Privacy Enhancing Technologies*, (pp. 46–66). Springer.

Clarke-Salt, J. (2009). *SQL Injection Attacks and Defense*. Elsevier.

Cowan, C., Pu, C., Maier, D., Walpole, J., Bakke, P., Beattie, S., Grier, A., Wagle, P., Zhang, Q., & Hinton, H. (1998). Stackguard: Automatic Adaptive Detection and Prevention of Buffer-Overflow Attacks. *USENIX Security Symposium*, *98*, 63–78.

Hossain, Shamim, & Muhammad. (2016). Cloud-Assisted Industrial Internet of Things (Iiot)–Enabled Framework for Health Monitoring. *Computer Networks, 101*, 192–202.

Hwang, Y. H. (2015). Iot Security & Privacy: Threats and Challenges. In *Proceedings of the 1st Acm Workshop on Iot Privacy, Trust, and Security*, (pp. 1–1). ACM.

Islam, Riazul, Kwak, Kabir, Hossain, & Kwak. (2015). The Internet of Things for Health Care: A Comprehensive Survey. *IEEE Access, 3*, 678–708.

Ma, M., Wang, P., Chu, C.-H., & Liu, L. (2014). Efficient Multipattern Event Processing over High-Speed Train Data Streams. IEEE Internet of Things Journal, 2(4), 295–309.

Moosavi, Gia, Nigussie, Rahmani, Virtanen, Tenhunen, & Isoaho. (2016). End-to-End Security Scheme for Mobility Enabled Healthcare Internet of Things. *Future Generation Computer Systems, 64*, 108–24.

Nazario, J. (2008). DDoS Attack Evolution. *Network Security*, (7), 7–10.

Paschou, Sakkopoulos, Sourla, & Tsakalidis. (2013). Health Internet of Things: Metrics and Methods for Efficient Data Transfer. *Simulation Modelling Practice and Theory, 34*, 186–99.

Project Freenet. (2019). *Freenet Project Documentation Page.* https://freenetproject. org/fr/pages/documentation.html

Razzaque, M. A., Milojevic-Jevric, M., Palade, A., & Clarke, S. (2015). Middleware for Internet of Things: A Survey. IEEE Internet of Things Journal, 3(1), 70–95.

Roman, Zhou, & Lopez. (2013). On the Features and Challenges of Security and Privacy in Distributed Internet of Things. *Computer Networks, 57*(10), 2266–79.

Shilton, K., Burke, J., Estrin, D., Govindan, R., Hansen, M., Kang, J., & Mun, M. (2009). *Designing the Personal Data Stream: Enabling Participatory Privacy in Mobile Personal Sensing. TPRC.*

Singh, J., Pasquier, T., Bacon, J., Ko, H., & Eyers, D. (2015). Twenty Security Considerations for Cloud-Supported Internet of Things. IEEE Internet of Things Journal, 3(3), 269–84.

Sliwa, J. (2016). A Generalized Framework for Multi-Party Data Exchange for Iot Systems. In *2016 30th International Conference on Advanced Information Networking and Applications Workshops (Waina)*, (pp. 193–98). IEEE. 10.1109/WAINA.2016.134

Weber, R. H. (2010). Internet of Things–New Security and Privacy Challenges. *Computer Law & Security Review, 26*(1), 23–30.

Yuehong, Zeng, Chen, & Fan. (2016). The Internet of Things in Healthcare: An Overview. *Journal of Industrial Information Integration, 1*, 3–13.

Zhu, Dhelim, Zhou, Yang, & Ning. (2017). An Architecture for Aggregating Information from Distributed Data Nodes for Industrial Internet of Things. *Computers & Electrical Engineering, 58*, 337–49.

Zhu, Diethe, Camplani, Tao, Burrows, Twomey, Kaleshi, Mirmehdi, Flach, & Craddock. (2015). Bridging E-Health and the Internet of Things: The Sphere Project. *IEEE Intelligent Systems, 30*(4), 39–46.

ENDNOTES

[1]   https://www.cpdpconferences.org/, accessed Feb 21, 2017.
[2]   https://youtu.be/7X-SxqophQA, accessed Feb 21, 2017.
[3]   http://esplab.epfl.ch/page-115053-en.html, accessed Feb 21, 2017.

Chapter 10
Information Security Management System:
A Case Study of Employee Management

Manoj Kumar Srivastav

https://orcid.org/0000-0002-5080-6796

Champdani Adarsh Shramik Vidyamandir, India

ABSTRACT

Security of information is always a challenging domain for any computer network organization. An organization always sets different types of policies with the course of time so that no information can be leaked. Some external or some internal factors of an organization play important roles in revealing the information. An organization mainly depends on its employees. An employee manages the data and information and there exists some chance among employees to reveal the data. There is need to study and set policies for employees so that no full information can be revealed. Information security management system (ISMS) has collection of different types of policies and procedures for systematically managing organizationally sensitive data. ISMSs have to deal with management of employees of an organization to minimize the risk of revealing information. This chapter studies employee management so that an organization can continue its business securely.

INTRODUCTION

A computer based network organisation works by communication/ transformation of information with the help of their employee. Therefore it is need to develop Information management system so that it is possible for an organisation to develop

DOI: 10.4018/978-1-7998-2444-2.ch010

the process for getting right information to the right person at the right place and at the right time. It is possible in an organisation that some employees can reveal secret/sensitive information. So, there need to develop some policies and procedures for systematically managing an organisation's sensitive data. It is necessary to manage data in proper way so that risk level with respect to secret/sensitive data should low. The goal of Information security management system should run an organisation smoothly and continuously by limiting the risk level very low. An ISMS mainly consists of (i) Human resource (HR) (ii) Organizational processes and procedures and (iii) Information and technologies. The key factors of ISMS are working on Data integrity, Availability and Confidentiality of information. (a)Data integrity: Access restriction and protection of data from unauthorized resources (b) Availability: Organizational information available to authorized resources without any issues. (c)Confidentiality: Protection of information from unauthorized resources. Employee management is the effort to help employee to their best. An organization always wants to take service from an employee with minimum cost expenditure and getting maximum profit. An employee has to do different types of tasks in Information Security Management System. [C.S.Park et al. 2010].To maintains information should be secure, the following criteria should be following with respect to employee in ISMS:-

1. Selection: Selection is initial stage of entry of employee in an organization. It is necessary to choose right person for doing right job so that ISMS can run properly.
2. Monitoring: The working process of an employee should be monitored. There should be some observation group for observing the whole process of employee and this will helpful manage performance of employee in ISMS.
3. Interaction: Employee should interact with each other properly and confidentially. The flow of information should be secure among employee so that ISMS can be implemented smoothly.
4. Reward: Employee should be rewarded with respect to their working ability and performance. This will work as catalyst among employee and organization performance will be tend in higher profit.
5. Discipline: The information of an organization will remain secure if some major disciplinary action against employee who is revealing information to unauthorized person. Role of an employee always plays an important role in an organization. An employee may leak all the information of an organization during working of job or after leaving the job.

The role of employee can greatly increase in maintaining a safe and secure environment after creating and maintaining an information security management.

Achieving information security is huge challenge for an organization. There is needed to look ISMS from some mathematical methods so that information can be remaining secure for an organization. IoT platform can help organization to reduce cost through improved process efficiency, assets utilization and productivity. In an organization employee can connect, analyze, integrate and take active participation with the help of IoT based technology. To make an organization secure IoT based technology should be apply to serve auto Shift / roster management, Email/SMS notifications of employee's attendance, automatically manages leave records of employees etc... Organization can establish their own policy for attendance, leave, ON duty, office time, and working place of employee and leave management system. The designing, developing, and maintaining and enabling the large technology to IoT system in an organization is quite complicated. In this paper some features related to security of information by the employee have discussed. As the devices of IoT interact and communicate with each other and do lot of task for an organization so it is required to discuss some security risk related from employee of an organization.

IMPLEMENTATION OF ISMS TO AN ORGANIZATION

The goal of information security management system (ISMS) is to protect the information of an organization. The implementation of ISMS will vary from organization to organization. Information security is major challenging task for any organization during implementation of ISMS. To make ISMS to be effective, it is need to analyze the information. It is needed to study value of each information. Security is challenging task with respect to employee working process. It is necessary to make analysis of security on each level of ISMS. There is need to create a controlling system to keep the information safe. Implementing ISMS is not a project with a fixed length. It is necessary ISMS should be able to handle challenging task with respect to information security. There is needed to make continuation of reassessment of information security. By frequently testing and assessing ISMS, an organization will know whether the information is still protected or need of modification in the system. By creating and maintaining an information security management system it is necessary to increase employee participation in maintain a safe and secure environment. Role of employee should be considered while implementing ISMS. The following issue should be considering while implementing ISMS.

Valuation of Information

An organization need to identify/differentiate about which information should be kept secret and which information should be public .It is necessary to study which information is more valuable. ISMS should study very deeply about risk based information. Activity of an employee should be manage in such a way that it will be ensure that information is exclusively accessible to authorized person only. Information among employee should be deployed in such a way that information should be access by authorized person in proper way.

All business procedures within companies depend on a regulated flow of information. Hence, it is essential to attain and maintain an appropriate level of information security. Information is most important resource of the organization. Managing the information means managing future. **According to Davis and Olson:** "Information is a data that has been processed into a form that is meaningful to recipient and is of real or perceived value in the current or the prospective action or decision of recipient." The parameters of a good quality are difficult to determine for information. Quality of information refers to its fitness for use, or its reliability. So, role of employee is more valuable in these prospects. There is need to manage role of employee with following characteristics features:

Timeliness

Timeliness means that information must reach the recipients within the prescribed timeframes. Working combination among employee must be effective, secured with respect to information and follow appropriate decision at the right time. Decision making process among employee should be appropriate. The ISMS with respect to employee management should be up-to-date i.e. follow status of current information.

Accuracy

Information should be accurate. It means that information should be free from mistakes, errors &, clear. Accuracy also means that the information is free from bias. Wrong information given to management would result in wrong decisions. Employee should give correct information to each other. There should need of a monitoring body to check accuracy of communication of information in ISMS.

Relevance

Information should be relevant during communication among employee as in ISMS each employee serve information to other. To run ISMS properly information should be relevant and useful.

Adequacy

Adequacy means information must be sufficient in quantity, i.e. Employee must provide proper and appropriate information during communication. Appropriate information plays important role in decision making and decision is needed to develop security in ISMS.

Completeness

The information which is given to an employee during working should be complete and should meet all his needs. Incomplete information may result in wrong decisions and thus may prove costly to the organization.

Explicitness

A report is said to be of good quality if it does not require further analysis by the monitoring team for maintain security in ISMS. The information is total secure in ISMS if it maintain good quality of analysis

Impartiality

Each employee should know their work properly and each of them should be assigned with proper knowledge of information. Impartial information contains no bias.

Balance Among Working Process of Employee of an Organization

Organization must manage a balance between securing information and making them accessible to authorized person .An authorized employee will be able to access data or information. Authorization is a security mechanism. It is used to determine access level of employee in an organization. This is the process of granting or denying access to employee. Each employee have unique identity .Based on their identity, employee can access their role in an organization. Most organization based on a two step process. The first steps are authentication, which ensures about the employee identity and second stage is authorization which allows employee to access the various resources based on employee's identity. ISMS depend on effectively designed authorization processes to facilitate employee management. Access control in ISMS relies on access policies and it is divided into two phases:

- *Policy definition phase where access is authorized*

Authorization is the process of giving someone permission to do or have something. In Information security management system there exist different types of working employee. A system administrator defines for the system which employees are allowed to access to the system and what information will be given to them for their work. Assuming that someone has logged in to an application, the administrator may apply to identify about employee is doing in that session or what the information or given to employee in that session. Thus, authorization is sometimes seen as both the preliminary setting up of permissions by a system administrator and the actual checking of the permission values that have been set up when an employee is getting access.

- *Policy enforcement phase where access requests are permitted or not permitted to employee*

When an employee attempts to access information, the access control process investigates that the employee has been authorized to use that information. Authorization services are implemented by the Security System which can control access at the level of individual employee or group of employee. Organization and employee that use computers can describe their needs for computer security and trust in system in terms of three major requirements:

- *Confidentiality*: Controlling which employee will get to read/access information.
- *Integrity*: Assuring that information and programs are changed only in a specified and authorized manner.
- *Availability*: Assuring that authorized employees have continued access to information and resources.

These three requirements may be emphasized differently in various applications.

Risk Assessment With Respect to Secure Information

The organization should analysis risk factor in securing information. The organization should observe the working process of an employee in an organization. There should be a monitoring body to analysis the working process of employee of an organization.

To make information secure in ISMS, there is need to develop some security plan where the approach and responsibilities will given some managerial level observing body to manage the security risk . It is needed to identify different types of risks regarding security of information. Information security management process has to study all areas of security from the working employee. ISMS have to determine sources of threat and risk (and potential events) that could affect the organization business. Security risk is divided into two steps:

1. Security risk assessment
2. Security risk treatment

Security Risk Assessment

It is comprehensive process to identify analysis and evaluation of security risk of information and determine practical steps to minimize the risk.

Security Risk Treatments

It is effective actions that are considered in the requirement to terminate the security risk in information.

Though there is some observing body to monitor the security risk in ISMS, the security concern is related to

1. Every Employee Of The Organization
2. The Decision Makers Who Takes Decision in an Organization.

Security management is logical and a systematic process. Security process identifies the risk environment in ISMS. Security process will study about level of risk which is acceptable or not. There is need to study the priorities and objective during risk assessment. It is necessary to study whether it is required to develop single risk assessment plan or multiple risk assessment plans. The security plan may be varying with time to time. It depends on how employee woks in an organization. It varies with demands of employee to run an organization. It is required to study level of threat, risk to its information which serves an assets in an organization and risk tolerance. Information Security Management System requires to review and manage their plan at least after some short period of time. Aim of ISMS to manage of security risk with changing in emerging threats. It is necessary to check security threats when the employee of an organization shift or leave the organization. ISMS determine the methods of review policy with respect to security and the role of employee. The monitoring body of ISMS will appoint the expert employee who can understand organization's strategic goals and objectives and the appropriate level of security risk management knowledge and expertise. There is need to develop positive security culture based on common understanding of security.

Table 1. Security risk environment

Goals and objective	Accountable monitoring committee has positive risk assessment to secure information.
Security risk environment	The environment in which the ISMS operates; the threats, risks and vulnerabilities effecting the organization's protection

Accountable authority can do the following for security of information:

1. Vigilance, resilience and adaptability of employee to security risk.
2. Safety of employee.
3. Protection of resources, information and assets held in the organization.
4. Possesses capacity to function during security incidents, disruption or emergencies.

When implementing the core requirement to detail threats, risks and vulnerabilities that affect the protection of employee, information and assets, organization:

- Identify the employee, information which is requiring to safe.
- Determine specific risks (including sharing of information's risks) by its employee.
- Identify the threats to employee, information which works as assets.(threat assessment)
- Accesses the degree of susceptibility and resilience to hazards (vulnerability assessment)
- Analysis and consequence of each risk occurring (risk analysis)

Establishment of ISMS

The rapid growth of information technology (IT) has created numerous business opportunities. At the same time, this growth has increased information security risk. IT security risk is an important issue in industrial sectors, and in organizations. Initially it is study about technical risk factors but in the present time employee factor also plays as risk factor.

"Information security is protecting the information through preserving their Confidentiality, Integrity and Availability along with the authenticity and reliability"

"ISO/IEC 27001 is an international standard which specifies requirements for **establishing**, implementing, maintaining and continually improving an organization's **ISMS"**. An organization should always work on establishment and implementation of ISMS. The following image represent specifies requirements for establishing, maintaining and continually improving an organization ISMS.

Figure 1. ISO 27001 ISMS

ISO 27001:2013 Standard have following properties:

- ISO 27001 is the International standard that provides guidelines for safeguarding an organization's asset
- ISO 27001:2005 was the first standard in the world dedicated to Information Security
- ISO 27001:2013 was published on the 25th September 2013 and it replaced ISO 27001:2005
- Comprehensive set of Clauses and Controls comprising best practices in information security
- A framework for building a risk based security management system

The formation of ISMS may vary from organization to organization. But there are some common factors which should be generally follows in all organization

Employee Password

Every employee of the organization should follow the following rule about their password

- Keep your passwords secret
- As per policy, password should be min 8 characters with alphabets, numbers, and special characters (#, @, *, $, &, %,)
- Use passwords that are easy to remember but difficult to guess
- Change passwords every 90 days to avoid password expiry

Every employee of the organization should not follow the following rule about their password

- Don't use passwords which are based on your personal info or words found in dictionary

- Don't write down or store passwords
- Don't share your passwords with anyone
- Don't reveal passwords in email, chat or other communication

Malware Protection

Malware is a 'Malicious Software' which is developed with intentions to cause harm to Confidentiality, Integrity and Availability of Information. Some common Malware are Virus, Worms, Trojans, spyware.

Every employee of the organization should follow the following rule about malware protection

- Ensure that the Antivirus is running on your desktops
- In case the antivirus is not present or not functional, report it immediately to IT service desk
- Scan all files coming from external sources (such as email, internet, USB).
- Do not open or download any executable files (.exe) from email attachment

Email Security

Every employee of the organization should follow the following rule about their email security

- Use Email only for business purposes
- Use only official email ids for official purposes
- Retain important emails for evidence/record purposes

Every employee of the organization should not follow the following rule about their email security

- Transmitting offensive material like political opinion, pornography and sexual harassment material;
- "Spamming" unsolicited messages, promotions, sending or forwarding chain letters;
- Creating, sending, receiving or storing materials that infringe the copyright or other intellectual property right of any third parties;

Clear Desk and Clear Screen

Every employee of the organization should do the following:

- Lock your desktop while leaving work place
- Ensure your desk is clear and no sensitive information lies around
- Be aware of shoulder surfers in office or in public places
- Be cautious while handling sensitive information
- Shred unwanted documents

Every employee of the organization should do not do the following:

- Don't forget to collect your printouts from printer
- Don't forget to clear white board while leaving meeting rooms
- Don't use / install any unauthorized software

Social Engineering

Every employee of the organization should do the following:

- Avoid discussing sensitive information with others in public
- Do not give out sensitive information over email/telephone without proper verification of identity.
- Always be assure of the other person's identity, when you receive a call which you are not expecting
- When discussing any important business issue make sure no one else is listening

Employment Policies and Practices

Employees and employment policies should be a major concern in ISMS. Employment policies can be used to protect information security assets by setting guidelines for the following:

1. *Background checks and security clearances:* It is need to check the basic and fundamental background of employee during his appointment. The organization should verify previous employment and other basic information provided as part of the application. For those in more sensitive positions, such as administrators and information security professionals, a further check into someone's background might be a consideration. As long as the checks are

disclosed, an organization can request access to credit and criminal records to verify the applicant's suitability for her position.

2. *Employment agreements and hiring and termination practices:* There is need to develop some agreement during employment of an employee. Employment agreements are used to protect the organization from something the employee can do. It is a protection from the insider threat. Agreement will belong with employee signature. Employee will follow the term and condition of organization otherwise termination policies will follows on his job.

3. *Setting and monitoring of job descriptions:* ISMS should have a monitoring body who will observe the activity of employee and also it will provide the details of job description of corresponding employee.

4. *Enforcement of job rotation:* Job rotation is the concept of not having one person in one position for a long period of time. Its purpose is to prevent single employee having too much control in an organization so that no single employee can misuse the information of organization. By enforcing job rotation, one person might not have the time to build the control that could place information assets at risk.

Information Security Is a Management Function

There are many technical aspects of creating information security. But to get some fruitful results there need to develop some managerial function .It is needed to study different types of policies and processes that protect an organization from misuse of information by employee.

Information Security Management System Is a Process

An organization business environment may change with use of advance technology .So information security management system must adapt to changing technological advances with proper planning.

An effective Information security management system includes:

1. *Awareness:* Every employee of organization should be aware about new technology. Technology awareness as is recently becoming popular. It is accepted in the market or industry. Awareness of technology is useful for the success of an organization. ISMS raise awareness to lower the overall risk related to information security in the organization.

2. *Education:* Every employee of the organization should be technically educated. They should be able to handle technical risk during their risk.

3. *Training:* Information security is not an IT responsibility; In general everybody in an organization is responsible for protecting information assets and more

specifically business manager. So every member of the organization should be properly given training to handle the information security risk.

4.   *Policies and Procedures:* An information security management system (**ISMS**) is a set of **policies and procedures** for systematically managing an organization's sensitive data. The goal of ISMS is to minimize risk and ensure business continuity by pro-actively limiting the impact of a security breach.

5.   *Separation of responsibilities to control:* Every employee should given separate responsibilities to tackle the security risks. There should be a controlling body who will give separate responsibilities to each employee.

6.   *Reviews:* A committee should be form in ISMS to monitor the risk factor and further improvement in the organization.

Information Security Management System and Use of IoT

The internet of things, or IoT, is a system of interrelated computing devices, mechanical and digital machines, objects, animals or people that are provided with unique identifiers (UIDs) and the ability to transfer data over a network without requiring human-to-human or human-to-computer interaction. An organization uses IOT to operate to give better service for the customers .IoT will help an organization to make control on the activity of its every employee .It will observe the performance of every employee and will focus for making betterment for customer service. IoT enables an organization to automate its working process and reduce labor cost. It also cuts down on waste and improves service delivery, making it less expensive to manufacture and deliver goods as well as offering transparency into customer transactions. [Weber R. H.(2010)]

IoT touches every industry, including healthcare, finance, retail and manufacturing. So different kind of organization can be able to apply IoT

Generally, the working process of IoT is as follows

1.   Collect data
2.   Collect and transfer data
3.   Analyze data and take action

Benefits of IoT:

IoT will acts as tool to improve the business strategies of an organization.

The internet of things offers a number of benefits to organizations, enabling them to:

*   Monitor their overall business processes;
*   Improve the customer experience;

- Save time and money;
- Enhance employee productivity;
- Integrate and adapt business models;
- Make better business decisions; and
- Generate more revenue.
- Ability to access information from anywhere at any time on any device;
- Improved communication between connected electronic devices;
- Transferring data packets over a connected network saves time and money;
- Automating tasks helps improve the quality of a business' services and reduces the need for human intervention.

Some disadvantages of IoT include:

- As the number of connected devices increases and more information is shared between devices, the potential that a hacker could steal confidential information also increases;
- Enterprises may eventually have to deal with massive numbers -- maybe even millions -- of IoT devices and collecting and managing the data from all those devices will be challenging.
- If there's a bug in the system, it's likely that every connected device will become corrupted;
- Since there's no international standard of compatibility for IoT, it's difficult for devices from different manufacturers to communicate with each other.

The "internet of thing" (IoT) is becoming a topic of conversation both in the work place and outside of it. The IoT is a giant network of connected "things" (which also includes people). The relationship will be between people-people, people-things, and things-things. The Internet of things (IoT) is a system of interrelated computing devices, mechanical and digital machines provided with unique identifiers (UIDs) and the ability to transfer data over a network without requiring human-to-human or human-to-computer interaction. Due to interconnectivity among network, Hackers may take chances to attack on weakly secured device of the employee which he brings to the office and assuming that these devices are connected to his corporate networks. The main data at risk is the employee's own personal information because that is what is usually used in the IoT device but there are other dangers related to organization as well. To make the system secure some precaution should be taken.

Use a Separate Network

An employee can create different types of Network to do work in an organization. Employee can minimize use of their personal device in the office work. In this method, it is possible to reduce the chance of leak of information. This is one of the easiest ways to protect the main network from IoT threats.

Use Strong and Unique Passwords

Password is the simplest and most commonly used authentication schemes .Like any security measure, device related to IoT security should be started with a strong password. Employees should be encouraged to use strong and unique passwords, especially if they are connecting their devices over a Wi-Fi network. One simple way to secure the password is to store it in encrypted form .The system employs a function (say, f(x)) to encode (encrypt) the entire password. Whenever an employee/ user attempts to log into the system, the password entered by him/her is first encrypted using the same function f(x) and then matched against the stored list of encrypted password. However, care should be taken to ensure that password would never be displayed on the screen in its decrypted form.[Khurana R. (2014)]

Do Not Use Universal Plug and Play

Most of IoT devices have universal plug and play features that make the employee easier to get connected to other devices. Without complex configuration, it may be easy for different devices like routers, printers, cameras and other to discover and connect to each other. So there exist chances of attack on the system as employee devices are little to open. In convenient way employee do not use universal plug and play always .The configuration of the system should be change with passage of time.

Disable Ex-Employee Accounts

There are two types of employee in an organization (i) Working Employees and (ii) Ex-working employee. Generally an organization think about working employee but there may be chances that ex-employee can create problem to that organization this one is so obvious but somehow, companies miss it. As soon as an employee leaves, all of his or her accounts should be turned off and especially those accounts that can be accessed remotely.

Change System Passwords Upon Administrative Employee Departure

There is need to change the shared password on all infrastructure and devices when the administrative employees of organization leave.

Authorized VPN Users

A virtual private network (VPN) extends a private network across a public network and enables users to send and receive data across shared or public networks as if their computing devices were directly connected to the private network. VPN technology was developed to allow remote users and branch offices to access corporate applications and resources. There should be strong control over authorized VPN user and make audit related to security with the help of technical support of the system.

Use Privileged Access Management (PAM)

Privileged access management (PAM) refers to a segment of network security solutions that control and monitor internal employee privileged user activity. These tools address the vulnerabilities that are introduced when users with high-level permissions require access to critical systems. These tools can allow secure access to all authorized employees without forcing them to remember many passwords. They can allow for multiple people to access the same account but who accessed the system is audited. When employees leave, they can be turned off on the PAM system without causing a disruption to operations for each individual system.

Better Policies, Guidelines, and Awareness

An awareness program should be conduct among employee to learn the use of Iot. An employee should be able to do Attendance, Registering meetings & trainings, track the colleague, Identify the availability of meeting rooms or working room etc. with the help of IoT based devices.

This is the responsibility of organization to prepare better policies, guideline and conduct awareness program among employee so that they can be able to work easily and securely in an organization.

MATHEMATICAL STUDY FOR IMPLEMENTATION EMPLOYEE MANAGEMENT WITH RESPECT TO INFORMATION IN INFORMATION SECURITY MANAGEMENT SYSTEM

Data and information are two important words for an organization. The word data and information are looking similar but there is some difference among them. Data are plain facts. The word "data" is plural for "datum." When data are processed, organized, structured or presented in a given context so as to make them useful, they are called Information. Information is data that has been processed in such a way as to be meaningful to the person who receives it. It is anything that is communicated.

Table 2. Comparision between Data and Information

Data example (Data is the name given to basic facts and entities such as names and numbers.)	Information example (Information is data that has been converted into a more useful or intelligible form. Information helps human beings in their decision making process)
Weights, prices, costs, numbers of items sold, employee names, product names, addresses, tax codes, registration marks etc.	Time Table, Merit List, Report card, Headed tables, printed documents, pay slips, receipts, reports etc

For security process, information of an organization can be made chunk. Chunking breaks long string of information into units.

Let, I be information. Suppose information I can be breaks into some finite numbers of units like $I_1, I_2, \ldots, I_n$. Therefore role of an employee is more important in making information secure.

ADVANTAGES

Benefits of implementing ISMS are:

Secure Your Information

An organization's information will remain secure. The chance of security related incident with respect to information will be low. An ISMS helps protect all forms of information, including digital, paper-based, intellectual property, company secrets, data on devices and in the Cloud, hard copies and personal information.

Protects Confidentiality, Availability and Integrity of Data

Help to preserve confidentiality, integrity and availability (CIA) of data. ISMS offer a set of policies, procedures, technical and physical controls to protect the confidentiality, availability and integrity of information.

Prepare an Environment of secure Culture

ISMS work to develop the responsibility of every employee in the organization. Information security risk will be minimized by every employee. So every employee will work in a friendly environment.

Table 3. Employee working process and validation of CIA

Case Study	Employee Working Process	Validation of CIA
Dependency among employee	$I= I_1 \cup I_2 \cup I_3 \cup \ldots\ldots\cup I_n$. n is a natural number. *CASE1:* $I_1, I_2, I_3, \ldots\ldots\ldots, I_n$ and make one to one correspondence with $emp_1, emp_2, \ldots\ldots emp_n$. Now, emp_1 pass information to emp_2 emp_2 pass information to emp_3 ……………………………………………………… ……………………………………………………… $emp_{(n-1)}$ pass information to emp_n emp_n pass information o customer Here, information is breaks into sequences. .All the employees are dependent are each other. So, information cannot be leak. .	Information is protected from unauthorized employee. All the information is available to authorized employee. No unauthorized user can make any modification. Since information is breaks into units and employee is dependent on each other so no information can be leak.
Independency among employee	Suppose, Information I can be divided into n units. And each unit is supplied to each employee. Employee 1 have information=$\{I_1,I_2,\ldots\ldots,I_n\}$, Employee 2 have information=$\{I_1,I_2,\ldots\ldots,I_n\}$, …………………………………………………… …………………………………………………… Employee N has information= $\{I_1,I_2,\ldots\ldots,I_n\}$. Here each employee knows whole information and any employee can leak the information. To overcome these problems, there is need to establish a monitoring body. To make an organization secure, when an employee of an organization will login the system, it is necessary to take permission from monitoring body.	Since there is a monitoring body in this system which will observe activity each employee, so information is secured in this system.
Grouping of information into manageable units.	Let I be information and information is breaks into distinct $I_1, I_2,\ldots\ldots,I_n$. Now, each information Ii made into subsequence of I_{ik} for k=1,2,……..m, m is natural number. Employee 1 have information $I_1=\{I_{11},I_{12},\ldots\ldots,I_{1m}\}$, Employee 2 have information $I_2=\{I_{21},I_{22},\ldots\ldots,I_{2m}\}$, ………………………………………………………… ………………………………………………………… Employee N have information $I_n=\{I_{n1},I_{n2},\ldots\ldots,I_{nm}\}$, Here each employee will manage the security of information $I_1, I_2,I_3,\ldots\ldots, I_n$ by making chunking of information I_i for i=1,2,3,…..n.	Here information is made into subsequence of units. So, the full information is protected from unauthorized user/ employee.

Protect Organization Assets

The risk assessment and analysis approach of ISMS manage to protect the assets of organization.

Decision Making

With development of new technology, the management will be able to take proper decision to reduce the security risk.

Provide a Centrally Managed Framework

ISMS provide a framework for keeping your organization's information safe and managing it all in one place.

Customer Satisfaction Will Grow

The customer satisfaction for any organization is final aim. Information security management system help to satisfy customer' demand.

CONCLUSION AND FUTURE SCOPE

An organization always wants to run in secure manner and therefore it depends on its employee. An employee plays an important role in communicating information. Some information is important for organization. So there exists a scope to manage the working process of employee of organization. In this paper it is tried to develop some working methods of employee of an organization and there exist future scope to develop the risk assessment of information. There also exists scope to develop the ISMS when some employee is not working properly. There exists scope to develop effective and continual improvement process in employee management. There exists scope to develop the importance of human resources and find the optimal methods to minimise the risk factor in an organization. With Internet of Things, we already have another wave of technology. IoT is going to play a significant impact on the working methods of employee and organization. Employees can use IoT devices in a system in such a way that the system will remain secure and also they become more efficient in their workplaces too.

REFERENCES

Al-Dhahri, S., Al-Sarti, M., & Aziz, A. A. (2017). Information Security Management System. *International Journal of Computer Applications, 158*(7), 29-33.

Amarachi, A. A., Okolie, S. O., & Ajaegbu, C. (2013). Information Security Management System: Emerging Issues and Prospect. *IOSR Journal of Computer Engineering, 12*(3), 96-102.

Authorization (n.d.)The Economic Times. https://economictimes.indiatimes.com/definition/authorization

Beckers, K. (2014). Goal-based establishment of an information security management system compliant to ISO 27001. *Theory and Practice of Computer, 8327*, 102–113. doi:10.1007/978-3-319-04298-5_10

Campbell, T. (2016). Evolution of a Profession. In Practical Information Security Management: A Complete Guide to Planning and Implementation. APress.

Deo, N. (2003). *Graph Theory with application to Engineering and Computer Science*. Prentice Hall of India Private Limited.

Distributed information security management model (DISMM). (2017, November 7). Identity Management Institute®.https://www.identitymanagementinstitute.org/distributed-information-security-management-model-dismm/

Employee management. (n.d.). BambooHR. https://www.bamboohr.com/hr-glossary/employee-management/

Employment policies and practices I CISSP security management and practices I Pearson IT certification. (n.d.). Pearson IT Certification: Videos, flash cards, simulations, books, eBooks, and practice tests for Cisco, CompTIA, and Microsoft exams.http://www.pearsonitcertification.com/articles/article.aspx?p=30287&seqNum=10

Hong, K.-S., Chi, Y.-P., Chao, L. R., & Tang, J.-H. (2003). An integrated system theory of information security management. *Information Management & Computer Security, 11*(5), 243–248. doi:10.1108/09685220310500153

Humphreys, E. (2008). Information security management standards: Compliance, governance and risk management. *Information Security Technical Report, 13*(4), 247–255. doi:10.1016/j.istr.2008.10.010

Information security management. (2007, May 12). Wikipedia, the free encyclopedia. Retrieved June 3, 2020, from https://en.wikipedia.org/wiki/Information_security_management

Information security management system. (2018, April 19). Quality Management System, ISO Certification Bodies In India.https://www.irqs.co.in/it-standards/information-security-management-system

Internet of things (IoT) security: 9 ways you can help protect yourself. (n.d.). Official Site | Norton™ - Antivirus & Anti-Malware Software. https://us.norton.com/internetsecurity-iot-securing-the-internet-of-things.html

Iqbal, Olaleye, & Bayoumi. (2016). A Review on Internet of Things (Iot): Security and Privacy Requirements and the Solution Approaches. *Global Journal of Computer Science and Technology, 16*(7).

ISMS - Security and value of information - TÜV TRUST IT GmbH Unternehmensgruppe TÜV Austria. (2015, August 31). TÜV TRUST IT GmbH Unternehmensgruppe TÜV AUSTRIA. https://it-tuv.com/en/leistungen/security-and-value-of-information/

Khurana, R. (2014). *Operating System*. Vikash Publishing House Pvt. Ltd.

Mapa, S. K. (1998). *Real Analysis*. Asoke Prakasan.

Mapa, S. K. (2000)., Higher Algebra. Sarat Book Distribution.

Nagpal, D. P. (2014). *Data Communications and Networking*. S. Chand & Company Pvt. Ltd.

Park, C.S., Jang, S.S., & Park, Y.T. (2010). A Study of Effect of Information Security Management System Certification on Organization Performance. *International Journal of Computer Science and Network Security, 10*(3).

Park & Lee. (2014). Advanced Approach to Information Security Management System Model for Industrial Control System. *E-Scientific World Journal*. doi:10.1155/2014/348305

Peltier, T. R. (2005). *Information Security Policies, Procedures and Standards, Guidelines for Effective Information Security Management*. CRC Press.

Ponnusamy, S. (2002). *Foundation of Functional Analysis*. Narosa Publishing House.

Reid, R. C., & Floyd, S. A. (2001). Extending the risk analysis model to include market-insurance. *Computers & Security, 20*(4), 331–339. doi:10.1016/S0167-4048(01)00411-4

Stewart, H., & Jürjens, J. (2017). Information security management and the human aspect in organizations. *Information and Computer Security*.

Suoa, H., Wana, J., Zoua, C., & Liua, J. (2012). Security in the Internet of Things: A Review. *International Conference on Computer Science and Electronics Engineering*, 648-651. 10.1109/ICCSEE.2012.373

Thakur, D. (n.d.). What do you understand by information? What are the characteristics of information. Computer Notes. http://ecomputernotes.com/mis/what-is-mis/what-do-you-understand-by-information-what-are-the-characteristics-of-information

Thakur, D. (n.d.). What is the difference between data and information? Computer Notes. http://ecomputernotes.com/fundamental/information-technology/what-do-you-mean-by-data-and-information

The benefits of implementing an ISMS (Information security management system) | IT governance UK. (n.d.). IT Governance - Governance, Risk Management and Compliance for Information Technology. https://www.itgovernance.co.uk/isms-benefits

Uranus. (2017). A Survey: Information Security Management System. *Journal of Analog and Digital Devices, 2*(3).

Weber, R. H. (2010). Internet of things – new security and privacy challenges. *Computer Law & Security Review, 26*(1), 23–30. doi:10.1016/j.clsr.2009.11.008

What is an information security management system? (n.d.). ISO Registration – Perry Johnson Registrars — ISO Registration Company.http://www.pjr.com/standards/iso-27001/information-security-management-system

What is information security management system (ISMS)? - Definition from WhatIs. com. (2011, January 25). WhatIs.com.https://whatis.techtarget.com/definition/information-security-management-system-ISMS

Zhang, Z. K., Cho, M. C. Y., Wang, C.W., Hsu, C.W., Chen, C.K., & Shieh, S. (2014). IoT Security: Ongoing Challenges and Research Opportunities. *IEEE 7th International Conference on Service-Oriented Computing and Applications.* 10.1109/SOCA.2014.58

Zhao, K., & Ge, L. (2013). A survey on the internet of things security. *Int'l Conf. on Computational Intelligence and Security (CIS),* 663-667.

Chapter 11
Vulnerabilities of Smart Homes

Suchandra Datta
St. Xavier's College, Kolkata, India

ABSTRACT

The concept of internet of things involves the establishment of ubiquitous computing devices that seamlessly integrate with our living environments, being interconnected via networks to gather information about the surroundings so as to enable the devices to interact with the ambient environment in favorable ways. With the growth of this concept and subsequent development of smart homes, it is to be borne in mind that security is of the utmost importance in such scenarios. In this chapter, the authors highlight the various vulnerabilities prevalent in smart homes, which might be exploited by unscrupulous individuals to launch cyberattacks.

INTRODUCTION

In the words of the man who is considered to be the father of ubiquitous computing, *"The most profound technologies are those that disappear. They weave themselves into the fabric of everyday life until they are indistinguishable from it."* Although computers and such-like devices are an integral part of different domains such as education, health, corporate offices these devices largely exist in a world of their own without being interweaved with our own. This perceptible difference between machines and our environment must cease to exist to achieve true ubiquitous computing(Mark Weiser, 1991). Devices will be embedded discreetly in different places which will interface with individuals through means other than a standard graphical set-up, for example heat sensors will automatically increase the rotational speed of a fan when the temperature rises. Construction of homes rich with sensors, which provide increased convenience to the inmates, where the devices are

DOI: 10.4018/978-1-7998-2444-2.ch011

connected via the internet to share, process and automate actions based on the data gathered could be a simplified definition for a smart home. X10 is a communication protocol for smart homes which involves radio frequency bursts of 120kHz which enables a transmitter to turn off the lights in a room when the room is empty for a specified period of time. X10 suffers from susceptibility to noise and inability to send information to a central computer. Soon smart home technology saw the introduction of wireless signals along with radio waves. To counter the problems of X10, Zigbee and Z-Wave were developed. WSN or wireless sensor networks reduce the complexity of installation of sensors, controllers and actuators minimizing cost of production(Ghayvat, H., Mukhopadhyay, S., Gui, X., & Suryadevara, N., 2015). WSN's offer a powerful way to monitor the different activities of the inhabitants. The lights in a room can regulate intensity with respect to sunlight and presence of occupants. Thermostats like Nest from Nest Labs Inc. are complete with integrated WiFi, allowing users to schedule, monitor and remotely control home temperatures. They learn occupant's behavior to automatically modify settings to provide residents with maximum comfort and efficiency. Surveillance is ensured via smart security cameras, smart locks and garage-door openers, motion sensors. Life can definitely be made easier by coffee makers that brew as soon as the alarm rings or at specified times, refrigerators that keep track of food items sending a signal to the occupants or ordering the items when it is consumed, keep track of expiration dates. System monitors may sense a surge and turn off electric appliances or sense leaking pipes, turn off the water supply in that part to avoid a disaster. A new technology which can be implemented involves usage of light bulbs to transmit information or provide access to internet connectivity, much like WiFi. Termed LiFi or light fidelity, it is a novel way of providing an eco-friendly alternative to radio waves based transmission; it is faster and only suffers from the condition that there must be an unhindered path between the light bulb and the device seeking connectivity. Although it does spell wonders for care of the elderly and handicapped, it opens up lots of avenues which can be investigated for a possible attack. The components will be controlled by some central controller, once it is breached, an attacker gets control over the security system disabling alarms, locking doors, disconnecting surveillance cameras. Connection to a network always introduces the possibility of attacks hence having a fail-safe security system for smart homes are of the utmost importance. This chapter aims to highlight the various vulnerabilities prevalent in modern day smart homes, with emphasis on the technology which might be used to exploit the latter. A comprehensive coverage of security issues include man in the middle attacks, device hijacking, data and identity theft, distributed denial of service attacks and its types, permanent denial of service attacks. An attempt is made to highlight some possible solutions of the same including encryption, security integrated within the hardware, security lifecycle management and the like.

TRENDING CHALLENGES

1. Man-In-The-Middle Attacks

As the name suggests, the attacker manages to intercept communication information between two authorized devices and to each device, pretends to be the other party in the communication, thereby being able to transmit signals which are treated to be valid even though it was never generated by any authorized source. Put simply, the attacker poses as the sender on both sides of the communication. Man in the middle attacks are one of the oldest forms of cyber attack. Computer scientists have been looking at ways to prevent threat actors tampering or eavesdropping on communications since the early 1980s.

Man in the middle attacks consists of sitting between the connection of two parties and either observing or manipulating traffic. This could be through interfering with legitimate networks or creating fake networks that the attacker controls. Compromised traffic is then stripped of any encryption in order to steal, change or reroute that traffic to the attacker's destination of choice (such as a phishing log-in site). Because attackers may be silently observing or re-encrypting intercepted traffic to its intended source once recorded or edited, it can be a difficult attack to spot.

Man in the middle attacks encompasses a broad range of techniques and potential outcomes, depending on the target and the goal. For example, in SSL stripping, attackers establish an HTTPS connection between themselves and the server, but with an unsecured HTTP connection with the user, which means information is sent in plain text without encryption. Evil Twin attacks mirror legitimate Wi-Fi access points but are entirely controlled by malicious actors, who can now monitor, collect or manipulate all information the user sends.

With respect to a smart home, a malicious entity may gain access to the temperature sensors of a home, causing it to heat up or more dangerous, turn off in severe winters with aged or disabled people in the house who would not be able to troubleshoot the problem on their own, if at all. Thermostats thrive on firmware updates which are brought about by cloud computing. The hacker can extract the firmware from one device, reverse-engineer it, send it back via HTTP to get control over the USB port. In 2016, an incident occurred in Lappeenranta, Finland where the hot water system and the central heating was shut down by attackers, perpetrating a reboot and hang in an endless loop with the temperature at that time being a miserable 20 degrees Fahrenheit. Man in the middle attacks maybe conducted in varied ways like DNS spoofing, SSL hijacking, side-jacking, evil twin, sniffing, ARP cache poisoning(Zoran Cekerevac, Zdenek Dvorak, Ludmila Prigoda, Petar Cekerevac, 2019). Cloud computing services typically store a session token after the first authentication which the attacker tries to access(Man in the cloud).

2. Data and Identity Theft

Data generated by unprotected wearables and smart appliances provide cyber attackers with an ample amount of targeted personal information that can potentially be exploited for fraudulent transactions and identify theft. The rush to bring products to market often results in compromising security. The WiFi network as a consequence maybe hacked through one of the connected devices like a smartphone or a personal health tracker. Fitness trackers offer a wealth of unique, sensitive data such as health statistics, workout routines, routes taken, susceptibility to certain health conditions. Once the data gets collected, fake identities are set-up to perpetrate crimes in the name of the lawful owner of the identity. Often the data or identity theft is masked by usage of everyday appliances like smart televisions, bulbs, security cameras, refrigerators coming together in a distributed denial of service attack which acts like an effective red herring from the greater calamity of identity theft. Identity is defined as the characteristics determining who or what a person or thing is. Identity theft is defined as someone's action of using any sort of an individual's(or a corporation's) private information with fraudulent intention mainly for financial gain. Identity fraud is the subsequent crime when a false identity is used in order to gain goods, services benefits or avoid obligations(Stilianos Vidalis, 2014). Common ways employed for this are IP spoofing and ARP spoofing. In the former, one device impersonates another using the IP address as the means of the impersonation. In the latter, the same principle is applied with the IP being replaced by the MAC address of the device. IP address spoofing, or IP spoofing, is the forging of a source IP address field in IP packets with the purpose of concealing the identity of the sender or impersonating another computing system. Fundamentally, source IP spoofing is possible because Internet global routing is based on the destination IP address. Or, more precisely, an Internet router with a default configuration (i.e. no special policy applied, like reverse path filtering) forwards packets from one interface to another looking up only the destination IP address. An application with sufficient privileges can modify the source IP address field of an IP packet to any syntactically correct value, and in most cases the packet will be sent through the network interface and in many cases will reach the destination. Of course, an incorrect source IP address may hinder normal operation of communications: responses from the destination application or intermediary nodes (e.g. ICMP responses) will not reach the sender. But attacks mounted using the spoofing technique do not rely on properly set up communication flows. On the contrary, they abuse this feature, directing traffic flow of responses to the target identified by the forged source IP address.

ARP Spoofing or ARP Poisoning has been used by hackers for decades to attack private networks. It is a form of network tapping that allows a malicious user to gain access to your local area network by imitating the router. This is a common vector for man in the middle (MITM) attacks. Every time we allow a new IoT device to enter the private network, or put our own hardware on somebody else's private network, we are susceptible to this attack. The only way to be protected on any network (including our own) is with encryption - the primary tool of a Virtual Private Network (VPN).

Network tapping hardware is everywhere. By definition, any IoT device is capable of compromising and snooping on the network if maliciously used. Any device that has a wireless chip can be used to find the location of wireless networks for future attack. The act of searching for wireless networks while we drive around is called "Wardriving." Wardriving devices can discover and remember the location of open wireless networks and nowadays can even illegally brute force access to the network password. Network tapping software is often used in conjunction with existing hardware or even specially designed network tapping hardware. Since its invention as "wardialing" decades ago, wardriving has become easier than ever as technology has advanced.

Global account director at IDT 311 a provider of identity theft protection and recovery services had this to say about the underlying mechanism, "What happens is the thieves exploit the Universal Plug and Play Protocol to gain access to one of the devices. Once they get in, they can access other devices through unsecure WiFi connections or a physical connection to another device such as a wearable device that's plugged into a laptop to charge. Each device may store different personal information. Once it is all aggregated, it could be enough to steal an identity."

3. Device Hijacking

The attacker hijacks and effectively assumes control of a device. These attacks are quite difficult to detect because the attacker does not change the basic functionality of the device. Moreover, it only takes one device to potentially re-infect all smart devices in the home. For example, an attacker who initially compromises a thermostat can theoretically gain access to an entire network and remotely unlock a door or change the keypad PIN code to restrict entry. Seven out of ten of the most commonly used Internet of Things (IoT) devices have "serious vulnerabilities", according to tech company Hewlett-Packard (HP). Tests revealed 250 flaws across the devices, including privacy concerns in eight cases, weak password policies in the same number, and a lack of transport encryption in seven cases. Daniel Miessler, practice principal at HP, said: "The current state of Internet of Things security seems to take all the vulnerabilities from existing spaces – network security, application security, mobile security and Internet-connected devices – and combine them into a new, even more insecure space, which is troubling." Six of the devices had user interfaces that concerned the company, and the same number had troubling software or firmware, including unencrypted updating protocols (Retrieved from https://www.cbronline.com/news/security/serious-vulnerabilities-on-the-internet-of-things-4330340 Access Time: 11.06.2019 at 12:47pm)

Smart hubs are a common part of any smart home, it is essentially the brain of the home, using dedicated protocols to communicate with each of the myriad devices and processing the data received. To control the hub using the Web portal, the user sends a synchronization command from the Web interface to the hub, a configuration file being assigned to a hub under a serial number. The file is sent over HTTP(not the secure HTTPS) with the serial number the only key used to identify the user. If the attacker knows the serial number, they could send a custom configuration file to the portal. Once the login and password information are extracted from the configuration file(depends on how good the encryption is but can be typically brute-forced), the attacker can wreck mayhem in the house. This technique of exploiting vulnerabilities to hijack the smart home has been published by Kaspersky(Retrieved from https://www.kaspersky.com/blog/mwc2018-insecure-iot/21343/ Access Time: 11.06.2019 at 01:10pm). Security critical devices like doorbells, cameras, baby monitors are not difficult to hack(Shachar Siboni, Vinay Sachidananda, Yair Meidan, Michael Bohadana, Yael Mathov, Suhas Bhairav, Asaf Shabtai, and Yuval Elovici, 2019). These are mass manufactured hence once a vulnerability is detected, it can be used against all individuals using that same device. The devices tested had passwords embedded to access settings but they were not always secure. Passwords such as 1234 were present which was easy to crack whilst the most difficult device, namely a baby monitor took only two days. Devices also store WiFi passwords so if it is compromised, chances are that the hacker could also get hold of the WiFi password and monitor the network's activity. This includes all online bank transactions, account information and the such-like sensitive information. The phantom device attack is an interesting thing to note with respect to this topic(Neal, Dave, 2016). Cloud based design and manufacturing services play an integral part in the set-up and smooth functioning of smart homes. Three entities need to interact to make this work, the CBDM service(the cloud), mobile app and smart home devices. The app provides users with an interface for initial set-up and subsequent monitoring of the devices. The latter uses the WiFi credentials to access the Internet and obtains the credential identification from the IoT cloud. It establishes a connection with the IoT cloud to routinely report its statuses and execute the remote control commands. In this scenario, enter the phantom device, which is simply a program that mimics a real device. CBDM services do not perform sufficient authorization checks for device side requests, supplying service simply by accepting sensitive commands without proper permission checking. Using these flaws, a phantom device can be leveraged that intervenes in the normal interaction of legitimate smart home devices, leading to unexpected state changes.

4. Distributed Denial of Service (DDoS)

A denial-of-service attack (DoS attack) attempts to render a machine or network resource unavailable to its intended users by temporarily or indefinitely disrupting services of a host connected to the Internet. In the case of a distributed denial-of-service attack (DDoS), incoming traffic flooding a target originates from multiple sources, making it difficult to stop the cyber offensive by simply blocking a single source. In fact, DDoS attacks doubled from 3% to 6% in 2016, primarily due to the lack of security in IoT devices. This isn't surprising, especially as a single compromised smart sensor on a network can infect similar devices running the same software. These infected devices are then forced to join vast botnet armies that execute crippling DDoS attacks. With home automation and surveillance, open IP addresses become the biggest challenge to overcome. The recent attacks from IoT devices on the DNS provider in the USA and the attack on the Internet in Libera were manifested by IoT unsecure IoT devices. How does these devices attack the global network of networks which has become the information super highway of the times and any delay or disturbance to the Internet introduces, among other things, financial loss and crippling inconvenience. Once a device is installed with an open IP address, it announces its presence to potential hackers by means of broadcasting its IP address. The device to be compromised is suppose a webcam. The address is known which means access to the device is also available. Hackers can insinuate themselves to the administration page of the device and try to login using standard usernames and passwords. The attackers on Dyn and Liberia used the Mirai toolkit(Neal, Dave, 2016) which tracks down devices with open IP addresses, finds the device type, tried standard username and password combinations and installs a service which can be remotely controlled, for instance a request to a specific web page. This service once installed on a substantially large number of devices, the hacker can make all of them access the web page at the same time hence causing a server crash. The attack on Dyn was excruciatingly successful since it interfered with translation of web addresses like www.google.com. The attack had a data rate of 1.2Tbps which the servers could not handle(Roger Hallman, Josiah Bryan, Geancarlo Palavicini, Joseph Divita and Jose Romero-Mariona, 2017). The IoT ecosystem has been the stage for several DDoS attacks which can be of several types like bandwidth depletion DDoS attacks which as the name suggests eats up the available range of frequencies allowed for transmission to the point that users are unable to use the system; flood attacks on the other hand involve a conscripted botnet army sending huge volumes of traffic to overwhelm the target network, it could be UDP packets in huge numbers of the Ping Of Death or ICMP flood attacks where the ping utility is used to create packets of size more than 65.536 bytes which will cause the victim network to crash or at least hang. Amplification attacks involve sending messages to a broadcast IP address, like sending packets to a subnet of networks from victim computer which must receive replies from all the other computers receiving the message(Roger Hallman, Josiah Bryan, Geancarlo Palavicini, Joseph Divita and Jose Romero-Mariona, 2017). Whilst discussing DDoS with respect to IoT devices and smart homes in particular, it will be inappropriate not to mention the 8 families of IoT malware which has been discovered(Internet Security Threat Report, Symantec, Volume 21 April 2016)

- Linux.Aidra spreads thpugh TCP looking for common username and password combinations to login to other devices. A backdoor is opened on the device and the infected device is added to the botnet army that employs UDP, TCP packet sor DNS requests to flood the victim network.
- XOR.DDos employs encryption to communicate with servers and in the malware code with the primary intention of opening a backdoor in the device to gegenrate a DDoS attack.
- Zollard is a worm which exploits PHP vulnerabilities to open a backdoor on TCP port to allow remote command execution.
- LizardStresser scans public IP's for telnet services, using the same tactics as Linux.Aidra to logon and report back to server for further instructions.
- Bashlite-infected devices enter the botnet army for DDoS attacks of EDP and TCP floods. Brute forcing password username combinations is also present and can even collect information from the CPU of infected devices.
- AES.DDoS uses the AES algorithm to encrypt communication with its C&C server.
- The Tsunami Trojan is used to launch DDoS attacks by modifying files such that it runs every time a user logs into a device or a device boots up. Tsunami will kill processes, download and execute various files, spoof IP addresses of the infected device making it quite a terror.
- PNScan is a Trojan that scans a networks segment for devices with an open port 22 and tries to brute force a log-in. It lacks botnet functionalities but maybe said to make up for that by downloading botnet malware like Tsunami.

The Internet of Things offers a wide variety of smart devices – all of which face the difficulty of securing overall privacy. As the devices are all so different their heterogenic nature is often used as an excuse by manufactures and owners alike to skip sufficient security controls. A DDoS attack means that it is administered with the same target from different sources – and here the Internet of Things must feel for hackers a bit like a toyshop would to children: millions of devices, all too often unprotected and unmonitored for long periods of time. The scale in which these attacks are now possible is rising tremendously with the advancement of the

Internet of Things. Hence it doesn't come as a big surprise that Akamai researchers say that nearly 21% of DDoS attacks now result from Internet of Things devices. It is predicted this will only keep increasing over the next few years. In the past DDoS attacks were limited to computers and internet connected machines, usually with a reasonable level of protection. The Internet of Things opens up a large variety of devices to potential attacks – from printers, to cameras, fridges, thermostats, sensors and routers to name a few. Not only is there a sheer amount of these devices, but they are often protected with very limited security, if any at all. It is all too easy to exploit those weaknesses and launch large-scale attacks without the knowledge of the owner. However, not only can connected devices be used for attacks, they can also become the target of said attacks. While a connected fridge that stops working for a while might be very unfortunate for the owner, think about the devices that have a huge impact on many people's lives, for example: control valves at power plants, sensors used in weather observations, door locks in prisons or traffic signals in called smart-cities.

5. Permanent Denial of Service (PDoS)

Permanent denial-of-service attacks (PDoS), also known as phlashing, is an attack that damages the device so badly that it requires replacement or reinstallation of hardware. BrickerBot, coded to exploit hard-coded passwords in IoT devices and cause permanent denial of service, is one such example. Another example could see fake data fed to thermostats in an attempt to cause irreparable damage via extreme overheating.

PDoS attacks can be carried out by uploading a corrupted BIOS to a device, or via remote administration of the management interface in general. One method is to exploit vulnerabilities to replace a device's basic software with a corrupt firmware image. This method is what is known as phlashing. PDoS attacks are also conducted physically. For instance, an article on Help Net Securityfeatured a USB stick referred to as USB Killer 2.0. This malicious tool can be plugged into any device that has a USB host interface, including routers, servers and modems. The USB stick uses a voltage converter to charge the device's capacitors to 220V and releases a negative electric surge into the USB port. These surges continue until the device can no longer draw power, and certain components must be replaced before the device can be operable again. There is a growing concern in the industry about the ability to use malware and bots to remotely overheat devices, damaging them and even setting them on fire.

An attacker could potentially cost a company millions by carrying out a PDoS attack to crash a few routers or servers, making their services unavailable until those devices could be repaired or replaced.

Experts have argued that PDoS attacks won't become common because they wouldn't be as lucrative for cyber criminals as other types of attacks. The attacks are irreversible, and so attackers could not demand a sum of money to stop the attack. The only way to make money would be to threaten a PDoS attack in the hopes an individual or organization would pay up to prevent it.

However, the recent global Petya attack proves that hackers can be motivated to conduct widespread attacks solely for the purpose of wreaking havoc, not for financial gain. Experts determined the Petya virus to be a wiper and not true ransomware. Victims were unable to get their files back, whether they paid the ransom or not. Experts say the ransom demand was likely a distraction to help cover the attackers.

Another reason to implement PDoS attacks is they could save attackers time and resources compared to the more common DDoS attacks. During a DDoS attack, attackers must continue to engage for as long as they want the attack to persist.

Lastly, the sheer number of devices connected to the Internet of Things provides more opportunity for these types of attacks with greater financial consequences.

PROPOSED METHODS

1. Secure Boot

Secure boot utilizes cryptographic code signing techniques, ensuring that a device only executes code generated by the device OEM or another trusted party. Use of secure boot technology prevents hackers from replacing firmware with malicious versions, thereby preventing attacks.

Implementing a secure boot process is critical to device integrity throughout its lifecycle for the simple reason that a compromised boot process allows hackers to inject malware or entirely replace firmware, leaving the entirety of a connected system vulnerable. A secure boot process also makes other security features possible by providing a necessary degree of trust. Indeed, a secure boot process is critical to extending a root of trust throughout an entire system. At its simplest, a secure boot process prevents the execution of unauthorized code at the time of device power up, and prevents the exposure of embedded boot code and software IP. A secure boot process can be accomplished in many different ways, including using digitally signed binaries, secure and trusted boot loaders, boot file encryption, and security microprocessors.

While most secure boot claims center around digitally signed boot files, unless those signatures are verifiable using some sort of an immutable root of trust, however, it is not secure. Here we do not intended to dive into the mechanics of secure boot, but rather layout the considerations that device designers must account for when implementing a secure boot process. These include:

- Protecting IP – Secure boot processes that do not protect a company's intellectual property (code) offer no real business benefit. If properly implemented, however, software IP such as proprietary algorithms can be protected from hackers.
- Trusted remediation – The ability to safely remediate in case of device failure or compromise is a critical ability that relies on having a secure boot process that checks the validity of the firmware image being booted with a root of trust.
- Secure firmware update – Validating incoming payloads intended to replace existing firmware images is critical to maintaining device integrity throughout the system lifecycle. The source of the payload and the payload itself must be validated prior to being applied, and with a properly implemented secure boot process, failure to validate results in a safe rollback to a known verified image.
- Secure connectivity to cloud resources – A secure boot process ensures that the device is authenticated with the cloud each time it attempts a connection through the use of embedded keys and certificates.

To boot securely a device must go through a series of steps to ensure the installation is as expected in order for the device to run correctly and securely. These steps could be along the lines of:

- Verify the initial bootloader executable is genuine and not been tampered with
- Run bootloader executable, which then…
- Checks the required sub-systems exist and function correctly. If OK then…
- Initiate basic logging
- Check for the existence of a new firmware update. If present, verify it is genuine, update the system to use the new firmware and the restart the system
- Verify all external services such as power supply, DNS, NTP etc. are operating correctly
- Verify the application code and run it if OK

The first stage, verifying that the bootloader is genuine and not been tampered with, is crucial. Only when this has been done can the rest of the boot process be assured. Verifying a bootloader executable file is usually done using public/private keys, more about which can be found in the IoTSF article on Encryption and online.

In essence, the manufacturer stores their private key very securely and never reveals it to anyone. When a device is manufactured, the public key associated with the private key is placed in secure storage on the device. The bootloader code is developed using a secure development process and then a cryptographic hash of it is digitally signed with the manufacturer's private key. Whenever bootloader firmware is to be installed on the device, the hash signature is checked against the embedded public key on the device to confirm that it is a genuine hash value from that manufacturer. The firmware code is then hashed again and compared with the signed hash. If this matches (which indicates the firmware code hasn't been altered), only then will the new firmware get installed.

Thereafter, whenever the device boots, the installed bootloader is again verified before being allowed to run. Cryptographic functions for these purposes and storage of keys can be provided by dedicated chips or modules such a Secure Access Modules (SAM) or Trusted Platform Modules (TPM).

The bootloader code knows which sub-systems to expect on the device so checks they exist and are functional. It can also check that there are no unexpected subsystems present.

If all is well then basic logging may begin, recording various start-up parameters and any issues found.

At some point the boot process may well need to check if there is an update to install, so will go away and verify new software as described before and possibly install and reboot, so the process starts again.

There may be other checks to ensure vital services are in place, possibly with security checks to ensure these services are indeed what they're expected to be.

If everything has been checked successfully up to this point, then now may be the time to run the device's functional applications. Again the signed application code can be verified against the embedded public key to ensure it is genuine. If that checks out OK then the applications can be started.

So every start-up stage is run only after the previous stage has been verified for authenticity and started successfully, with the whole process initiated by trusted bootloader code. ARM's TrustZone technology is particularly well suited to support a secure boot process. If an application uses a device equipped with ARM TrustZone, from the recently released Cortex-M23 and -M33 microcontrollers (MCUs) through Cortex-A-class applications processors, the device contains two operating systems (OSs) – a Trusted Execution Environment (TEE), which is a secure OS that manages access to a secure enclave of the device, as well as a rich OS or rich execution environment (REE) that executes primary applications.

The TEE plays a critical role in the secure boot process in that the TEE boots after the initial ROM boot but before the REE. Indeed, the TEE can boot the REE as part of the boot sequence, and doing so allows the REE image to be verified so that remedial action can be taken, if necessary.

2. Mutual Authentication

Every time a smart home device connects to the network it should be authenticated prior to receiving or transmitting data. This ensures that the data originates from a legitimate device and not a fraudulent source. Cryptographic algorithms involving symmetric keys or asymmetric keys can be utilized for two-way authentication. This ensures that the data originates from a legitimate device and not a fraudulent source. Cryptographic algorithms involving symmetric keys or asymmetric keys can be utilized for two-way authentication. For example, the Secure Hash Algorithm (SHA-x) can be used for symmetric keys and the Elliptic Curve Digital Signature Algorithm (ECDSA) for asymmetric keys. Despite growing awareness of the need for security, developers too often find themselves taking shortcuts in security for connecting IoT devices to the cloud. In many cases, the conflicts between the complexity of suitable security mechanisms, the limited memory and processing resources available in tiny battery powered IoT devices, and the need to ship product, seem insurmountable. To address these problems and simplify implementation of security features in IoT devices, Microchip Technology and Google collaborated to create an approach that combines Microchip's secure hardware capabilities with a simple data structure called a JSON Web Token (JWT). The result is an easy method for ensuring mutual authentication between IoT devices and Google Cloud IoT Core services(Retrieved from https://www.digikey.in/en/articles/techzone/2019/jan/an-easier-solution-for-securely-connecting-iot-devices-to-the-cloud Access Time: 13.06.2019 at 10:03pm). Specialized security devices such Microchip Technology's CryptoMemory and CryptoAuthentication ICs feature hardware-based mechanisms to protect private keys and other secret data. Integrated in these devices, an EEPROM array provides secure storage that can only be reached through cryptographically secure mechanisms accessed through the device's SPI or I²C serial interface (shown below). As a result, these devices provide a simple method to add secure storage and other security features to any IoT device design.

Microchip CryptoAuthentication devices offer hardware-based ultra secure key storage to ensure that a product with the consumables it uses, firmware it runs, accessories that supports it, and the network nodes it connects to are not cloned, counterfeited, or tampered with. Keeping products genuine helps maintaining a customer revenue flow by ensuring that only legitimate products can work with the host system. Microchip offers the industry's widest selection of authentication devices featuring hardware-based root of trust storage and cryptographic countermeasures that can fight off even the most aggressive attacks. Because attackers cannot see secret keys that are stored in protected hardware, they cannot attack.

JSON Web Token (JWT) is an open standard (RFC 7519) that defines a compact and self-contained way for securely transmitting information between parties as a JSON object. This information can be verified and trusted because it is digitally signed. JWTs can be signed using a secret (with the **HMAC** algorithm) or a public/ private key pair using **RSA** or **ECDSA**.

Although JWTs can be encrypted to also provide secrecy between parties, we will focus on *signed* tokens. Signed tokens can verify the *integrity* of the claims contained within it, while encrypted tokens *hide* those claims from other parties. When tokens are signed using public/private key pairs, the signature also certifies that only the party holding the private key is the one that signed it(Retrieved from https://jwt.io/introduction/ Access Time: 13.06.2019 at 10:47pm). The JSON web token consists of three parts separated by dots which are namely, header, payload and signature. The header consists of 2 parts, the type of the token which is JWT and the signing algorithm being used such as HMAC SHA256 or RSA. For instance, { "alg": "HS256", "typ": "JWT" } means JSON is Base64Url encoded to form the first part of the JWT. The payload contains the claims which are statements about an entity and additional data. There are three types of claims: registered, public and private. Registered claims are predefined claims which are not compulsory but recommended to provide a set of useful, interoperable claims. Public claims are defined at will but to avoid collisions they should be defined in the IANA JSON web token registry or be defined as a URL that contains a collision resistant namespace. Private claims are the custom claims created to share information between parties that agree on using them and are neither registered or public claims. Finally to create the signature, the encoded header, payload, secret and algorithm specified is taken and signed. The signature is used to verify the message was not changed along the way. In case of tokens signed with private key, it can also verify that the sender of the JWT is indeed who he claims to be or establishment of proof of identity. JWT are better than Simple web tokens(SWT) or Security Assertion Markup Language Tokens(SAML). JSON is less verbose than XML hence gets encoded to a smaller size so more compact than SAML. SWT can only be symmetrically signed by a shared secret using the HMAC algorithm. However, JWT and SAML tokens use public/private key pair in the form of a X.509 certificate for signing. Signing XML with XML Digital signature without introducing obscure security holes is very difficult compared to the simplicity of signing JSON. JSON parsers are common in programming languages as they map directly to objects. XML does not have a natural document to object mapping which makes JWT easier to work with than SAML assertions.

Hardware security primitives like PUFs can be used for securing IoT systems(Muhammad Naveed Aman, Kee Chaing Chua, and Biplab Sikdar, 2018). OTP based authentication needs multiple iterations and the requirement of computing OTP using public or private keys increases computational complexity. Group authentication protocol and sharing of keys amongst multiple nodes puts all of them at risk even if only one is compromised. Certificate-based authentication suffers from the drawback that the credential information is stored in the edge node, inviting cloning attacks. A PUF is regarded as a distinguishing feature of a device like the biometric features of humans. It cannot be reproduced using crytopgraphic primitives, it is extremely hard to produce a physical clone of a PUF. It is a physical unclonable function that maps a set of challenges to a set of responses based on an intractably complex physical system(G. E. Suh, and S. Devadas, 2007).

3. Secure Communication (Encryption)

Protecting data in transit between a device and its service infrastructure (the cloud). Encryption ensures that only those with a secret decryption key can access transmitted data. For example, a smart thermostat that sends usage data to the service operator must be able to protect information from digital eavesdropping. The most common encryption methods are Data Encryption Standard(DES), TripleDES, RSA, Advanced Encryption Standard(AES) which is the trusted US government standard and Twofish. Protecting smart home devices does not entail usage of any one single solution as one needs to take into consideration varied control platforms, servers, connectivity domains and protocols. IoT devices employ machine learning to generate huge datasets and inferences from it which needs to be encrypted else anyone who has access to it can try to take advantage of it. Different encryption algorithms have been used for the purpose of securing smart homes. These include models based on SDN(Software defined networking) with its ability to extend their security area to access the network(F. Olivier, G. Carlos, N. Florent, 2015). Hybrid encryption has been proposed where the home resident has a public key that is generated by AES(Amirhossein Safi, 2017). The messages are encrypted by asymmetric encryption and sent to receptors which are the devices in the smart home like refrigerator, doors and the like. Each receptor also possesses their own private key that the home resident is unaware of. By combining the algorithms of AES and NTRU encryption and decryption can be done much faster with less memory requirements. Hybrid models combining AES and ECC algorithms have also been applied to the domain of smart home security(M. Xin, 2015). ECC or elliptic curve cryptography is a public key encryption technique based on elliptic curves that create smaller, faster cryptographic keys. Tradional method of key generation relies on the fact that prime numbers are the basic building blocks of all numbers and they are irregular or totally random in their occurrence. ECC generates keys based on the elliptic curve equation. Since it helps to establish high-performance security using lower computing power and resource usage, it is increasingly popular for mobile applications. Other encryption methods include security frameworks with SM2 encryption algorithm, blowfish algorithm on FPGA by the use of VHDL programming language which had supervision on some of the FPGA resources. Blowfish algorithm shows good performance with FPGA implementation and is a good alternative for network security in IoT. Hash encryption is also a well-established method of enforcing security. DES and DSA combined offer risk reduction in IoT environments. DES and RSA is a hybrid model that finds application is Bluetooth connections.

4. Security Monitoring and Analysis

Captures data on the overall state of the system, including endpoint devices and connectivity traffic. This data is then analyzed to detect possible security violations or potential system threats. Once detected, a broad range of actions formulated in the context of an overall system security policy should be executed, such as quarantining devices based on anomalous behavior. This monitor- analyze-act cycle may execute in real time or at a later date to identify usage patterns and detect potential attack scenarios. It is critical to ensure that endpoints devices are secured from possible tampering and data manipulation, which could result in the incorrect reporting of events. Smart home security is characterized by devices which once shipped cannot be upgraded to enhance their security, the devices are special purpose and need special purpose security solutions, they are typically running real-time operating systems like VxWorks or INTEGRITY and cannot implement the standard security solutions for Linux or Windows based systems and users cannot install third party solutions onto their devices which makes security solutions for these devices much different from those implemented in other areas. OEMs who build devices must ship their products with security embedded in it, although often the latter throw the responsibility of security enforcement to the OS vendors. The OEM is responsible however for specifying security requirements, testing the product, selecting the OS, security protocols, secure authentication and protection mechanism such as an endpoint firewall. The OS vendor ensures the security of the OS. Communication protocols and services are bundled with the OS which provide the main attack vectors for cyber-attacks. Chip vendors lead the way in embedded device security. Processors with built-in code verification capability, physical tampering detection, encryption engines are novel ways to secure the devices at the hardware level. These allow OEMs to develop devices that verify they are running authentic code and detect when someone has physically opened a device. Once detected, the device can shut itself down or report against tampering. It is the responsibility of the end user to ensure the device is deployed in a secure manner. Setting sufficiently strong passwords and enable authentication are the least measures which can be taken but they are amazingly effective to ward off possible attacks.

Monitoring and analysis calls for home security system kits. What comes in a security system starter kit? That will vary from one manufacturer to another, but the typical kit will include:

- A hub that connects to the router, either wirelessly or with an ethernet cable. This is the "brains" of the system. There will be a siren to warn and frighten an intruder, and a keypad for use to arm the system when home owners are absent or retired for the night, and disarm when they come home or wake up and start the day. In some systems, the alarm, hub, and keypad will all be in the same enclosure.
- More advanced hubs will contain a battery backup and a cellular radio, so that alerts are sent even in case of loss of power or broadband connection goes down. In most cases, however, a monthly fee needs to be paid for that peace of mind.
- Door/window sensors: These are small, typically two-piece devices that attach to doors and windows via tape or screws. One side of the sensor has a magnet and the other a small piece of steel. Separating the two breaks the magnetic field between them and sends a signal to the hub to report that the door or window has been opened. The hub can typically be programmed with a delay that allows to open a door, walk to the keypad, and disarm the system before the alarm goes off. Window sensors trigger an immediate alarm, since no one should be entering or exiting the home via a window.
- At least one motion sensor that will detect movement within its field of view. When one plans to remain in the house, the system is armed with commands "home" or "stay," and the hub will ignore messages from the motion sensor. When one leaves the house and arm the system "away," any unexpected movement will trigger the hub to go into an alarm state. Most motion sensors include a pet mode that will prevent small animals from triggering false alarms.

Some home security systems provide or allow to add other security components, such as:

- A remote key fob or a secondary keypad: The most frequent interactions with the security system will probably occur via a smartphone app, but better systems offer more flexibility. One might set up a second keypad at another entry location, or push a button on a remote control on the keychain to arm and disarm the system. Nest Labs offers an NFC-enabled remote that one taps on its hub to disarm its Nest Secure system, which might be easier for children to work with.

- Glass break/vibration sensors: These sensors either listen for the specific pitch of glass breaking or adhere to a window, monitoring for the vibrational shock of damage, tripping the alarm if a break is detected.
- Smoke and/or carbon monoxide detectors: Many security vendors have been expanding their definition of security by adding the option to protect homes and its occupants from smoke, fire, and carbon monoxide.
- Water leak sensors: Insurance claims for water damage from burst pipes and similar disasters are far more common than fires, so a system that can warn of the presence of water where it shouldn't be can deliver big benefits.
- A security camera: Surprisingly, most security systems do not include cameras as part of their base package, but many offer them as an add-on, or they partner with a third-party provider to incorporate cameras.

The IoT environment, unlike an IT one, has three layers to it: edge, platform/cloud and enterprise. Most edge devices work in constrained environments, that is, they have low compute, memory and storage capabilities. Gateway devices can still hold some power, but that deteriorates with the growing volume of devices connecting to it. The sheer volume of connected devices in geo-dispersed clusters makes it impossible to work-unlike in an IT environment. Also, the edge layer is not equipped with any logging framework and, even if it were present, it may not have any standard logging format and the ability to capture all events. What makes the edge layer most vulnerable to attacks is its lack of physical and logical controls. This layer could be porous, allowing spurious data to creep in and lead to flawed analytics, thereby impacting business decision-making. These devices can be used for PDOS (permanent denial of service) and DDOS attacks, causing major disruptions. Even though these are low powered, the volume makes a huge difference. Hence, it is crucial to have rules for these scenarios in security monitoring solutions. The edge layer, in an IoT environment, must be firmly integrated with the IT security framework and should have standards and policies in place. In the platform/cloud layer, there are the CSPs, software service providers and multiple parties involved, who take care of core capabilities for IaaS, PaaS and SaaS. All these, which together define the IoT suite, are physically dispersed and loosely coupled when compared with a traditional IT application. IoT, a critical business driver today, is more in the discovery phase of the security monitoring journey. It is imperative to build a solution where IT and IoT frameworks can co-exist. The traditional approach can no longer work in an IoT format. IoT security monitoring must embrace all tiers, along with security monitoring tools, such as the SIEM (Security Incident and Event Monitoring) tool. One way can be for organizations to establish standards in IoT, so they can put in their own policies and standards as an extension of the IT landscape. This, however, is unlikely to happen in the short term because it adds to the complexity of the situation as IoT technology is at a different level of maturity and is much more diverse. The other way can be to "innovate" a model that encompasses the needs of both IT and IoT environments, thereby bridging existing gaps. Agent-less tools need to be used at the edge layer to ensure that it doesn't impact any device functionality while cloud-based solutions need to excel on PaaS capabilities. So, the idea here is to initially segment the solution and then add specific security monitoring layers before we capture the context/behavior of each segment. We close the loop by building an integration layer, encompassing all segments-edge, platform/cloud and enterprise. Finally, by being cognizant of the threat intelligence feed generated post integration of all segmented components, organizations can be prepared for likely IoT attacks(Retrieved from https://www.wipro.com/content/dam/nexus/en/service-lines/applications/latest-thinking/iot-security-monitoring.pdf Access Time: 15.06.2019 at 01:02pm).

5. Security Lifecycle Management

The lifecycle management feature allows service providers and OEMs to control the security aspects of IoT devices when in operation. Rapid over the air (OTA) device key(s) replacement during cyber disaster recovery ensures minimal service disruption. In addition, secure device decommissioning ensures that scrapped devices will not be repurposed and exploited to connect to a service without authorization. Design philosophy for IoT devices is completely different from that prevalent in other computing systems. Due to hardware limitations, signature-based blacklisting is not an option(https://www.trendmicro.com/us/iot-security/content/main/document/IoT%20Security%20Whitepaper.pdf Access Time: 15.06.2019 at 02:12pm).

Typical lifecycle of IoT devices include:

- The device boots up or loads the firmware and starts to work as defined.
- Once the boot-up is complete, reading configuration, establishing connections, synchronization of data are the next steps.
- The device operated as per customer requirements.
- In case of any updates, new firmware is installed and the device reboots and loads the new firmware.

What Is AAA Protection?

Authentication, authorization, and accounting (AAA) is a term for a framework for intelligently controlling access to computer resources, enforcing policies, auditing usage, and providing the information necessary to bill for services. These combined processes are considered important for effective network management and security.

As the first process, authentication provides a way of identifying a user, typically by having the user enter a valid user name and valid password before access is granted. The process of authentication is based on each user having a unique set of criteria for gaining access. The AAA server compares a user's authentication credentials with other user credentials stored in a database. If the credentials match, the user is granted access to the network. If the credentials are at variance, authentication fails and network access is denied.

Following authentication, a user must gain authorization for doing certain tasks. After logging into a system, for instance, the user may try to issue commands. The authorization process determines whether the user has the authority to issue such commands. Simply put, authorization is the process of enforcing policies: determining what types or qualities of activities, resources, or services a user is permitted. Usually, authorization occurs within the context of authentication. Once you have authenticated a user, they may be authorized for different types of access or activity.

The final plank in the AAA framework is accounting, which measures the resources a user consumes during access. This can include the amount of system time or the amount of data a user has sent and/or received during a session. Accounting is carried out by logging of session statistics and usage information and is used for authorization control, billing, trend analysis, resource utilization, and capacity planning activities.

Authentication, authorization, and accounting services are often provided by a dedicated AAA server, a program that performs these functions. A current standard by which network access servers interface with the AAA server is the Remote Authentication Dial-In User Service (RADIUS).

What Is KMS?

A key management system (KMS), also known as a cryptographic key management system (CKMS), is an integrated approach for generating, distributing and managing cryptographic keys for devices and applications. They may cover all aspects of security - from the secure generation of keys over the secure exchange of keys up to secure key handling and storage on the client. Thus, a KMS includes the backend functionality for key generation, distribution, and replacement as well as the client functionality for injecting keys, storing and managing keys on devices. A critical cryptosystem component, key management is also one of the most challenging aspects of cryptography because it deals with many types of security liabilities beyond encryption, such as people and flawed policies. It also involves creating a corresponding system policy, user training, interdepartmental interactions and proper coordination.

For a multicast group, security is a large issue, as all group members have the ability to receive the multicast message. The solution is a multicast group key management system, in which specific keys are securely provided to each member. In this manner, an encryption using a specific member's key means that the message can only be accessed and read by that group member.

A popular example of a key management system is public key infrastructure (PKI), which is used in Secure Sockets Layer (SSL) and Transport Layer Security (TLS).

What Is PKI?

A public key infrastructure (PKI) supports the distribution, revocation and verification of public keys used for public key encryption, and enables linking of identities with public key certificates. A PKI enables users and systems to securely exchange data over the internet and verify the legitimacy of certificate-holding entities, such as webservers, other authenticated servers and individuals. The PKI enables users to authenticate digital certificate holders, as well as to mediate the process of certificate revocation, using cryptographic algorithms to secure the process.

PKI certificates include a public key used for encryption and cryptographic authentication of data sent to or from the entity that was issued the certificate. Other information included in a PKI certificate includes identifying information about the certificate holder, about the PKI that issued the certificate, and other data including the certificate's creation date and validity period.

Without PKI, sensitive information can still be encrypted, ensuring confidentiality, and exchanged between two entities, but there would be no assurance of the identity of the other party. Any form of sensitive data exchanged over the internet is reliant on the PKI for enabling the use of public key cryptography because the PKI enables the authenticated exchange of public keys.

Security guidelines to be followed during the device life cycle of IoT devices:

- Boot-up: To ensure that the firmware has not been modified or tampered with by others a firmware integrity check needs to be issued either by means of embedded checksum or secure password. Encrypting firmware with PKI or public/private certification to secure the whole boot-up process can also be done.
- Initialisation:

- ○ AAA protection: Usage of proper encryption to avoid user/device hijack. Default account credentials appear on many IoT devices. Best practices call for an activation process which needs end-user to change the default password.
  - ○ Using a KMS(Key Management System) or CMS(Certification Management System) to protect encryption/decryption keys or store those keys in a TPM(Trusted Platform Module).
  - ○ Communication protection involves securing the communication between device and device, device and Internet or device and user interface(through web or mobile apps) by encryption like HTTPS, AES 128, 256 and the like.
  - ○ Identity protection involves a KMS or CMS to prevent fake identity within the communication group.
- Operation:
  - ○ AAA protection: Remove all backdoor debug user accounts. From several studies, it was found that many IoT devices keep accounts for debugging purposes in the system which multiplies chances of penetration.
  - ○ The device must implement knowledge to detect abnormal operations and in the event that such an abnormality surfaces, provide a warning to the backend or the user.
  - ○ Runtime integrity checks can prevent the device from being captured or compromised during the operation. Cloud technology with two-way integrity checks is effective.
  - ○ Risk management like virtual patching or a host IPS to reduce risk before FOTA or Firmware Over the air Triggers.

CONCLUSION

IoT device driven smart homes will definitely emerge as a commonality in the future. The world will dissolve into habitation centers with their own central processing facilities which look after all aspects of home management whilst the residents can devote their time to more fruitful endeavors. Living in a land of autonomous homes and interconnected machines entails establishment of strong security measures else unscrupulous individuals will easily gain access to the hub and launch widespread cyber attacks. The traditional burglary will be replaced by hackers trying to gain access to our very homes with malicious network signals which would allow them to virtually control all connected devices in the home which is more worrisome as to combat it one cannot simply call the police. Advancement of technology is imperative to progress but it should not be so as the cost of personal and general safety. Smart homes of the future would not be unique entities but similar in its working provided obtained from the same manufacturer. This implies the added danger of widespread attacks, once a home is compromised, the same technique or methodology might be used to attack other neighboring homes, resulting in widespread mayhem.

Whilst full autonomy is imperative for elderly care centers and invalids, it may be of interest to keep a provision for supervised human control so as not to feel overwhelmed residing in places chiefly controlled via the cloud. In this chapter we have explored the major areas in smart homes which are susceptible to external attacks and touched upon certain ways in which these vulnerabilities can be protected. Awareness of the dangers is the first step in combating it as well as understanding the role of the home owners in security enforcement by proper usage of strong passwords and the like.

The goal of smart homes is to have smart household devices delivering services needed for efficient home functioning with minimum human intervention. Smart home devices have to deal with security and privacy issues. The concept of digitalization has led to several interesting application using Internet of Things (IoT). The IoT finds application, such as smart homes, buildings, cities, retail and public safety. Most of the current smart home systems use digital door lock having an interface for customers to input a PIN (personnel identification number) thus eliminating the customer burden of carrying keys. Survey from vendors like August and Kwikset Kevo smart locks have demonstrated critical vulnerabilities in their devices. Many products are being developed by companies around the world for smart homes application and services. Even though smart homes offer desirable qualities, it can cause security and privacy vulnerability. Overcoming stolen private information due to vulnerabilities in smart homes is a critical challenge for wide adoption. Even if private information is not stolen by adversaries, customers still have issues about their private information being gathered, shared and exploited. Smart homes offer all in one applications that allow a user can easily control lights, TVs, appliances, thermostat, and locks on an array of touchpad sensors.

Smart homes are susceptible to security intimidation. Most Security problems are related to weak customer and their tool supervision methods. Current security research has focused on separate devices, and how they are interacting with each other. For example, the My Q garage system can be turned into a surveillance tool, alerting would-be thieves when a garage door opened and then closed, and allowing them to remotely open it again after the residents had left(Abdiladif Said, Abdisalan Jama, Faysal Mahamud, Jayabalaji Mohan, Prakash Ranganathan, 2018). Veracode performed a security analysis of several smart home hubs, including Smart Things . The security analysis focused on organization protection such as whether SSL/TLS is used, whether there is again an attack protection, and whether strong passwords are used. The Veracode study found that the SmartThings hub had correctly established all studied infrastructural security mechanisms with the exception of an open telnet re-correcting the interface on the hub, which has since been fixed. In addition, we would perform an analysis which is based on our experiment of the SmartThings platform (Earlence Fernandes, 2016).

With greater connectivity comes the threat of more damaging attacks since networks are the life blood of cyber attacks, greater the number of devices connected to that network the better. However the future is not all that bleak. With proper security measures, it is indeed exciting to think of how different our lives would be when the devices in our homes work together to make our lives easier and more productive.

REFERENCES

Aman, Chua, & Sikdar. (n.d.). *Mutual Authentication in IoT Systems using Physical Unclonable Functions*. Academic Press.

Cekerevac, Dvorak, Prigoda, & Cekerevac. (n.d.). Internet of things and man in the middle attacks-security and economic risks. *MEST Journal, 5*(2), 15-25.

Fernandes. (2016). Security Analysis of Emerging Smart Home Applications. *IEEE Symposium on Security and Privacy*, 636-654.

Ghayvat, H., Mukhopadhyay, S., Gui, X., & Suryadevara, N. (2015). WSN- and IOT-Based Smart Homes and Their Extension to Smart Buildings. *Sensors, 15*(5), 10350–10379. doi:10.3390150510350

Hallman, Bryan, Palavicini, Divita, & Romero-Mariona. (2017). *IoDDoS — The Internet of Distributed Denial of Service Attacks A Case Study of the Mirai Malware and IoT-Based Botnets*. IoTBDS 2017 - 2nd International Conference on Internet of Things, Big Data and Security.

Neal, D. (2016). Mirai botnet: DDoS attack takes out Liberia communications networks. *The Inquirer*. Available at: https://www.theinquirer.net/inquirer/news/2476458/miraibotnetddosattacktakesoutliberiacommunicationsnetworks

Olivier, F., Carlos, G., & Florent, N. (2015). *New Security Architecture for IoT Network. Procedia Computer Science* , 52.

Safi. (2017). Improving the Security of Internet of Things Using Encryption Algorithms. *World Academy of Science, Engineering and Technology International Journal of Computer and Information Engineering, 11*(5).

Said, A., Jama, A., Mahamud, F., Mohan, J., & Ranganathan, P. (2018). Smart Home Vulnerabilities – A Survey. *Int'l Conf. Embedded Systems, Cyber-physical Systems, & Applications ESCS'18.*

Siboni, Sachidananda, Meidan, Bohadana, Mathov, Bhairav, Shabtai, & Elovici. (2019). Security Testbed for Internet-of-Things Devices. *IEEE Transactions on Reliability, 68*(1).

Suh, G. E., & Devadas, S. (2007). Physical Unclonable Functions for Device Authentication and Secret Key Generation. *Proceedings of IEEE/ACMDAC,* 9-14.

Vidalis & Angelopoulou. (n.d.). Assessing Identity Theft in the Internet of Things. *IT CoNvergence PRActice (INPRA), 2*(1), 15-21.

Weiser. (1991). The Computer for the 21st Century. *Scientific American, 265*(3), 94-105.

Xin, M., & China, H. (2015). A Mixed Encryption Algorithm Used in Internet of Things Security Transmission System. *International Conference on Cyber-Enabled Disributed Computing and Knowledge Discovery*, 62-65. 10.1109/CyberC.2015.9

Chapter 12
IoT–Controlled Railway Gate System With ML Object Detection Approach:
Applied Approach for a Secured IoT System

Megha Kamble
 https://orcid.org/0000-0001-7466-1504
Lakshmi Narain College of Technology, India

Jaspreet Mehra
Lakshmi Narain College of Technology, India

Monika Jain
Lakshmi Narain College of Technology, India

ABSTRACT

The growing demand of internet of things (IoT) has rendered advancement in the practical fields towards society. In spite of recent advancements and cost effective IoT solutions for smart railway infrastructure, presently, most of the railway gates in India are opened and closed manually. This is a time-consuming process. It is an error-prone system and raises the accident probability. This chapter evaluates and demonstrates the applicability of IoT to resolve the problem of unmanned automatic railway crossing. The aim is to propose a prototype that will control with the help of microcontroller board, IoT sensor integration, and integrating it to machine learning-based image analysis to detect the intermediate real time obstacle (obstacle on the track). This kind of IoT system will also invite potential attacks, and traditional security countermeasures can be inefficient in dynamic IoT environments. So open challenges related to IoT security threats and emerging security mechanisms for security of the proposed smart railway crossing system are also elaborated.

DOI: 10.4018/978-1-7998-2444-2.ch012

INTRODUCTION

The emerging industrial concept of "internet of things" (IoT) has had a major impact on the all domains of industry. IoT is essentially a platform where embedded devices are connected to the internet, so they can collect and exchange data with each other. It enables devices to interact, collaborate and, learn from each other's experiences just like humans do. This work is focused on impact of IoT on transportation industry. With the advent of autonomous vehicles and improved public transportation including the railways, there are many use cases and potential of IoT that has been explored all over the world. Traditionally in the railway industry, the concept of IoT has been about connected sensors for real time operation and analysis. IoT of today is extending the scale and scope of sensors, data accessibility and applications. By adopting new technologies existing railway system can be converted to more efficient for day-to-day operations and for the passengers. There are many solutions which are proposed for effective day-to-day operations of smart railway. Railway crossings are part of urban areas and also important part of society and day-to-day safety. This work is focused on IoT based solution for railway crossings in city areas and the idea is to propose IoT based unmanned solution for automatic operation of closing and opening of railway crossing taking care of ignorance of passers by during train transition.

Before coming to the suggested solution, it is essential to throw some light on broad domain of the solution which is Internet of things. This section is describing the different fundamental concepts behind IoT and the basic technologies as well as connectivity devices that are required to design internet of things, objects, real world entities and an overall understanding of making of IoT and its functionality.

All the different things that are that we are seeing around us and that we have around us are the part of IoT and working together as a part of network and responding with its functionality. They are all going to be interconnected. To provide us IoT based services exactly like internet based services we enjoy at present. Internet based services is basically A connection of different computers and computing devices all over the world is able to provide us Internet based services. Scope of this internet is going to be expanded beyond computing and computer devices being connected and is going to interconnect different physical objects in our day-to-day life such as lights, fans, ACs and everything in our home similarly any manual mechanism we consider in the businesses, different machines office gates, vehicle gates, Dam gates, railway signals every possible thing of internetworking equipments which can provide us automization and be interconnected to provide us advanced levels of services that can be offered for peaceful life.

These IoT systems fit with embedded systems, embedded electronics and information technology, so that they have some basic computing platform attached to them and then, they are going to be acting as different nodes of that particular internet, the IoT internet of things.

In this way, they will help in connecting different other things that are around them and depending on the business application requirements, to form a much bigger internet than the current internet of computers and this will be known as internet of things. IoT is one of the building blocks that is considered to be of use for developing smart homes and smart cities.

There are two ways to build IoT, one way is to expand the scope of the current internet means, the internet of computers and the other approach is to build a separate internetwork of these physical objects from scratch. In short, internetwork of things is not a single technology. There can be the different types of physical devices having different configuration and different specifications. Each of these supported through different other systems such as cloud technology, big data machine and computer vision and also from the technologies from electrical sciences and mechanical sciences are required in order to build IoT. The number of things that are connected to the internetwork of things are going to send lot of data. This data has to be handled properly, this data have to be analyzed using data science mechanism.

There are different enabling technologies for internet of things and some are identified as IoT enablers: RFID, nanotechnology, sensors, and smart networks.

- RFID is one we know at present in the market places and different places in the society being used RFID tags, RFID readers etc. So, RFID based devices are required for building internet of things.
- Sensors is another one which is one of the most important enabling device or enabling technology for building internet of things. Sensors and actuators and the other networking devices, different connectivity, and different communication paradigms are also required in order to connect these different sensors, RFIDs and different other physical devices that have to be internetwork to form the IoT.
- At present there is lot of interest in the nanotechnology domain. So, nanosensors can also be the option for building internet of nano things.

Desire Characteristics

IoT, is mostly about networking of physical objects and these physical objects are embedded with the different embedded electronics. They communicate and sense and interact with the internal states or interact with internal and inter external environment. They also interact with the external environment in which they are operating. So, either they are interacting with each other, they change their different states and they interact with the environment in which they are operating.

There are different characteristics of IoT.

- Efficiency: IoT which will be designed and developed should be efficient. It has to serve efficiently the requirements of the applications for which they are deployed.
- Scalability: They have to be scalable because IoT systems consist of millions of things, So, even if the number of sensors and the sensing devices IoT devices are going to increase, the overall network performance should not be compromised.

Essential Elements of IoT

- Connectivity: There are three layers of connectivity service:
  - Service Layer: for service layer, there are different communication technologies, such as services that can be offered to different application areas, such as health care, agriculture, businesses, factories, plants, banks and so on.
  - Local connectivity: for local connectivity we have components such as the gateway
  - Global connectivity: For global connectivity, the internet is used
- Baseline Technology

There are quite a few baseline technologies that can be used. Machine to machine(M2M) communication is one of the baseline technique and this idea is also based on M2M. In machine to machine communication, one machine directly talks to another machine, communicates with another machine without any human intervention. M2M offers the means for managing devices and device interaction while also collecting computer/sensor data.

- Sensors and actuators

The sensors basically sense the physical phenomena that are occurring around them and the actuators basically based on the sensed information. The actuators, actuate, means, they perform some actions on the physical environment and take some actions based on what has been sensed.

The stepwise design:

Step 1: identify the sensors which sense different parameters depending on the application. For example, temperature, pressure,humidity conditions, lighting conditions and so on. Then, sensed information is sent over a connected system.

That means, over a network that information will be passed, it can also involve cloud. Finally that information is transmitted and based onthe requirements, some physical action is going to be taken by an actuator.

IoT Camera sensors senses the movement and obstacle and generate signal based on visuals. I this way, these sensors have different unique functionalities. They are fabricated to measure a certain physical property and they come in different shapes and sizes. They can be very small, they can be very big. For ex. An intelligent device such as a traffic camera, monitors the railway tracks for traffic congestion, accidents and communicate this data to a common gateway. This gateway also receives data and signals the information to mechanical sensor for gate movement.

The same sensors can be mechanical sensors, these can be electrical sensors, they can be electronic sensors, they can be chemical sensors. There are so many different types of sensors and fabrication of a sensor is a completely different. So, the sensors based on certain stimuli, the different stimuli might be there. They can measure the thing in the physical characteristics of the environment of the system and so on and these changes are basically converted to electrical signals. Based on the output, the sensors can be classified as analog or digital and based on the data type, they can be classified as scalar or vector sensors. So, in the analog sensor, what we have these sensors give continuous analog output. Then, scaler sensors basically measure scalar variables which can measure only the changes in the magnitude whereas, the vector senses not only the magnitude, but also the direction. For example, the camera sensor or the accelerometer sensor whose values are dependent on the orientation or on the direction and so on direction in which the sensor is being put and the weight is measured, will determine outcome of the actuator. Then, we have for force, we have the strain, strain gauge and pressure. Pressure switch for position, we have potentiometers, encoders, opto couplers. With opto couplers we can sense the speed as optical rays are obstructed and based on the position information can be obtained.

- There is another basic element, transducer which is a collective term which includes sensors as well as the actuators. An electric actuator is generally powered by a motor that converts electrical energy into mechanical torque. So, this electrical energy is used to actuate the equipment, such as the solenoid valve which control the flow of water in pipes in response to electrical signals. Then, we can have the mechanical actuators which basically converts rotary motion into linear motion to execute some movements.

In short, IoT components comprises of Device (the thing), Local network, Internet, Backend services, ICT application. So hybrid application where IoT sensors are collecting data, cloud providing data storage and ML based application to analyse the data for future use is the requirement of future.

IoT applications are expected to equip billions of everyday objects with connectivity and intelligence. It is already being deployed extensively, in various domains, and some promising areas of applications of IoT are business manufacturing, healthcare, retail, agriculture, smart home, smart city and security. This work describes Modern day IoT application in railways. Nowadays, the railway industry is in a position where it is able to exploit the opportunities created by the IIoT (Industrial Internet of Things). Analysis of latest research provides various options of implementation of IoT for maintenance, smart infrastructure, advanced monitoring of assets, video surveillance systems, railway operations, Passenger and Freight Information Systems (PIS/FIS), train control systems, safety assurance, signaling systems, cyber security and energy efficiency in railway infrastructure. The aim of this article is to provide a detailed examination of the state-of-the-art of IoT technologies for railway crossing automatic monitoring that will revolutionize the railway industry towards citizen safety and will give better solution in train transition even in rural and urban areas and serve mankind in better manner releasing stress of railway workers.

The Role of Data Analytics in IoT System for Railways

The role of big data in IoT is to process a large amount of data on a real-time basis and storing them using different storage technologies. A large amount of unstructured data is generated by IoT devices which are collected in the big data system. IoT and data remain essentially linked together. In the proposed system, IoT system monitors the trains on track for 24 hours and so data consumed and produced keeps on growing at faster rate and repetitive manner. The data generated from IoT devices is treated to be of valuable only if it gets analysed and this can be done with data analytics. Data Analytics is defined as a process, which is used to examine big and small data sets with varying data properties to extract meaningful conclusions. These conclusions are usually in the form of trends, patterns, and statistics that help the organizations in proactively working with data to implement effective decision-making at real time for safety, utility and optimization purpose. There are various forms of analytics which can be applied in case of proposed IoT controlled system. Following details are listed:

- **Streaming Analytics:** This form of data analytics is also referred as event stream processing and it analyzes real time motion data sets. Real time data streams are analyzed in this process to detect urgent situations and immediate actions for safety. IoT applications of railways for traffic analysis and gate controlling can be done with this analytics.

- **Spatial Analytics:** This is the data analytics method that is used to analyze geographic patterns to determine the spatial relationship between the physical objects. Location-based IoT applications like proposed system with track location and train location can utilize this to track and monitor the location based data, to control the operation of gate in real time manner.

- **Time Series Analytics:** This form of data analytics is based upon the time-based data which is analyzed to reveal time based patterns and time span wise analysis, how many times controlling to be done, what are the day hours during which track are relatively less crowded and more crowded and time limit can be varied dynamically based on time based pattern analysis.

- **Prescriptive Analysis:** This form of data analytics is the combination of descriptive and predictive analysis. It is applied to understand the sequence of actions that can be taken in a particular situation. Railway gate or crossing monitoring IoT applications can make use of this form of data analytics to gain better conclusions about prediction of approaching of train towards gate and obstacle descriptions with image datasets.

IoT analytics will also allow the increased safety and surveillance abilities through video sensors and application of data analytics methods which is core part of this proposed system.

- **IoT analytics:** The potential of sensors lies in their ability to gather data about the physical environment, which can then be analyzed or combined with other forms of data to detect patterns. In the proposed system, we are applying IoT sensors in such a manner that it will be always connected to environment.

Large-scale sensor deployments assist with understanding and enhancing the experiences of participants and connected events.. The internet of things is expanding to include cameras as rich data sources alongside sensors, in order to analyze the same situation from different perspectives. So camera sensors can be part of video analytics, particularly a form of analytics based on machine learning and used for video anomaly detection. This kind of video analytics takes the raw input from a camera and learns the scene and contribute to estimation of free track for safety purpose.

Video Analytics for Surveillance and Safety-Protecting infrastructure such as Raiway crossing, track movement goes beyond predictive maintenance, and frequently people need protection from infrastructure that can be effectively provided with integration IoT and Machine Learning.

The proposed system incorporates traffic management system based on real time video analytics. Human operators monitoring the sensor can adjust the time threshold dynamically with ML prediction here. Some anomalous events (a delayed vehicle at crossing, a car moving on the track, passers by crossing etc.) hampers the threshold and hence require the dynamic setting of machine to operate. If the analytics detect a strong movement on track at crossing from both the direction, that's an indication of an accident and the analytics will trigger an alarm. Such technologies are useful for adjusting operations, as well as for ensuring safety. Such kind of video analytics are also being used to manage crowd movements on track near crossing. This is included in this proposed system.

Big data means a large dataset of structured, unstructured or semi-structured data and analyzing those data to get the insights of the controlling event.

IoT big data processing follows following broad steps –

1. A large amount of unstructured data is generated by IoT devices which are collected in the big data system.
2. In the big data system the huge amount of data is stored in big data files.
3. Analyzing the stored IoT big data using data analytics tools.
4. Generating the reports and observe the patterns of analyzed data.

With reference to proposed IoT system for railway crossing. as more and more IoT devices are deployed in uncontrolled, complex, and hostile environments of railway infrastructure, securing this IoT system presents a number of security challenges. With sensors and remote sensors security is most important aspect of IoT. As per the architecture of proposed IoT system is concerned, some security issues to be taken care by are security constraints of devices such as sensors and actuators, authorization and authentication of devices, managing device updates, secure communication among the IoT enables and data backup and software unit, data privacy and integrity, ensuring high availability, detection and prevention of vulnerabilities, predicting and preempting unknown security issues. After describing the IoT system architecture, some light has been thrown on security mechanisms using conventional IoT practices and some of the emerging IoT security practices.

BACKGROUND

Rail transport is by far the least expensive method of transportation used by the general public. It is preferred the most over the other means of transportation. In routine life, general public come across many accidents due to the mismanagement of the railway crossing gate management. Human handling of railway gates, lack of synchronization mechanism, ignorance of general public are multiple causes of railway crossing related accidents. In these types of accidents sometimes demise rate is quite high. The void caused by the loss of mankind can never be replenished. Therefore, there is an necessity to take some precautionary steps to enhance railway crossing security.

Presently, most of the railway crossings are taken care by gatekeeper ie human being and some are unmanned using various sensor mechanisms. Even literature presents number of techniques for automation of railway gates. Current scenario is of IOT and ML based intelligent and cloud basing controlling proven technology.

The Internet of Things (IoT) also called the Internet of objects, refers to a wireless network between objects by embedding short range mobile transceivers into a wide array of additional gadgets and everyday items. IoT enables new form of communication between people and things and among the objects themselves. This is emerging technology and research disciplines that enables the internet to reach out into the real world of physical objects. The Internet of Things (IoT) permits objects to be detected and controlled remotely over existing system structure. Allowing more straight forward combination of the physical world into. computer based frameworks leads to enhanced productivity, precision, effective communication and financial advantage. The IOT application covers smart environments in various domains and found very useful in case of automation railway gate controlling.

This article presents a framework by integrating IoT hardware and sensors with machine learning algorithm that would help in preventing rail-transport accidents upto a greater extent. IoT sensors sense the track for train presence, generating signal to trigger controlling system automatically without human intervention where as there will be short interval in which still obstacle will be there until the track is entirely clear. For this short duration, track images will be clicked by automatic camera. These images are analysed using ML object localization to identify exact location and object detection to classify them and warning time will be given before train approached the crossing gates. So the aim is by controlling the opening and closing of the railway gates without any human assistance and object detection, obstacles on the track are removed upto great extent so as to avoid the accidents.

Manual Railway gate controlling is the popular present system. When a train leaves any station, the station master of current station intimates upcoming crossing's gatekeeper about the arrival of the train by a telephonic call. On receiving the manual information, the gatekeeper comes into action to close the the gate manually and the time interval for the said process is approximate time interval which is varying on daily basis. The time interval is approximated by manual calculation by considering the distance traveled by the train from a station to the crossing gate. However, the gate remains closed for a long time even if the train is late for some reasons. If number of trains are crossing, until the entire track is free, then only gates are opened. The natural human tendency triggers the usage of track although crossing is closed leading the track to accident prone area. Unmanageable delays, human handling and unawareness of crowd to hurriedly crossing the track these are the some of the problems to be taken care by automation system. By keeping the limitations of existing system, survey of existing automatic railway gate controlling system is done. The system is redesigned by using a sensor near to the railway gate on track, that detects the arrival of the train and signals the closing of the gate. Similarly cameras are operational on crossing, generating the images of the track after gate closing to ensure all object removal from the track before crossing of the train. Hence, this can be utilized in an unmanned railway gates which are more prone to accidents due to presence on track even after gate is closed.

Present Scenario of Railway System

Presently IoT has wide application in smart city development. Here smart means in terms of the services that are given to the respective stake holders of these cities. So citizens are able to do things in a better manner in an improved manner then usual and how is that made possible that is made possible with the help of nothing, but the ICT technologies information and communication technologies which also includes electronics embedded electronics different other advanced topologies in electrical in a electrical sciences and so on. So, computers electronics put together in form of IoT can make these cities smart.

The objective of this work is to conceive an IoT as a very complex system involving sensors, actuators, networks, local area, wide area internet and different servers, different algorithms, machine learning and so on, all executing together to make the system function as as one single entity towards smart city concept.

Existing Solutions of IoT for Railway System

There are various technologies available for automatic railway gate controlling system based on IR sensors, radar system, pressure sensors, ultrasonic sensors integrated on electronic board. The brief study of some good examples is stated as follows:

R.Ekalya et al.(2018) suggested an efficient method to control the opening or closing of the railway gates using the help of Internet of Things(IoT) pressure sensors, embedded on Arudino board. Pressure sensors are bulky sensors and can be calibrated manually, so they are less accurate and prone to error. So the suggested system is less reliable and also obstacle detection between the level crossing gates at peak time is not handled.

Dr.S.Anila et al.(2017) proposed a prototype for the automation of the level crossing gates at the railway station using IR sensors and intermediate obstacle detection using Ultrasonic sensors and GSM network. IR sensors work with line of sight between transmitter and receiver. The limitations of this system are: IR sensors are not able to distinguish between the objects with similar thermal energy level irradiation. They are not cost effective. They can control only one device at one time. They are not able to sense the objects which are not in LOS (Line of Sight). And above all they support shorter range and hence their performance degrade with longer distances. The sensing accuracy of the ultrasonic sensors is affected by climatic changes in the nature and hence they are not durable. These sensors also support short range of communication.

The paper proposes signal and data communication with GSM network which provide limited data rate capability and then complete system is dependent on GSM network availability. At time, this may delay the data transmission making entire system unreliable.

The authors of Pranav Sharma et al.(2015) proposed a system using RFID, Pressure sensor, and servo motor to control mechanical movement of the gate.. But it suffered from the drawback that it cannot be used for very high speed trains and also at the hilly areas where the pressure sensor may not perform accurately.

The authors of k.Sato et al.(1998) have developed a new obstruction detector, that can be useful for all railway lines including ones in snow-covered areas, by studying ultrasonic-based obstruction detection at a crossing. In this paper, the authors explained the structure and the methods of the ultrasonic-based obstruction detector first, then about the safety logic of the detection.

Pretty early work of P. Longrigg (1975) discussed early railroad operations and expressed the situation of poor safety performance at grade crossings. Many lives are lost each year in accidents at crossings, to say nothing of costly injuries and property damage sustained. The situation has gotten worse with the advent of soundproofed cars, being driven at high speed in conditions of poor visibility. The authors stated the need of some improved method of warning motorists at the crossing. Analysis of a critical encounter between a road vehicle and a railway locomotive reveal that the presently used equipment is inadequate to meet the needs of present day high-speed vehicles. A system of vehicular movement warning devices is described in this paper to improve the safety of crossing to some extent. Two methods are detailed in paper using traditional techniques of static directional sonic devices positioned at the crossing and cattle guard in the roadway, to issue a tactile warning. Both systems are designed to give adequate warning to a motorist in a critical encounter situation as he approaches the crossing with a convergent locomotive on the track(s).

The authors of A.Ready et al.(2017) aimed to develop a prototype that control the railway gate using the micro-controller. Whenever train touches base at the sensor, caution is activated at the railway crossing so that the general population get instruction that entryway will be shut. At that point the control module initiates and shuts the gates on either side of the track. Once the train crosses, this module naturally lifts the gate. For mechanical operation of a gate DC adapted engines are utilized. We are utilizing an installed controller worked around the 8051 family (AT89C52) for the control. As per the instructions produced at the microcontroller, the proper action (i.e., shut or lift) will be made. This logic was implemented in Embedded C and dumped to the Raspberry PI. This prototype was tested and successfully shuts the gate at the time of train arrival and lifts after train crosses other end.

The work of Kumar, s barani. (2015) tried to focus on feasibility issues of safety at crossing of Indian railways. There has been an increase in the road traffic as well as the rail traffic, accidents at level crossing has increased and this has caused the concern for the indian railways. There are certainly many ways to solve this issues but there are major concerns regarding its feasibility for the current environment. Along this factor the cost factor remains the major concern. The paper proposed a simple solution for the level crossing with fixing the radio frequency tag (rf tag) on the train and the dynamic real time information is sent to the database server through internet of things (iot).

Theoretically, there exists a number of ways for the railway gate control system but every system has some drawbacks. Similarly only providing mechanical system may not work in the real world, it must be supported by image analysis and data analytics features. Automated railway gate at a level crossing is generally used to replace a gatekeeper who operates it manually. It manages two operations. First, it reduces the gate closing and waiting time. Second, it provides safety to the users and prevents accidents.

The proposed system has to be secured against common IoT threats discussed in [4] and it is suggested that some extended security measures[5] will be beneficial in this case.

The next section presents proposed system prepared by integrating some less complex but effective sensors and machine learning abilities.

PROPOSED SOLUTION

Functional components of IoT application can be listed as

1. Components for interaction and communication with other IoT
2. Components for processing and analysis of operations
3. Components of internet interaction
4. Components for handling web services of applications
5. Components to integrate application services
6. User interface to access IoT

Proposed work is about railway infrastructure domain for IoT implementation. This section describes overall architecture consisting of hardware, IoT sensors to judge the train movement on track and automatic railway crossing gate handling. In addition to this, during buffer closure time, the citizens tend to use the tracks which is really unsafe. Here Machine Learning application is initiated to track the obstacles and movement on the track during buffer closure time. The application will take the images clicked by camera and predict the time when all the obstacles will be removed from the track after warning bell. Automatically barriers will be closed and secure train transition will be there without much human intervention. To achieve this integrated projects, set of IoT sensors are applied on tracks, near crossings and ML module is with gatekeeper to track the last minute movement.

Proposed Architecture and Circuit

Whenever a train touches the base of the sensor, alert signals get activated at the railway crossing, to aware the general population about the arrival of the train and closing of the railway gate. After this warning, the control module initiates and shuts down the gates on both side of the track. Once the train crosses, the module lifts up the gate according to the received signals. For mechanical operation of the gate dc adapted engines are utilized. The proposed prototype makes use of an installed controller whose working revolves around the 8051 family (at89c52) for the control. As per the instructions produced at the microcontroller, the appropriate action (i.e., shut or lift) is made. This logic is implemented in embedded c and dumped to the arduino board. The prototype successfully shuts the gate at the time of train arrival and lifts the gate as the train departs from the other end as shown in fig.5. Circuit is operating from approx. 3km from crossing gates, sometimes variable depending upon train dimension. Machine Learning algorithm implemented in the system near crossing to signal final gate closure to arudino in case of obstacles on the track even after warning bell.

Figure 1 shows the array of load sensors embedded on Arduino board placed on track from 3 km distance from railway crossing. When train transition occurs, load sensor signals actuator. Near crossing gate, another arduino board embedded with mechanical sensor to lift the gate is available. But during buffer closure time, lot many passersby will try to cross the track and so camera sensors work is to check obstacle on track. It will monitor it continuously for duration of warning period while alarm is ringing as soon as load sensors sense the train on track. When camera senses last movement on the track and there is no obstacle it actuates the mechanical sensor to close the railway crossing. The circuit is consisting of following salient components:

Figure 1. Proposed Circuit

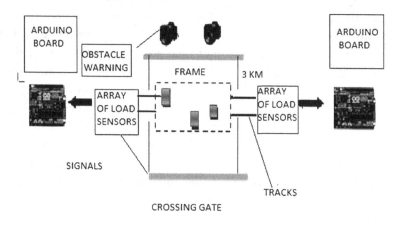

Elements Applied

A. Microcontroller

Microcontroller is utilized in this structure. AT89C52 is a 8-bit microcontroller and has a place with Atmel's 8051 family AT89C52 has 8KB of Flash programmable and erasable read just memory (PEROM) and 256 bytes of RAM. AT89C52 has a perseverance of 1000 Write/Erase cycles which implies that it very well may be deleted and modified to a limit of multiple times.

Figure 2. Microcontroller

B. Sensors

The sensor faculties and reacts to occasions happening in the physical condition. It is equipped for estimating a physical marvel (like temperature, weight, warmth, moistness, etc) and changes it into an electric flag which can additionally be utilized for playing out a specific task.

In this system, load sensors are utilized for the equivalent sensing. A heap cell is a transducer that is utilized to make an electrical flag whose extent is legitimately corresponding to the heap being estimated. At least one burden cells can be utilized for detecting a solitary burden. More sensors are utilized for huge holders or stages, or high loads.

Here crafted by the heap sensor is to detect the approaching burden and along these lines create electric signs. These signs are then sent to the microcontroller. Microcontroller forms these signs.

Figure 3. Load Cell

C. Stepper Motor

A stepper engine, otherwise called venture engine or venturing engine, is a brushless DC electric engine that isolates a full revolution into various equivalent advances. The engine's position would then be able to be told to move and hold at one of these means with no position sensor for criticism (an open-circle controller), as long as the engine is painstakingly measured to the application in regard to torque and speed.

Figure 4. Stepper Motor

D. Arduino Borard

Arduino board structures utilize an assortment of chip and controllers. The sheets are outfitted with sets of advanced and simple information/yield (I/O) sticks that might be interfaced to different extension sheets or breadboards (shields) and different circuits. The microcontrollers are normally modified utilizing a tongue of highlights from the programming dialects C and C++. Notwithstanding utilizing customary compiler toolchains, the Arduino venture gives an incorporated advancement condition (IDE) in view of the Processing language venture.

Figure 5. Arduino Board

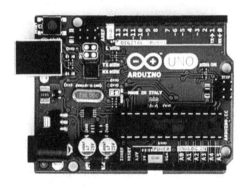

ML Module for Object Detection

The high resolution cameras are available on railway gates. Periodically on interval of 10 msec-1sec, image of gap between two gates- track part between two gates is taken. The computer can be trained to detect and classify multiple objects within an image with high accuracy.

Object detection comprises of object localization refers to identifying the location of an object in the image. An object localization algorithm will output the coordinates of the location of an object with respect to the image.

The popular algorithm from computer vision to localize an object in an image is to represent its location with the help of bounding boxes.

For ex. Image is consisting of single or multi -class images. Multi classes can be car, truck,bike and pedestrian.

The target variable for a multi-class image classification problem is defined as a vector of multiple classes

$y = [ci1, ci2, ci3, ci4]$

where, ci = Probability of the ith class the object belongs to the image

Then it will be checked against bounding box,

pc = Probability/confidence of an object

(i.e the four classes) being present in the bounding box and

bx, by, bh, bw = Bounding box coordinates.

This is one mechanism to get coordinates of objects in the image. Another approach for an object detection is to first build a classifier that can classify closely cropped images of an object. Neural network model is trained on a dataset of closely cropped images of a vehicle/or any object present on the track and the model predicts the probability of an image being a vehicle/pedestrian.

To capture number of cropped images for more accurate detection, a sliding window mechanism may be applied. The size of the crop is the same as the size of the sliding window and repetitively image is cropped and passed to convolution network model or neural network model, which in turn predicts the probability of the cropped image is a vehicle/pedestrian.

SOLUTIONS AND RECOMMENDATIONS

Preceding section has given overview about IoT controlled system for unmanned railway crossing. However, involvement of number of sensors and image data analysis will give rise to security and privacy issues in IoT system.

Issues

The proposed work is consists of Analog sensor- load sensor, Camera Sensor- Digital sensor. There are some issues related to Quantization error and Aliasing error.

Sensors are going to be active for some time and they are going to be in the sleep state for some time, how to power them because these are very small sized an d they are very resource staved sensors. So, basically the power unit in these sensor nodes these are very small in size. So, basically consequently and this is one of the challenges in these embedded devices.

IOT service oriented architecture is affected by issues of sensors, actuators, power consumption, availability and vulnerability.

Consumer IoT Device communication within the locally networked device and so communication issues in heterogeneous environment is another challenge.

If local communication is done via WiFi, limited connectivity and security issues are another challenges.

So, security on privacy issues are per amount in IoT because there are heavy concerns because dealing with resource constraint nodes with communication constraints, bandwidth constraints, processing constraints, energy constraints and so on. So, these nodes become very much valuable to different type of attacks, different types of security breaches and also because IoT systems are very much detailed intensive, there is lot of information that frozen through the network as a consequence of which the privacy of the individuals of the organizations might be at stake. So, security and privacy and trust also which is not mentioned over here, these are very much important to power IoT technologies.

Security Problems

Defining the security policies for IoT systems is also urgent task due to the unification of physical and data domains, which can severely increase the risks of cyber attacks. The proposed IoT system is working in heterogeneous IoT environment and integrated application of data collection, data decision and IoT implementation. So the the definition of IoT security here includes safety and security of sensors, managing their updation, data analysis. The specific features of IoT requires software-driven network security policies, extended security framework and relevant protection mechanism.

Some Security threats identified in proposed IoT applications are

- Malicious worm/virus
- Application data leakage
- Malicious scripts
- Man-in-the middle attack
- Routing attacks
- Inconsistent software patches

Security Countermeasures

IoT system setup includes the devices able to interact with the physical environments, by leveraging identification, sensing, and actuation capabilities. Through their enveloping capabilities, IoT devices represent the bridge between the physical and cyber domains. The main technologies generally adopted by networking of things are RFID technologies and Wireless Sensor Networks (WSNs).

The main application scenario for RFID tags deals with the identification and tracking of goods [4].Therefore, RFID tags present extremely low costs and can be battery-free by leveraging electromagnetic energy harvesting [4]. WSNs have been used in manifold application scenarios, such as environmental monitoring, agriculture, military scenarios, and smart cities, and represent a key enabler for IoT adoption [4]. So with IoT systems, hardware trojen, replication, battery draining, tampering are some common security threats which we also consider while developing IoT controlled system for railways.

Conventional mechanisms for security monitoring in IoT are authentication aand authorization of devices.

Authentication and authorization for IoT uses authentication protocol based on cryptography. This is also known as AAA framework[4], for intelligent access control or resources and security policy enforcement The majority of current IoT authentication protocols rely on mutual authentication, which refers to two or more IoT devices authenticating each other, providing privacy and data integrity. This can be based on

1. symmetric cryptography, which generates unique symmetric keys for each session based on a shared algorithm, and
2. public cryptography, which uses a combination of public and private keys for each entity.

This conventional framework offers protection against multiple vulnerabilities, such as insecure network services, insecure interfaces, and privacy concerns.

Authentication is the process of proving the user's or device's ID and credentials. The framework uses a combination of a username and a corresponding password. This is a simple traditional secure private topology that can be implemented in smart railway infrastructure and railway crossings.

Another conventional practice is Traffic filtering and firewall. This work consists of routing all traffic through a component such as Raspberry Pi, with gateway which secures the communications of IoT devices with the cloud database. The relevant firewall is implemented at the gateway level.

A firewall, also known as packet filter, is a network security appliance which analyzes incoming/outcoming packets,checking for matches to any of the pre-configured filtering rules, to either drop or forward the packets accordingly.

The literature has presented specially designed a high-performance lightweight deep-packet anomaly detection solution which is feasible for such resource constrained devices. This approach uses "n-gram bit-patterns" to make a fast and efficient packet classification decision. Although the illustrated results show low level of false alerts and high efficiency, the authors have not evaluated the power consumption of this solution.

In comparison to this, there are some extended security systems such as software driven network (SDN) and Virtualization that guarantees enhanced network programmability. This will decouple the control and forwarding functions. In this way, network management can be done separately, without affecting data flows, and can be carried out by a centralized controller. Software defined networking (SDN) and network function virtualization (NFV) have the potential to reshape the landscape of cybersecurity for IoT systems.

The adoption of virtualization technologies within network environments has recently changed the landscape of many more domains such as telecommunication systems, similarly it wll do it form IoT.

CONCLUSION

In this research work, an effective railway crossing system is proposed based on Internet of Things (IoT) and Machine Learning (ML). The prototype developed for this purpose successfully verifies the opening and closing of the railway gate during the train arrival and further helps in detecting the intermediate obstacle. It is user friendly and cost effective, and has acquired options, which can be utilized for performing desired operations. The outcomes achieved are: a. Reduced manpower b. The opening and closing of railway gates has now become more tractable c. Load sensors are easily available d. Efficient use of the sensors on the track e. Reduced the count of accidents due to human intervention f. Flexible for future enhancement.

This research work has improvised the present situation of railway gates with the help of prevailing technologies. It has helped the people living in accident prone areas to a great extent.

In this chapter, a broad overview on major security threats for IoT systems and conventional security countermeasures is presented. Data analytics integration with the relevant state-of-the-art solutions for IoT systems is included. This article covers different potential deployment environments, such as IoT access networks, core networks, and cloud/edge data centers, illustrating how SDN and NFV security mechanisms in brief. The article can be concluded by presenting this IoT controlled system by bringing two technologies IoT for improved resource planning, decision support system and secured operational technology to manage field equipments in heterogeneous railway infrastructure.

The most promising research areas are towards the broad deployment of SDN/NFV based security solutions in IoT systems. Accounting for the complexity of railway crossing and secured IoT systems, this discussion aims at providing an overview of potential IoT threats, conventional and cutting-edge security mechanisms to extend security mechanisms in heterogeneous environment of railway infrastructure. However, this article gives an idea and basic concept towards one aspect of smart railway crossing. In future, complete railway operations can be monitored by powerful IoT systems using platform server and crossing server and secured IoT devices. In this direction, there is lot of scope for IoT development.

REFERENCES

Abhinay, M. (2018). Automation of railway gate using IoT. *IJERT*, *6*(14), 1–4.

Anila, Saranya, Kiruthikamani, & Devi. (2017). Intelligent System for Automatic Railway Gate Controlling And Obstacle Detection. *International Journal of Scientific Research & Growth*, *4*(8), 24-28.

Asplund & Nadjm-Tehrani. (2016). Attitudes and Perceptions of IoT Security in Critical Societal Services. *IEEE Access, 4,* 2130-2138. . doi:10.1109/ACCESS.2016.2560919

Ekalya, Pavithran, & Biswas. (2018). Controlling Railway Gate Using Arduino. *Journal of Network Communications and Emerging Technologies*, *8*(4), 1–14.

Farris.(2019). A Survey on Emerging SDN and NFV Security Mechanisms for IoT Systems. *IEEE Comm. Surveys & Tutorials*, *21*(1), 812-834.

Farris, I., Taleb, T., Khettab, Y., & Song, J. (2019). Survey on emerging SDN and NFV security mechanisms for IoT systems. *IEEE Communications Surveys and Tutorials*, *21*(1), 812–837. doi:10.1109/COMST.2018.2862350

Fraga-Lamas. (2017). Towards the Internet of Smart Trains: A Review on Industrial IoT-Connected Railways. *Sensors 2017*, *17*(1457). doi:10.339017061457.1-44

Hellaoui, H. (2016). TAS-IoT: Trust-based Adaptive Security in the IoT. In *Proceedings of IEEE 41st Conference on Local Computer Networks* (pp. 599-602). 10.1109/LCN.2016.101

Jha, Agrawal, & Bhaumik. (2012). Automatic alert generation from train to the people at unmanned level crossings using principles of IoT. *Lecture Notes in Computer Science*, *7266*.

Jo. (2018). IoT for smart railway: feasibility and applications. *IEEE Internet of Things*, *5*(2), 482-490.

Joseph. (n.d.). Smart railway automation system using IoT- a literature survey. *IJCESR*, *5*(4), 42-57.

Kumar. (2015). *Automatic level crossing gate using IoT*. doi:10.13140/rg.2.1.2320.3368

Longrigg, P. (1975). Railroad-highway vehicular movement warning devices at grade crossings. IEEE Transactions on Industry Applications, 11(2), 211-221.

Mansingh, Selvakumar, & Kumar. (2015). Automation in unmanned railway level crossing. In *Proceedings of IEEE 9th international conference on intelligent systems and control (ISCO)* (pp. 1-4). IEEE.

Mavropoulos. (2017). *ASTo: A Tool for Security Analysis of IoT Systems. Proceedings IEEE SERA 2017*.

Reddy, Kavati, Rao, & Kumar. (2017). A secure railway crossing system using IoT. In *Proceedings of international conference of electronics, communication and aerospace technology (ICECA)* (pp. 196-199). 10.1109/ICECA.2017.8212795

Sato, K., Arai, H., Shimizu, T., & Takada, M. (1998). Obstruction detector using ultrasonic sensors for upgrading the safety of a level crossing. In *Proceedings of International conference on developments in mass transit systems*. (Vol.453, pp. 190-195). 10.1049/cp:19980140

Sharma, Kumar,& Sarika. (2015). Automatic Railway Gate Control System Based on RFID, pressure sensor and servo motor. *Journal of Network Communications and Emerging Technologies (JNCET)*, *5*(2), 153-156.

Siboni. (2019). Security Testbed for Internet-of-Things Devices. *IEEE Transactions on Reliability, 68*(1), 23-44.

Vishwanatha, Vidya Shree, & Kumar. (2018). *Smart railway gate system using IoT*. doi:10.23883/ijrter.2018.4128.w1usi

KEY TERMS AND DEFINITIONS

IoT: A geographic and cultural region of the Mideastern United States. The population in media is portrayed as suspicious, backward, and isolated.

Machine Learning: The belief that family is central to wellbeing and that family members and family issues take precedence over other aspects of life.

Sensors: A belief that one's own culture is superior to other cultures.

Compilation of References

'walkie-talkie' skyscraper melts jaguar car parts. (n.d.). http://www.bbc.co.uk/news/uk-england-london-23930675

Abdic, I., Fridman, L., McDuff, D., Marchi, E., Reimer, B., & Schuller, B. (2016). Driver frustration detection from audio and video in the wild. In *KI 2016: Advances in Artificial Intelligence: 39th Annual German Conference on AI*. Springer.

Abhinay, M. (2018). Automation of railway gate using IoT. *IJERT*, *6*(14), 1–4.

Abomhara, M., & Køien, G. M. (2014). Security and privacy in the Internet of Things: current status and open issues. In *International Conference on Privacy and Security in Mobile Systems (PRISMS)*. IEEE. 10.1109/PRISMS.2014.6970594

Abusalah, L., Khokhar, A., & Guizani, M. (2008). "A survey of secure mobile ad hoc routing protocols," IEEE Commun. *Surveys & Tutorials, IEEE*, *10*(4), 78–93. doi:10.1109/SURV.2008.080407

Acıiçmez, O. (2007). Yet another microarchitectural attack: exploiting I-Cache. In *Comp* (pp. 11–18). Security Arch. WS.

Acıiçmez, O., Gueron, S., & Seifert, J. P. (2007). New Branch Prediction Vulnerabilities in OpenSSL and Necessary Software Countermeasures. *International Conference on Cryptography and Coding (IMA)*. 10.1007/978-3-540-77272-9_12

Ahmad, S., Lavin, A., Purdy, S., & Agha, Z. (2017). Unsupervised real-time anomaly detection for streaming data. *Neurocomputing*, *262*, 134–147. doi:10.1016/j.neucom.2017.04.070

Aitken, C., & Taroni, F. (2004). *Statistics and the Evaluation of Evidence for Forensic Scientists*. Wiley. doi:10.1002/0470011238

Akhtar, N., & Mian, A. (n.d.). *Threat of adversarial attacks on deeplearning in computer vision: A survey*. https://arxiv.org/abs/1801.00553

Al-Dhahri, S., Al-Sarti, M., & Aziz, A. A. (2017). Information Security Management System. *International Journal of Computer Applications, 158*(7), 29-33.

Al-Fuqaha, Guizani, Mohammadi, Aledhari, & Ayyash. (2015). Internet of Things: A Survey on Enabling Technologies, Protocols, and Applications. *IEEE Communications Surveys & Tutorials, 17*(4), 2347–76.

Aman, Chua, & Sikdar. (n.d.). *Mutual Authentication in IoT Systems using Physical Unclonable Functions*. Academic Press.

Amara, Chebrolu, Vinayakumar, & Soman. (2018). *A Brief Survey on Autonomous Vehicle Possible Attacks, Exploits and Vulnerabilities*. Academic Press.

Amarachi, A. A., Okolie, S. O., & Ajaegbu, C. (2013). Information Security Management System: Emerging Issues and Prospect. *IOSR Journal of Computer Engineering, 12*(3), 96-102.

Amer, M., & Goldstein, M. (2012, August). Nearest-neighbor and clustering based anomaly detection algorithms for rapidminer. In *Proc. of the 3rd RapidMiner Community Meeting and Conference (RCOMM 2012)* (pp. 1-12). Academic Press.

Amer, M., Goldstein, M., & Abdennadher, S. (2013, August). Enhancing one-class support vector machines for unsupervised anomaly detection. In *Proceedings of the ACM SIGKDD Workshop on Outlier Detection and Description* (pp. 8-15). ACM.

Andrea, I., Chrysostomou, C., & Hadjichristofi, G. (2015, July). Internet of Things: Security vulnerabilities and challenges. In *2015 IEEE Symposium on Computers and Communication (ISCC)* (pp. 180-187). IEEE.

Andy, S., Rahardjo, B., & Hanindhito, B. (2017). Attack scenarios and security analysis of MQTT communication protocol in IoT system. In *4th International Conference on Electrical Engineering, Computer Science and Informatics (EECSI)*, (pp. 1–6). IEEE. 10.1109/EECSI.2017.8239179

Angin, O., Campbell, A., Kounavis, M., & Liao, R. (1998, August). The Mobiware Tollkit: Programmable Support for Adaptive Mobile Computing. *IEEE Personal Communications Magazine, Special Issue on Adapting to Network and Client Variability, 5*(4), 32–44. doi:10.1109/98.709367

Angiulli, F., & Fassetti, F. (2007, November). Detecting distance-based outliers in streams of data. In *Proceedings of the sixteenth ACM conference on Conference on information and knowledge management* (pp. 811-820). ACM. 10.1145/1321440.1321552

Anila, Saranya, Kiruthikamani, & Devi. (2017). Intelligent System for Automatic Railway Gate Controlling And Obstacle Detection. *International Journal of Scientific Research & Growth, 4*(8), 24-28.

Antonakakis, M., April, T., Bailey, M., & Bernhard, M. ElieBursztein, Jaime Cochran, ZakirDurumeric (2017). Understanding the mirai botnet. *26th USENIX Security Symposium (USENIX Security 17)*, 1093-1110.

Aranha, Barbosa, Cardoso, Mariano, & Diego. (2017). *Nizkctf: A Non-Interactive Zero-Knowledge Capture the Flag Platform*. https://arxiv.org/abs/1708.05844.X

Arias, O., Wurm, J., Hoang, K., & Jin, Y. (2015). Privacy and Security in Internet of Things and Wearable Devices. IEEE Transactions on Multi-Scale Computing Systems, 1(2), 99–109. doi:10.1109/TMSCS.2015.2498605

Arjaria & Khan. (2011). Busy Tone Based IG-MAC Protocol Using Multiple Data Rates In Ad-Hoc Networks. *Proceedings of International Journal of Advance in Communication Engineering, 3*.

Arjaria. (2013). A Scalable MAC Scheme Supporting Multimedia Applications in Wireless Ad-hoc Networks. *International Journal of Modern Engineering Management Research*.

ARM. (2018). *Vulnerability of speculative processors to cache timing side-channel mechanism.* Developer support of security update.

Armentano, R., Bhadoria, R. S., Chatterjee, P., & Deka, G. C. (2018, October). The Internet of things: foundation for smart cities, eHealth and ubiquitous computing. Boca Raton, FL: CRC Press. ISBN 9781498789028

Ashton, K. (2009). That 'internet of things' thing. *RFID Journal, 22*(7), 97–114.

Asplund & Nadjm-Tehrani. (2016). Attitudes and Perceptions of IoT Security in Critical Societal Services. *IEEE Access, 4,* 2130-2138. . doi:10.1109/ACCESS.2016.2560919

Atzori, L., Iera, A., & Morabito, G. (2010). The internet of things: A survey. *Computer Networks, 54*(15), 2787–2805. doi:10.1016/j.comnet.2010.05.010

Authorization (n.d.)The Economic Times. https://economictimes.indiatimes.com/definition/authorization

Badr, S., Gomaa, I., & Abd-Elrahman, E. (2018). Multi-tier blockchain framework for IoT-EHRs systems. *Procedia Computer Science, 141,* 159–166. doi:10.1016/j.procs.2018.10.162

Banks, A., Briggs, E., Borgendale, K., & Gupta, R. (2019). *MQTT Version 5.0.* https://docs.oasis-open.org/mqtt/mqtt/v5.0/mqtt-v5.0.html.X

Beckers, K. (2014). Goal-based establishment of an information security management system compliant to ISO 27001. *Theory and Practice of Computer, 8327,* 102–113. doi:10.1007/978-3-319-04298-5_10

Benoist, E., & Sliwa, J. (2014). How to Collect Consent for an Anonymous Medical Database. HEALTHINF, 405–12.

Bensaou, B., Wang, Y., & Ko, C. C. Fair Medium Access in 802.11 Based Wireless Ad-Hoc Networks. *First Annual IEEE & ACM International Workshop on Mobile Ad Hoc Networking and Computing.*

Bharghavan, V., Lee, K., Lu, S., Ha, S., Li, J. R., & Dwyer, D. (1998). Timely Adaptive Resource Management Architecture. *IEEE Personal Communication Magazine, 5*(8), 20-31.

Bharghavan, V., Demers, A., Shenker, S., & Zhang, L. (1994). MACAW: A Media Access Protocol for Wireless LANs. *Proc. of ACM SIGCOMM '94.* 10.1145/190314.190334

Bianchi, G. (2000, March). Performance Analysis of the IEEE 802.11 Distributed Coordination Function. *IEEE Journal on Selected Areas in Communications, 18*(3), 535–547. doi:10.1109/49.840210

Bianchi, G., Fratta, L., & Oliveri, M. (1996). Performance Evaluation and Enhancement of the CSMA/CA MAC Protocol for 802.11 Wireless LANs. *Proc. of PIMRC '96*, 392–396. 10.1109/PIMRC.1996.567423

Birrer, S. (2010). *Analyse systématique et permanente de la délinquance sérielle: place des statistiques criminelles: apport des approches situationnelles pour un système de classification: perspectives en matière de coopération.* Academic Press.

Bitzer, S., Albertini, N., Lock, E., Ribaux, O., & Delémont, O. (2015). *Utility of the clue — From assessing the investigative contribution of forensic science to supporting the decision to use traces* (Vol. 55). Academic Press.

Bojarski, M., Del Testa, D., Dworakowski, D., Firner, B., Flepp, B., Goyal, P., Jackel, L. D., Monfort, M., Muller, U., & Zhang, J. (2016). *End to end learning for self-driving cars.* arXiv preprint arXiv:1604.07316

Bonomi, F., Milito, R., Zhu, J., & Addepalli, S. (2012, August). Fog computing and its role in the internet of things. In *Proceedings of the first edition of the MCC workshop on Mobile cloud computing* (pp. 13-16). ACM.

Bosch. (2019). *Multiple Vulnerabilities in ProSyst mBS SDK and Bosch IoT Gateway Software.* https://psirt.bosch.com/Advisory/BOSCHSA-562575.html

Cali, Conti, & Gregori. (n.d.). *Dynamic Tuning of the IEEE 802.11 Protocol to Achieve a Theoretical Throughput Limit.* Academic Press.

Cali, F., Conti, M., & Gregori, E. (2000, December). Dynamic tuning of the IEEE 802.11 protocol to achieve a theoretical throughput limit. *IEEE/ACM Transactions on Networking, 8*(6), 785–799. doi:10.1109/90.893874

Cali, F., Conti, M., & Gregori, E. (2000, September). IEEE 802.11 Protocol: Design and Performance Evaluation of an Adaptive Backoff Mechanism. *IEEE Journal on Selected Areas in Communications, 18*(9), 1774–1786. doi:10.1109/49.872963

Campbell, T. (2016). Evolution of a Profession. In Practical Information Security Management: A Complete Guide to Planning and Implementation. APress.

Canedo, J., & Skjellum, A. (2016, December). Using machine learning to secure IoT systems. In *2016 14th Annual Conference on Privacy, Security and Trust (PST)* (pp. 219-222). IEEE.

Canella, C., Van Bulck, J., Schwarz, M., Lipp, M., Von Berg, B., Ortner, P., Piessens, F., Evtyushkin, D., & Gruss, D. (2018). *A Systematic Evaluation of Transient Execution Attacks and Defenses.* arXiv:1811.05441

Carlini, N., & Wagner, D. (2017). Towards evaluating the robustness of neural networks. *Proc. IEEE Security and Privacy Symposium*. 10.1109/SP.2017.49

Carrier, B. (2003). Defining digital forensic examination and analysis tools using abstraction layers. *International Journal of Digital Evidence, 1*(4), 1-12.

Casey, E. (2002) "Error, Uncertainty, and Loss in Digital Evidence" International Journal of Digital Evidence, Volume 1, Issue 2

Casey, E. (2007). What does "forensically sound" really mean? *Digital Investigation, 4*(2), 49–50. doi:10.1016/j.diin.2007.05.001

Casey, E. (2011). *Digital Evidence and Computer Crime - Forensic Science* (3rd ed.). Computers and the Internet.

Casey, E., & Jaquet-Chiffelle, D.-O. (2017). Do Identities Matter? *Policing. Journal of Policy Practice, 13*(1), 21–34.

Casey, E., Ribaux, O., & Roux, C. (2019). The Kodak syndrome: Risks and opportunities created by decentralization of forensic capabilities. *Journal of Forensic Sciences, 64*(1), 127–136. doi:10.1111/1556-4029.13849 PMID:29975983

Catarinucci, L., De Donno, D., Mainetti, L., Palano, L., Patrono, L., Stefanizzi, M. L., & Tarricone, L. (2015). An Iot-Aware Architecture for Smart Healthcare Systems. IEEE Internet of Things Journal, 2(6), 515–26. doi:10.1109/JIOT.2015.2417684

Cecchinel, C., Jimenez, M., Mosser, S., & Riveill, M. (2014, June). An architecture to support the collection of big data in the internet of things. In *2014 IEEE World Congress on Services* (pp. 442-449). IEEE. 10.1109/SERVICES.2014.83

Cekerevac, Dvorak, Prigoda, & Cekerevac. (n.d.). Internet of things and man in the middle attacks-security and economic risks. *MEST Journal, 5*(2), 15-25.

Champod, C., & Meuwly, D. (2000). The inference of identity in forensic speaker recognition. *Speech Communication, 31*(2), 193–203. doi:10.1016/S0167-6393(99)00078-3

Chernikova, Oprea, Nita-Rotaru, & Kim. (2019). *Are Self-Driving Cars Secure? Evasion Attacks against Deep Neural Networks for Steering Angle Prediction.* arXiv:1904.07370v1

Chisum, W. J., & Turvey, B. E. (2011). *Crime reconstruction.* Academic Press.

Choi, N., Seok, Y., & Choi, Y. (2003). Multi-channel MAC Protocol for Mobile Ad Hoc Networks. *Proc. IEEE VTC 2003.*

Chung, H., Park, J., & Lee, S. (2017). Digital forensic approaches for Amazon Alexa ecosystem. *Digital Investigation, 22*, S15–S25. doi:10.1016/j.diin.2017.06.010

Cisco. (2014). *The Internet of Things Reference Model.* Retrieved from http://cdn.iotwf.com/resources/71/IoT_Reference_Model_White_Paper_June_4_2014.pdf,2014

Compilation of References

Clarke, Miller, Hong, Sandberg, & Wiley. (2002). Protecting Free Expression Online with Freenet. *IEEE Internet Computing, 6*(1), 40–49.

Clarke, Sandberg, Wiley, & Hong. (2001). Freenet: A Distributed Anonymous Information Storage and Retrieval System. In *Designing Privacy Enhancing Technologies*, (pp. 46–66). Springer.

Clarke-Salt, J. (2009). *SQL Injection Attacks and Defense*. Elsevier.

Common Vulnerabilities and Exposures. (n.d.). https://cve.mitre.org

Commonwealth of Pennsylvania, Appellant v. Tyler Kristian MANGEL, Matthew Robert Craft. Commonwealth of Pennsylvania, Appellant v. Tyler Kristian Mangel, Matthew Robert Craft., No. 181 A.3d 1154 (2018) (Superior Court of Pennsylvania 2018).

Cowan, C., Pu, C., Maier, D., Walpole, J., Bakke, P., Beattie, S., Grier, A., Wagle, P., Zhang, Q., & Hinton, H. (1998). Stackguard: Automatic Adaptive Detection and Prevention of Buffer-Overflow Attacks. *USENIX Security Symposium, 98*, 63–78.

Creator, Q. T. (2019). *Software development made smarter*. Retrieved from https://www.qt.io

CVE-2017-11578. (2017). https://nvd.nist.gov/vuln/detail/CVE-2017-11578

CVE-2018-11629. (2018).Retrieved from https://nvd.nist.gov/vuln/detail/CVE-2018-11629

CVE-2018-11925. (2018). Retrieved from https://nvd.nist.gov/vuln/detail/CVE-2018-11925

CVE-2018-11967. (2018). Retrieved from https://nvd.nist.gov/vuln/detail/CVE-2018-11967

CVE-2018-13908 .(2018).Retrieved from https://nvd.nist.gov/vuln/detail/CVE-2018-13908

CVE-2018-13913. (2018). Retrieved from https://nvd.nist.gov/vuln/detail/CVE-2018-13913

CVE-2018-13914. (2018). Retrieved from https://nvd.nist.gov/vuln/detail/CVE-2018-13914

CVE-2018-8119. (2018). Retrieved from https://nvd.nist.gov/vuln/detail/CVE-2018-8119

CVE-2018-8531. (2018). Retrieved from https://nvd.nist.gov/vuln/detail/CVE-2018-8531

CVE-2019-0729. (2019) Retrieved from https://nvd.nist.gov/vuln/detail/CVE-2019-0729

CVE-2019-11219. (2019). Retrieved from https://nvd.nist.gov/vuln/detail/CVE-2019-11219

CVE-2019-11220. (2019). Retrieved from https://nvd.nist.gov/vuln/detail/CVE-2019-11220

CVE-2019-11603. (2019). https://nvd.nist.gov/vuln/detail/CVE-2019-11603

CVE-2019-1644. (2019). Retrieved from https://nvd.nist.gov/vuln/detail/CVE-2019-1644

CVE-2019-1845. (2019). Retrieved from https://nvd.nist.gov/vuln/detail/CVE-2019-1845

CVE-2019-1957. (2019). Retrieved from https://nvd.nist.gov/vuln/detail/CVE-2019-1957

CVE-2019-2255. (2019). Retrieved from https://nvd.nist.gov/vuln/detail/CVE-2019-2255

CVE-2019-2278. (2019). Retrieved from https://nvd.nist.gov/vuln/detail/CVE-2019-2278

CVE-2019-9750. (2019). https://nvd.nist.gov/vuln/detail/CVE-2019-9750,2019

CWE-798: Use of Hard-coded Credentials. (2018). Retrieved from http://cwe.mitre.org/data/definitions/798.html

Deepika, N., & Variyar, V. V. S. (2017). Obstacle classiðcation and detection for vision based navigation for autonomous driving. *2017 International Conference on Advances in Computing,Communications and Informatics (ICACCI)*, 2092–2097. 10.1109/ICACCI.2017.8126154

Deo, N. (2003). *Graph Theory with application to Engineering and Computer Science*. Prentice Hall of India Private Limited.

Dessimoz, D., & Champod, C. (2008). Linkages between biometrics and forensic science. In *Handbook of biometrics* (pp. 425–459). Springer. doi:10.1007/978-0-387-71041-9_21

Ding, Z., & Fei, M. (2013). An anomaly detection approach based on isolation forest algorithm for streaming data using sliding window. *IFAC Proceedings Volumes, 46*(20), 12-17.

Disselkoen, C., Kohlbrenner, D., Porter, L., & Tullsen, D. (2017). Prime+Abort: A Timer-Free High-Precision L3 Cache Attack using Intel TSX. Usenix Security.

Distributed information security management model (DISMM). (2017, November 7). Identity Management Institute®.https://www.identitymanagementinstitute.org/distributed-information-security-management-model-dismm/

Ditzler, G., & Polikar, R. (2012). Incremental learning of concept drift from streaming imbalanced data. *IEEE Transactions on Knowledge and Data Engineering, 25*(10), 2283–2301. doi:10.1109/TKDE.2012.136

Du, J., Masters, J., & Barth, M. (2004). Lane-level positioning for in-vehicle navigation and automated vehicle location (avl) systems. In *Intelligent Transportation Systems, 2004. Proceedings. The 7th International IEEE Conference on*. IEEE. 10.1109/ITSC.2004.1398868

Ekalya, Pavithran, & Biswas. (2018). Controlling Railway Gate Using Arduino. *Journal of Network Communications and Emerging Technologies, 8*(4), 1–14.

El Mouaatamid, O., Lahmer, M., & Belkasmi, M. (2016). Internet of Things Security: Layered classification of attacks and possible Countermeasures. *Electronic Journal of Information Technology*, (9).

Employee management. (n.d.). BambooHR. https://www.bamboohr.com/hr-glossary/employee-management/

Employment policies and practices | CISSP security management and practices | Pearson IT certification. (n.d.). Pearson IT Certification: Videos, flash cards, simulations, books, eBooks, and practice tests for Cisco, CompTIA, and Microsoft exams.http://www.pearsonitcertification.com/articles/article.aspx?p=30287&seqNum=10

Erfani, S. M., Rajasegarar, S., Karunasekera, S., & Leckie, C. (2016). High-dimensional and large-scale anomaly detection using a linear one-class SVM with deep learning. *Pattern Recognition*, *58*, 121–134. doi:10.1016/j.patcog.2016.03.028

Evtimov, I., Eykholt, K., Fernandes, E., Kohno, T., Li, B., Prakash, A., Rahmati, A., & Song, D. (n.d.). *Robust physical-world attackson machine learning models*. https://arxiv.org/abs/1707.089455

Evtyushkin, D., Ponomarev, D. V., & Abu-Ghazaleh, N. B. (2016). Jump over ASLR: Attacking branch predictors to bypass ASLR. MICRO.

Farahani, B., Firouzi, F., Chang, V., Badaroglu, M., Constant, N., & Mankodiya, K. (2018). Towards fog-driven IoT eHealth: Promises and challenges of IoT in medicine and healthcare. *Future Generation Computer Systems*, *78*, 659–676. doi:10.1016/j.future.2017.04.036

Farris.(2019). A Survey on Emerging SDN and NFV Security Mechanisms for IoT Systems. *IEEE Comm. Surveys & Tutorials*, *21*(1), 812-834.

Farris, I., Taleb, T., Khettab, Y., & Song, J. (2019). Survey on emerging SDN and NFV security mechanisms for IoT systems. *IEEE Communications Surveys and Tutorials*, *21*(1), 812–837. doi:10.1109/COMST.2018.2862350

Felson, M., Clarke, R. V. G., & Great Britain Home Office, P. a. R. C. U. (1998). *Opportunity makes the thief: practical theory for crime prevention*. London: Home Office, Policing and Reducing Crime Unit, Research, Development and Statistics Directorate.

Fernandes. (2016). Security Analysis of Emerging Smart Home Applications. *IEEE Symposium on Security and Privacy*, 636-654.

FHIR Work Group. (2011). *HL7 FHIR Release 4*. Retrieved from https://hl7.org/fhir/

Fraga-Lamas. (2017). Towards the Internet of Smart Trains: A Review on Industrial IoT-Connected Railways. *Sensors 2017*, *17*(1457). doi:10.339017061457.1-44

Franklin. (2019). *Peer-to-Peer Vulnerability Exposes Millions of IoT Devices*. Retrieved from https://www.darkreading.com/vulnerabilities—threats/peerto-peer-vulnerability-exposes-millions-of-iot-devices/d/d-id/1334564

Fridman, Brown, Glazer, Angell, Dodd, Jenik, Terwilliger, Patsekin, Kindelsberger, Ding, Seaman, Mehler, Sipperley, Pettinato, Seppelt, Angell, Mehler, & Reimer. (n.d.). *MIT Autonomous Vehicle Technology Study: Large-Scale Deep Learning Based Analysis of Driver Behavior and Interaction with Automation*. arXiv:1711.06976v3

Fullmer, C. L., & Garcia-Luna-Aceves, J. J. (1997). Solutions to Hidden Terminal Problems in Wireless Networks. *Proc. ACM SIGCOMM '97*. 10.1145/263105.263137

Gen, H. P.-C. S. A. (2015). *Controllers, R. Hewlett-Packard Enterprise Development LP.*

Ge, Q., Yarom, Y., Cock, D., & Heiser, G. (2018). A survey of microarchitectural timing attacks and countermeasures on contemporary hardware. *J. Cryptographic Engineering, 8*(1), 1–27. doi:10.100713389-016-0141-6

Ghayvat, H., Mukhopadhyay, S., Gui, X., & Suryadevara, N. (2015). WSN- and IOT-Based Smart Homes and Their Extension to Smart Buildings. *Sensors, 15*(5), 10350–10379. doi:10.3390150510350

Giry, D. (2008). *Keylength – Cryptographic Key Length Recommendation.* http://www.keylength.com

Giuseppe Nebbione and Maria Carla Calzarossa. (2020). *Security of IoT Application Layer Protocols: Challenges and Findings.* MDPI, Future Internet.

Gomes. (2014). *Hidden obstacles for googles self-driving cars: Impressive progress hides major limitations of googles quest for automated driving.* Academic Press.

Govindaswamy, V., Blackstone, W. L., & Balasekaran, G. (2011). Survey of Recent Position Based Routing Mobile Ad-hoc Network Protocols. Proceedings of *2011 UKSim 13th International Conference on Modelling and Simulation,* 467-471. 10.1109/UKSIM.2011.95

Gruss, D., Maurice, C., Fogh, A., Lipp, M., & Mangard, S. (2016) Prefetch Side-Channel Attacks: Bypassing SMAP and Kernel ASLR. CCS.

Gruss, D., Maurice, C., Wagner, K., & Mangard, S. (2016). Flush+Flush: A Fast and Stealthy Cache Attack. DIMVA'16.

Gruss, D., Spreitzer, R., & Mangard, S. (2015). Cache Template Attacks: Automating Attacks on Inclusive Last-Level Caches. *USENIX Security Symposium.*

Guido, M., Brooks, M., Grover, J., Katz, E., Ondricek, J., Rogers, M., & Sharpe, L. (2016). Generating a Corpus of Mobile Forensic Images for Masquerading user Experimentation. *Journal of Forensic Sciences, 61*(6), 1467–1472. doi:10.1111/1556-4029.13178 PMID:27545967

Guimar, R., Morillo, J., Cerd, L., & Barcel, J. (2004). *Quality of service for mobile Ad-hoc Networks: An Overview.* Technical Report UPC-DAC-2004-24, Polytechnic University of Catalonia.

Gullasch, D., Bangerter, E., & Krenn, S. (2011). Cache Games - Bringing Access-Based Cache Attacks on AES to Practice. IEEE: Security & Privacy.

Gunes, M., & Reibel, R. (2002). An IP address configuration algorithm for Zeroconf mobile multihop ad hoc networks. *Proceedings of International Workshop on broadband wireless ad hoc networks and services.*

Guth, J., Breitenbucher, U., Falkenthal, M., Fremantle, P., Kopp, O., Leymann, F., & Reinfurt, L. (2018). *A Detailed Analysis of IoT Platform Architectures: Concepts, Similarities, and Differences. In Internet of Everything.* Springer.

Hallman, Bryan, Palavicini, Divita, & Romero-Mariona. (2017). *IoDDoS — The Internet of Distributed Denial of Service Attacks A Case Study of the Mirai Malware and IoT-Based Botnets.* IoTBDS 2017 - 2nd International Conference on Internet of Things, Big Data and Security.

Han, G., Xiao, L., & Poor, H. V. (2017, March). Two-dimensional anti-jamming communication based on deep reinforcement learning. In *2017 IEEE International Conference on Acoustics, Speech and Signal Processing (ICASSP)* (pp. 2087-2091). IEEE.

Hao, F. (2017). *Schnorr Non-Interactive Zero-Knowledge Proof.* RFC 8235. https://tools.ietf.org/rfc/rfc8235.txt.X

Haque, A., DeLucia, A., & Baseman, E. (2017, November). Markov chain modeling for anomaly detection in high performance computing system logs. In *Proceedings of the Fourth International Workshop on HPC User Support Tools* (p. 3). ACM.

Hellaoui, H. (2016). TAS-IoT: Trust-based Adaptive Security in the IoT. In *Proceedings of IEEE 41st Conference on Local Computer Networks* (pp. 599-602). 10.1109/LCN.2016.101

Heller, K., Svore, K., Keromytis, A. D., & Stolfo, S. (2003). *One class support vector machines for detecting anomalous windows registry accesses.* Academic Press.

Hong, K.-S., Chi, Y.-P., Chao, L. R., & Tang, J.-H. (2003). An integrated system theory of information security management. *Information Management & Computer Security, 11*(5), 243–248. doi:10.1108/09685220310500153

Horn, J. (2018). *Speculative execution, variant 4: speculative store bypass.* Retrieved from https://bugs.chromium.org/p/project-zero/issues/detail?id=1528

Horsman, G. (2018). *"I couldn't find it your honour, it mustn't be there!" – Tool errors, tool limitations and user error in digital forensics* (Vol. 58). Academic Press.

Hossain, Shamim, & Muhammad. (2016). Cloud-Assisted Industrial Internet of Things (Iiot)–Enabled Framework for Health Monitoring. *Computer Networks, 101*, 192–202.

Humphreys, E. (2008). Information security management standards: Compliance, governance and risk management. *Information Security Technical Report, 13*(4), 247–255. doi:10.1016/j.istr.2008.10.010

Hwang, Y. H. (2015). Iot Security & Privacy: Threats and Challenges. In *Proceedings of the 1st Acm Workshop on Iot Privacy, Trust, and Security,* (pp. 1–1). ACM.

IAIK. (2018). *Meltdown Proof-of-Concept.* Retrieved from https://github.com/IAIK/meltdown

Inci, M. S., Gulmezoglu, B., Irazoqui, G., Eisenbarth, T., & Sunar, B. (2016). Cache Attacks Enable Bulk Key Recovery on the Cloud. CHES'16. doi:10.1007/978-3-662-53140-2_18

Information security management system. (2018, April 19). Quality Management System, ISO Certification Bodies In India.https://www.irqs.co.in/it-standards/information-security-management-system

Information security management. (2007, May 12). Wikipedia, the free encyclopedia. Retrieved June 3, 2020, from https://en.wikipedia.org/wiki/Information_security_management

INTEL. (2016). *Intel Software Guard Extensions (Intel SGX).* Retrieved from https://software.intel.com/en-us/sgx

INTEL. (2017a). *Intel Xeon Processor Scalable Family Technical Overview.* Retrieved from https://software.intel.com/en-us/articles/intel-xeon-processor-scalable-family-technical-overview

INTEL. (2017b). *Intel 64 and IA-32 Architectures Optimization Reference Manual.* INTEL.

INTEL. (2018). *Intel Analysis of Speculative Execution Side Channels.* Retrieved from https://software.intel.com/security-software-guidance/api-app/sites/default/files/336983-Intel-Analysis-of-Speculative-Execution-Side-Channels-White-Paper.pdf

Internet of things (IoT) security: 9 ways you can help protect yourself. (n.d.). Official Site | Norton™ - Antivirus & Anti-Malware Software. https://us.norton.com/internetsecurity-iot-securing-the-internet-of-things.html

Iqbal, Olaleye, & Bayoumi. (2016). A Review on Internet of Things (Iot): Security and Privacy Requirements and the Solution Approaches. *Global Journal of Computer Science and Technology, 16*(7).

Irazoqui, G., Eisenbarth, T., & Sunar, B. (2016). Cross processor cache attacks. AsiaCCS. doi:10.1145/2897845.2897867

Irazoqui, G., Eisenbarth, T., & Sunar, B. (2015). S$A: A shared cache attack that works across cores and defies VM sandboxing—and its application to AES. *IEEE Security & Privacy.* doi:10.1109/SP.2015.42

Islam, Riazul, Kwak, Kabir, Hossain, & Kwak. (2015). The Internet of Things for Health Care: A Comprehensive Survey. *IEEE Access, 3*, 678–708.

ISMS - Security and value of information - TÜV TRUST IT GmbH Unternehmensgruppe TÜV Austria. (2015, August 31). TÜV TRUST IT GmbH Unternehmensgruppe TÜV AUSTRIA. https://it-tuv.com/en/leistungen/security-and-value-of-information/

Jackson, G., Jones, S., Booth, G., Champod, C., & Evett, I. (2006). *The Nature of Forensic Science Opinion – A Possible Framework to Guide Thinking and Practice in Investigation and in Court Proceedings* (Vol. 46). Academic Press.

James, J. (2017). IoT Forensic Challenge, 2017-2018. Retrieved from https://github.com/jijames/DFRWS2018Challenge

Jan, S.-S., & Tao, A.-L. (2016). Comprehensive comparisons of satellite data, signals, and measurements between the beidou navigation satellite system and the global positioning system. *Sensors, 16*(5), 689. doi:10.339016050689 PMID:27187403

Jaquet-Chiffelle, D.-O. (2008). The Model: A Formal Description, Section 7.2. In D.-O. Jaquet-Chiffelle, B. Anrig, E. Benoist, & R. Haenni (Eds.), *Virtual Persons and Identities, FIDIS deliverable 2.13*. Available at http://www.fidis.net/fileadmin/fidis/deliverables/fidis-wp2-del2.13_Virtual_Persons_v1.0.pdf

Jaquet-Chiffelle, D.-O. (2009a). Identification, Section 4.2. In D.-O. Jaquet-Chiffelle & H. Buitelaar (Eds.), *Trust and Identification in the Light of Virtual Persons, FIDIS deliverable 17.4*. Available at http://www.fidis.net/fileadmin/fidis/deliverables/new_deliverables/fidis-wp17-del17.4_Trust_and_Identification_in_the_Light_of_Virtual_Persons.pdf

Jaquet-Chiffelle, D.-O. (2009b). Identity Core Components, Section 7.2. In D.-O. Jaquet-Chiffelle, H. Zwingelberg, & B. Anrig (Eds.), *Modelling New Forms of Identities: Applicability of the Model Based on Virtual Persons, FIDIS deliverable 17.1*. Available at http://www.fidis.net/fileadmin/fidis/deliverables/fidis-wp17-del17.1.Modelling_New_Forms_of_Identities.pdf

Jha, Agrawal, & Bhaumik. (2012). Automatic alert generation from train to the people at unmanned level crossings using principles of IoT. *Lecture Notes in Computer Science, 7266*.

Jo. (2018). IoT for smart railway: feasibility and applications. *IEEE Internet of Things, 5*(2), 482-490.

Joglekar, S. (2015). *Self-Organizing Maps with Google's Tensor Flow*. Retrieved from https://codesachin.wordpress.com/2015/11/28/self-organizing-maps-with-googles-tensorflow/

Joseph. (n.d.). Smart railway automation system using IoT- a literature survey. *IJCESR, 5*(4), 42-57.

Jovanbulck. (2019). *Foreshadow*. Retrieved from https://github.com/jovanbulck/sgx-step/tree/master/app/foreshadow

Karimi, M., & Pan, D. (2009). Challenges for Quality of Service (QoS) in Mobile Ad-Hoc Networks (MANETs). *Proceedings of IEEE 10th Annual Wireless and Microwave Technology Conference, WAMICON '09*, 1-5. 10.1109/WAMICON.2009.5207262

Khurana, R. (2014). *Operating System*. Vikash Publishing House Pvt. Ltd.

Kiriansky, V., & Waldspurger, C. (2018). *Speculative Buffer Overflows: Attacks and Defenses*. arXiv:1807.03757

Kirk, P. L. (1963). The ontogeny of criminalistics. *The Journal of Criminal Law, Criminology, and Police Science, 54*(2), 235. doi:10.2307/1141173

Kocher, P. (1996). Timing Attacks on Implementations of Diffie-Hellman, RSA, DSS, and Other Systems. Proc. Advances in Cryptology (CRYPTO '96), 104-113.

Kocher, P., Horn, J., Fogh, A., Genkin, D., Gruss, D., Haas, W., Hamburg, M., Lipp, M., Mangard, S., Prescher, T., Schwarz, M., & Yarom, Y. (2019). Spectre attacks: Exploiting speculative execution. *IEEE Security & Privacy*. doi:10.1109/SP.2019.00002

Kohonen, T. (1982). Self-organized formation of topologically correct feature maps. *Biological Cybernetics*, *43*(1), 59–69. doi:10.1007/BF00337288

Kohonen, T. (1990). The self-organizing map. *Proceedings of the IEEE*, *78*(9), 1464–1480. doi:10.1109/5.58325

Kolias, C., Kambourakis, G., Stavrou, A., & Voas, J. (2017). DDoS in the IoT: Mirai and Other Botnets. *Computer*, *50*(7), 80–84. doi:10.1109/MC.2017.201

Koruyeh, E. M., Khasawneh, K., Song, C., & Abu-Ghazaleh, N. (2018). Spectre returns! speculation attacks using the return stack buffer. WOOT.

Koscher, K., Czeskis, A., Roesner, F., Patel, S., Kohno, T., Checkoway, S., McCoy, D., Kantor, B., Anderson, D., & Shacham, H. (2010). Experimental security analysis of a modern automobile. *2010 IEEE Symposium on Security and Privacy*, 447–462. 10.1109/SP.2010.34

Kriegel, H. P., Kröger, P., Sander, J., & Zimek, A. (2011). Density-based clustering. *Wiley Interdisciplinary Reviews. Data Mining and Knowledge Discovery*, *1*(3), 231–240. doi:10.1002/widm.30

Kumar Sarkar, S., Basavaraju, T. G., & Puttamadappa, C. (2008). *Ad-hoc Mobile Wireless Networks Principles, Protocols, and Applications*. Auerbach Publications.

Kumar. (2015). *Automatic level crossing gate using IoT*. doi:10.13140/rg.2.1.2320.3368

Kwan, Q. (1977). *Inference of Identity of Source (PhD diss), Sociology*. University of California.

Lee, J., Jang, J., Jang, Y., Kwak, N., Choi, Y., Choi, C., Kim, T., Peinado, M., & Kang, B. B. (2017). Hacking in darkness: Return-oriented programming against secure enclaves. In USENIX Security (pp. 523–539). Academic Press.

Lee, S. B., Gahng-Seop, A., Zhang, X., & Campbell, A. T. (2000, April). INSIGNIA: An IP-based Quality of Service Framework for Mobile Ad-hoc Networks. *Journal of Parallel and Distributed Computing*, *60*(4), 374–406. doi:10.1006/jpdc.1999.1613

Lee, S., Shih, M., Gera, P., Kim, T., Kim, H., & Peinado, M. (2017). Inferring Fine-grained Control Flow Inside SGX Enclaves with Branch Shadowing. *USENIX Security Symposium*.

Li, Cai, & Xu. (2007). Spanning-tree based autoconfiguration for mobile ad hoc networks", Wireless Personal Communications. *Springer Science, 43*(4).

Li, K. L., Huang, H. K., Tian, S. F., & Xu, W. (2003, November). Improving one-class SVM for anomaly detection. In Proceedings of the 2003 International Conference on Machine Learning and Cybernetics (IEEE Cat. No. 03EX693) (Vol. 5, pp. 3077-3081). IEEE.

Li, L., Cai, Y., & Xu, X. (2009). *Cluster based autoconfiguration for mobile ad hoc networks. Wireless Personal Communications* , 49.

Lipp, M., Schwarz, M., Gruss, D., Prescher, T., Haas, W., Fogh, A., Horn, J., Mangard, S., Kocher, P., Genkin, D., Yarom, Y., & Hamburg, M. (2018). Meltdown: Reading Kernel Memory from User Space. *USENIX Security Symposium.*

Liu, F., Yarom, Y., Ge, Q., Heiser, G., & Lee, R. (2015). Last level cache side channel attacks are practical. *36th IEEE Symposium on Security and Privacy (S&P 2015).* 10.1109/SP.2015.43

Liu, F. T., Ting, K. M., & Zhou, Z. H. (2012). Isolation-based anomaly detection. *ACM Transactions on Knowledge Discovery from Data, 6*(1), 3. doi:10.1145/2133360.2133363

Locard, E. (1920). *L'enquête criminelle et les méthodes scientifiques.* E. Flammarion.

Loh, P. K. K., & Loh, B. W. Y. (2016). Celles — A novel IOT security approach. In *Conf. Rec. 2016 IEEE Int. Conf. TENCON* (pp. 3716– 3719). IEEE.

Longrigg, P. (1975). Railroad-highway vehicular movement warning devices at grade crossings. IEEE Transactions on Industry Applications, 11(2), 211-221.

Luo, H., Lu, S., Bharghavan, V., Cheng, J., & Luo, H. (2004). A Packet Scheduling Approach to QoS Support in Multi-hop Wireless Networks. *Mobile Networks and Applications, 9*(3), 193–206. doi:10.1023/B:MONE.0000020643.70011.c7

Ma, M., Wang, P., Chu, C.-H., & Liu, L. (2014). Efficient Multipattern Event Processing over High-Speed Train Data Streams. IEEE Internet of Things Journal, 2(4), 295–309.

Mahmoud, R., Yousuf, T., Aloul, F., & Zualkernan, I. (2015, December). Internet of things (IoT) security: Current status, challenges and prospective measures. In *2015 10th International Conference for Internet Technology and Secured Transactions (ICITST)* (pp. 336-341). IEEE.

Maisuradze, G., & Rossow, C. (2018). Ret2spec: Speculative execution using return stack buffers. CCS.

Malik, M. I., McAteer, I. N., Hannay, P., Firdous, S. N., & Baig, Z. (2018). XMPP architecture and security challenges in an IoT ecosystem. *Proceedings of the 16th Australian Information Security Management Conference,* 62.

Mansingh, Selvakumar, & Kumar. (2015). Automation in unmanned railway level crossing. In *Proceedings of IEEE 9th international conference on intelligent systems and control (ISCO)* (pp. 1-4). IEEE.

Mapa, S. K. (2000)., Higher Algebra. Sarat Book Distribution.

Mapa, S. K. (1998). *Real Analysis.* Asoke Prakasan.

Marquis, R., Biedermann, A., Cadola, L., Champod, C., Gueissaz, L., Massonnet, G., . . . Hicks, T. (2016). *Discussion on how to implement a verbal scale in a forensic laboratory: Benefits, pitfalls and suggestions to avoid misunderstandings* (Vol. 56). Academic Press.

Martin, J.-C., & Delémont, O. (2002). *Investigation de scène de crime: fixation de l'état des lieux et traitement des traces d'objets.* Presses polytechniques et universitaires romandes.

Martini, B., & Choo, K.-K. R. (2012). An integrated conceptual digital forensic framework for cloud computing. *Digital Investigation*, *9*(2), 71–80. doi:10.1016/j.diin.2012.07.001

Mavropoulos. (2017). *ASTo: A Tool for Security Analysis of IoT Systems. Proceedings IEEE SERA 2017.*

Minerva, R., Biru, A., & Rotondi, D. (2015). Towards a definition of the Internet of Things (IoT). *IEEE Internet Initiative*, *1*, 1–86.

Mirhahhak, M., Schult, N., & Thomson, D. (2000). Dynamic Quality-of-Service for Mobile Ad-hoc Networks. *Proceedings of the 1st ACM International Symposium on Mobile Ad-hoc Networking & Computing*, 137 - 138.

Mohsin, M., & Prakash, R. (2002). IP address assignment in a mobile ad hoc network. *Proceedings of the IEEE MILCOM 2002*. 10.1109/MILCOM.2002.1179586

Moosavi, Gia, Nigussie, Rahmani, Virtanen, Tenhunen, & Isoaho. (2016). End-to-End Security Scheme for Mobility Enabled Healthcare Internet of Things. *Future Generation Computer Systems*, *64*, 108–24.

Msmania. (2018). *Meltdown/Spectre Proof-of-Concept for Windows*. Retrieved from https://github.com/msmania/microarchitectural-attack

Mulay, S. A., Devale, P. R., & Garje, G. V. (2010). Intrusion detection system using support vector machine and decision tree. *International Journal of Computers and Applications*, *3*(3), 40–43. doi:10.5120/758-993

Muniyandi, A. P., Rajeswari, R., & Rajaram, R. (2012). Network anomaly detection by cascading k-Means clustering and C4. 5 decision tree algorithm. *Procedia Engineering*, *30*, 174–182. doi:10.1016/j.proeng.2012.01.849

Murphy, K. P. (2012). *Machine learning: a probabilistic perspective*. MIT Press.

Murthy, C. S. R., & Manoj, B. S. (2004). *Ad-hoc Wireless Networks Architectures and Protocols*. Prentice Hall.

Nagpal, D. P. (2014). *Data Communications and Networking*. S. Chand & Company Pvt. Ltd.

National Research Council. (2003). *Who goes there?: Authentication through the lens of privacy*. National Academies Press.

Nazario, J. (2008). DDoS Attack Evolution. *Network Security*, (7), 7–10.

Neal, D. (2016). Mirai botnet: DDoS attack takes out Liberia communications networks. *The Inquirer*. Available at: https://www.theinquirer.net/inquirer/news/2476458/miraibotnetddosattacktakesoutliberiacommunicationsnetworks

O'Donnell. (2020). *Threat post*. https://threatpost.com/half-iot-devices-vulnerable-severe-attacks/153609/

O'Hanlon, B. W., Psiaki, M. L., Bhatti, J. A., Shepard, D. P., & Humphreys, T. E. (2013). Real-time gps spoofing detection via correlation of encrypted signals. *Navigation, 60*(4), 267–278. doi:10.1002/navi.44

Olivier, F., Carlos, G., & Florent, N. (2015). *New Security Architecture for IoT Network. Procedia Computer Science* , 52.

OPenest. (n.d.). https://openest.io/en/2020/01/03/mqtts-how-to-use-mqtt-with-tls/

Oriwoh, E., & Sant, P. (2013). *The Forensics Edge Management System: A Concept and Design.* Paper presented at the 2013 IEEE 10th International Conference on Ubiquitous Intelligence and Computing and 2013 IEEE 10th International Conference on Autonomic and Trusted Computing.

Oriwoh, E., Jazani, D., Epiphaniou, G., & Sant, P. (2013). *Internet of Things Forensics: Challenges and approaches.* Paper presented at the 9th IEEE International Conference on Collaborative Computing: Networking, Applications and Worksharing.

Osvik, D. A., Shamir, A., & Tromer, E. (2006). Cache Attacks and Countermeasures: The Case of AES. CT-RSA.

OWASP Foundation. (n.d.). https://owasp.org/

Park & Lee. (2014). Advanced Approach to Information Security Management System Model for Industrial Control System. *E-Scientific World Journal.* doi:10.1155/2014/348305

Park, C.S., Jang, S.S., & Park, Y.T. (2010). A Study of Effect of Information Security Management System Certification on Organization Performance. *International Journal of Computer Science and Network Security, 10*(3).

Parkinson, Ward, Wilson, & Miller. (2017). Cyber Threats Facing Autonomous and Connected Vehicles: Future Challenges. *IEEE Transactions on Intelligent Transportation Systems, 18*(11).

Paschou, Sakkopoulos, Sourla, & Tsakalidis. (2013). Health Internet of Things: Metrics and Methods for Efficient Data Transfer. *Simulation Modelling Practice and Theory, 34*, 186–99.

Peltier, T. R. (2005). *Information Security Policies, Procedures and Standards, Guidelines for Effective Information Security Management.* CRC Press.

Perdisci, R., Gu, G., & Lee, W. (2006, December). Using an Ensemble of One-Class SVM Classifiers to Harden Payload-based Anomaly Detection Systems. In ICDM (Vol. 6, pp. 488-498). doi:10.1109/ICDM.2006.165

Pereira, C., Guimarães, D., Mesquita, J., Santos, F., Almeida, L., & Aguiar, A. (2018). Feasibility of Gateway-less IoT E-health Applications. In *2018 European Conference on Networks and Communications (EuCNC)*, (pp. 324-328). IEEE. 10.1109/EuCNC.2018.8442531

Perera, S. (2015). *Introduction to Anomaly Detection: Concepts and Techniques.* Retrieved from https://iwringer.wordpress.com/2015/11/17/anomaly-detection-concepts-and-techniques/

Perkins, Malinen, Wakikawa, Belding-Royer, & Sun. (2001). *IP address autoconfiguration for ad hoc networks*. IETF draft.

Perumal, S., Norwawi, N. M., & Raman, V. (2015). *Internet of Things(IoT) digital forensic investigation model: Top-down forensic approach methodology*. Paper presented at the 2015 Fifth International Conference on Digital Information Processing and Communications (ICDIPC). 10.1109/ICDIPC.2015.7323000

Pollitt, M. (2008). *Applying Traditional Forensic Taxonomy to Digital Forensics*. Paper presented at the Advances in Digital Forensics IV, Boston, MA.

Pollitt, M., Casey, E., Jaquet-Chiffelle, D.-O., & Gladyshev, P. (2018). *A Framework for Harmonizing Forensic Science Practices and Digital/Multimedia Evidence*. Retrieved from : doi:10.29325/OSAC.TS.0002

Pollitt, M. (2013). Triage: A practical solution or admission of failure. *Digital Investigation, 10*(2), 87–88. doi:10.1016/j.diin.2013.01.002

Ponnusamy, S. (2002). *Foundation of Functional Analysis*. Narosa Publishing House.

Pour, M., Bou-Harb, E., Varma, K., Neshenko, N., Pados, D., & Raymond Choo, K.-K. (2019). *Comprehending the IoT Cyber Threat Landscape: A Data Dimensionality Reduction Technique to Infer and Characterize Internet-scale IoT Probing Campaigns* (Vol. 28). Academic Press.

Project Freenet. (2019). *Freenet Project Documentation Page*. https://freenetproject.org/fr/pages/documentation.html

Radovanović, M., Nanopoulos, A., & Ivanović, M. (2014). Reverse nearest neighbors in unsupervised distance-based outlier detection. *IEEE Transactions on Knowledge and Data Engineering, 27*(5), 1369–1382. doi:10.1109/TKDE.2014.2365790

Raza, S., Wallgren, L., & Voigt, T. (2013). SVELTE: Real-time intrusion detection in the Internet of Things. *Ad Hoc Networks, 11*(8), 2661–2674. doi:10.1016/j.adhoc.2013.04.014

Razzaque, M. A., Milojevic-Jevric, M., Palade, A., & Clarke, S. (2015). Middleware for Internet of Things: A Survey. IEEE Internet of Things Journal, 3(1), 70–95.

Reddy, Kavati, Rao, & Kumar. (2017). A secure railway crossing system using IoT. In *Proceedings of international conference of electronics, communication and aerospace technology (ICECA)* (pp. 196-199). 10.1109/ICECA.2017.8212795

Reid, R. C., & Floyd, S. A. (2001). Extending the risk analysis model to include market-insurance. *Computers & Security, 20*(4), 331–339. doi:10.1016/S0167-4048(01)00411-4

Reif, M. (2019). *L'implémentation de CASE aux extractions Cellebrite* (Master Degree Mémoire de Maîtrise). Université de Lausanne.

Ribaux, O. (2014). *Police scientifique: Le renseignement par la trace*. PPUR, Presses polytechniques et universitaires romandes.

Ristenpart, T., Tromer, E., Shacham, H., & Savage, S. (2009.) Hey, you, get off of my cloud: exploring information leakage in third-party compute clouds. CCS. doi:10.1145/1653662.1653687

Roman, Zhou, & Lopez. (2013). On the Features and Challenges of Security and Privacy in Distributed Internet of Things. *Computer Networks, 57*(10), 2266–79.

Roux, C., Ribaux, O., & Crispino, F. (2012). *From Forensics to Forensic Science* (Vol. 24). Academic Press.

Sadigh, D., Driggs-Campbell, K., Puggelli, A., Li, W., Shia, V., Bajcsy, R., Sangiovanni-Vincentelli, A. L., Sastry, S. S., & Seshia, S. A. (2014). *Datadriven probabilistic modeling and verification of human driver behavior*. Formal Verification and Modeling in Human-Machine Systems.

Safi. (2017). Improving the Security of Internet of Things Using Encryption Algorithms. *World Academy of Science, Engineering and Technology International Journal of Computer and Information Engineering, 11*(5).

Said, A., Jama, A., Mahamud, F., Mohan, J., & Ranganathan, P. (2018). Smart Home Vulnerabilities – A Survey. *Int'l Conf. Embedded Systems, Cyber-physical Systems, & Applications ESCS'18*.

Sato, K., Arai, H., Shimizu, T., & Takada, M. (1998). Obstruction detector using ultrasonic sensors for upgrading the safety of a level crossing. In *Proceedings of International conference on developments in mass transit systems*. (Vol.453, pp. 190-195). 10.1049/cp:19980140

Sebastian, M. (2018). *Intel admits Meltdown/Spectre patches cause severe reboots*. Retrieved from https://www.datacenterdynamics.com/news/intel-admits-meltdownspectre-patches-cause-server-reboots/

Servida, F., & Casey, E. (2019). IoT forensic challenges and opportunities for digital traces. *Digital Investigation, 28*, S22–S29. doi:10.1016/j.diin.2019.01.012

Shabo, A., Sahama, T. R., Hofdijk, J., Hafen, E., Bignens, S., Goossen, W., Yasnoff, W., & Ball, M. (2016). *IMIA Working Group on Health Record Banking-How Complex Systems Can Cooperate Towards Having Individual's Consolidated Data*. Academic Press.

Shacham, H. (2007). The geometry of innocent flesh on the bone: Return- into-libc without function calls (on the x86). CCS.

Shama, D., Puhlmann, F., Morrish, J., & Bhatnagar, R. M. (2019). *Enterprise IoT, Strategies and Best Practices for Connected Products and Services*. O'Reilly Media Inc.

Sharma, Kumar,& Sarika. (2015). Automatic Railway Gate Control System Based on RFID, pressure sensor and servo motor. *Journal of Network Communications and Emerging Technologies (JNCET), 5*(2), 153-156.

Sharma, M., & Siddiqui, A. (2010, April). RFID based mobiles: Next generation applications. In *2010 2nd IEEE International Conference on Information Management and Engineering* (pp. 523-526). IEEE.

Shepard, D. P., Humphreys, T. E., & Fansler, A. A. (2012). Evaluation of the vulnerability of phasor measurement units to gps spoofing attacks. *International Journal of Critical Infrastructure Protection, 5*(3), 146–153. doi:10.1016/j.ijcip.2012.09.003

Shilton, K., Burke, J., Estrin, D., Govindan, R., Hansen, M., Kang, J., & Mun, M. (2009). *Designing the Personal Data Stream: Enabling Participatory Privacy in Mobile Personal Sensing*. TPRC.

Siboni, Sachidananda, Meidan, Bohadana, Mathov, Bhairav, Shabtai, & Elovici. (2019). Security Testbed for Internet-of-Things Devices. *IEEE Transactions on Reliability, 68*(1).

Siboni. (2019). Security Testbed for Internet-of-Things Devices. *IEEE Transactions on Reliability, 68*(1), 23-44.

Simon, S. O. (2009). *Haykin Neural Networks and Learning Machines*. Academic Press.

Sindhu, S. S. S., Geetha, S., & Kannan, A. (2012). Decision tree based light weight intrusion detection using a wrapper approach. *Expert Systems with Applications, 39*(1), 129–141. doi:10.1016/j.eswa.2011.06.013

Singh, J., Pasquier, T., Bacon, J., Ko, H., & Eyers, D. (2015). Twenty Security Considerations for Cloud-Supported Internet of Things. IEEE Internet of Things Journal, 3(3), 269–84.

Sliwa, J. (2016). A Generalized Framework for Multi-Party Data Exchange for Iot Systems. In *2016 30th International Conference on Advanced Information Networking and Applications Workshops (Waina)*, (pp. 193–98). IEEE. 10.1109/WAINA.2016.134

Soltan, S., Mittal, P., & Poor, H. V. (2018). *BlackIoT: IoT botnet of high wattage devices can disrupt the power grid*. Academic Press.

Stecklina, J., & Prescher, T. (2018). *LazyFP: Leaking FPU Register State using Microarchitectural Side-Channels*. arXiv:1806.07480

Stephen, N. (2018). *Intel: Problem in patches for Spectre, Meltdown extends to newer chips*. Retrieved from https://www.reuters.com/article/us-cyber-intel/intel-problem-in-patches-for-spectre-meltdown-extends-to-newer-chips-idUSKBN1F7087

Stewart, H., & Jürjens, J. (2017). Information security management and the human aspect in organizations. *Information and Computer Security*.

Stop Secret Surveillance Ordinance. (2019). *File #190110*. C.F.R.

Stottelaar, B. G. (2015). *Practical cyber-attacks on autonomous vehicles*. Available: http://essay.utwente.nl/66766/

Sugiyama, M., & Borgwardt, K. (2013). Rapid distance-based outlier detection via sampling. In Advances in Neural Information Processing Systems (pp. 467-475). Academic Press.

Suh, G. E., & Devadas, S. (2007). Physical Unclonable Functions for Device Authentication and Secret Key Generation. *Proceedings of IEEE/ACMDAC*, 9-14.

Sun, Y., & Belding-Royer, E. M. (2003). *Dynamic address configuration in mobile ad hoc networks.* UCSB Technical Report 2003-11.

Sunde, N., & Dror, I. E. (2019). Cognitive and human factors in digital forensics: Problems, challenges, and the way forward. *Digital Investigation, 29,* 101–108. doi:10.1016/j.diin.2019.03.011

Suoa, H., Wana, J., Zoua, C., & Liua, J. (2012). Security in the Internet of Things: A Review. *International Conference on Computer Science and Electronics Engineering,* 648-651. 10.1109/ICCSEE.2012.373

Swarnapriyaa, U. G., & Vinodhini, S. Anthoniraj, R., & Anand. (2011). Auto Configuration in Mobile Ad Hoc Networks. *Proceedings of the National Conference on Innovations in Emerging Technology,* 61-66.

Tan, L., & Wang, N. (2010, August). Future internet: The internet of things. In *2010 3rd international conference on advanced computer theory and engineering (ICACTE)* (Vol. 5, pp. V5-376). IEEE.

Tan, Z., Jamdagni, A., He, X., Nanda, P., & Liu, R. P. (2013). A system for denial-of-service attack detection based on multivariate correlation analysis. *IEEE Transactions on Parallel and Distributed Systems, 25*(2), 447–456.

Tayal, A. P., & Patnaik, L. M. (2004). An address assignment for the automatic configuration of mobile ad hoc networks. *Personal and Ubiquitous Computing, 8*(1), 47–54. doi:10.100700779-003-0256-5

Thakur, D. (n.d.). What do you understand by information? What are the characteristics of information. Computer Notes. http://ecomputernotes.com/mis/what-is-mis/what-do-you-understand-by-information-what-are-the-characteristics-of-information

Thakur, D. (n.d.). What is the difference between data and information? Computer Notes. http://ecomputernotes.com/fundamental/information-technology/what-do-you-mean-by-data-and-information

The benefits of implementing an ISMS (Information security management system) | IT governance UK. (n.d.). IT Governance - Governance, Risk Management and Compliance for Information Technology. https://www.itgovernance.co.uk/isms-benefits

Threat Post. (n.d.). https://media.threatpost.com/wp-content/uploads/sites/103/2020/03/11092116/word-image-24.png

Tobagi, F. A., & Kleinrock, L. (1978). The Effect of Acknowledgment Traffic on the Capacity of Packet-Switched Radio Channels. *IEEE Transactions on Communications, 26*(6), 815–826. doi:10.1109/TCOM.1978.1094159

Tompson, J. J., Jain, A., LeCun, Y., & Bregler, C. (2014). Joint training of a convolutional network and a graphical model for human pose estimation. *Advances in Neural Information Processing Systems,* 1799–1807.

Treat, J. R., Tumbas, N. S., McDonald, S. T., Shinar, D., Hume, R. D., Mayer, R. E., Stanisfer, R. L., & Castellan, N. J. (1977). *Tri-level study of the causes of traffic accidents.* Report No. DOT-HS-034-3-535-77 (TAC).

Turvey, B. E. (2011). *Criminal profiling: An introduction to behavioral evidence analysis.* Academic Press.

Uranus. (2017). A Survey: Information Security Management System. *Journal of Analog and Digital Devices, 2*(3).

Ut austin researchers successfully spoof an $80 million yacht at sea. (n.d.). https://news.utexas.edu/2013/07/29/ut-austin-researchers-successfullyspoof-an-80-million-yacht-at-sea

Vaidya, N. H. (2002). Weak duplicate address detection in mobile ad hoc networks. *Proceedings of the ACM mobi-Hoc 2002*, 206–216. 10.1145/513800.513826

Van Bulck, J., Minkin, M., Weisse, O., Genkin, D., Kasikci, B., Piessens, F., Silberstein, M., Wenisch, T. F., Yarom, Y., & Strackx, R. (2018). Foreshadow: Extracting the Keys to the Intel SGX Kingdom with Transient Out-of-Order Execution. *Proceedings of the 27th USENIX Security Symposium.*

Van Bulck, J., Piessens, F., & Strackx, R. (2017). SGX-Step: A practical attack framework for precise enclave execution control. In *Proceedings of the 2nd Workshop on System Software for Trusted Execution.* ACM. 10.1145/3152701.3152706

Veerappan, C. S., Loh, P. K. K., Tang, Z. H., & Tan, F. (2018). Taxonomy on Malware Evasion Countermeasures. In *Conf. Rec. 2018 IEEE Int. Conf. WF-IoT* (pp. 558-563). IEEE.

Verdult, R., Garcia, F. D., & Ege, B. (2015). Dismantling megamos crypto: Wirelessly lockpicking a vehicle immobilizer. *Supplement to the 22nd USENIX Security Symposium (USENIX Security 13)*, 703–718.

Vidalis & Angelopoulou. (n.d.). Assessing Identity Theft in the Internet of Things. *IT CoNvergence PRActice (INPRA), 2*(1), 15-21.

Vidhyasanker, Manoj, & Siva Ram Murthy. (2006). Slot Allocation Schemes for Delay Sensitive Traffic Support in Asynchronous Wireless Mesh Networks. *International Journal of Computer and Telecommunications Networking, 50*(15), 2595-2613.

Vishwanatha, Vidya Shree, & Kumar. (2018). *Smart railway gate system using IoT.* doi:10.23883/ijrter.2018.4128.w1usi

Wang, P., Chen, P., Yuan, Y., Liu, D., Huang, Z., Hou, X., & Cottrell, G. (2017). *Understanding convolution for semantic segmentation.* arXiv preprint arXiv:1702.08502

Wang, H., Fan, W., Yu, P. S., & Han, J. (2003, August). Mining concept-drifting data streams using ensemble classifiers. In *Proceedings of the ninth ACM SIGKDD international conference on Knowledge discovery and data mining* (pp. 226-235). ACM. 10.1145/956750.956778

Wang, Y., & Garcia-Luna-Aceves, J. J. (2002). Performance of Collision Avoidance Protocols in Single-Channel Ad Hoc Networks. *Proc. of IEEE ICNP 2002*. 10.1109/ICNP.2002.1181387

Wang, Y., Wong, J., & Miner, A. (2004, June). Anomaly intrusion detection using one class SVM. In *Proceedings from the Fifth Annual IEEE SMC Information Assurance Workshop*, 2004. (pp. 358-364). IEEE. 10.1109/IAW.2004.1437839

Weber, R. H. (2010). Internet of Things–New Security and Privacy Challenges. *Computer Law & Security Review, 26*(1), 23–30.

Weber, R. H. (2010). Internet of things – new security and privacy challenges. *Computer Law & Security Review, 26*(1), 23–30. doi:10.1016/j.clsr.2009.11.008

Weichbrodt, N., Kurmus, A., Pietzuch, P., & Kapitza, R. (2016). Asyncshock: exploiting synchronization bugs in Intel SGX enclaves. In *European Symposium on Research in Computer Security*. Springer. 10.1007/978-3-319-45744-4_22

Weiser. (1991). The Computer for the 21st Century. *Scientific American, 265*(3), 94-105.

Weisse, O., Vanbulck, J., Minkin, M., Genkin, D., Kasikci, B., Piessens, F., Silberstein, M., Strackx, R., Wenisch, T. F., & Yarom, Y. (2018). *Foreshadow-NG: Breaking the Virtual Memory Abstraction with Transient Out-of-Order Execution*. Technical report.

Weniger & Zitterbart. (2004). Address Autoconfiguration in Mobile Ad Hoc Networks: Current approaches and Future Directions. *IEEE Network*, 6-11.

Weniger & Zitterbart. (2004). *Address Autoconfiguration in Mobile Ad Hoc Networks: Current approaches and Future Directions*. IEEE Network.

Weniger, K. (2003). Passive duplicate address detection in mobile ad hoc networks. *Proceedings of the IEEE WCNC 2003*. 10.1109/WCNC.2003.1200609

Weniger, K. (2005, March). PACMAN: Passive autoconfiguration for mobile ad hoc networks. *IEEE JSAC, Special Issue on Wireless Ad Hoc Networks, 23*(3), 507–509. doi:10.1109/JSAC.2004.842539

What is an information security management system? (n.d.). ISO Registration – Perry Johnson Registrars — ISO Registration Company.http://www.pjr.com/standards/iso-27001/information-security-management-system

What is information security management system (ISMS)? - Definition from WhatIs.com. (2011, January 25). WhatIs.com.https://whatis.techtarget.com/definition/information-security-management-system-ISMS

Wu, M., Lu, T. J., Ling, F. Y., Sun, J., & Du, H. Y. (2010, August). Research on the architecture of Internet of Things. In *2010 3rd International Conference on Advanced Computer Theory and Engineering (ICACTE)* (Vol. 5, pp. V5-484). IEEE.

Wu, L., & Varshney, P. (1999). Performance Analysis of CSMA and BTMA Protocols in Multihop Networks (I). Single Channel Case. Information Sciences. *Elsevier Sciences Inc.*, *120*, 159–177. doi:10.1016/S0020-0255(99)00047-X

Wu, S.-L., Lin, C.-Y., Tseng, Y.-C., & Sheu, J.-P. (2000). A New Multi-Channel MAC Protocol with On-Demand Channel Assignment for Mobile Ad Hoc Networks. *Int'l Symp. on Parallel Architectures, Algorithms and Networks (I-SPAN)*, 232-237.

Xiao, H., Seah, W. G., Lo, A., & Chua, K. C. (2000). A Flexible Quality of Service Model for Mobile Ad-hoc Networks (FQMM). *Proceedings of IEEE Vehicular Technology Conference (VTC 2000- Fall)*, 397-413.

Xiao, L., Wan, X., Lu, X., Zhang, Y., & Wu, D. (2018). *IoT security techniques based on machine learning*. arXiv preprint arXiv:1801.06275

Xiao, L., Li, Y., Han, G., Liu, G., & Zhuang, W. (2016). PHY-layer spoofing detection with reinforcement learning in wireless networks. *IEEE Transactions on Vehicular Technology*, *65*(12), 10037–10047. doi:10.1109/TVT.2016.2524258

Xiao, L., Yan, Q., Lou, W., Chen, G., & Hou, Y. T. (2013). Proximity-based security techniques for mobile users in wireless networks. *IEEE Transactions on Information Forensics and Security*, *8*(12), 2089–2100. doi:10.1109/TIFS.2013.2286269

Xin, M., & China, H. (2015). A Mixed Encryption Algorithm Used in Internet of Things Security Transmission System. *International Conference on Cyber-Enabled Disributed Computing and Knowledge Discovery*, 62-65. 10.1109/CyberC.2015.9

Yang, S. (2017). IoT stream processing and analytics in the fog. *IEEE Communications Magazine*, *55*(8), 21–27. doi:10.1109/MCOM.2017.1600840

Yang, Y., Zheng, X., Guo, W., Liu, X., & Chang, V. (2018). Privacy-preserving fusion of IoT and big data for e-health. *Future Generation Computer Systems*, *86*, 1437–1455. doi:10.1016/j.future.2018.01.003

Yarom, Y., & Falkner, K. (2014). FLUSH+RELOAD: A High Resolution, Low Noise, L3 Cache Side-Channel Attack. In *23rd USENIX Security Symposium* (pp. 719–732). San Diego, CA: USENIX Association.

Yasumoto, K., Yamaguchi, H., & Shigeno, H. (2016). Survey of real-time processing technologies of iot data streams. *Journal of Information Processing*, *24*(2), 195–202. doi:10.2197/ipsjjip.24.195

Yuan, X., He, P., & Zhu, Q. (2018). *Adversarial Examples: Attacks and Defenses for Deep Learning*. arXiv:1712.07107v3

Yuehong, Zeng, Chen, & Fan. (2016). The Internet of Things in Healthcare: An Overview. *Journal of Industrial Information Integration*, *1*, 3–13.

Zarpelao, B. B., Miani, R. S., Kawakani, C. T., & de Alvarenga, S. C. (2017). A survey of intrusion detection in Internet of Things. *Journal of Network and Computer Applications, 84,* 25–37. doi:10.1016/j.jnca.2017.02.009

Zawoad, S., & Hasan, R. (2015). *FAIoT: Towards Building a Forensics Aware Eco System for the Internet of Things.* Paper presented at the 2015 IEEE International Conference on Services Computing.

Zhang, Y., Juels, A., Reiter, M. K., & Ristenpart, T. (2012). Cross-VM side channels and their use to extract private keys. In CCS (pp. 305–316). doi:10.1145/2382196.2382230

Zhang, Y., Juels, A., Reiter, M. K., & Ristenpart, T. (2014). Cross-tenant side-channel attacks in PaaS clouds. In CCS (pp. 990– 1003). doi:10.1145/2660267.2660356

Zhang, Z. K., Cho, M. C. Y., Wang, C.W., Hsu, C.W., Chen, C.K., & Shieh, S. (2014). IoT Security: Ongoing Challenges and Research Opportunities. *IEEE 7th International Conference on Service-Oriented Computing and Applications.* 10.1109/SOCA.2014.58

Zhang, Y., Ge, Z., Greenberg, A., & Roughan, M. (2005, October). Network anomography. In *Proceedings of the 5th ACM SIGCOMM conference on Internet Measurement* (pp. 30-30). USENIX Association.

Zhao, X., Veerappan, C. S., Loh, P. K. K., Tang. Z. H., & Forest, T. F. (2018) Multi-Agent Cross-Platform Detection of Meltdown and Spectre. In *Proc. 2018 IEEE Conference on Control, Automation, Robotics and Vision* (pp. 1834—1838). 10.1109/ICARCV.2018.8581146

Zhao, H., Shi, J., Qi, X., Wang, X., & Jia, J. (2017). Pyramid scene parsing network. *The IEEE Conference on Computer Vision and Pattern Recognition (CVPR).*

Zhao, K., & Ge, L. (2013). A survey on the internet of things security. *Int'l Conf. on Computational Intelligence and Security (CIS),* 663-667.

Zhao, S., Aggarwal, A., Frost, R., & Bai, X. (2011). A Survey of Applications of Identity-Based Cryptography in Mobile Ad- Hoc Network. *IEEE Communications Surveys and Tutorials.*

Zhou, J., Fu, Y., Wu, Y., Xia, H., Fang, Y., & Lu, H. (2009). Anomaly detection over concept drifting data streams. *Journal of Computer Information Systems, 5*(6).

Zhu, Dhelim, Zhou, Yang, & Ning. (2017). An Architecture for Aggregating Information from Distributed Data Nodes for Industrial Internet of Things. *Computers & Electrical Engineering, 58,* 337–49.

Zhu, Diethe, Camplani, Tao, Burrows, Twomey, Kaleshi, Mirmehdi, Flach, & Craddock. (2015). Bridging E-Health and the Internet of Things: The Sphere Project. *IEEE Intelligent Systems, 30*(4), 39–46.

Ziegler, J., & Urbas, L. (2011, September). Advanced interaction metaphors for RFID-tagged physical artefacts. In *2011 IEEE International Conference on RFID-Technologies and Applications* (pp. 73-80). IEEE. 10.1109/RFID-TA.2011.6068619

About the Contributors

Parag Chatterjee is a research profssor at the National Technological University (*Universidad Tecnológica Nacional*) in Buenos Aires, Argentina and an assistant professor at the University of the Republic (*Universidad de la República*), Uruguay. He obtained his MSc in Computer Science from the University of Calcutta in 2015, and is currently working in the transdisciplinary areas of Internet of Things and Artificial Intelligence applied to healthcare, especially in the domain of intelligent prediction and prevention. He is a member of editorial and reviewer boards of 20+ international journals and conferences, and has delivered talks and keynotes in 30+ conferences and events, including *ExpoInternet LatinoAmérica*, IoT Week Geneva and TED[x].

Emmanuel Benoist is a professor of Computer Sciences at the Bern University of Applied Sciences. He teaches Web Security and low-level programming (C and Assembler) and conducts research activities at the Research Institute for Security in the Information Society (RISIS). He works on the link between security and privacy. This includes understanding privacy issues and the way they are solved for instance for criminal and illegal activities on the Darknet, based on which, he created a Darknet Observatory.

Asoke Nath is an associate professor of Computer Science at St. Xavier's College Kolkata, University of Calcutta, in India. After receiving PhD in 1984 from the Indian Association of Cultivation of Science, he has performed extensive research, having 250+ publications in international journals and conferences. He has experience of working in multiple domains in parallel, including cryptography and network security, MOOCs, image processing and green computing, and has delivered invited talks and keynotes in several international conferences.

* * *

Kavitha Ammayappan completed her PhD., with specialization in cyber security from University of Hyderabad, India. To her credit she has publications in international conferences and international journals. She has filed patent applications. She has worked in academics and in MNCs in the area of cyber security. Her name appeared in Marquis Who's Who. Her areas of interest include system security and interdisciplinary research on system security.

Arundhati Arjaria was born in Chhatarpur, India, in 1988. She received the Bachelors of Engineering degree in Information Technology from Oriental Institute of Science & Technology (UIT/RGPV) Bhopal, India, in 2009, and the Masters of Engineering degree in Computer Engineering from Shri Govindram Seksaria Institute of Technology & Science (UIT/RGPV), Indore, in 2012, respectively. In 2013 she joined the Department of Computer Engineering, University of Technology, Rajiv Gandhi Proudyogiki Vishwavidyalaya, Bhopal as a Assistant Professor (Temporary Basis). From April 2016 till now she is working as an assistant professor (Computer Engineering) in Digital Institute of Computer Applications. She has published several research papers in Mobile Ad hoc networks and cloud computing in international and national journals.

Serge Bignens is Professor in the department of medical informatics of the University of Applied Sciences. He is the director of the research institute I4MI.

Eoghan Casey is professor of Digital Forensic Science and Investigation in the School of Criminal Sciences at the University of Lausanne. He has extensive experience working in digital forensic laboratories in the public and private sectors, and he has analysed many types of digital evidence to support complex cases, and he has delivered expert testimony in civil and criminal matters. He has helped develop new capabilities for extracting and analysing digital evidence, including smartphones and networks. He wrote the foundational book Digital Evidence and Computer Crime, now in its third edition, and he created advanced smartphone forensics courses taught worldwide. He has also coauthored several advanced technical books including Malware Forensics, and the Handbook of Digital Forensics and Investigation. Since 2004, he has been Editor-in-Chief of Digital Investigation: The International Journal of Digital Forensics & Incident Response, publishing cutting edge work by and for practitioners and researchers. He serves on the Digital Forensic Research Workshop (DFRWS) Board of Directors and helps organize biannual digital forensic research conferences. He also contributes to forensic science definitions, guidelines, and standards as Executive Secretary of the Digital/Multimedia Scientific Area Committee (DMSAC) of the NIST Organization for Scientific Area Committees (OSAC).

Phidahunlang Chyne is a Research Scholar in the Department of Information Technology, NEHU, India. She completed her Master of Technology (Information Technology) in 2015 from NEHU, India, and Bachelor of Engineering in Computer Science from the University of Pune in 2013. Her area of interests includes Wireless Mobile Communications, Computer Networks, IoT Architectures, Machine Learning. She has published several papers in reputed journals and conference proceedings till date.

Suchandra Datta completed B.Sc. Computer Science with first class from St. Xavier's College (Autonomous), Kolkata. Currently pursuing M.Sc. Computer Science at St. Xavier's College (Autonomous), Kolkata. Fields of interest include machine learning and cryptography.

David-Olivier Jaquet-Chiffelle is full professor at the School of Criminal Justice, University of Lausanne, Switzerland. He is head of the Master program in forensic science, orientation digital investigation and identification. His current research covers cybercrime, digital traces, security and privacy, new forms of identities in the information society, as well as authentication, anonymization and identification processes, especially in the digital world.

Megha Kamble has completed B.E. and M.Tech in Computer Science and PhD. in Faculty of IT in the domain of channel allocation for cellular network using multi agent system framework. She possess 6 years industrial and 17 years of teaching experience of UG and PG engineering courses. Her specialization includes Multi gent System, Machine Learning, Soft Computing, Cellular Network, Channel Allocation, Software Engineering, computer graphics and multimedia. She has 17 International and 11 National Publications in Conference Proceedings and reputed Journal. She is Gold Medalist in NPTEL certification for R software and IBM TGMC mentor, Smarthackathon mentor.

Reto König is Professor at the Bern University of Applied Sciences (BFH). He received a PhD from the University of Freiburg (Switzerland). He conducts research in the Research Institute on Security in the Information Society (RISIS). His research areas are privacy and security in eVoting and in the Internet of Things.

Alexander Kreutz is senior software developer for the midata project since 12/2014. He graduated in information technologies in Passau, Germany in 2001. Since then he was involved in the development of various database application servers for ERP, XQuery processing, online gaming and a wiki platform. Since December 2014 he is main developer of the backend of the midata platform.

Lukas Laederach has a BSc in information technology specialized in distributed systems and IoT. He is passionate about secure communication, location based services (LBS) and Distributed systems and IoT in general.

Peter Loh is Director of the Centre for Operational Technology – Information Security, Deputy Program Director (Information Security) and an Associate Professor at the Singapore Institute of Technology. His research interests are in information and cyber security, fault-tolerant and high-performance networks and AI. He has successfully managed more than USD 4 million of research funding spanning these areas. He has set up and headed research centers in Information and Cybersecurity, Software Engineering and High-Performance Computing. He had also set up and headed the Software Systems Cluster which supported undergraduate level IT-based practicum as well as undergraduate project work. He has authored or coauthored over 100 research publications and talks, 37 of which were published in international, peer-reviewed books, monographs and journals. Currently, Peter is the Principal Investigator of an MOE-TIF funded project which involves the design and development of a cross-platform, real-time security framework for IoT endpoints. Concurrently, he is also collaborating with the Ministry of Home Affairs on the design and development of a vulnerability analysis and remediation tool for drones. Peter is also a member of the Singapore Cybersecurity Consortium steering committee and the Telecoms Standard Advisory Committee. From 2001 to 2002, he served as an Expert Mentor to the Ministry of Education's Innovation Program. As a Principal Research Scientist and Program Manager of Computer Security at Temasek Labs at NTU, Peter single-handedly developed and provided oversight to the Computer Security research program that covered research domains in Systems Security, Security Analytics, Mobile Phone Security and Software Code Protection. The Computer Security lab that he had set up in 2009 and helmed, had supported almost USD 3 million worth of research projects. In teaching, Peter has planned, developed, coordinated and delivered curriculum for both undergraduate and graduate level student cohorts and he was twice nominated for the Best Teacher of the Year Award in 2000 and 2003. Professionally, he has trained commissioned officers in the Singapore Armed Forces as well as working professionals pursuing the BSc in Computing and Info Systems program at Singapore Institute of Management in collaboration with the University of London.

Atul Negi holds a PhD., and is a professor in University of Hyderabad, India. To his credit, he has many publications in international conferences and international journals. His areas of research widely cover system security, pattern recognition applications such as principal component analysis, palm print recognition, clustering algorithms and optical character recognition.

Arun Babu Puthuparambil is currently a Member of Technical Staff at the Indian Institute of Science, Bengaluru. He obtained his PhD at Indira Gandhi Centre for Atomic Research, Kalpakkam; and holds an M.Tech degree from University of Hyderabad. His areas of interests are Cybersecurity and software engineering.

Elénore Ryser has a MSc in Forensic Science and is a PhD student at the University of Lausanne. Her main areas of research cover a typology of digital traces, interpretation of digital traces as well as geo-localisation evidence.

Francesco Servida has a MSc in Forensic Science and is a PhD student focused on Digital Investigation and Identification at the University of Lausanne. In the context of his master thesis, he prepared the IoT Forensic Challenge scenario for the 2018-2019 DFRWS conference.

Jan Sliwa was research assistant at the Bern University of Applied Sciences (BFH) 2010-2018. He graduated from the Silesian University of Technology in Automation and informatics in 1977. He worked as a software engineer for various firms. He joined the MEMdoc project of the University of Bern (2005-2010) where he developed a privacy preserving medical register.

Hannes Spichiger has a MSc in Forensic Science and is a PhD student at the University of Lausanne. In addition, he works part time at the Neuchâtel police force as a specialist for digital investigation. His main areas of research are the evaluation of smart phone evidence and the use of a Bayesian framework in a digital forensics context.

Manoj Kumar Srivastav has completed his MSc in Pure mathematics from University of Calcutta., He has completed his MCA from Indira Gandhi National Open University. He has more than 20 published research papers in national and international journal.

Chandra Sekar Veerappan is a professional officer (project) in the ICT cluster at the Singapore Institute of Technology. He has a master's degree in Computer Applications and a special diploma in IoT. He has over 12 years of experience in software design and development. His research interests revolve around cybersecurity, secure coding, ethical hacking, and malware analysis. He works on various aspects of machine learning in cybersecurity and aims is to develop secure systems by combining novel ways techniques from artificial intelligence. He is a professional member of Singapore computer society, IEEE and ACM.

Cédric von Allmen has a BSc in information technology specialized in distributed systems and IoT. He is passionate about secure communication, location based services (LBS) and Distributed systems and IoT in general.

Xinxing Zhao is a research engineer, specialises in information and cyber security, currently he is with the Singapore Institute of Technology (SIT). His current project is investigating and researching on a cross-platform, real-time security framework. He received his Bachelors (Communication Engineering) in 2008 and his Master of Engineering (Signal and Information Processing) in 2011. After that, he had been working in Nanyang Technological University (Singapore) as a research engineer. While working full-time there, he pursued and received his second Master of Engineering (in Secure Communications and Networks in 2016). In 2017, he joined SIT as a research engineer.

Index

Ensure Quality Research is Introduced to the Academic Community

Become an IGI Global Reviewer for Authored Book Projects

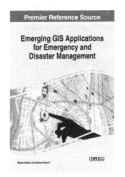
Premier Reference Source

Emerging GIS Applications for Emergency and Disaster Management

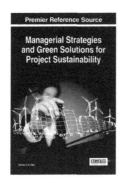
Premier Reference Source

Managerial Strategies and Green Solutions for Project Sustainability

Premier Reference Source

Comparative Approaches to Using R and Python for Statistical Data Analysis

Premier Reference Source

Solutions for High-Touch Communications in a High-Tech World

The overall success of an authored book project is dependent on quality and timely reviews.

In this competitive age of scholarly publishing, constructive and timely feedback significantly expedites the turnaround time of manuscripts from submission to acceptance, allowing the publication and discovery of forward-thinking research at a much more expeditious rate. Several IGI Global authored book projects are currently seeking highly-qualified experts in the field to fill vacancies on their respective editorial review boards:

Applications and Inquiries may be sent to:
development@igi-global.com

Applicants must have a doctorate (or an equivalent degree) as well as publishing and reviewing experience. Reviewers are asked to complete the open-ended evaluation questions with as much detail as possible in a timely, collegial, and constructive manner. All reviewers' tenures run for one-year terms on the editorial review boards and are expected to complete at least three reviews per term. Upon successful completion of this term, reviewers can be considered for an additional term.

If you have a colleague that may be interested in this opportunity, we encourage you to share this information with them.

IGI Global Proudly Partners With
eContent Pro International
Receive a 25% Discount on all Editorial Services

Editorial Services

IGI Global expects all final manuscripts submitted for publication to be in their final form. This means they must be reviewed, revised, and professionally copy edited prior to their final submission. Not only does this support with accelerating the publication process, but it also ensures that the highest quality scholarly work can be disseminated.

English Language Copy Editing

Let eContent Pro International's expert copy editors perform edits on your manuscript to resolve spelling, punctuaion, grammar, syntax, flow, formatting issues and more.

Scientific and Scholarly Editing

Allow colleagues in your research area to examine the content of your manuscript and provide you with valuable feedback and suggestions before submission.

Figure, Table, Chart & Equation Conversions

Do you have poor quality figures? Do you need visual elements in your manuscript created or converted? A design expert can help!

Translation

Need your documjent translated into English? eContent Pro International's expert translators are fluent in English and more than 40 different languages.

Email: customerservice@econtentpro.com   www.igi-global.com/editorial-service-partners

Printed in the United States
By Bookmasters